D1547853

The German Diplomatic Service, 1871–1914

The German Diplomatic Service, 1871-1914

Lamar Cecil

PRINCETON UNIVERSITY PRESS, PRINCETON, NEW JERSEY

For
LINDSEY AND DICK HUDDLESTON
JANE AND DONALD MATHEWS
MAXINE AND DICK SOLOWAY
with affection and gratitude

Contents

List of Tables

Preface

This is a book about diplomats, not about diplomacy. In investigating the German Foreign Office from 1871 to 1914 I have examined the men who conceived and executed German diplomacy rather than the policies and stratagems through which they attempted to advance the Fatherland's interest. I have attempted to analyze a group of persons, identified by their common employment in a branch of the imperial and Prussian bureaucracy, and then to depict the circumstances under which they pursued their careers.

The first chapter delineates the structure of the Foreign Office; chapters two and three deal with the conditions of entry imposed by the Wilhelmstrasse.[1] Chapter four treats the association of these novice diplomats, as well as their more senior colleagues, with the military element, which after 1871 found increasing accommodation in all ranks of the diplomatic establishment. Chapter five is an analysis of the career patterns of German diplomats. The remaining four chapters portray the changing, and generally deteriorating, conditions under which diplomats practiced their craft, first under Bismarck and William I and thereafter under an immature monarch and a succession of epigoni.

My indebtedness to various individuals and institutions is very great and it is one I am happy to acknowledge. H.S.H. Prince Otto von Bismarck, H.S.H. Prince Siegfried zu Castell-Rüdenhausen, Count Paul zu Münster and Baroness Anne-Katrin von Ledebur graciously allowed me ac-

[1] The Foreign Office was located at Wilhelmstrasse 76. Throughout this book the term Wilhelmstrasse, whether or not followed by this numeral, is understood to mean the Foreign Office and not other government agencies also located on the street.

cess to their private archives in order to examine papers of diplomat forebears or relatives. My colleagues at Chapel Hill, Richard Allen Soloway and Samuel Ruthven Williamson, Jr., manfully waded through the manuscript, purging it of many flaws and suggesting lines of investigation that I had not perceived with clarity, if at all. Hans W. Gatzke of Yale went to considerable trouble to help me deal with an aggravating problem, and the generous hospitality on different sides of the Atlantic of Hannelore Countess zu Pfaffendorf and David Dickinson made many of my research missions pleasant as well as productive. I owe a particular debt to Dr. and Frau Sareyko of the Political Archive of the German Foreign Office in Bonn, who sifted through inaccessible personnel records of former diplomats in order to provide me with many biographical details. The exemplary staff of the Bundesarchiv in Koblenz, and in particular Professor Dr. Kahlenberg and Dr. Reiser, as usual went out of the way to expedite the use of its vast collections. R. Miriam Brokaw and Scotia W. MacRae of Princeton University Press shepherded the manuscript through the process of publication with masterful acumen. Finally, the Research Council of the University of North Carolina helped sustain me in Germany amidst the painful and bewildering distress inflicted by the collapse of the dollar.

Lamar Cecil
Chapel Hill
October 20, 1975

Acknowledgment

I am indebted to Vandenhoeck & Ruprecht Verlagsbuchhandlung for permission to quote from Rudolf Vierhaus, ed., *Das Tagebuch der Baronin Spitzemberg geb. Freiin v. Varnbüler: Aufzeichnungen aus der Hofgesellschaft des Hohenzollernreiches*, 2d ed. (Göttingen, 1960).

Abbreviations

The following abbreviations are used in the footnotes. The sources are described more fully in the bibliography.

Persons:

BvB	Bernhard von Bülow (1899, Count; 1905, Prince von Bülow)
FvH	Friedrich von Holstein
HvB	Count Herbert von Bismarck
KvR	Count Kuno von Rantzau
OvB	Prince Otto von Bismarck-Schönhausen
PzE	Count (1900, Prince) Philipp zu Eulenburg-Hertefeld
W2	William II, German Emperor and King of Prussia

Sources:

Asseverat 45	Eulenburg *Nachlass*, Asseverat 45
BisN	Bismarck *Nachlass*
BüN	Bülow *Nachlass*
BuschN	Busch *Nachlass*
CN	Castell-Rüdenhausen *Nachlass*
Dd 122	Deutschland 122 No. 2
Dd 135	Deutschland 135 No. 1, no. 1
Dd 149	Deutschland 149
EN	Eulenburg *Nachlass*
GN	Gebhardt *Nachlass*
Gen 1 AA.a.40	Generalia 1 AA.a. 40
Gen 1 AA.a.61	Generalia 1 AA.a.61
Gen 1 AA.a.68	Generalia 1 AA.a. 68

GW	Herman von Petersdorff et al., eds., *Bismarck: die gesammelten Werke*, 15 vols. (Berlin, 1923–33).
HA	Haus Archiv
HardenN	Harden *Nachlass*
HepkeN	Hepke *Nachlass*
HHStA	Haus-, Hof-, und Staatsarchiv
HohN	Hohenlohe *Nachlass*
HolN	Holstein *Nachlass*
HP	Norman Rich and M. H. Fisher, eds., *The Holstein Papers*, 4 vols. (Cambridge, 1955–63)
KayserN	Kayser *Nachlass*
Kl.Erwb.	*Kleine Erwerbung*
KWN	Kiderlen-Wächter *Nachlass*
LoebellN	Loebell *Nachlass*
MichahellesN	Michahelles *Nachlass*
MiquelN	Miquel *Nachlass*
MünsterN	Münster *Nachlass*
PourtalèsN	Pourtalès *Nachlass*
Reichstag	*Stenographische Berichte über die Verhandlungen des Reichstags* (Berlin, 1871 ff.)
RichthofenN	Richthofen *Nachlass*
RottenburgN	Rottenburg *Nachlass*
SchlözerN	Schlözer *Nachlass*
StoedtenN	Lucius von Stoedten *Nachlass*
ThimmeN	Thimme *Nachlass*
TN	Treutler *Nachlass*

The German Diplomatic Service, 1871–1914

CHAPTER I

The Organization of the Foreign Office

The broad sweep of the Unter den Linden from the Brandenburg Gate to the Royal Palace defined the northern perimeter of the heart of imperial Berlin. South of the thoroughfare, between the Tiergarten and the palace, imposing public edifices, great department stores, and banking houses were wedged among the stately mansions of the newly rich and those still the property of royalty and of ancient noble families such as Arnim, Redern, Pless, Hatzfeldt-Wildenburg, and Stolberg-Wernigerode. The most elegant address in the area was the Wilhelmstrasse, a narrow street running south from the Linden. It took its name from King Frederick William I, who had ordered it laid out at the turn of the eighteenth century. In the 1870s, the Wilhelmstrasse was unpaved except for a narrow spur of cobblestones down the middle reserved for court carriages. The street was bordered by embassies, private residences as well as government buildings, many of them converted relics of aristocratic pretension. The most important of these bureaucratic offices were the three contiguous houses at numbers 75, 76, and 77.

Number 76 had been built in 1736 by a Prussian colonel as a comfortable and unimposing house for his family. Seventy years later, Max von Alopäus, the envoy to Berlin of Tsar Alexander I, acquired the property. He considerably enlarged the house and made a number of decorative alterations reflecting the prevailing Egyptian craze. In 1819, the Russian government sold the building, together with its furnishings, to Prussia for 80,000 thalers. The residence became the headquarters of the Prussian Ministry for Foreign

3

Affairs, which after 1871 acquired the codesignation of Foreign Office of the German Empire. The only entrance was through the wide wooden doors of the carriageway, over which was affixed a blue enameled plaque with the number 76. No inscription or fluttering ensign revealed the official nature of the premises. In 1874, the imperial government purchased the equally modest building at number 77, a 130-year-old dwelling formerly owned by the Radziwill family. In 1878 it became the residence of the imperial chancellor. Meanwhile, in 1877 the government took over a small house set in a park at number 75 belonging to the Decker publishing firm, and a villa, designed to serve as the residence of the state secretary of the Foreign Office, was erected in the spacious garden. Doors were cut between all these structures, and Bismarck and subsequent chancellors were therefore able to be in immediate contact with the personnel of the Foreign Office.[1]

All three buildings, placed directly on the sidewalk and scantly relieved by decorative embellishments, were drab and monotonous. The interiors were correspondingly wan, save for the pair of Nilotic sphinxes, a legacy of Alopäus, which flanked the stairs at 76. All the Bismarcks were notorious for their defective sense of chic, and Caprivi and Hohenlohe were equally immune to decorative taste.[2] It was not until Bernhard von Bülow and his cosmopolitan

[1] For a description of the buildings, see Moritz Busch, *Tagebuchblätter*, 3 vols. (Leipzig, 1899), II, 177–219, and Walter Zechlin, *Diplomatie und Diplomaten* (Stuttgart, 1935), pp. 64–85.

[2] "In Berlin society I have often heard Bismarck's establishment [Wilhelmstrasse 77] ridiculed," Count Philipp zu Eulenburg-Hertefeld wrote. "The Prussian nobility should rather be proud that it was not renounced by the greatest of its own, for we *Altpreussen* have always been tasteless." Johannes Haller, ed., *Aus 50 Jahren: Erinnerungen, Tagebücher und Briefe aus dem Nachlass des Fürsten Philipp zu Eulenburg-Hertefeld* (Berlin, 1923), pp. 117–18; also Rudolf Vierhaus, ed., *Das Tagebuch der Baronin Spitzemberg . . . : Aufzeichnungen aus der Hofgesellschaft des Hohenzollernreiches*, 2d ed. (Göttingen, 1960), pp. 171–72, 407.

wife moved to number 75 in 1897 that the state secretary's residence acquired any elegance. Marie Bülow transformed the garden villa into a house that charmed even the dour Friedrich von Holstein. Emboldened by this success, when in 1900 her husband became chancellor, she spent 240,000 marks decorating number 77.[3] Few structural changes were made over the years in either 75 or 76, except for the construction shortly after 1900 by State Secretary Baron Oswald von Richthofen of an *altdeutsche Bierstube* in the cellar of number 75.

The buildings at 75 and 76 were as uncomfortable in their interior appointments as they were ignoble in appearance. Neither had been designed for the bureaucratic purposes they were called upon to serve. Number 75, for example, had no interior corridors until it was renovated a few years before the outbreak of the First World War. Bismarck's parsimony as well as his hostility to modern devices, notably the telephone, was perpetuated by his successors.[4] Not until 1907 was the Foreign Office provided with electricity, and until that time smoky and malodorous oil lamps had been distributed to the staff on the basis of rank. A section chief or *Direktor* was entitled to two desk lamps and one ceiling fixture; a counselor *(Vortragender Rat)* was allowed only the desk lamps, while an assistant *(Hilfsarbeiter)* had to grope by the aid of a single fixture on his writing table. Telephones were also allotted according to title and position. Rudolf Nadolny, a young assistant at the turn of the century who in 1933 would become Hitler's first envoy to the Soviet Union, left an account of the advent of the telephone. Nadolny's chief, Counselor Rudolf Goebel von Harrant, had long been alarmed that if such devices penetrated the Wilhelmstrasse diplomats would eventually dare to ring

[3] Vierhaus, *Tagebuch; Spitzemberg*, p. 407; Ottomar von Mohl, *Aegypten* (Leipzig, 1922), p. 124; Sidney Whitman, *German Memories* (London, 1912), pp. 213–14.

[4] Ottomar von Mohl, *Fünfzig Jahre Reichsdienst: Lebenserinnerungen* (Leipzig, 1921), p. 240.

up the kaiser himself. While Goebel was away on vacation, a telephone was installed in his office. On his return, Goebel, aghast at the discovery of this affront, promptly cut the lines with his desk scissors. Nadolny, as a mere assistant not entitled to a phone, was given his chief's apparatus and became the envy of his junior colleagues.[5] Some rooms in the labyrinth at 76 were so cold and dank that they required heating ten months of the year. Moritz Busch, Bismarck's Francophobe minion, who spent many years in the building, pronounced it fit for comparison only with the prefecture of a middling French city.[6]

By 1914, the Berlin headquarters (*Zentralstelle*) of the Foreign Office, after four decades of gradual expansion, consisted of the state secretary, an under state secretary, three directors, four assistant directors (*Dirigenten*) and twenty-three counselors. Each of these bureaucrats was freighted with the titles and distinctions so vital in what Chancellor Hohenlohe deplored as the Wilhelmstrasse's "Chinese ordering of ranks."[7] A man who received the nod from on high translated from a mere *Legationsrat* to *Wirklicher Legationsrat und Vortragender Rat*, to *Geheimer Legationsrat*, and finally—ne plus ultra—to *Wirklicher Geheimer Legationsrat mit Prädikat Exzellenz*. Serving as underlings to the counselors were the twenty-seven assistants, the more fortunate of whom were eventually promoted to the dignity of counselor or given assignments abroad. The lower reaches of the Foreign Office consisted of cadres of decipherers, archivists, paymasters, and couriers, whose futures were limited almost without exception to becoming the heads of their respective services.[8]

[5] Nadolny, *Mein Beitrag* (Wiesbaden, 1955), p. 23.

[6] Busch, *Tagebuchblätter*, II, 179.

[7] Wilhelm Ohnesseit, *Unter der Fahne schwarz-weiss-rot: Erinnerungen eines kaiserlichen Generalkonsuls* (Berlin, 1926), p. 15.

[8] The discussion which follows, insofar as it concerns the *Zentralstelle*, does not include any personnel below the rank of assistant, since between 1871 and 1914 men in inferior positions were rarely

The state secretary was the superior officer of the Wilhelmstrasse, but in the imperial era the ultimate authority was the chancellor. In the Foreign Office, but not in the other branches of the federal government, the chancellor bore the title of *Chef*, and it was he and not the secretary who, with royal assent, appointed all Wilhelmstrasse personnel above the clerical level. The position of under state secretary was created in 1880 to take some of the administrative burden from the state secretary and was assigned to Clemens Busch, then serving as consul general in Budapest.[9] Busch was always very compliant toward Bismarck, and the state secretary, Count Herbert von Bismarck, the chancellor's son, was a forceful personality who made the most of his prerogative. In 1886, a Bavarian, Count Max von Berchem, assumed the post and soon found that the Bismarcks, father and son, did not intend to let him have any meaningful authority. Berchem attempted to abandon the position in favor of an envoyship, but he had already become the victim of an intrigue launched by Holstein, the senior counselor in the Political Division. In time the Bismarcks and Holstein virtually excluded Berchem from political affairs, and in 1890, unable to secure a suitable foreign post, he resigned.[10] His successors as under state secretary—Baron Wolfram von Rotenhan (1890–97), Baron

---

promoted to assistant or given field assignments in the diplomatic service, although some did later serve as consuls. The official listing of diplomatic personnel is found in Prussia, Staatsministerium, *Handbuch über das königlichen preussischen Staat und Hof* (Berlin, 1873–1919) and in Germany, Reichskanzlei, *Handbuch für das deutsche Reich* (Berlin, 1873–1919).

[9] Ludwig Raschdau, *Unter Bismarck und Caprivi: Erinnerungen eines deutschen Diplomaten aus den Jahren 1885–1894*, 2d ed. (Berlin, 1939), p. 165.

[10] Ibid.; BvB to Lindenau, Sept. 18, 1887, BüN 99; Berchem to KvR, June 16, 1890, BisN FC 2954/291–93; PzE to FvH, Aug. 1, 1890, HolN 3855/H192177–78; Mohl, *Fünfzig Jahre*, p. 249; John C.G. Röhl, *Germany without Bismarck: The Crisis of Government in the Second Reich, 1890–1900* (Berkeley, 1967), p. 59.

Oswald von Richthofen (1897–1900), Otto von Mühlberg (1900–07), Wilhelm Stemrich (1907–11) and Arthur Zimmermann (1911–16)—were essentially unobtrusive administrative functionaries rather than policy makers. The real work of the Foreign Office conducted in Berlin was performed by the counselors, who reported to the state secretary. Initially no formal distinction was made with respect to area of competence among these figures other than that, after 1879, one was in charge of personnel, but as the scope of business increased they were differentiated into divisions. In 1881, the Political Division, administratively denominated as Division I, was created and placed under the direct supervision of the state secretary and under state secretary. It was entrusted with surveying dispatches from field personnel, making policy recommendations to the state secretary and chancellor, handling press affairs, and determining the disposition of diplomatic and consular posts. In 1885, the Political Division was subdivided into section A, which handled diplomatic and press affairs, and section B, responsible for personnel.[11] Section B, headed either by a director or assistant director after 1890, was kept very subordinate to A, its counselors seldom ascended into the A section and only rarely were they given any opportunity for service in the field. Under Chancellor Caprivi, Holstein began to detach the more important appointments from section B and to entrust such matters to his confidants among the counselors in A. This arrangment became official in 1895 and continued through 1918.[12] After 1910, one of the counselors served as director of section A.

[11] The counselors in section B handling personnel were Otto von Bülow (1879–81), Johannes Humbert (1881–95), Lothar von Eichhorn (1895–1903), Georg von Schwartzkoppen (1903–12), and Theodor Matthieu (1912–14).

[12] Julius von Eckardt, *Lebenserinnerungen*, 2 vols. (Leipzig, 1910), II, 114–15; Mohl, *Fünfzig Jahre*, p. 283. In the 1896 edition of the *Handbuch über das königlichen preussischen Staat und Hof* the rubric "ausschliesslich derjenigen des diplomatischen Dienstes etc." first

Division II dealt with trade treaties, emigration, the protection of German nationals and their property in foreign lands, passports, patent questions, extraditions, border violations, and in addition superintended consular personnel appointments and examined drafts of legislation coming to the Foreign Office from other branches of the government. By the mid-1880s, it was dealing with eighty percent of the Foreign Office's annual crop of 70,000 reports.[13] In 1885, the division was designated the *Handelspolitische Abteilung*, and thereafter the lack of interest of the Political Division in economic matters — and in Division II — was pronounced.[14] A legal division (Division III, or *Rechtsabteilung*) was established in 1885, and in 1890 still another division, the *Kolonial Abteilung*, was formed. Divisions II, III, and the *Kolonial Abteilung* were each headed by a director under whom the counselors and their assistants served. The *Kolonial Abteilung* was unique in that its director had the right of direct access to the emperor.

The character of the Political Division was markedly different from that of the other sections. It was more important, for its officials were involved in making policy while the other divisions for the most part merely rendered opinions or executed orders. Consequently, Bismarck himself handpicked the counselors who served there, and they were the only ones who enjoyed the privilege of direct intercourse with the chancellor.[15] Service in the Political Divi-

---

appears following "B. Personalien." After I–A "Politische" the notice "und Personalien des diplomatischen Dienstes" appears for the first time.

[13] Memo dated Jan. 1878 from the Bucher correspondence in BisN FC 2957/528–35; Reichstag, Dec. 15, 1884, p. 356 (Busch).

[14] Otto Hammann, *Der neue Kurs: Erinnerungen* (Berlin, 1918), p. 56.

[15] Ludwig Raschdau, "Fürst Bismarck als Leiter der Politischen Abteilung: aus der schriftlichen Nachlass der Unter Staatssekretärs Dr. Busch," *Deutsche Rundschau*, CLI (1912), 48; Eckardt, *Lebenserinnerungen*, II, 113.

sion conferred a special luster on a diplomat when he went into the field, for he was known to have firsthand acquaintance with the highest officials in the Wilhelmstrasse.[16] So great was the repute of the division that a counselor with long service there regarded being appointed minister to a minor German state as a demotion, while an envoy reassigned to Berlin considered being placed in any section other than the Political Division a similarly deplorable fate.[17]

The staff of the Political Division was the most aristocratic and the most Prussian contingent in the Wilhelmstrasse, and its snobbish counselors indulged in little traffic, social or professional, with their colleagues in the other divisions.

TABLE 1

PERSONNEL IN FOREIGN OFFICE DIVISIONS
(DIRECTORS, ASSISTANT DIRECTORS, COUNSELORS)

Section	Period	% Noble	% Prussian	% Prussian Noble	% E. Prussian Noble
Political Division (I-A only)	1881–1914	61.36	63.64	38.64	27.27
Handelspolitische Abteilung (II)	1881–1914	55.17	58.62	24.14	24.14
Rechtsabteilung (III)	1881–1914	28.57	57.14	19.05	19.05
Kolonial Abteilung	1890–1907	27.27	36.36	13.64	13.64

A counselor in Division II responsible for following the economic affairs of a foreign power could only in exceptional cases persuade the Political Division to let him examine the intelligence it had assembled on the nation in question.[18] Moreover, the Political Division counselors do not appear

[16] Monts to Marie von Bülow, Nov. 6, 1902, BüN 106; undated memo by Wilhelm von Stumm, in ThimmeN 24, pp. 4–7.

[17] Raschdau, *Unter Bismarck*, p. 352; HvB to BvB, Dec. 25, 1886, BüN 66.

[18] Hammann, *Neue Kurs*, p. 56.

to have had to work as tirelessly as their counterparts in the other sections, and Bismarck became sufficiently alarmed to compel them to account for their time.[19] Not surprisingly, the Political Division was resented, but it had to be handled warily because of its control of personnel. To run afoul of its counselors—and particularly of the éminence grise, Holstein—could adversely affect one's future. On the other hand, a diplomat could use contacts there to further his career. Bernhard von Bülow, to take one example, was careful to maintain close relations with several officials there during his extended service (1888–94) in remote Rumania. He corresponded regularly with Karl von Lindenau, an assistant, while another of his friends was Ludwig Raschdau, an influential counselor, who in the early 1890s warned Bülow that the humorless Caprivi was not amused by his gossipy *Alkoven-Geschichten* regarding the peccadillos of Crown Prince Ferdinand.[20]

Another feature which differentiated the Political Division from the other sections was the continuing interplay between its staff and diplomats in the field. On entry into the service, each fledgling diplomat was temporarily assigned to a Political Division counselor or assistant, who was responsible for introducing him to the regimen of the Wilhelmstrasse. Once assigned abroad, every diplomat came under the supervision of the counselor charged with the geographical area in which his post lay. The counselor observed the diplomat's behavior, surveyed his dispatches, and recommended changes in his assignments. The desirability of an individual post was therefore in part deter-

---

[19] FvH to HvB, June 16, and Sept. 22, 1880, BisN FC 2966/440, 500.

[20] BvB to Lindenau, May 9, 1890, Apr. 25, 1891, BüN 99; Friedrich Thimme, ed., *Front wider Bülow: Staatsmänner, Diplomaten und Forscher zu seinen Denkwürdigkeiten* (Munich, 1931), p. 22. Bülow was also in continuous contact with Holstein, for which see HolN 3854–55.

mined by the counselor under whose jurisdiction it fell.[21] The division of responsibility among the counselors shortly after the turn of the century was as follows. Holstein treated France, Italy, Switzerland, Spain, Tunis, Algeria, and Morocco. Bülow's friend Lindenau, now a counselor, was responsible for Great Britain and the United States, together with their colonies, as well as Afghanistan. Otto Hammann dealt with the press, while Reinhold Klehmet supervised Germany, the Vatican, China, Japan, Korea, Siam, and religious affairs excepting those in the Orient. Otto von Below-Schlattau managed Austria, Russia, the Pamirs, Belgium, and the Netherlands as well as personnel affairs; Friedrich Rosen had Turkey, Rumania, Serbia, Greece, Montenegro, Bulgaria, Egypt, Persia, and Oriental religious matters. Alexander von Kries' bailiwick was Denmark, Sweden, Norway, Luxemburg, Portugal, Mexico and South America, Africa, and the German colonies. He was additionally entrusted with keeping a watch on the anarchist movement insofar as the legal division did not deal with this conspiracy under police affairs.[22]

After their introductory training, novice diplomats, who up to this point had received no wages and only occasionally scant per diem allowances, were sent to their first assignments. When these apprentice years were over, many young secretaries of legation returned temporarily to Berlin as assistants or as counselors, usually in the Political Division. Some diplomats assigned to this department early in their careers stayed there for years, finally being rewarded for their long service by being accredited as ministers to foreign courts. In some cases, the inability of counselors and other Foreign Office officials to get along with each other

---

[21] Ludwig Raschdau, *In Weimar als preussischer Gesandter: ein Buch der Erinnerungen an deutsche Fürstenhöfe, 1894–1897* (Berlin, 1939), pp. 164–66.

[22] Undated memo (ca. 1906) in Dd 149, vol. 10, T–149/280/ 00383–85. Below's jurisdiction in personnel affairs affected only matters not covered by the personnel counselor in section I–B.

resulted in one of the parties being sent abroad in order to eliminate the friction in Berlin.[23] Twenty-five of the forty-four men who at various times were assigned as counselors in the Political Division later served as envoys, while thirty-two (72.73 percent) had some record of diplomatic or consular service. At every level, a protégé relationship prevailed between the younger diplomats and their superiors in the Political Division. If the association was cordial, their futures proceeded smoothly, but those who occasioned difficulties were packed off to dreary diplomatic posts or, worse, assigned to the consular service.

The careers of men in the other divisions were more static. Most assistants or counselors in these sections had been stationed in Berlin since their entry into the service, though some had earlier been posted abroad as consuls. An official in these less distinguished divisions was seldom given assignment in the field, and then usually only in the twilight of his career for a terminal appointment as minister to a South American republic.[24] Bismarck was dissatisfied with this differentiation in the careers of his staff, for he felt that Political Division personnel spent so much time abroad that they lost sight of domestic affairs, while men in the other divisions often did not have enough service abroad to appreciate foreign problems. He therefore saw to it that young diplomats, all of whom were likely candidates for later service in the Political Division, did some time in the Wilhelmstrasse before being posted abroad to their initial assignments. He also attempted, but only with moderate success, to introduce the personnel of the other divisions to foreign duty.[25] Finally, as a physical symptom of the pre-

[23] Max von Philippsborn, a senior counselor in the Political Division, found that he could not work with Under State Secretary Busch and in 1880 asked for and received the ministership in Copenhagen. KvR to HvB, Sept. 19, 1880, BisN FC 3028.

[24] Mohl, *Fünfzig Jahre*, pp. 145–46; Arthur von Brauer, *Im Dienste Bismarcks: persönliche Erinnerungen* (Berlin, 1936), p. 94.

[25] Reichstag, Mar. 24, 1873, pp. 64–65 (Bismarck).

ferred status of the Political Division, it alone was housed with the state secretary at number 76.[26] Until the late 1880s, the other divisions were exiled to temporary quarters several doors down the street and thereafter crowded together at number 75. The *Kolonial Abteilung*, which was regarded with disdain by counselors in the Political Division and by other diplomats as a dumping ground for failures from other departments of the Foreign Office, was permanently banished to Wilhelmstrasse 62.[27]

Just as there were numerous distinctions between the Political Division and the other sections of the Berlin headquarters, so diplomatic posts were of various levels of significance and prestige. In 1871, the combined Prussian-German Foreign Office took over the eighteen diplomatic posts which the Prussian Foreign Ministry had previously managed for the North German Confederation, retaining all the incumbents in office. The ambassadorship in Paris was, for the moment, unoccupied. The eight Prussian ministers to the other German states were all retained. The formation of the empire thus occasioned hardly any change except that envoys stationed outside of Germany, with the exception of the Prussian minister to the Vatican, were now to be styled as imperial dignitaries.

The seven great European ambassadorships—Constantinople, London, Madrid, Paris, Rome, St. Petersburg, and Vienna—were the premier diplomatic plums.[28] The ministerial posts in the remaining European capitals were next in importance. These ministries, with the dates of their establishment if after 1871, were Belgium, Bulgaria (1909),

[26] On the separation of the Political Division see Mohl, *Fünfzig Jahre*, pp. 34, 145–46; Brauer, *Im Dienste Bismarcks*, pp. 94–95; Raschdau, *In Weimar*, p. 78; Otto Hammann, *Um den Kaiser: Erinnerungen aus den Jahren 1906–1909* (Berlin, 1919), pp. 36–37; Raschdau, *Unter Bismarck*, pp. 10, 168–69.

[27] Karl F. Nowak and Friedrich Thimme, eds., *Erinnerungen und Gedanken des Botschafters Anton Graf Monts* (Berlin, 1932), p. 365.

[28] Constantinople was raised to embassy status in 1874, Rome in 1876, and Madrid in 1888.

Denmark, Greece, Luxemburg (1890), Montenegro (1906), the Netherlands, Norway (1906), Portugal, Rumania (1881), Sweden, Switzerland, and Serbia (1880). These positions differed widely in their significance. Bulgaria, Sweden, and Norway were posts of little political consequence, disliked by those who held them, and they were not places of apprenticeship for the seven European embassies. The only exception was Count Carl von Wedel, a military figure who served briefly, and under protest, in Stockholm (1893–94) before eventually moving on to Italy in 1899 and Vienna in 1902. The other European ministries were proving grounds for fifteen of the thirty-five men who filled the seven European embassies. Belgium, which was regarded as the leading ministry, headed the list, followed by Denmark, Greece, the Netherlands, and Rumania. Switzerland was relatively insignificant. As one German diplomat posted there modestly observed, Berne was a place to which the powers sent envoys who were impossible anywhere else. Diplomats who were accredited there did little but complain about their fate.[29] The remote American, African and Asian ministries were, with the exception of Washington and Tokyo, unwelcome assignments of relative inconsequence.

The Prussian ministries to the German states were by and large of limited significance, and the business transacted there was neither important nor taxing. An envoy's responsibility consisted largely of dutiful attendance at court functions and of accommodating, or in some cases frustrating, the prince's concern that Berlin treat him as a German sovereign by keeping him informed of imperial diplomatic developments.[30] Prince Alexander von Hohenlohe, whose

[29] Alfred von Bülow to BvB, Aug. 11, 1888, BüN 14; HvB to Wilhelm von Bismarck, May 2, 1876, BisN FC 3011/133–34.

[30] For princely anxiety on this point see State Secretary Bernhard Ernst von Bülow to the Foreign Office, Mar. 2, 1874, Gen 1 AA.a.61, vol. 1, 279/00548–51; same to Wentzel (minister to Hesse), ibid., 00580; Derenthall (minister to Württemberg) to Chancellor Bülow,

father was chancellor and who served briefly as a diplomat, held the lesser of the ministries to be inferior in importance to the office of *Regierungspräsident*, a position which he later held in Colmar.[31]

In addition to the imperial and Prussian posts, there were also consular positions available to junior diplomats.[32] A young man eager to join the foreign service had to decide whether he would apply for the diplomatic or the consular branch. Some who chose the latter did so intending it as a lifetime career; others selected it in the expectation that their consular status would eventually be converted into a diplomatic appointment.[33] A consular official could apply for transfer to the diplomatic service, but usually such a move came only when a young consul's reports caught Bismarck's eye or struck a counselor in the Political Division as especially promising. He might then be transferred to Berlin as an assistant or given a diplomatic appointment as secretary of legation.[34] In rare instances, a senior consul

---

Dec. 5, 1901, Dd 149, vol. 7, T–149/280/00282–84; Count Henckel (minister to Oldenburg) to same, Dec. 8, 1902, ibid., 00298; Count Dönhoff (minister to Saxony) to same, Apr. 22, 1905, ibid., vol. 9, 00361–62; Bülow (minister to Oldenburg) to Chancellor Bethmann Hollweg, Nov. 21, 1910, ibid., vol. 13, 00506.

[31] Alexander Hohenlohe to Chlodwig Hohenlohe, July 21, 1898, HohN, XXII.A.14.

[32] The classic study of the German consular service is Bernhard W. von König, *Handbuch des deutschen Konsularwesens*, 7th rev. ed., 2 vols. (Berlin, 1909). See also Anon., "Die diplomatische und die Consularvertretung des deutschen Reiches," *Preussische Jahrbücher*, XLVII, no. 4 (1881), 380–96. In 1908 there were 126 professional, salaried consular officials (*Berufskonsuln*) and another 634 *Wahlkonsuln*, who lived off their fees and with whom diplomatic personnel did not mingle. Movements of consular personnel are listed in Germany, Reichskanzlei, *Central-Blatt des deutschen Reiches* (Berlin, 1873–1919).

[33] Alfred von Kiderlen-Wächter to Carl Weiszäcker, June 21, 1880, in Kl. Erwb, 458F, 6.

[34] Brauer, *Im Dienste Bismarcks*, pp. 30, 50; Ludwig Raschdau, "Meine ersten dienstlichen Beziehungen zu Fürst Bismarck," in Ar-

might temporarily assume a counselor's duties.[35] Sometimes the transition was in the opposite direction, for consular positions were also later given to men who had entered the service as diplomatic appointees. Bismarck felt that some exposure to consular affairs was desirable training for Wilhelmstrasse personnel, and he and other Foreign Office dignitaries also used the consular service as a means of ridding themselves of diplomats whom they found incapable or obnoxious.[36]

The ultimate consular post, a general consulship, was given to relatively young candidates, and many general consuls were therefore anxious to move on to still more choice positions in the diplomatic service before reaching the age of retirement. The Foreign Office sometimes obliged by elevating them to ministerships, but with very few exceptions they were accredited only to South American and minor Asian capitals. Another link between the consular and diplomatic services was the position of dragoman in several African and Near Eastern posts. The dragoman's duty, in addition to serving as translator, was to draw up *Kapitulationen* with foreign governments prescribing the extraterritorial rights of German citizens. Dragomen held appointments as consuls but some won transfers to the diplomatic service, and one sandwiched a term as minister to Morocco between long periods as first dragoman in the embassy in Constantinople.[37] Baron von Richthofen, the state secretary

thur von Brauer et al., eds., *Erinnerungen an Bismarck: Aufzeichnungen von Mitarbeitern und Freunden des Fürsten* . . . , 4th ed. (Stuttgart, 1915), p. 27; Mohl, *Fünfzig Jahre*, p. 145; Raschdau, *In Weimar*, pp. 1–2.

[35] Count Siegfried zu Castell-Rüdenhausen, "Kurze Aufzeichnungen über das Jahr 1888," CN, IeVI/29.

[36] Reichstag, Mar. 24, 1873, pp. 64–65 (Bismarck); FvH to HvB, July 5, 1882, BisN FC 2966/207.

[37] Nadolny, *Mein Beitrag*, pp. 18, 24, discusses the dragomen but is in error in stating that these positions were eliminated before 1914. See also Hajo Holborn, ed., *Aufzeichnungen und Erinnerungen aus dem Leben des Botschafters Joseph Maria von Radowitz*, 2 vols. (Berlin, 1925), II, 208–10.

from 1900 to 1906, entered the foreign service as a dragoman, as did Baron Klemens von Ketteler, whose career met
an untimely end when, as minister to China, he was assas-
sinated by the Boxer rebels in the legation compound in
Peking.

Athough there was some resentment by regular diplomatic personnel at the absorption of consuls into the diplomatic service and although the Political Division was
adamantly opposed to any merger of the diplomatic and
consular services, a discernible relationship gradually
emerged between the two.[38] About one of every four diplomats, including some of the most well known—Bernstorff,
Metternich, Radowitz, Monts, to name but a few prominent
envoys—combined consular with diplomatic careers.[39] The
connection between the two services was further strengthened by the fact that about a third of the Foreign Office
personnel whose service was otherwise restricted to Berlin
also held positions as consuls before or after transferring to
the diplomatic service.

The task of determining who should fill what positions
became more complicated as Germany's position in the
world expanded. In 1872, the first year for which definitive
figures are available, the civil personnel stationed in Berlin
in the ranks of assistant and above numbered only eighteen,

[38] See BvB to PzE, Apr. 24, 1893, in EN, XXIV, 215–19, complaining of the decline in Foreign Office morale because of the introduction of consular and military personnel into the diplomatic
service. For testimony on the closeness of the consular and diplomatic
services see Richard von Kühlmann, *Die Diplomaten* (Berlin, 1939),
pp. 85–86; State Secretary Baron Wilhelm von Schoen's remarks in
the Reichstag, Mar. 16, 1910, pp. 2168–69; Nadolny, *Mein Beitrag*,
p. 24; and Mohl, *Fünfzig Jahre*, pp. 145–46.

[39] Of the 548 persons serving between 1871 and 1914 in the ranks
of assistant or secretary of legation, or above, 158 (28.83%) held
consular appointments at one time or another in the course of their
careers. Of the 187 envoys, 75 (40.11%) and 54 of the 128 counselors (42.19%) held such appointments.

the civil personnel in thirty-four diplomatic (but not consular) posts came to fifty, exclusive of dragomen, secretarial, medical, and religious staff, for a total of sixty-eight. In 1914, the corresponding figures were fifty-nine persons in Berlin, not including colonial administrators, who in 1907 had been removed from the Foreign Office to an independent *Kolonial Amt*. There were another ninety-three men stationed in forty posts around the world. In addition, during this forty-year period there had been a striking increase in the number of military officers attached to foreign missions. In 1872, eight officers had been so assigned, but by 1914 the figure had risen to thirty-eight, in addition to which another five were assigned to Berlin. The cost

TABLE 2

FOREIGN OFFICE PERSONNEL

		1872		1914	
		#	%	#	%
Berlin:	Civil	18	23.68	59	30.26
	Military	—	—	5	2.56
Field:	Civil	50	65.79	93	47.69
	Military	8	10.53	38	19.49
	Total	76	100.00	195	100.00

of maintaining this diplomatic establishment, which by 1912 stood at slightly more than 19,000,000 marks per year, was twice what it had been twenty years earlier.[40] By the outbreak of the First World War, the German diplomatic service, by its own reckoning, was not only considerably larger than that of any other major European nation but also handled a greater volume of business and a greater work load per man. Next to the actual conduct of diplomacy, the Wilhelmstrasse's principal concern was to attract to the service

[40] Germany, Finanzministerium, *Reichshaushalts-Etat*, 1891–92, p. 26; ibid., 1912, p. 20.

TABLE 3
FOREIGN OFFICE WORK LOAD, 1907

	Germany	Great Britain	France	Russia	Austria	Italy	USA
		Number of documents					
Political Division	26,290	23,372	—	8,467	—	—	—
Trade Division	41,507	20,136	—	17,000	—	—	—
Legal Division	61,262	7,146	—	—	—	—	—
Other	50,790	1,904	—	13,499	—	—	—
Total	179,849	52,558	—	[38,966]	99,000+	92,000	105,125
		Number of officials					
Senior Officials*	52	56	84	214	95	84	64
Junior Officials*	198	50	166	—	100	67	63
Total	250	106	250	214	195	151	127
Reports per Senior Official*	3,459	938	—	1,821	1,042**	1,095	1,643

* In the original table, designated *Hohe Beamte* and *Bureau Beamte*, respectively.

** In the original table, this number was given incorrectly as 1,368.

SOURCE: This table was assembled by the Foreign Office for a Reichstag speech by State Secretary Kiderlen-Wächter on Aug. 11, 1908, and is located in Dd 122, vol. 3, T–149/280/00795–97. The figures for the United States are taken from Dd 149, vol. 12, T–149/280/00462.

men who would be aware of Germany's increasingly important role in world affairs and at the same time be emblematic of its tradition of aristocratic statecraft.

## CHAPTER II

Intelligence and Income

The German diplomatic service was a career open to talent, but also to connections. For all aspirants, a maze of requirements, first for admission and later for advancement, had to be satisfied. But for every rule there was an exception, for every seemingly insuperable barrier an avenue of appeal. Where talents or qualifications were pale, family and friends often proved effective surrogates. As a result, the imperial diplomatic corps was an assemblage of men of real ability in some cases, of little other than luminous lineage in others. Not a few diplomats could provide evidence of both.

Any young man, provided he was twenty-five years old and a citizen of one of the German states, could apply directly to the Foreign Office for admission to the diplomatic or to the consular service. If already a member of the consular service, the candidate could request transfer to the diplomatic branch. Those born with patrician pedigrees could frequently depend on the nepotism of relatives already in the service or on connections at court or in the bureaucracy. It was not unusual for an ambassador to request that a son or nephew be assigned to his mission as an unsalaried civil attaché. These subalterns did not receive diplomatic commissions, but attaché service facilitated their subsequent absorption into the regular Foreign Office staff. Two ambassadors to France, Prince Chlodwig zu Hohenlohe-Schillingsfürst and Baron Wilhelm von Schoen, were joined in Paris by their sons. Radowitz at Madrid sent for his son, while young Count Hatzfeldt-Wildenburg served under his father at the Court of St. James. Uncles were similarly useful in smoothing the entry of their nephews into the diplomatic service. When Count Karl von Pückler, a junior army officer, desired to become a diplomat, he asked his uncle, Prince Heinrich VII Reuss, the ambassador to Austria-Hungary, to request that he be assigned to the embassy. Pückler's father made a similar entreaty to General Emil von Albydyll, the chief of the Military Cabinet, noting that he had provided his son with an annual allowance of 15,000 marks. Pückler shortly thereafter appeared in Vienna as a member of Reuss' staff.[1] There were other cases of avuncular patronage among various Bülows, Schlözers, Stumms, Metternichs and Rotenhans.

Chancellors and state secretaries were also adept at obtaining places for their sons or nephews in the service. The later chancellor, Bernhard von Bülow, entered the service while his father was state secretary. Bülows *fils* understandably did not object when much later, during his tenure as chancellor, a son of his state secretary, Baron von Richthofen, was introduced into the service. He also saw to it that his own relatives, as well as those of his wife, won diplomatic preferment even when their talents were minimal.[2] Bismarck arranged for both of his sons to serve in the Foreign Office, and the elder, Herbert, ascended to the state secretaryship while his father was chancellor. The Hohenlohe connection was especially involved in nepotism. Prince Hohenlohe, who as ambassador in Paris had had one son join his mission, later as chancellor had another given a position in the Wilhelmstrasse. In 1900, Hohenlohe ordered Darmstadt vacated in order to make it available for his nephew, Prince Hans zu Hohenlohe-Oehringen. Still another nephew, Prince Max von Ratibor und Corvey, was tireless in using Uncle Chlodwig to advance his career. Ratibor, like other Hohenlohes, was fearful that the chancellor, who was seventy-five when he took office in 1894,

---

[1] GN, 1071; Pückler, *Aus meinem Diplomatenleben* (Schweidnitz, 1934), p. 7.

[2] Count Kuno von Rantzau, "Autobiographische und andere Aufzeichnungen," BisN FC 3030/643.

might die before he had secured a satisfactory post. Finally in 1900, several months before Hohenlohe's resignation, Ratibor was made minister at Weimar. Chlodwig's own son Alexander, an able official but an acerbic personality, did not fare so well, for his tongue had offended William II, who therefore declined to offer him an envoyship.[3]

There were altogether twenty-four diplomat fathers who produced twenty-nine diplomat sons in the period from 1871 to 1914. At least two families—the Bülows and the Richthofens—were represented by three generations of diplomats in this period. Finally, there were ten sets of brothers, seven uncle-nephew connections, one grandfather-grandson, and some eighty-nine cousins (all but six of them noble), with the Bülows leading the count with ten members. A great many other diplomats enjoyed various degrees of kinship through birth or marriage. Count Nicolas von Wallwitz, for example, married the daughter of Count Karl von Dönhoff, longtime Prussian minister at Dresden. Dönhoff's wife divorced him and then married Bernhard von Bülow, who thus became Wallwitz's stepfather-in-law. Wallwitz, who had been minister to Sweden, was promoted to Brussels shortly after Bülow became chancellor in 1900 and left the service after Bülow's fall, when it became apparent that he would receive no further advancement. For the German nobility, the Foreign Office was a family operation.

Protégés of chancellors, state secretaries, or envoys were by no means always members of their families. Bismarck kept an eye out for young men who offered some prospect of maturing into accomplished diplomats. The Iron Chan-

---

[3] Ratibor to Alexander Hohenlohe, Apr. 26 and May 12, 1896, HohN, XXII.A.8; Alexander to Chlodwig Hohenlohe, July 13 and 20, 1897, ibid., XXII.A.11; Heinrich O. Meisner, ed., *Denkwürdigkeiten des General-Feldmarschalls Alfred Grafen von Waldersee*, 3 vols. (Stuttgart, 1923–25), II, 439. Other Hohenlohe kinsmen, notably Prince Karl Max von Lichnowsky, found their connections an advantage.

cellor himself selected Bernhard von Bülow, still in his twenties but already celebrated for his charm.[4] Others brought themselves to Bismarck's attention through requests to be admitted to the diplomatic service. Karl von Schlözer, whose candidacy doubtless owed its inspiration to his distinguished Uncle Kurd, then minister to the Vatican, applied personally to the chancellor. He was accepted and went on to have a distinguished career as minister to Bavaria.[5] Richard von Kühlmann, who would serve briefly as state secretary in 1917, is an interesting example of the chancellors' highly personal manner of selecting fresh material. Kühlmann's father had known Chancellor Hohenlohe since the 1860s, and Hohenlohe had once told him that if one of his sons should ever desire a diplomatic appointment to send him to Berlin. Young Richard did eventually apply directly to the chancellor, who forwarded his application to the Political Division. Here it encountered objections, so Hohenlohe took matters into his own hands. He summoned Kühlmann to dinner at Wilhelmstrasse 77, asking him to arrive early. Hohenlohe placed the young man at his side at the head of the stairs. When the guests arrived they proved to be diplomatic dignitaries, and the chancellor's greeting to each was "May I introduce you to Herr von Kühlmann, who is entering the Foreign Office at my wish." Later that evening Kühlmann's commission arrived.[6]

Bernhard von Bülow, first as ambassador, then as state secretary and finally as chancellor, was instrumental in gaining entry for several aspiring diplomats. He favored some applications because they happened to come from relatives of his friends. Gottlieb von Jagow, for example, was admitted largely because his brother had served in the hus-

[4] Bülow, Denkwürdigkeiten, 4 vols. (Berlin, 1930–31), IV, 288–89.

[5] Karl von Schlözer, Menschen und Landschaften: aus dem Skizzenbuch eines Diplomaten (Berlin, 1926), p. 96.

[6] Kühlmann, Erinnerungen (Heidelberg, 1948), pp. 118–20. For a Caprivi protégé see Edgar Stern-Rubarth, Graf Brockdorff-Rantzau: Wanderer zwischen zwei Welten, 2 vols. (Berlin, 1936), I, 27.

sars with Bülow. Bülow's old comrade-in-arms wrote in 1895 asking that the ailing Gottlieb be attached to Bülow's sunny Italian embassy. He agreed, and a career was launched which would culminate in 1913 in Jagow's appointment as state secretary.[7] Among other state secretaries, Herbert von Bismarck was particularly active in encouraging his friends to enter the service. Two of the least attractive diplomatic personalities of Wilhelmine Germany, Prince Philipp zu Eulenburg-Hertefeld and Baron Hermann von Eckardstein, owed their admission to his suggestion, and Eulenburg himself was later engaged in recruiting talent for the Wilhelmstrasse.[8] Ambassadors as well as counselors in the Political Division were also involved in recruiting diplomatic material.[9]

The Foreign Office was remarkably independent in engaging young men for the diplomatic service, choosing those whom it found attractive, rejecting those whose qualifications seemed deficient. Only rarely was its freedom of choice encroached upon by external forces. There were only a few cases of influence being applied to secure the admission of candidates already, or likely to be, rejected by the Wilhelmstrasse. Usually, pressure from outside the Foreign Office consisted of little more than the recommendation to the Wilhelmstrasse by rulers, anxious parents, and military commanders of names of potential diplomats. The

---

[7] Bülow, *Denkwürdigkeiten*, III, 33–34. For an example of Bülow's patronage as chancellor see MiquelN, 00186–87.

[8] Eckardstein, *Lebenserinnerungen u. politische Denkwürdigkeiten*, 3 vols. (Leipzig, 1919–21), I, 83–88; Eulenburg, *Aus 50 Jahren: Erinnerungen, Tagebücher und Briefe* (Berlin, 1923), pp. 50–51. For Eulenburg's activity as a recruiter see his letters to HvB of Oct. 7, 1880, and Oct. 9, 1881, and to OvB of July 19, 1882, in BisN FC 2961/1143–44, 1163–64, 1210; and his letters to HvB of Mar. 23, 1882, Aug. 13, 1887, and May 20, 1888, in ibid., FC 2962/9–10, 143–44, 158–59.

[9] Rudolf Vierhaus, ed., *Das Tagebuch der Baronin Spitzemberg* . . . : *Aufzeichnungen aus der Hofgesellschaft des Hohenzollernreiches*, 2d ed. (Göttingen, 1960), pp. 397–98; Count Castell-Rüdenhausen's memo entitled "Das Jahr 1888," CN, IeVI/29.

Foreign Office in most cases acted as it pleased on such suggestions.[10]

*

Formal admission to the diplomatic service was in most cases contingent on passing a series of examinations. In order to qualify for a four-year assignment as a probationary, unsalaried attaché, a candidate had to certify that he had passed the primary legal examination (*Referendarexamen*). This examination, for which one stood after three or four years of university study, was administered by the federal states and was an arduous affair. The Bavarian test, for example, consisted of sixty-four hours of questioning spread over eight days.[11] After this internship, the neophyte was promoted to a regular position as a salaried secretary of legation. As an alternate path to a diplomatic career, a university student on completion of his *Referendar* could practice law or serve in the bureaucracy for four years and then present himself for the secondary legal examination (*Assessorexamen*). If successful, he received the doctor juris degree and was then granted a one year probationary term as an unpaid attaché, after which he was made a salaried secretary. In exceptional cases, men without either the *Referendar* or the *Assessor* certificate might be admitted as attachés, but in such cases their probationary period was set at five years and during this period they were expected to attend university lectures in law, history, economics, and other appropriate subjects.[12] The Foreign Office preferred

[10] For examples of parental pressure see Helmuth Rogge, ed., *Friedrich von Holstein: Lebensbekenntnis in Briefen an eine Frau* (Berlin, 1932), p. 183, and Arthur von Brauer et al., eds., *Erinnerungen an Bismarck* (Berlin, 1915), pp. 343–44.

[11] Kühlmann, *Erinnerungen*, p. 114.

[12] Ibid., p. 117; Great Britain, House of Commons, Accounts and Papers, 1912–13 session, Command Paper #6268, misc. no. 9, "Return showing the conditions of entry into the Austro-Hungarian, Ger-

candidates in possession of the *Assessor* certificate, for the law, with its precision of argument and expression, was the most exacting training for those who would as diplomats have to draft watertight conventions and treaties or draw up unambiguous directives for their colleagues stationed in foreign capitals. Just under one-third of the 548 diplomats holding the rank of assistant or secretary of legation or above between 1871 and 1914 held the doctor juris degree.

TABLE 4
LEGAL DEGREES OF FOREIGN OFFICE PERSONNEL

Position	# Persons	# Dr. Juris	% Dr. Juris
State/Under State			
Secretaries	9	—	—
Envoys	187	43	22.99
Directors/			
Counselors	109	41	37.61
Jr. Field			
Personnel	121	35	28.93
Assistants	82	32	39.02
Attachés	40	11	27.50
Total	548	162	29.56

NOTE: Each person is ranked in ultimate position achieved.

Candidates also had to negotiate examination hurdles administered by the Foreign Office. These consisted of a written examination, which lasted eight hours and for which the candidates were allowed to use printed materials in composing their answers, and then an oral interrogation conducted in French and English.[13] Count Ulrich von Brockdorff-Rantzau, formidable even in youth, managed to finesse entirely his oral examination in French. The first question addressed to him concerned William II's birthday,

---

man, Italian and Russian diplomatic services," pp. 142–45; John C.G. Röhl, "Beamtenpolitik im wilhelmischen Deutschland," in Michael Stürmer, ed., *Das kaiserliche Deutschland: Politik und Gessellschaft, 1870–1918* (Düsseldorf, 1970), p. 292.

[13] Castell diary, Mar. 23, 1889, CN, IeVI/29.

27

which was being celebrated on that day. Brockdorff dismissed the question, as well as the examiner, by observing that, "Heute am Kaisers Geburtstag, sprechen wir lieber Deutsch."[14] The interrogator was offended, but Brockdoff passed without having had to speak any French.

Next came the *grosses diplomatisches Examen*, which was usually taken two years after being admitted as attaché.[15] Every attaché entering the provisional ranks was assigned three subjects on which he was expected to prepare essays in his spare time. One, to be composed in German, was to deal with an aspect of history, law, or economics. The other two consisted of analyses of specific diplomatic problems. Until 1908, one of these essays was to be in French and one in German; thereafter the German paper had to be composed in English.[16] The topics of these essays varied greatly, but the Foreign Office tried to assign subjects on which a candidate could be expected to have some familiarity. The record for Count Brockdorff-Rantzau's examination in 1896 is particularly full. Brockdorff's *historisch-politische Arbeit* concerned "Joseph II et l'insurrection des Pays-Bas." In the second paper (*öffentlich-rechtliches Thema*), the candidate was asked to describe existing emigration laws in Germany and to formulate an improved statute, while on the third exercise, the *staatswissenschaftliches Thema*, he was required to describe the economic value to Belgium of the Congo. This last question was tail-

[14] Stern-Rubarth, *Brockdorff-Rantzau*, I, 38–39. On preparing for the language exams, see Werner Otto von Hentig, *Mein Leben—eine Dienstreise*, 2d ed. (Göttingen, 1963), pp. 19–20, and Rudolf Nadolny, *Mein Beitrag* (Wiesbaden, 1955), pp. 17–18.

[15] The exam might be taken within six months of becoming an attaché but it could not be postponed more than three years. Nadolny, *Beitrag*, p. 18. Both the draft and the final version of Count Castell-Rüdenhausen's exam are preserved in CN, IeVI/4 and IeVI/25.

[16] Herbert von Bismarck, as state secretary, had considered requiring an English paper as early as 1887. HvB to BvB, Oct. 11, 1887, BüN 66.

ored for Brockdorff, since he had just finished a year's tour as an attaché at the ministry in Brussels, and he scored a *genügend* on parts one and two, but a *recht gut* on the third. Brockdorff then passed the oral examination with marks of *genügend* and *ausreichend*, a performance which was not regarded as distinguished.[17]

Once the written examinations had been successfully passed, the candidate had to present himself for an elaborate oral examination. If a reserve officer, he was required to appear in full dress uniform. This trial, which was held before a panel chaired by the state secretary or under state secretary, was conducted in German, French, and English and covered seven areas: European history since 1648, political geography, German constitutional law, constitutional law of major foreign nations, international law, political economy, and international finance and commerce. In addition, an impromptu disquisition on documents chosen from the Foreign Office archives was required.[18] Herbert von Hindenburg, who had taken the precaution of consulting a well-known tutor who specialized in preparing noble candidates, left an account of his interrogation, which took place about 1900. At the examination, one judge concentrated on legal questions; Dr. Otto von Glasenapp, vice president of the Reichsbank, drilled Hindenburg on commercial law, banking, and coinage; another examiner asked for an account in French of the history of the period from 1800 to 1840. The exam concluded with the chairman, Under State Secretary von Mühlberg, testing the candidate's

[17] GN, 201–2. For examples of exams see Eulenburg, *50 Jahre*, p. 51; Schlözer, *Menschen und Landschaften*, p. 121; Hajo Holborn, ed., *Aufzeichnungen und Erinnerungen aus dem Leben des Botschafters Joseph Maria von Radowitz*, 2 vols. (Berlin, 1925), I, 44; Rogge, *Holstein: Lebensbekenntnis*, p. 30; Ernst Jäckh, ed., *Kiderlen-Wächter der Staatsmann und Mensch: Briefwechsel und Nachlass*, 2 vols. (Berlin, 1924), I, 85.

[18] Great Britain, House of Commons, Command Paper #6268, misc. no. 9, pp. 142–45.

familiarity with various aspects of diplomatic practice. Hindenburg acquitted himself well and was subsequently posted to Rome as third secretary.[19] In the case of those who had passed the *Assessor* examination, the oral consisted only of European history since 1648 and the archival analysis. If the written examinations were of a high level of distinction, the candidate might be excused from the oral. Karl von Schlözer, who completed his written exercises in the extraordinarily short period of two months, was so exempted, as was Philipp Eulenburg, part of whose examination was later published.[20]

This rigorous examination schedule chastened many a candidate into enrolling in cram courses given by knowledgeable docents or led them to sojourn abroad to perfect their French or English. The Foreign Office expected candidates whose background for the financial and commercial questions was weak to take positions in banks or business houses.[21] It is doubtful, however, that the examinations, in spite of the terror they instilled in those who took them, were in fact very arduous. The written portions were, after all, "take-home" examinations and ample time was allowed for preparation. Candidates borrowed books and old exams from their friends among more seasoned diplomats and gave their finished essays to them for criticism before submitting their work to the Wilhelmstrasse. In 1874, Bernhard Bülow sent Herbert Bismarck reading material to help him with the exams they would soon take. Both passed with ease, and the books were sent on to Bülow's brother Alfred, who also hoped to enter the diplomatic service. Bismarck in turn provided his friend Philipp Eulenburg with information about the exams. Such help was apparently not

[19] Hindenburg, *Am Rande zweier Jahrhunderte: Momentbilder aus einem Diplomatenleben* (Berlin, 1938), p. 136.

[20] BvB to HvB, June 20, 1886, BisN FC 2958/580–81.

[21] Hindenburg, *Am Rande*, pp. 92–94, 135; Hentig, *Mein Leben*, pp. 19–20; Holborn, *Aufzeichnungen, Radowitz;* I, 44; Great Britain, House of Commons, Command Paper #6268, misc. no. 9, pp. 142–45.

judged inconsistent with the oath which had to accompany the essays that they were the candidate's own work.[22]

The level of proficiency for the English-language qualification, according to one successful candidate, could be handled with the energetic use of a dictionary and the assistance of an English lady for the necessary corrections.[23] The questions were often deliberately designed to treat the examinee's expertise, and the grading system—consisting of fluid terminology such as satisfactory (*befriedigend*), sufficient (*ausreichend, genügend*), good (*gut*), excellent (*vorzüglich*), and so forth—were applied with leniency.[24] There were, moreover, a number of ways through which an applicant could be exempted from all or part of the oral or written examinations. Transfers from the military to the diplomatic service were sometimes allowed to substitute an essay on jurisprudence for either the *Referendar* or *Assessor* examinations, and it appears that they were also frequently exempted from the *grosses diplomatisches Examen* as well. And some candidates who were not military officers but who had influential connections in the Wilhelmstrasse were given full or partial exemptions.[25]

The ease with which examinations could be diluted or

---

[22] HvB to BvB, Dec. 1, 1874, and Apr. 1, 1876, BisN FC 2958/ 349–50, 353; PzE to HvB, Sept. 13, 1879, ibid., FC 2961/1141; HvB to BvB, Mar. 22, 1875, BüN 65; Alfred von Bülow to Paul Kayser, Apr. 10, June 23, and June 29, 1882, KayserN 5. See also Georg Cleinow, "Diplomaten-Erziehung: eine Erinnerungen zu Bismarcks Geburtstag," *Die Grenzboten*, LXXII, no. 13 (1913), 590–91, 597, containing correspondence by Kiderlen.

[23] Nadolny, *Mein Beitrag*, pp. 17–18.

[24] TN, XII, 1, in which Holstein decreed that one *vorzüglich* and one *befriedrigend* were equal to two *guts* and that Treutler could therefore be exempted from the third question.

[25] Count Friedrich zu Limburg-Stirum to HvB, Nov. 4, 1880, BisN FC 2370/362. Count Kuno von Rantzau, who entered the service as a military officer, apparently took no examinations. See his "Autobiographische und andere Aufzeichnungen," ibid., FC 3030/580f. For another example see FvH to Pietro Blaserna, Apr. 11, 1900, HolN 3851/H188767–69.

avoided suggests that they were not taken entirely seriously by the Foreign Office. There is ample evidence to indicate that, as an index of a candidate's suitability, his performance on the tests was considered less important than the impression which he created. Grace in society and sprightliness of mind were preferred to academic training and intellectual profundity. No one was more susceptible than Bismarck to subjective standards of measurement, and no one was more suspicious of self-styled experts. "Diplomacy," he declared, "is not a craft which can be learnt by years and developed by rote on a roller. Diplomacy is an art . . . [There is a] kind of Privy Counsellor who understands everything, knows nothing, and can do nothing. I will give you a whole cart-load of these Privy Counsellors, jurists, theologians, and even philologists, all of them with first-class qualifications, and you will not be able to make more out of them than a man who compiles some spiritless local paper with a pair of scissors."[26] Bismarck cared not a whit for the examinations and was mistrustful of formal education as a preparation for diplomacy. Practical skills were what was needed.[27] There were men in the Foreign Office who believed that the Iron Chancellor preferred to make diplomats out of candidates who in fact had failed their exams. Perhaps that is what Herbert Bismarck had in mind when he warned his good friend Bülow that doing *too* well on the exams might prove to be to his disadvantage.[28] Herbert gave the same advice to another of his comrades, Baron Ludwig von Scheel-Plessen, and advised him to call on the examination committee once or twice in order

[26] Heinrich von Poschinger, *Conversations with Bismarck* (London, 1900), p. 124; Arthur von Brauer, *Im Dienste Bismarcks: persönliche Erinnerungen* (Berlin, 1936) p. 302.

[27] Richard Krauel, *Persönliche Erinnerungen an den Fürsten Bismarck* (Stuttgart, 1915), pp. 13–14; Reichstag, Mar. 14, 1877, p. 159 (Bismarck); Brauer, *Im Dienste Bismarcks*, p. 302. For this attitude in other diplomats see MiquelN, 00187; Hindenburg, *Am Rande*, pp. 127, 332.

[28] Letter of Sept. 11, 1875, BüN 65.

to sound out the sort of questions he might be asked. The examiners, he warned Plessen, only wanted to hear their own views parroted. "If you listen to them with an intent face," Bismarck continued, "one which expresses the greatest wonder at their knowledge and powers of interpretation, they will consider you to be very learned and give you the highest marks."[29]

Chancellor Bismarck did not hestitate to take men into the Foreign Office who had been disqualified for other branches of the bureaucracy because of their failure on examinations.[30] In the presence of academic disaster, connections could be put to work. After considerable intervention by his family with Holstein and the Bismarcks, Alfred von Bülow was permitted to present himself in 1881 for a third, and finally successful, attempt at the *Assessor* examination. One of his brothers admitted that this exception had resulted almost entirely because of the standing of his family. Bülow was, after all, the son of a former state secretary and the brother of Bernhard, one of the rising figures in the ranks of younger diplomats, as well as of Adolf, a major on the General Staff who was widely regarded as a man with a career to watch.[31] Once Bismarck had decided to send a young diplomat abroad, it ceased to matter whether or not he had even taken the examinations.[32]

The chancellor refused to be bound by the results of a candidate's performance on the examinations. Ambassador Bernstorff related that Bismarck inserted a marginal comment in his own hand in the instructions for the diplomatic examination: "I reserve the right to accept the candidate for

[29] HvB to Plessen, June 19, and July 8, 1876, BisN FC 3015/ 942–44.

[30] GN, 248 (concerning Hans Adolf von Bülow); HvB to Count Wilhelm von Bismarck, June 13, 1877, BisN FC 3011/164; HvB to KvR, Oct. 22, 1881, ibid., FC 3014/745.

[31] Alfred von Bülow to BvB, undated letter (ca. 1881), BüN 14, pp. 29–33.

[32] HvB to FvH, Sept. 30, 1888, HolN 3853/H190798.

the diplomatic service if I think him suitable, even though he may not have passed the exam." Another diplomat related at second hand that the chancellor, on being asked a question concerning a revision in the examination, answered: "The diplomatic examination must be constructed in such a way that a candidate whom I wish to have in the service cannot fail, while such examinees whom I cannot use will have to fail, no matter how intelligent they may be."[33] Although himself a superior linguist, Bismarck was sometimes willing to relax the language requirements. In a remark which he undoubtedly did not mean seriously, but which was widely circulated, the chancellor observed to a mother anxious to introduce her multilingual son into the Wilhelmstrasse that a gift for languages was essential in headwaiters but that for a diplomat he would prefer a man "with an open mind who spoke *Plattdeutsch* to an ass who could prattle in seven tongues."[34]

Bismarck believed that the best method of evaluation was to scrutinize a candidate in a social setting to measure his nimbleness in conversation, his social ease, and his capacity for drink, a qualification easily tested by Bismarck's notoriously bibulous hospitality. This would reveal whether or not the man in question had the proper style, a virtue Bismarck referred to as the *Kavalierperspektiv*. To Bismarck, tactlessness was the worst defect in a diplomat, and this was a failing which could be detected only by personal contact.[35] Baron von Eckardstein, a slick parvenu who doubt-

[33] Count Johann-Heinrich Bernstorff, *Memoirs*, trans. Eric Sutton (New York, 1936), p. 38; TN, XII, 1; also John C.G. Röhl, "Higher Civil Servants in Germany, 1890–1900," *Journal of Contemporary History*, II, no. 3 (July 1967), 106.

[34] Brauer et al., eds., *Erinnerungen an Bismarck*, pp. 343–44; GW, XV, 7; Baron Robert Lucius von Ballhausen, *Bismarck-Erinnerungen* (Stuttgart, 1921), p. 86.

[35] BvB to Friedrich von Loebell, Jan. 29, 1912, LoebellN 7; Helmuth Rogge, ed., *Holstein und Hohenlohe* . . . (Stuttgart, 1957), pp.

less received approbation on all counts, related in his memoirs that he was invited to dinner so that Bismarck could look over his talents as a prospective diplomat. Eckardstein drank prodigiously, spoke discreetly, and displayed his manners handsomely. He shortly was admitted as an attaché and began what would be a brief and unsavory career.[36] Under the chancellor's successors, candidates continued to be evaluated in much the same way. The fastidious Prince Karl Max von Lichnowsky, who had been exempted from the examinations, served from 1899 to 1904 as the Political Division counselor responsible for admissions. He like to find "social culture" in applicants and confessed that "as a general rule examination marks do not count so much as personality . . . I made it a practice to watch the candidate as he entered the room. Then I knew pretty well with whom I had to deal. The conversation that ensued soon showed what sort of intelligence he possessed."[37] Similarly, to Holstein an important desideratum was a sure command of "*usage du monde*," while to Chancellor Bülow the requisite qualities were "intuition, tact, a feeling for nuance and a refinement of judgment."[38] *Exzel-*

179–80; HvB to Hohenlohe, Nov. 22, and 24, 1882, HohN, XX.B.3; HvB to FvH, Nov. 22, 1882, HolN 3824/E343556–57; also Holstein's diary for Jan. 11, 1883, ibid., 3860/H195690–93.

[36] Eckardstein, *Lebenserinnerungen*, I, 83–88. Bülow, who disliked Eckardstein, declared that he had impressed Herbert von Bismarck by leaving a restaurant from a second-story window. Bülow, *Denkwürdigkeiten*, I, 343. For Bismarck's supper interviews see also TN, XII, 1; GW, VIII, 371–72; Count Anton Monts, "Unsere Diplomatie," in his *Politische Aufsätze* (Berlin, n.d. [ca. 1917]), p. 80. The chancellor also used this method for examining candidates for appointment to other branches of the bureaucracy. See Brauer, *Im Dienste Bismarcks*, p. 161.

[37] Lichnowsky, *Heading for the Abyss: Reminiscences* (New York, 1928), p. 85.

[38] Johannes Haller, ed., *Aus dem Leben des Fürsten Philipp zu Eulenburg-Hertefeld* (Berlin, 1924), p. 13; Karl F. Nowak and

lenz von Glasenapp of the Reichsbank, who sat on the Foreign Office examination board from 1899 to 1914, rendered the following Sanskrit adage as a prescription for aspiring diplomats. The order in which Glasenapp ranked the virtues is significant.

Sieben Gaben muss ein Gesandter haben.
Er sei aus edlen Geschlecht entsprossen,
Beredt geschickt und zur Tat entschlossen,
Muss freundliche Worte zu reden verstehn,
Genau berichten, was er gesehn,
Und ein gutes Gedächtnis haben,
Das sind die sieben Gaben.[39]

Good form—in appearance, manners, and accomplishments—was much in demand. One had to converse with delicacy, in French as well as in German, be agile on the dance floor, and remain tireless in the execution of social rituals. Some posts, especially Munich and Vienna, insisted on a special gloss in deportment, while some sovereigns— Pope Leo XIII, for one—were especially susceptible to grace of person.[40] In 1913, Prince Lichnowsky, who was then ambassador in London, advised Chancellor Bethmann Hollweg that General Count Carl von Wedel was just the

---

Friedrich Thimme, eds., *Erinnerungen und Gedanken des Botschafters Anton Graf Monts* (Berlin, 1932), p. 330. Walter Struve, *Elites against Democracy: Leaderships Ideals in Bourgeois Political Thought in Germany, 1890–1933* (Princeton, 1973), p. 36, indicates that this basis for selection prevailed in the entire German bureaucracy. This is confirmed by Otto Hintze, "Der Beamtenstand," in Gerhard Oestreich, ed., *Soziologie und Geschichte: gesammelte Abhandlungen zur Soziologie, Politik und Theorie der Geschichte*, 2d ed. (Göttingen, 1964), p. 101.

[39] Walter Zechlin, *Diplomatie und Diplomaten* (Stuttgart, 1935), pp. 69–70.

[40] On Vienna see Karl A. von Müller, ed., *Fürst Chlodwig zu Hohenlohe-Schillingsfürst: Denkwürdigkeiten der Reichskanzlerzeit* (Stuttgart, 1931), p. 14; on Munich, HP, III, 163–64; on the Pope, Nowak and Thimme, *Erinnerungen; Monts*, pp. 84–85.

man to assume the vacant ambassadorial position in Rome. Lichnowsky's recommendation, which reveals the importance, not to say the preeminence, which the Foreign Office placed on social rather than intellectual qualities, ran as follows: "His intelligence is sufficient for the post. What [Rome] essentially requires is tact, good form, and social grace. These attributes he possesses. He has a presentable wife, plays a good game of bridge, has enough money, and besides is a jolly fellow [*bon enfant*] and will know how to get along with everyone."[41]

No family exhibited the flair for diplomatic behavior with more expertise than the Bülows. Bülow *père*, a tiresome zealot, was celebrated for the punctiliousness of his language. He was scrupulous in referring to all deceased potentates in the exact phraseology prescribed for their equivalents among the quick. An associate declared that Bülow "would never have allowed himself to speak other than of the mistakes of His Majesty the Emperor Nero, or of the lamentable errors committed by His Majesty King Herod."[42] His son Bernhard, successively secretary of legation, minister, ambassador, state secretary and chancellor, was well known for his virtuosic powers of social intercourse. The "eel," as he was called by some of his colleagues, once revealed his recipe for diplomatic sociability. Diplomats, he confided to the deputies of the Reichstag, had to be chameleons in the manner of Alcibiades, who was "intellectual among the Athenians, abstimenious in Sparta, and wrapped in a caftan when with the Persians."[43] But to Bülow, charm was the root of diplomacy. Count Botho von Wedel, who served as minister to Weimar while Bülow was chancellor, recalled that Bülow always had the Foreign Of-

---

[41] Lichnowsky to BvB, Jan. 3, 1913, BüN 98; a similar appraisal of what was needed in Rome is in BvB to HvB, Apr. 12, 1887, BisN FC 2958/767–69.

[42] Holborn, *Aufzeichnungen, Radowitz;* 1: 281; GW, III, 386–87.

[43] Reichstag, Nov. 14, 1906, pp. 3648–49.

fice press division provide him with thumbnail sketches of people he was to meet at dinner. In one such case, the chancellor was to dine with an important newspaper owner whose father, he was informed, had been a "forty-eighter." Bülow greeted the son by declaring that "decades had to pass by before I might make the acquaintance of the son of a man whom I revered from childhood as a great patriot." The press lord felt enormously honored and his paper was thereafter solidly behind the chancellor, who later laughingly confessed to his staff that he had never before heard of either the newspaperman or his father. "Das war echt Bülow," Wedel noted.[44]

The Bülows were not unique in their gifts. Ambassador Robert von Keudell in Rome, for example, was not only a very popular envoy but a pianist of sufficient stature to perform duets with the Abbé Liszt. Philipp Eulenburg in Vienna was equally gifted, both socially and musically, while Lichnowsky in London and Radolin in Paris were the very eponyms of the grand seigneur. Such attributes were essential for the business of diplomacy. As Lichnowsky noted shortly after taking up his post at the Court of St. James, "the whirl of society is certainly now and then rather tiring, but it is absolutely part of the profession and cannot properly be avoided. It is also the only way to make oneself known."[45]

A few German diplomats, some of whom succeeded in rising to eminent positions, were notoriously lacking in social graces or physical attractiveness. Münster was arrogant beyond redemption and rather a bore; Kiderlen-Wächter, quite apart from his irregular liaison with Frau Kypke, was

---

[44] Friedrich Thimme, ed., *Front wider Bülow: Staatsmänner, Diplomaten und Forscher zu seinen Denkwürdigkeiten* (Munich, 1931), p. 282. Bülow was frank to admit once that "there are moments in life when one cannot stick strictly to the truth." See Princess Herbert Bismarck, "Meine Erinnerungen an Bernhard von Bülow," BisN FC 2958/979–80.

[45] Lichnowsky to BvB, Apr. 30, 1913, BüN 98.

bawdy, while Marschall was excessively gruff. Monts was frighteningly sarcastic; Klehmet's clothes were ill-fitting; Werthern was antisocial and eccentric; Kurd von Schlözer was grotesquely ugly and sometimes embarrassingly parsimonious. But all of these men, and other diplomats whose appearance or manner left something to be desired, atoned for these shortcomings either by establishing themselves as popular envoys, by entertaining in style, or by displaying gifts for ferreting out and ably reporting sensitive information.

✸

No requirement was so carefully observed as the rule, formally in effect until 1908, that candidates had to have independent incomes. This was a common European practice, enforced also in England, Austria-Hungary, Russia, and Italy.[46] The Wilhelmstrasse had first insisted in the 1880s that candidates give evidence of private wealth, with the annual figure set at 6,000 marks. The amount rose with inflation, and by 1900 it stood at 10,000 marks.[47] This sum represented more than what a fledgling secretary could expect to make in his initial assignment. In 1892, for example, the average annual pay for beginning secretaries was only 7,967 marks. There could be no question that some additional income was imperative. The case of Alfred von Bülow is particularly revealing because his attempt in 1884 to enter the diplomatic service came at the same moment that he was striving to win the hand of a charming but only moderately wealthy Württemberg countess. Bülow consequently had to reckon the fiscal expectations of his marriage very closely in terms of his professional prospects. His mother had five other sons for whom she had to make pro-

---

[46] Great Britain, House of Commons, Command Paper #6268, misc. no. 9, pp. 140–41.

[47] Monts, "Unsere Diplomatie," p. 83; Richard von Kühlmann, *Die Diplomaten* (Berlin, 1939), p. 124.

vision and she therefore advised Alfred that she could make him a wedding settlement of "only" 6,000 marks a year, the minimum allowance required for diplomatic recruits. Bülow's salary as secretary of legation, in addition to his paternal inheritance, would come to only 9,000 to 10,000 annually, while his bride's dowry of 100,000 marks would at best provide an annual yield of five percent. This represented a total income of about 20,000 a year. Such an amount might barely suffice for a secretary, but if Bülow's private income did not increase it would not enable him to advance to higher ranks. He therefore appealed to his mother to inflate her largesse, and she eventually raised her contribution to 10,000 per annum. Bülow married the countess, entered the service, and proceeded (constantly complaining of his expenses) to have a modest career culminating as minister to Saxony.[48]

In 1908, the formal requirement for an independent income was abolished and thereafter candidates were required to furnish only a statement of their financial position.[49] In practice, however, the Foreign Office continued to insist as firmly as ever that applicants be independently wealthy. In 1912, State Secretary Kiderlen-Wächter defended the custom before the Reichstag by arguing that diplomacy was only one of many professions which required money. Merely obtaining the necessary legal training restricted the diplomatic corps to those who could afford to be educated, and this was not inexpensive.[50] By the end of the nineteenth century, the cost involved in securing the doctor juris degree ran to at least 9,000 marks if a student lived in a university city to as much as 25,000 if he did

[48] Alfred von Bülow to BvB, Feb. 3 and 17, 1884, BüN 14, pp. 263–72; ibid., 13, same to same, Feb. 27, 1884 (2 letters).

[49] Great Britain, House of Commons, Command Paper #6268, misc. no. 9, p. 142.

[50] Reichstag, May 18, 1912, p. 2103 (Kiderlen). In 1877 Treutler received an annual allowance of 1,700 marks as a university student, a sum regarded at the time as modest. TN, VI, 2.

not. Service as an army officer, which was frequently the path to diplomacy, was, at a cost of 6,000 marks a year for preparatory training, also quite taxing.[51] By 1912, the Wilhelmstrasse reckoned the minimum private fortune requisite for a diplomatic career to be 15,000 marks a year, and it seems to have insisted that candidates provide assurances that they possessed this degree of wealth.[52] Such a sum represented a heavy charge even on those from comfortable backgrounds, for on the eve of the First World War a German family required an income of 30,000 marks to be considered "well-to-do."[53] In the case of a particularly desirable candidate who could muster some but not all of the essential private income, the Foreign Office might waive the stipulation. This, however, appears to have been an unusual practice.[54]

Many diplomats, young and old, had great riches at their command. In the lists of German diplomats there were names well known for affluence coming from sources as varied as Mumm's vineyards to Schoen's tanneries. One junior secretary owned a yacht of such cyclopean displacement that it excited the envy of William II, while another stationed in Paris managed to acquire one of the original castings of Rodin's "Kiss." Baron Hellmuth Lucius von Stoedten, a twenty-eight-year-old junior official in France, had a private income of 75,000 marks a year. In addition,

51 F. von Schulte, "Adel im deutschen Offizier- und Beamtenstand: eine soziale Betrachtung," *Deutsche Revue*, XXI, no. 1 (1896), 186.

52 Hans Adolf von Moltke, whose father was Prussian minister of interior, applied for admission in January 1913, his father having previously agreed to provide him with 15,000 marks a year. GN, 935–36. See also Reichstag, May 18, 1912, p. 2087 (David).

53 Karl von Stutterheim, *The Two Germanys*, trans. Moffat Freet (London, 1939), p. 110. The enormity of the 15,000 requirement becomes apparent when compared with the annual wages of skilled German workers in 1913, which ranged between 1,646 and 2,106 marks. See Gerhard Bry, *Wages in Germany, 1871–1945* (Princeton, 1960), p. 438.

54 Monts, "Unsere Diplomatie," p. 84; Lichnowsky, *Abyss*, p. 85.

he was married to a Stumm-Hallberg and had yet to receive his patrimony.[55] Examples abound, but a cross-section of the staff in the embassy in London during 1913 and 1914 will serve to illustrate the prosperity of some diplomats. Ambassador Lichnowsky was a rich Silesian landowner; his first secretary, Richard von Kühlmann, was the son of a railroad entrepreneur and the husband of a Saarland Stumm. The father of the second secretary, Carl von Schubert, had also cornered a Stumm. Leopold Hoesch, who served as third secretary and who would die in London in 1936 as Hitler's ambassador, was the scion of an immensely wealthy Ruhr industrial dynasty. Finally, one of the attachés, the source of whose riches was well advertised by his name, was Baron Albert von Goldschmidt-Rothschild. There were also plutocrats among the officials in the Wilhelmstrasse. One was Willibald von Dirksen, who had married a wealthy banker's daughter and acquired a title. Dirksen was himself the owner of huge estates which had once belonged to the *uradelige* von Jagows.[56] Some diplomats, of course, were relatively impoverished, but even among these some managed to escape privation by marrying heiresses.[57]

The requirement of a private income and the obvious expenses involved in diplomatic careers led some men to abandon their attempts to enter the foreign service. Some candidates who feared they could not afford to become diplomats but who yearned to live abroad turned instead to the consular service, which had no probationary period and

[55] GN, 835; Hindenburg, *Am Rande*, pp. 128, 136, 190; Holstein, *Lebensbekenntnis*, p. 182; Holborn, *Aufzeichnungen; Radowitz*, I, 281; HP, II, 186–87; Ottomar von Mohl, *Fünfzig Jahre Reichsdienst: Lebenserinnerungen* (Leipzig, 1921), p. 28; BvB to HvB, June 9, 1886, BisN FC 2958/573.

[56] TN, XI, 1–2.

[57] An enumeration of diplomats who married wealth would be very long, but among the more familiar names who made off with heiresses are Keudell, Monts, Raschdau, Flotow, Tschirschky, and Kühlmann.

paid salaries from the outset. Consular promotions were regular, and one might expect to become a consul general within ten or fifteen years. In 1879, Kiderlen-Wächter, for example, had to weigh very carefully whether to choose the consular service, which would rapidly lead to financial independence but mean living in remote places, or diplomacy, more attractive but initially less remunerative. Kiderlen's mother apparently agreed to make the necessary sacrifice, and he became a diplomat.[58] Applicants who were determined to become diplomats had to make certain that their fathers were prepared to make provision to cover the private income requirement.[59] Holstein was of the opinion that Bismarck would not have been able to afford a diplomatic career for his son Herbert had it not been for the enormous dotations he received from William I in gratitude for the victories won in the wars of unification.[60] Young men had to calculate whether their patrimony was sufficient to withstand the costs of the service. Baron Paul von Schoenaich, who described himself as "rather well off" (*ziemlich wohlhabend*) after the death of his parents, decided to leave the navy for diplomacy only after determining that his income was "with the utmost strain sufficient for this most costly of all careers." He never acted on his decision, however, and settled instead on becoming an army officer.[61] Hans von Miquel, a young secretary at the turn of the century, observed that "one enters the diplomatic service for two reasons: either from an interest in the profession or in order to acquire an imposing social position and to lead a pleasant life. There is also another reason, which

[58] Cleinow, "Diplomaten-Erziehung," p. 589. For another example see a letter of Count Castell-Rüdenhausen to his mother, Sept. 21, 1888, CN, IeIII/76.

[59] Pückler, *Diplomatenleben*, p. 7; Nowak and Thimme, *Erinnerungen*; *Monts*, p. 39; TN, X, 3–4.

[60] Holstein diary, Jan. 14, 1884, HolN 3860/H195749.

[61] Schoenaich, *Mein Damaskus: Erlebnisse und Bekenntnisse* (Berlin, 1926), pp. 13, 46.

is important in other professions but which [in diplomacy] is nonexistent: making money."[62]

No member of the German foreign service, whether he was stationed in Berlin or in the field as a diplomatic or consular official, grew rich through his profession. On the eve of the First World War, the state secretary received 50,000 marks, 14,000 of which was earmarked for entertainment, as well as the furnished residence at Wilhelmstrasse. The under state secretary was paid 25,000, directors 20,000 each. Counselors' pay ranged between 8,000 and 13,500 marks, depending on years of service and job function. Assistants, whose salaries also reflected considerations of seniority, were paid from 5,400 to 7,800. Counselors and assistants were also granted housing allowances, which averaged 1,358 marks per year. These salaries had changed little since William II came to the throne in 1888 except for those of directors, who in the budget of 1891 to 1892 had received only 9,000 to 11,400, and those of counselors, whose wages had been 7,500 to 9,000. While these salary scales were adequate, they did not put any of these bureaucrats, except the state secretary, within the ranks of well-to-do Germans. The Foreign Office did not pay its staff appreciably better wages than other departments of the imperial government, but its salaries were somewhat higher than those provided by the Prussian government for comparable positions.

The pay of a diplomat in the field was determined both by his years of service and by the position he held. There were wide differentials among various posts. Sometimes cost-of-living considerations led to a greater salary for a diplomat in a relatively unimportant post than for an envoy in a major European ministry. Buenos Aires, which was forever in the grip both of ruinous inflation and Brazilian pretension, paid more than Copenhagen, The Hague, Stockholm, or Berne. In other cases, the demands of entertain-

[62] MiquelN, 00185.

ment, which varied according to local tastes, caused salaries to be increased. The Foreign Office broke down all diplomats' pay into expenses and wages. An envoy could draw his wages during protracted absences from his post, but after fourteen days away from his assignment the allotment for expenses stopped. Prince Hohenlohe, ambassador in Paris from 1873 to 1885, on realizing that his expense credit comprised no less than 102,000 of his 120,000 salary, determined not to linger on vacation.[63] An envoy's salary was not always proportional to his rank. Although all ambassadors made more than any minister, some ministers were outdistanced in pay by ministers-resident or general consuls. Moreover, base salary rates were often improved by the inclusion of a free residence or by housing allowances. A move resulting in an advance in title might not necessarily mean an increase in wages, nor was a reassignment to a politically more important post necessarily a financial promotion as well.

The Foreign Office budget for 1912 reflects the varying pay scales of various posts and of positions within these posts. A contrast with the wages paid from 1891 to 1892 indicates how little salaries rose in this twenty-year period.

The possession of private wealth was necessary for a variety of reasons, some relating to a man's training for a diplomatic career, others to his performance as a diplomat. Without an adequate supply, the appropriate cosmopolitan background enriched by travel and polite society was hardly possible.[64] A candidate might occasionally receive a per diem allowance during his apprenticeship, but it did not begin to cover his expenses. Count Siegfried zu Castell-Rüdenhausen, for example, began his career with an honorarium of 2,160 marks a year. Fortunately he could also draw on a private income of between 6,000 and 7,000

[63] Hohenlohe diary, July 1, 1883, HohN, CC.X.11.

[64] Baron Magnus von Braun, *Von Ostpreussen bis Texas: Erlebnisse und zeitgeschichtliche Betrachtungen eines Ostdeutschen*, 2d ed. (Stollhamm, 1955), pp. 38–39.

TABLE 5

PAY SCALES OF SELECTED POSTS

Post	1891–1892	1912
State Secretary	50,000 marks	50,000 marks
Under State Secretary	25,000	25,000
Directors	9,000/11,400	20,000
Counselors	7,500/9,900	8,000/13,500
Assistants	4,200/7,200	5,400/7,800
Ambassador, London	150,000	150,000
Ambassador, Paris	120,000	120,000
Ambassador, Rome	100,000	100,000
Minister, Athens	42,000	42,000
Minister, Copenhagen	36,000	40,000
Minister, Teheran	60,000	60,000
Minister-Resident, Santiago	36,000	36,000
Minister-Resident, Tangiers	30,000	36,000
*Legation Secretary, London	17,400	17,400
*Legation Secretary, Athens	7,200	7,200
*Legation Secretary, Bucharest	9,000	9,000
*Legation Secretary, Rio de Janeiro	10,500	11,500
*Legation Secretary, Tokyo	12,000	13,200
General Consul, New York City	48,000	53,000
General Consul, London	40,000	40,000

* First Secretary or equivalent post.
SOURCE: The salaries are from Germany, Finanzministerium, *Reichshaushalts-Etat*, 1891/92 and 1913.

marks.[65] As a rule, however, an attaché received no pay until he had passed his diplomatic examinations, a barrier which might take as long as three years to clear.[66] In the interim, he had to draw on private income or on parental allowances. After an attaché became a secretary of legation his need of private funds did not abate. Although he now received a salary, no subsidy was paid for entertainment,

[65] Castell diary, June 4, 1889, CN, IeVI/29; GN, 301. Some years earlier, when Castell's father had only 2,000 a year to give his son, Castell had decided on the consular service. See PzE to HvB, Oct. 9, 1881, BisN FC 2961/1163–64.

[66] Herbert von Hindenburg, *Das Auswärtige Amt im Wandel der Zeiten* (Frankfurt/Main, 1932), p. 16; Hindenburg, *Am Rande*, p. 107; Brauer, *Im Dienste Bismarcks*, p. 29.

which was required of junior as well as senior officials. In a social oasis such as St. Petersburg, a first secretary might spend more on entertaining than a minister at a more somnolent post. Bernhard Bülow, first secretary in St. Petersburg from 1884 to 1888, declared that his salary barely covered a quarter of the expenses required for purposes of entertainment, the handsome execution of which was necessary if a diplomat expected to accomplish anything in the Romanov capital.[67] The cost of getting settled in a new assignment could amount to as much as 3,000 marks, while travel expenses between posts had in some cases to be paid out of one's own pocket.[68]

Professional success brought prestige and satisfaction, but also increased expense. Ministers and ambassadors were paid entertainment allowances but these usually did not suffice to cover expenditures. "An ambassador," one diplomat laconically observed, "cannot be rich enough."[69] In a day when the salon was often the locus of a diplomatic offensive or the source of an important confidential disclosure, the envoy had to be prepared to dispense staggering amounts of hospitality. Entertainment was consequently the principal charge on a diplomat's time and means. The Foreign Office, from Bismarck's era until the outbreak of the war in 1914, was insistent that its servants provide a suitably elegant *Repräsentation* in their posts. Bismarck declared that the style in which German envoys lived should be commensurate with the important position Germany occupied in world affairs, for otherwise Germany's impact would be lessened and it would be given short shrift. An envoy, he noted, should always "act in a manner appropriate not to his rank but to the greatness and dignity of the

[67] BvB to HvB, Apr. 12, 1887, BisN FC 2958/767–69.

[68] Zechlin, *Diplomatie und Diplomaten*, p. 74; Reichstag, Mar. 31, 1909, pp. 7914–16 (Schoen): BvB to Adolf von Bülow, Jan. 6, 1885, BüN 13; Elisabeth von Heyking, *Tagebücher aus vier Weltteilen, 1886/1904* 2d ed. (Leipzig, 1926), p. 132.

[69] Hindenburg, *Am Rande*, pp. 62, 252.

German empire."[70] Entertainment was, of course, not without its practical side. Karl Georg von Treutler, as first secretary in Tokyo in the late 1890s, managed to wrest a number of valuable secrets from his taciturn Russian counterpart by involving him in poker parties at which champagne was liberally uncorked. Treutler was rewarded by a citation from Berlin.[71]

The demands on an envoy's time and money were enormous, and most of both were invested in society. In Constantinople in 1883, for example, Ambassador Joseph Maria von Radowitz christened his new residence by inviting 750 guests, whom he diverted with a musical ensemble of 250 members. Twenty-nine house servants stood ready to fulfill the guests' desires.[72] The social regimen which afflicted Eugen von Jagemann, the minister of Baden to Prussia from 1893 to 1900, was doubtless one shared by his colleagues in the Prussian-imperial service. Jagemann estimated that during the period of his ministry he entertained 8,136 people. That came to more than three guests per day every day of the year, and Jagemann's figure did not include hundreds of Badeners visiting in Berlin who were invited to drink a beer with the envoy.[73] In addition to their formal entertaining, ministers in remote stations found that their residences were used as refuges for other lonely European diplomats in search of companionship. The German ministry in Rio de Janeiro, according to the envoy, was really a sort of club for such displaced persons.[74]

No scrutiny of the mores of society was more exacting than that exercised by Philipp Eulenburg. Anxious to cut an imposing figure but troubled by the fact that his fortune

[70] Reichstag, Nov. 16, 1871, p. 298; also State Secretary Bülow's remarks in ibid., Mar. 14, 1877, pp. 158–59.

[71] TN, XIII, 7.

[72] Holborn, *Aufzeichnungen; Radowitz*, II, 226, 236.

[73] Jagemann, *Fünfundsiebzig Jahre des Erlebens und Erfahrens (1849–1924)* (Heidelberg, 1925), p. 209.

[74] TN, XIIIe, 2.

was only modest, his descriptions of the receptions he gave as ambassador in Vienna were almost invariably followed by a querulous notation of their ruinous expense. Eulenburg scorned Franz Josef's niggardly court balls, where tea that was hard to obtain and bouillon hardly fit to drink was often all that was provided to sustain the guests. Eulenburg noted with pride, mingled perhaps with condescension, that *he* served champagne and sat people down to dinner. But he complained that some of his guests, especially visiting Germans, could quaff an entire bottle of champagne, or more. When the German kaiser came to Vienna, the ambassador had to hire a dozen extra footmen at enormous cost. However, their powdered hair and Eulenburg livery did not fail to win William II's approbation.[75]

The burden of entertainment worsened after the turn of the century, and Foreign Office officials noted that the mounting taste for luxury of the belle époque as well as the increased cost of living in metropolitan centers was outpricing the means of even wealthy diplomats. The embassy in Rome is a case in point. Count Anton Monts, a secretary there in the mid-1880s and one well known for his parsimony, described the social life of diplomats in Rome in those days as simple, with the embassy having a staff of only four servants. This was partly due to the penny-wise calculations made by Frau von Keudell, the ambassador's wife, in assembling her menu. Although an heiress, she usually estimated on the short side and saw to it that the Germans present at her dietetic fêtes ate the slender pickings left in the wake of her Italian guests, who were always served first. By the time Monts returned as ambassador in 1902, Roman society, goaded by the lavish expenditures of rich Americans and infected with gambling, had become fearfully sumptuous. Monts' predecessor, Count Wedel, had found it necessary to lay forty-eight covers for dinner each week

[75] PzE to W2, Feb. 1, 1898, EN, L, 15–16; Eulenburg memo of Sept. 18, 1898, ibid., LII, 289.

merely to keep up with his heavy social obligations.[76] Rome, however, was a bargain in comparison with St. Petersburg, the most expensive duty in the service, where a single reception might cost 10,000 marks. If one ambassador entertained magnificently, the others had to follow suit. Unfortunately, as one German envoy observed, the French and the Austrians would spend any amount to make an opulent impression.[77]

Although entertaining was the major drain on an envoy's or a secretary's money, meeting the demands of society was not the only reason a diplomat needed to have a private income. Even younger staff sometimes had body servants or secretaries accompany them to their posts, and their wages represented a sizeable claim on diplomatic pay.[78] Diplomats often had to assume travel expenses. These might be considerable if an ambassador, such as Count Friedrich von Pourtalès, posted to St. Petersburg in 1907, elected to drag along sixteen van loads of his own furniture.[79] Temporary duty involving travel was not always covered by per diem allowances. In some posts an envoy was responsible for providing housing for his staff, and the embassy itself might serve as

[76] Nowak and Thimme, *Erinnerungen; Monts*, pp. 50–51, 90–92, 335–36; Hindenburg, *Am Rande*, pp. 174–75, 247; Count Robert Zedlitz-Trützschler, *Zwölf Jahre am deutschen Kaiserhof: Aufzeichnungen* (Berlin, 1924), p. 17; Alfred von Bülow to BvB, n.d. [1885], BüN 14, p. 147.

[77] See, for example, BvB's letters to Karl von Lindenau of July 20, Aug. 1, and Dec. 25, 1887, in BüN 99; Radolin to FvH, Jan. 30, and Feb. 15, 1896, HolN 3860/H195204, 195207–8; Count Gustav von Lambsdorff, *Die Militärbevollmächtigte Kaiser Wilhelms II. am Zarenhofe, 1904–1914* (Berlin, 1937), p. 73; Walter Bussmann, ed., *Staatssekretär Graf Herbert von Bismarck: aus seiner politischen Privatkorrespondenz* (Göttingen, 1964), p. 434.

[78] Holstein complained in 1871 that his servant received 800 thalers a year while his own salary was only 2,000. Rogge, *Holstein: Lebensbekenntnis*, p. 116.

[79] Hindenburg, *Am Rande*, p. 210. On Pourtalès' luxurious establishment in St. Petersburg, see Count Karl Luxburg, *Nachdenkliche Erinnerungen* (Aschach/Saale, 1953), p. 23.

a residence not only for the ambassador but for many of his assistants, all of whom he had to feed. In the event that an audit revealed any irregularities in a post's bookkeeping, the head of mission was required to set the matter right out of his own funds.[80] Then there was the question of dress. Diplomatic uniforms, afire with gilt braid, epaulettes and egret plumes, were impressive but very expensive. When Eulenburg was appointed minister to Oldenburg, he was aghast to find that his caparison cost 2,100 marks, the equivalent of a month's pay in his new post.[81]

Diplomats were expected to spend a great part of their salaries and to dip into their own means to maintain themselves on a fitting plane. Bülow, as first secretary in St. Petersburg, declared that he had been forced to spend 38,000 of his own money in order to live with suitable elegance.[82] Even minor posts such as the Prussian ministries in Germany entailed a generous outlay for social purposes. In 1898, Karl von Eisendecher in Karlsruhe complained to Chancellor Hohenlohe that he had to spend 8,000 to 10,000 marks a year out of his own pocket; a single ball set him back 4,000. The demands of entertainment in the Baden capital, Eisendecher noted, were even greater than those in his former post as minister in Washington, although his salary now was less than half as much.[83]

In ambassadorial ranks, expectations and consequently

[80] Karl-Heinz Janssen, ed., *Die graue Exzellenz . . . : aus den Papieren des kaiserlichen Gesandten Karl Georg von Treutler* (Frankfurt/Main, 1971), p. 130; Rogge, *Holstein: Lebensbekenntnis*, p. 118; Holborn, *Aufzeichnungen; Radowitz*, II, 251.

[81] Eulenburg diary, Nov. 4, 1888, EN, IV, 165–66.

[82] BvB to HvB, Apr. 12, 1887, BisN FC 2958/767–69; also Bülow's letters to Lindenau of July 20, Aug. 1, Sept. 18, and Dec. 25, 1887, BüN 99. There is, however, a letter by Bülow to his brother Alfred of Nov. 12, 1884, in which he frets about where to invest his money. BüN 13.

[83] Eisendecher to Hohenlohe, Nov. 6, 1898, HohN, XXII.A.15. For the same complaint by a German envoy in Washington see HolN 3819/E340556–57.

expenditures were correspondingly enhanced. In the 1860s, Bismarck himself had been a victim of the burdens borne by German diplomats. As ambassador to Russia he had had to spend his capital, and in 1879 he declared that as chancellor he was forced to lay out 50,000 to 60,000 thalers (about 150,000 to 180,000 marks) of his own money, much of it doubtless destined for the same sort of entertaining he expected of his diplomats.[84] Ambassador Hohenlohe found himself in an even tighter position in Paris in the mid-1870s. Thanks in part to the peculations of the embassy's maître d'hôtel, Hohenlohe ended his first year as ambassador with a deficit of 56,000 marks. Merely outfitting the embassy with silver, crystal, china and linens, in addition to assembling the necessary coaches and teams, came to between 40,000 and 48,000 marks. "A Frenchman," Hohenlohe complained, "loves nothing so much as to be invited to dinner." In the ensuing three years, expenditures again outdistanced the envoy's salary and allowances, and Hohenlohe was forced to consider resigning his position. When he tried to cut back on entertainment, the royal entourage in Berlin complained to the Foreign Office, which in turn suggested that the ambassador be more generous in his invitations.[85]

Without the support of adequate salaries, the amount of debt incurred in the diplomatic service could be serious, if

[84] Hohenlohe diary, Oct. 28, 1879, HohN, CC.X.7. On Bismarck's complaints about his expenditures as ambassador to Russia, see GW, III, 240, 252–53, 292; ibid., XIV(1), 5, 19–20, 552–53, 565–68; and two undated memos by Holstein in HolN 3842/H196771 and H196932–33.

[85] Draft of a letter by Hohenlohe to Bismarck, n.d. (ca. Jan. 1879), HohN, XX.E.1A; State Secretary Count Hatzfeldt to Prince Max von Ratibor, May 23, 1884, and Hohenlohe to Ratibor, Apr. 19, 1884, ibid., XX.E.6; Hohenlohe diary, Nov. 2, 1884, ibid., CC.X.12. For the financial difficulties of other diplomats see Ludwig Raschdau, *In Weimar als preussischer Gesandter: ein Buch der Erinnerungen an deutsche Fürstenhöfe, 1894–1897* (Berlin, 1939), pp. 67–68, 113–14.

not ruinous. Obligations piled up, and appeals had to be addressed to relatives for additional funds. Count Wilhelm von Redern, a secretary in the embassy in London in the 1870s and a popular member of the Prince of Wales' extravagant Marlborough House set, ran up £37,000 in debts in a single year. His father assumed this indebtedness and the Foreign Office transferred Redern to the socially less giddy ministry in Stockholm.[86] Some diplomats in financial straits applied to bankers for loans or paid their bills and their servants' wages irregularly. Others were forced to moonlight to make ends meet. Baron von Richthofen, a man of slender means, supplemented his income by writing.[87] The cost of becoming a German representative abroad sometimes made nominees reluctant to accept ministries or ambassadorships, while the position of state secretary, less generously salaried but requiring copious entertaining, was still less popular.[88] A few envoys managed to live on their salaries and even to save a portion of their pay, but this seems to have been accomplished either by neglecting their social roles or by performing them in a beggarly fashion. Those who allegedly managed credit balances were subjected to criticism by officials in Berlin and by diplomats who entertained more openhandedly.[89] On the other hand,

[86] GN, 1150–51.

[87] Holstein diary, Mar. 7, 1885, HolN 3861/H195965; Nowak and Thimme, *Erinnerungen; Monts*, p. 41.

[88] See, for example, Count Erhard von Wedel, ed., *Zwischen Kaiser und Kanzler: Aufzeichnungen des General-adjutanten Grafen Carl von Wedel aus den Jahren 1890–1894* . . . (Leipzig, 1943), pp. 173–75; also Holborn, *Aufzeichnungen; Radowitz*, II, 185–86.

[89] For envoys who apparently managed to save money, see Raschdau, *In Weimar*, pp. 113–14; Hindenburg, *Am Rande*, p. 175. For junior diplomats or those in Berlin who lived within their means, see Ludwig Raschdau, *Unter Bismarck und Caprivi: Erinnerungen eines deutschen Diplomaten aus den Jahren 1885–1894*, 2d ed. (Berlin, 1939), p. 87; Kühlmann, *Diplomaten*, p. 124. For complaints against those who saved, see Bussmann, *Herbert Bismarck*, pp. 283–84, and the Hohenlohe materials in note 85 above.

consular personnel and counselors in Berlin, who had few if any entertainment duties, sometimes succeeded in saving part of their wages.[90] The Foreign Office admitted that diplomatic salaries, while somewhat higher than the pay for comparable positions in some other branches of the bureaucracy, lagged behind those paid to diplomats by other major nations and were by no means sufficient to cover most diplomats' expenses.[91] The juggling of funds within the Wilhelmstrasse for the benefit of impoverished envoys was virtually impossible. The *Oberrechnungskammer*, whose scrutiny of the accounting practices of government departments was very rigorous, would not allow salary supplements to be paid from regular appropriations. The chancellor, however, had discretionary funds which he occasionally used to bail out impecunious diplomats.[92] The Reichstag alone could grant the requisite funds for salary increases, but the Wilhelmstrasse was unwilling to press that body to increase pay scales to the point that private incomes were no longer necessary.

This negative attitude was based on reasoning which was both tactical and professional. The Reichstag, few of whose members were familiar with or sympathetic to the exalted social spheres in which diplomats moved, was always reluctant to boost salaries, which it believed already excessive.

[90] Holstein diary, May 8, 1884, HolN 3860/H195902; Rogge, *Holstein: Lebensbekenntnis*, p. 147. The expense of consular posts in Russia, like those in the diplomatic service, could not be covered by wages. See Mohl, *Fünfzig Jahre*, p. 167.

[91] Reichstag, Nov. 16, 1871, p. 298 (Bismarck); ibid., Feb. 25, 1878, pp. 202–3 (Bismarck); ibid., Mar. 14, 1877, p. 160 (Richter); Lichnowsky, *Abyss*, p. 87.

[92] Limburg-Stirum to HvB, Oct. 28, 1880, BisN FC 2370/128; Moritz Busch, *Tagebuchblätter*, 3 vols. (Leipzig, 1899), III, 3. There is a cryptic letter from OvB to W2 of Aug. 30, 1889, which indicates that Bismarck may have intended to help Count Hatzfeldt, ambassador in London, pay the unmanageable debts of his wife. BisN FC 2896/402–3.

It occasionally refused Bismarck's requests to grant ambassadors and state secretaries even modest pay increases. To appeal to the Reichstag was therefore merely courting defeat. Besides, any inflation in diplomatic wages, already somewhat out of line with posts in the Prussian bureaucracy, would aggravate other government departments. As State Secretary von Jagow observed in 1913, envoys' pay could not be allowed to fall into "crass contradiction" with that meted out to other high officials. One diplomat, who fortunately had a sufficiency of private funds, noted that if fledgling diplomats were paid enough to cover their expenses, their salaries would have to equal those paid to Prussian *Regierungspräsidenten* or even cabinet ministers.[93]

If the Foreign Office's requests for salary increases had to be kept moderate, it was nevertheless essential that envoys not be reduced to poverty because of their service. If that were allowed, old families with a tradition of service would have to abandon diplomacy and the Wilhelmstrasse would degenerate into a preserve of the very rich, a prospect which Bismarck regarded as most undesirable. Ambassadors, the Iron Chancellor declared, had usually been drawn from the ranks of landowning nobles, whose estates, as he knew from his own long service abroad, suffered because of their long absences at their posts.[94] Consequently, salaries had to be kept high enough to attract such men to the diplomatic service and to offer them at least partial compensation for the sacrifices in behalf of the Fatherland. Where wages did not suffice, some relief might be afforded by assigning diplomats to posts in which the cost of living or the demands of entertainment were less burdensome, or they might be given one of the well-endowed seats on the

[93] MiquelN, 00185–86.

[94] Reichstag, Feb. 25, 1878, pp. 202–3. See also ibid., Mar. 14, 1877, pp. 158–59 (State Secretary Bülow). See also Hohenlohe to Prince Max von Ratibor, Apr. 19, 1884, HohN, XX.E.6, in which Hohenlohe complains that his diplomatic career was interfering with the management of his landed estates and thereby resulting in a fall in his income.

international Egyptian Debt Commission.[95] Appointment
to an important general consulship was an alternate way
out of insolvency, for these posts paid more than some diplomatic assignments. The general consul in New York, for
example, received 53,000 marks in 1912, while the minister
in Berne had to be content with less metropolitan surround-
ings and only 31,000 marks. Those who protested that they
could not live on their salaries and for whom no relief could
or would be provided were either ignored or advised to
resign.[96]

Although the position of many diplomats was thus un-
easy, if not impossible, the Foreign Office discerned a number of professional advantages in keeping salaries low
enough to insure that independent incomes were absolutely
necessary. A wealthy man was more likely to be immune
from falling under the sway of undesirable foreign or domestic influences; he could afford to adopt an independent
attitude toward both the state to which he was accredited
and officials in Berlin. Ludwig Raschdau, a bourgeois of
modest beginnings who nevertheless rose to become minister to the Saxon states in the 1890s, observed that one of the
happy advantages of his marriage to an heiress while still
a counselor in the Political Division was that his new wealth
enabled him to stand up to his superiors in the Wilhelmstrasse. Shortly after Raschdau's marriage, Holstein noted
rather sourly that he had become "unpleasant, arrogant and
purse-proud [*protzig*]. His rich old Jewess [bride] is probably responsible."[97] Moritz Busch, Bismarck's scribe, was

[95] Nowak and Thimme, *Erinnerungen; Monts*, p. 41; Jäckh, *Kiderlen-Wächter*, II, 79, 96–97.

[96] Heinrich von Poschinger, ed., *Also sprach Bismarck*, 3 vols.
(Vienna, 1910–11), I, 332 note 2. For the Wilhelmstrasse's lack of
interest in diplomats' financial problems see TN, XIIIe, 5.

[97] FvH to PzE, Aug. 9, 1890, EN, XII, 522–23; Raschdau, *Unter
Bismarck und Caprivi*, p. 87. For a similar complaint on the effect
of the wealthy Frau Paul Kayser on her husband, the head of the
Kolonial Abteilung, see Eulenburg's "Eine Erinnerungen an den
'kleinen Kayser,'" EN, IX, 225–32.

explicit on this point. "A diplomat," he wrote, "must keep his financial affairs in order, incur no debts, be independent from any need which might occasion him to have to say that 'you can't take five from four, so I'll borrow.' He must have no inclination to speculate on the exchange in either stocks or commodities, because in doing so he runs the risk of having to accommodate himself to *Finanzjuden* at the cost of the interests or honor of his country."[98]

Even if a prospective diplomat could successfully move through the prescribed course of examinations and meet the requirements of an independent income, there were still other barriers which had to be negotiated before his admission would become assured or, once in the Wilhelmstrasse, his career advanced. For if there were objective requirements for those who aspired to become diplomats, the Foreign Office also imposed a number of subjective qualifications. To become a diplomat, a candidate had to avoid the perils rooted in prejudice as well as those erected in the name of standards.

[98] Busch, *Unser Reichskanzler: Studien zu einem Charakterbilde*, 2 vols. (Leipzig, 1884), I, 228–29. In his strictures against indebtedness to Jews, Busch was probably thinking of Count Hatzfeldt, whose disorderly financial and personal affairs had allegedly made him dependent on loans from Gerson von Bleichröder. It appears that Bleichröder had made loans to Hatzfeldt to the amount of 360,000 to 400,000 marks. See HvB to KvR, Aug. 3, 1880, and July 12, 1881, BisN FC 3014/627, 660. See also Hohenlohe diary for May 30, 1880, HohN, CC.X.8, and for June 18, 1881, ibid., CC.X.9; Holstein diary for Feb. 8, 1884, HolN 3860/H195786–87. Bismarck's son-in-law, Count Kuno von Rantzau, believed that Holstein, who wanted Hatzfeldt to become state secretary, had encouraged Bleichröder to come to Hatzfeldt's assistance. Rantzau, "Autobiographische Aufzeichnungen," BisN FC 3030/687. There is additional information on the Hatzfeldt-Bleichröder connection in Holborn, *Aufzeichnungen; Radowitz*, II, 185–86; Raschdau, *Unter Bismarck und Caprivi*, p. 207; Rudolf Morsey, *Die oberste Reichsverwaltung unter Bismarck, 1867–1890* (Münster, 1957), p. 121 note 120. Robert von Keudell, ambassador to Italy in the 1870s and 1880s, was, in Holstein's opinion, also in Bleichröder's toils. See Holstein diary for May 8, 1884, HolN 3860/H195904.

## CHAPTER III

Birth and Background

The Foreign Office prized no quality so much as noble lineage. The Wilhelmstrasse, as one of Germany's leading bourgeois businessmen observed, was a "club into which one had to be admitted by and through birth."[1] It was reluctant, however, to admit that familial descent played a role in the selection of diplomats, and Bismarck and his successors often denied charges of aristocratic favoritism.[2] Under the Iron Chancellor, the prejudice in behalf of the well-born resided less in Bismarck than in some of his assistants. Arthur von Brauer, who knew Bismarck well and who had been admitted into the diplomatic service before his father's ennoblement by the Grand Duke of Baden, attributed the preference given to noble candidates to the inclination of the counselors in the Political Division.[3] Two counselors who played important roles in personnel matters between 1891 and 1904, Count Friedrich von Pourtalès and Prince Karl Max von Lichnowsky, both had a clear predilection for noble applicants.[4] The Political Division was notable for its aristocratic, Prussian composition, one which it apparently hoped to perpetuate by choosing young diplomats with care

[1] Lamar Çecil, *Albert Ballin: Business and Politics in Imperial Germany, 1888–1918* (Princeton, 1967), p. 123.

[2] GW, XV, 15; Reichstag, Mar. 31, 1909, pp. 7914–16 (Schoen), and Mar. 16, 1910, pp. 2168–69 (Schoen).

[3] Brauer, "Die deutsche Diplomatie unter Bismarck," *Deutsche Revue*, XXXI, no. 2 (1906), 71–72. See also Wilhelm Ohnesseit, *Unter der Fahne schwarz-weiss-rot: Erinnerungen eines kaiserlichen Generalkonsuls* (Berlin, 1926), pp. 11–12.

[4] MiquelN, 00186; Lichnowsky, *Heading for the Abyss: Reminiscences* (New York, 1928), p. 87.

and discrimination. The absorption by the Political Division in 1895 of all personnel matters affecting heads of mission and their staffs consequently had the effect of favoring the aristocratic interest.[5]

The Foreign Office enjoyed a sufficiently formidable reputation of being the privileged preserve of wealthy nobles to deter bourgeois candidates, especially those of modest means, from attempting to enter the diplomatic service. As late as 1910, two years after a declaration before the Reichstag by State Secretary von Schoen that diplomacy had become a career open to talent, Under State Secretary Wilhelm Stemrich persuaded an impecunious *Referendar*, Hans Riesser, who was eager to become a diplomat, to abandon his aspiration. Stemrich warned Riesser that, without a title, a bourgeois diplomat could compete successfully with aristocratic colleagues only if he possessed great wealth.[6] Since the consular service made no demands with respect to birth or income, some men who might have preferred a diplomatic career contented themselves with consular positions in distant commercial centers. Even sons of bourgeois diplomats were intimidated from attempting the calling of their fathers. Hans von Miquel, who acquired his noble predicate in 1897 through his father's elevation, recalled such a case. The person in question would not risk applying because he was "too proud as a *Bürgerlicher* to expose himself to the refusal that seemed likely." And Miquel's father, who was the Prussian Minister of Finance and a conservative who enjoyed wide entrée with the aristocracy, warned his son that his future as a diplomat would be difficult because he had no family connections among the nobility, a caveat later repeated by Holstein. Miquel fortu-

[5] Herbert von Hindenburg, *Das Auswärtige Amt im Wandel der Zeiten* (Frankfurt/Main, 1932), p. 8.

[6] Riesser, *Von Versailles zur UNO: aus der Erinnerungen eines Diplomaten* (Bonn, 1962), p. 35. Only in the Weimar Republic did Riesser secure admission to the diplomatic service.

nately ingratiated himself with State Secretary Bülow, who allowed him to choose his initial assignment and who thereafter, as chancellor, took an active interest in his career.[7]

The Foreign Office's attitude as to the desirability of titles was expressed clearly, if somewhat cynically, by Herbert von Bismarck. In 1886, Bernhard von Bülow asked for Bismarck's help in securing the admission of his cousin, Martin Rücker-Jenisch, a wealthy reserve lieutenant from the elegant Hamburg suburb of Klein Flottbek. Bismarck at once acceded to his friend's request, but he added that if he were Rücker-Jenisch he would obtain a title. Since the candidate was a rich officer a patent of nobility would be easy to obtain. Besides, "Baron" or "Count von Flottbek" had an impressive ring.[8] The usefulness of a noble pedigree was confirmed by Karl Georg von Treutler, whose father was awarded his title in 1884, a few years before Treutler entered the service. Treutler declared that his acceptance by the Wilhelmstrasse would not have been possible without this distinction.[9]

Securing places in the diplomatic service for their sons was a matter of concern to many noble families, whose conception of suitable employment for their male heirs was very restricted. Herbert von Beneckendorff und von Hindenburg, a cousin of the field marshal, grandson of Ambassador Prince Münster, and himself a diplomat, observed that in the late nineteenth century there were only three *standesgemäss* professions for men of his station: the army, diplomacy, and service in certain branches of the bureaucracy.[10] To the nobility, diplomacy was a birthright, an ac-

[7] Walter Zechlin, *Fröhliche Lebensfahrt: diplomatische und undiplomatische Erinnerungen* (Stuttgart, 1936), p. 41; Ohnesseit, *Unter der Fahne*, pp. 10–11; MiquelN, 00186, 00192–93.

[8] HvB to BvB, June 24, 1886, BüN 66. He became a baron in 1906.

[9] TN, VII, 1.

[10] Hindenburg, *Am Rande zweier Jahrhunderte: Momentbilder aus einem Diplomatenleben* (Berlin, 1938), pp. 46–47. Prior to the wars

ceptable and pleasant career insuring one's social status. Young diplomats delighted in engraving *Beschäftigt im Auswärtigen Amt* on their calling cards, and as such they were sought after by the doyennes who superintended the intricacies of Berlin society.[11] A diplomatic career, moreover, provided opportunities for a pleasant life in interesting places rather than a stagnant routine in Berlin or in the provinces. The diplomatic service also seemed to offer a stability of tenure, while officials in more politicized branches of the government were subjected to the caprices of political fortune. A diplomat was, at least in theory, above faction, while a Prussian *Landrat*, the preferred bureaucratic position of many nobles, stood in the midst of party conflict. A diplomat might fall for incompetence, but a *Landrat* could perish because of his political identification.[12]

The attitude of young nobles on their entry into the diplomatic service was often distinctly cavalier. Doubtless many felt that they had been forced into diplomacy only because it was one of the few pursuits socially suitable for men of their birth. A fate imposed by destiny could be treated with a more ample measure of nonchalance than a predicament which was voluntary. One young secretary confessed that he had opted for diplomacy only because it was the path of least resistance, while a mediatized count joined the Foreign Office because he could not get along

---

of unification, the multiplicity of German states created an extraordinary number of diplomatic positions for young nobles. With the consolidation of the empire, there were fewer posts, a fact which perhaps accounted for some of the aristocratic hostility to unification. See Moritz Busch, *Unser Reichskanzler: Studien zu einem Charakterbilde*, 2 vols. (Leipzig, 1884), I, 229–30.

[11] Ludwig Raschdau, *Wie ich Diplomat wurde: aus dem Leben erzählt* (Berlin, 1938), p. 42.

[12] Alfred von Bülow to BvB, n.d. (ca. 1881), BüN 14, pp. 37–39. For the *Landräte* see Lysbeth Walker Muncy, *The Junker in the Prussian Administration under William II, 1888–1914* (Providence, 1944).

with his father.[13] Philipp Eulenburg admitted that he had been attracted to diplomacy by contemplating the free time it would provide for his artistic interests. One of his good friends was pleased to note that after almost a decade in the service, Eulenburg seemed to have developed a much greater enthusiasm for professional affairs than had formerly been the case.[14] The real affection of most of these nobles was for their ancestral estates and for life upon the land, and diplomacy, however socially acceptable, inevitably meant a rupture with the delights of rustication. Count Harry Kessler, a worldly and perceptive Prussian who grew to maturity among men preordained to become diplomats, courtiers, or generals, wrote of this species that since they were never able to uproot themselves from the soil "they exhibited a certain detachment from the bureaucracy . . . , and in some of them this aloofness passed into faint doubts as to the utility or the necessity of the roles for which they were intended."[15] Furthermore, not a few young diplomats, bourgeois as well as aristocratic, found their initial tasks at the Foreign Office trivial and boring. They entered with visions of participating in the highest diplomatic negotiations but instead were instructed to handle petty affairs such as the retrieval of personal property misplaced in railroad stations by itinerant and absentminded Germans.[16]

Even among titled applicants, the Foreign Office was careful to draw distinctions. In the competition for admission to the Wilhelmstrasse after 1871, aristocrats of royal, mediatized, and *uralt* houses, as well as those whose titles

[13] Gerhard von Mutius, *Abgeschlossene Zeiten* (Hermannstadt, n.d. [ca. 1929]), p. 106; GN, 301 (on Count Siegfried zu Castell-Rüdenhausen).

[14] MiquelN, 00185; Johannes Haller, *Aus dem Leben des Fürsten Philipp zu Eulenburg-Hertefeld* (Berlin, 1924), p. 12. See Hindenburg, *Am Rande*, pp. 177, 192, for a junior diplomat's sufficiency of free time.

[15] Kessler, *Gesichter und Zeiten: Erinnerungen* (Berlin, 1962 [1935]), p. 201.

[16] Julius von Eckardt, *Lebenserinnerungen*, 2 vols. (Leipzig, 1910), II, 117.

were old but not ancient, vied with sons of bourgeois industrialists and bankers, some of them recently ennobled. So marked was the taste of these aristocratic parvenus for diplomacy that they were sometimes referred to contemptuously as *Diplomatenadel*.[17] One object of aristocratic derision was Baron Hermann ("Specki") Speck von Sternburg, the descendant of a Bavarian shepherd who had perfected a breed of superior woolliness, amassed a great fortune, acquired landed estates, and in 1829 received a title from King Ludwig I. Another was the champagne magnate, Baron Alfons Mumm von Schwarzenstein, who was known familiarly to his fellow diplomats as "Cliquot" or "Extra-dry." Mumm's Prussian baronial coronet dated only from 1903, his *von* (a grant to his father) from 1873. The triumph of wealth had produced in the German haute bourgeoisie a taste for imitating their social superiors.[18] If diplomacy was an aristocratic pursuit, then it was one which was attractive to such late arrivals. Bismarck claimed that he did what he could to facilitate the introduction of bourgeois into the service but that his attempts failed because of opposition on the part of the *Heroldsamt* or of the Prussian Civil Cabinet to allow patents of nobility to be awarded to would-be middle-class candidates.[19] There is, however, no evidence that the Iron Chancellor or his successors tried very earnestly to attract *Neuadel* to the diplomatic service. The offspring of new wealth and new titles were only modestly represented in the Foreign Office lists. Of the 377 nobles serving in the Wilhelmstrasse or in the field between 1871 and 1914 in the rank of assistant or secretary of legation or above, thirty-six (9.55 percent) owed their titles to Prussian grants to their fathers; another sixteen (4.24 per-

[17] Prince Alexander von Hohenlohe, *Aus meinem Leben* (Frankfurt/Main, 1925), p. 328.

[18] See the interesting remarks of Franz Oppenheimer in his *Erlebtes, Erstrebtes, Erreichtes: Erinnerungen* (Berlin, 1931), p. 73.

[19] Baron Robert Lucius von Ballhausen, *Bismarck-Erinnerungen* (Stuttgart, 1921), p. 373.

cent) were similarly indebted to other German sovereigns. In addition, Prussian titles were awarded to twelve bourgeois diplomats, while another five were elevated by other rulers. Combining these, *Diplomatenadel* constituted only 18.30 percent of the aristocratic element in the Foreign Office. Like their unennobled brethren, who represented a more significant segment of German diplomatic personnel, they seldom rose to the highest positions.

The more ancient a candidate's ancestry and the more lofty his title, the greater the disposition which could be made of his services. Within the diplomatic profession, as in noble society at large, an invidious distinction was drawn between old and new nobles. Diplomats of old aristocratic families, especially those who had become impecunious, were sometimes intolerant of their colleagues whose titles were recent, considering them in all respects, except nomenclature, to be indistinguishable from bourgeois.[20] Count (later Prince) Georg Herbert zu Münster, ambassador in Paris from 1885 to 1900, was notorious for his aristocratic hauteur and he had a low opinion of the social quality of almost all diplomats. He protested that his second secretary, Wilhelm von Schoen, whose Hessian title dated only from 1885 and who was the heir to a great Rhenish tannery fortune, "smelled of leather."[21] Peers of venerable origin argued that only in their own ranks were to be found diplomats who would maintain an independent judgment. Furthermore, aristocrats of standing, in a gracious exercise of

[20] Karl F. Nowak and Friedrich Thimme, eds., *Erinnerungen und Gedanken des Botschafters Anton Graf Monts* (Berlin, 1932), pp. 50–51; Hohenlohe, *Meinem Leben*, pp. 328–29. Not all diplomats shared this attitude, however. See Alfred von Bülow to BvB, Sept. 10, 1889, BüN 14, and Florian von Thielau to HvB, Aug. 8, 1879, BisN FC 2982/1020.

[21] Bernhard von Bülow, *Denkwürdigkeiten*, 4 vols. (Berlin, 1930–31), I, 395; III, 31. Münster eventually overcame his distaste for Schoen. See his letter to Hohenlohe, May 17, 1895, HohN, XXII.D.3, and his letters to FvH of Feb. 22, 1889, and Dec. 30, 1895, HolN 3859/H194679, 194738.

noblesse oblige, would be more inclined to consort with the common people of the land in which they served. Newly minted nobles, ever aspiring to social triumphs, would in parvenu fashion be eager only to grovel before the pillars of society.[22] An ancient or an exalted title was especially desirable in places, such as Vienna, which were notable for aristocratic punctiliousness. Ambassador Eulenburg, never one to minimize his effectiveness, on being raised by William II from count to prince in 1900 gushed to State Secretary Bülow that in the Habsburg capital his elevation was regarded as an act of courtesy to the Dual Monarchy. He noted in his diary that the Austrian government regarded his having been accorded the honor as a "very shrewd political coup."[23]

A mediatized title, or one derived from a royal morganatic marriage, was sometimes useful, for in such cases the envoy might well be related to the sovereign to whose court he was accredited. Berlin society itself was not overly impressed by these scions of once regnant houses. At least one mediatized princeling serving in the Wilhelmstrasse deplored the inability of Berlin to appreciate his exalted status. He found the capital's salons dreary, the Foreign Office suffused with *"preussisch-Bureaukraten-Pedantismus,"* and yearned to be posted overseas.[24] Bismarck appears to have been aware of the advantage of enlisting *Standesherren* in the diplomatic corps, but not all mediatized princes and counts who wanted to enter the Foreign Office were admitted.[25] Some who did secure positions, such as Count

[22] Lichnowsky, *Abyss*, p. 87; Nowak and Thimme, *Erinnerungen; Monts*, pp. 50–51, 118; GW, VIc, 64–65; Hohenlohe, *Meinem Leben*, p. 329.

[23] PzE to BvB, Jan. 13, 1900; PzE notes for Jan. 3 and 4, 1900, EN, LV, 14–15, 28.

[24] Castell diary for June 24, 1889, Feb. 12, 1890, Mar. 26, 1893, CN, IeVI/29; Castell to his mother, Sept. 21, 1888, ibid., IeIII/76.

[25] Otto von Bülow to HvB, Nov. 25, 1879, BisN FC 2958/1145–47, concerning a Prince of Erbach-Erbach, who did not win admittance.

65

Albert von Quadt-Wykradt-Isny and Prince Max von Ratibor und Corvey, had inflated notions of their abilities and were placed in backwater posts. But some of Germany's most effective emissaries, such as Prince Hohenlohe, were drawn from the ranks of formerly sovereign houses, and a few, such as the arrogant but able Prince Heinrich VII Reuss, were members of still regnant houses.[26] At various times between 1871 and 1914, there were twenty-four members of mediatized families as well as four collateral relatives of such lines, four scions of regnant houses, and four products of royal morganatic marriages. Of these thirty-six men, all but one served abroad for most of their careers. The exception was Ernst von Wildenbruch, the playwright laureate and a descendant of a Hohenzollern mésalliance, whose position as a permanent assistant was designed as a sinecure to enable him to compose his sodden dramas glorifying the royal house.

Altogether, of the 548 Foreign Ministry officials under examination, 377 (68.80 percent) bore titles of nobility. Of these 377, 330 (87.53 percent) had some service in the field, while the remaining forty-seven were stationed permanently in Berlin. Titled diplomats were clearly more effectively employed abroad than in the Wilhelmstrasse, where work went on behind closed doors rather than in the fulsome light of society.[27] The Foreign Office had no difficulty in formulating justifications for the large percentage of nobles in its ranks. It was, after all, in the tradition of European

See also Busch, *Unser Reichskanzler*, I, 227–28, which undoubtedly reflects Bismarck's opinion. See Hindenburg, *Am Rande*, p. 237, for State Secretary von Jagow's liking for mediatized diplomats.

[26] For Hohenlohe's serviceability in London because of his kinship to Queen Victoria, see BvB to HvB, Aug. 23, 1884, BisN FC 2958/386–87.

[27] The Bavarian diplomatic service showed a similar distribution between 1871 and 1914. Even *Neuadel* were less likely to be assigned abroad. See Walter Schärl, *Die Zusammensetzung der bayerischen Beamtenschaft von 1806 bis 1918* (Kallmünz, 1955), pp. 307–46.

monarchical statecraft, and even the new French republic endorsed the practice until about 1890.[28] With their innate refinement, aristocrats, and particularly those drawn from old houses, were more likely to possess the social attributes Berlin considered desirable in the conduct of diplomacy. Such nobles could also draw upon the cosmopolitan connections of their families. How convenient for Prince Hugo von Radolin, ambassador in Paris from 1900 to 1910, that his mother-in-law was a Talleyrand; for Count Gustav von Lambsdorff, the military plenipotentiary in St. Petersburg, that his uncle, another Count Lamsdorf, was at the same time the tsar's foreign minister; and for the ambassador to Italy from 1894 to 1897, Bernhard von Bülow, that his effervescent wife, née Princess Camporeale, was the stepdaughter of a celebrated Italian statesman and the daughter of the grande dame of Roman society.

Moreover, there were also the stupefyingly complex interrelationships of German diplomatic families. The Hohenlohes were kin to the Lichnowskys and to the Arnims, who in turn had connections with the Bismarcks, Flemmings, and Heykings. The Bülows, Brockdorffs, and Rantzaus were intertwined and all had genealogical tentacles that embraced various Wallwitzes, Dönhoffs, and Bismarcks. The enumeration of such strategic ties both in Germany and abroad would be endless. The German bourgeoisie, whatever its talent for moneymaking, lacked the experience, the sophistication, and the connections to be found in the nobility.[29] Middle-class men were simply less effective than nobles and they could prove an embarrassment, for bourgeois envoys were sometimes slighted by aristocratic courts,

[28] Of French envoys accredited between 1870 and 1914, 44.79% were noble. The incidence of such aristocrats fell from 88.98% in the period 1871–78 to 7.14% in the period from 1903 to 1914. I am indebted to Lt. Col. Walter S. Barge, USA, for providing these statistics.

[29] See the interesting remarks on this point by *ganz edler* Herr zu Putlitz in the Reichstag, Mar. 31, 1909, pp. 912–13.

a painful experience for those diplomats and an affront to German or Prussian honor. Count Gustav Kálnoky von Körös-Patek, the Austro-Hungarian foreign minister from 1881 to 1895, was notorious for his arrogance to diplomats. One French envoy, a gentle man of humble birth, was a particular object of Kálnoky's contempt, and he treated him, as another diplomat stationed in Vienna described it, "like a shoeshine boy."[30] Good relations were poorly served by such incidents and they had to be avoided. Bourgeois diplomats therefore tended to be sent to out-of-the-way posts or to consular stations, or they were kept permanently in Berlin.

In some posts, the presence of a noble was more than desirable: it was imperative. Even the National Liberal lead-

TABLE 6

DISTRIBUTION OF DIPLOMATIC POSTS TO NOBLES AND BOURGEOIS

Position	Nobles		Bourgeois	
	#	%	#	%
European ambassador	30	7.96	—	—
European minister	43	11.41	4	2.34
Prussian minister	28	7.43	1	.58
Major non-European ambassador or minister*	26	6.90	6	3.51
Other non-European minister	26	6.90	15	8.77
Lower field position	147	38.98	16	9.36
Berlin position	77	20.42	129	75.44
Total	377	100.00	171	100.00

* Argentina, Brazil, China, Japan, Morocco, Mexico, Persia, United States.
NOTE: Each diplomat is tabulated in highest post achieved.

[30] Nowak and Thimme, *Erinnerungen; Monts*, p. 122. For a rebuff to a middle-class Prussian envoy see Ludwig Raschdau, *In Weimar als preussischer Gesandter: ein Buch der Erinnerungen an deutsche Fürstenhöfe, 1894–1897* (Berlin, 1939), p. 77. For the hostility of the Prussian court to bourgeois envoys see Marie von Bunsen, *Zeitgenossen die ich erlebte, 1900–1930* (Leipzig, 1932), p. 76, and Helmuth Rogge, ed., *Friedrich von Holstein: Lebensbekenntnis in Briefen an eine Frau* (Berlin, 1932), p. 334.

er, Ernst Bassermann, often a determined critic of aristocratic influence in the Foreign Office, publicly conceded the point.[31] Aristocratic pomp was meet and right in Edwardian London, while nobles of South German lineage were considered particularly effective in the important general consulate in Budapest.[32] In Vienna, the Habsburgs' fanatical devotion to the "Spanish etiquette," with its arcane snobberies and vacant rituals, and the hauteur of the capital's aristocratic society—"Olympia," it was called—conspired to make it obligatory for legations there to be blue-blooded. An ambassador of the French republic, himself a marquis, was careful to have none but noblemen on his staff, an insistence his German counterpart regarded as a "very shrewd maneuver."[33] Philipp Eulenburg, as ambassador in Vienna, noted that "secretaries from small beginnings, without money or manners, are impossible here."[34] Only one bourgeois ever served as a secretary in the German embassy in the Habsburg capital. This was Martin Rücker-Jenisch, the kinsman of the Bülows and a young man of considerable wealth and polish, who served there for less than a year in 1889. How he fared in society is not on record, but the staff believed that his lack of title was a disadvantage. "You know," one member of the embassy wrote to his diplomat brother, "that in the lofty reaches of society here humanity begins with counts. But it is certainly fitting that we show them that there are excellent people [*vornehme Leute*] in Germany who are not from the nobility."[35]

[31] Reichstag, Mar. 29, 1909, p. 7812.

[32] Alfred von Tirpitz, *Politische Dokumente*, 2 vols. (Stuttgart, 1924–26), I, 383; Monts to BvB, Nov. 16, 1891, BüN 106.

[33] Undated note (ca. 1900) by PzE, EN, LV, 113. The vanity of Viennese society was enough to give qualms to an *uralt* Bülow. See Alfred von Bülow to BvB, Nov. 9, 1888, BüN 14.

[34] PzE to FvH, Jan. 11, 1895, HolN 3855/H193376–77.

[35] Alfred von Bülow to BvB, Sept. 10, 1889, BüN 14. Rücker had 300,000 marks in securities and a number of landed properties in Prussia and in Denmark. BvB to HvB, June 9, 1886, BisN FC 2958/573.

The Wilhelmstrasse believed that Russia could be most effectively covered by an east Elbian diplomat or a military figure—or by somone who might possess both qualifications. Such a man would by origin be likely to favor an eastern orientation of German policy and be endowed with a certain knowledgeability about the problems of a hierarchical, agrarian society. At the same time, the German ambassador should be able to acquit himself opulently enough to satisfy the limitless expectations of St. Petersburg society. Its salons, attendance at which was crucial for a diplomat in search of information, were hostile to bourgeois diplomats. On the other hand, caution had to be taken in accrediting a Junker to certain courts. Munich posed problems because of the Wittelsbachs' highly developed particularist notions and their resentment of Prussian hegemony in Germany. At the same time, the Bavarian court demanded an envoy of old-fashioned elegance and decorum.[36]

At the other ideological extreme from such aristocratic courts was republican France, but it too was purposely staffed with men of old, and usually exalted, lineage. Count Karl von Pückler, a diplomat who was a collateral descendant of the mediatized Pückler und Limburgs, reflecting on the success and popularity of the elegant Prince von Radolin as ambassador in Paris, noted that it was a "well-founded experience that the grand seigneur is most winning where he is least likely to encounter his equals."[37] William II believed that this principle had applied to Radolin's predecessor, the elegant and icy Prince Münster, for French workingmen, the kaiser claimed, stood transfixed

[36] On the Russian post see HvB to FvH, Mar. 1 and 8, 1884, HolN 3853/H190676, 190682; on Munich PzE to FvH, July 16, 1886, ibid., 3855/H192092–94.

[37] Count Karl von Pückler, *Aus meinem Diplomatenleben* (Schweidnitz, 1934), p. 56. Bernhard von Bülow, who had served in Paris, believed, however, that bourgeois birth could be an advantage, but only if an envoy had style and money. BvB to HvB, Aug. 23, 1884, BisN FC 2958/386.

whenever the envoy appeared in public.[38] Of the five ambassadors who served in Paris from 1871 to 1914, only Baron von Schoen possessed a recent title. The other four —Arnim, Hohenlohe, Münster, and Radolin—were all members of *uralt* houses, all but Arnim were princes, and Hohenlohe was the head of a mediatized line. Hohenlohe, a calm Bavarian grandee who served in Paris from 1874 to 1885, was a particularly brilliant success. At first Parisian society and political leaders, wounded by France's recent defeat, boycotted the German embassy, but gradually the charm and sympathetic bearing of both the ambassador and his Russian wife won over the most ardent republicans as well as the *gratin* of the elegant faubourgs. One account wistfully reported that the éclat of receptions at the embassy, with the powdered footmen in black Hohenlohe livery, were "almost royal" and reminiscent of the Second Empire.[39] Berlin also invariably sent noblemen to Washington, although few were of remote lineage and none bore princely or mediatized titles.

Finally, there were posts—*Hofämter*—in which diplomats were required to display tolerance for court ritual rather than expertise in negotiation. In such capitals what was needed was glistening courtliness, a virtue which the nobility believed it monopolized. One of Hohenlohe's nephews, Prince Max Ratibor, implored his uncle to send him as minister to Weimar rather than that "rough diamond" Ludwig Raschdau, who was being considered for the post. Hohenlohe, who recognized that his kinsman's abilities were quite ordinary, chose Raschdau. The appointment of a bourgeois was initially frowned on by the Grand Duke of Saxe-Weimar, but he later came to have a high regard for the polished Raschdau.[40]

---

[38] PzE to BvB, July 22, 1899, EN, LIV, 178–79.

[39] Clipping from an unnamed English newspaper, dated Feb. 24, 1877, HohN, XX.J.5.

[40] Ratibor to Alexander Hohenlohe, May 12, 1896, ibid., XXII.A.8; Raschdau, *In Weimar*, pp. 3, 17, 77, 170; Raschdau, *Unter Bismarck*

Even where the special attributes of a post were not factors in the appointment of noble envoys, considerations of a general nature often prompted such a choice. For one thing, aristocrats would be politically reliable. The striking absence of political abstractions or ideological conceptions in the papers of German diplomats, and the failure of the Foreign Office to provide its diplomats with any formulation of political belief indicate that the Wilhelmstrasse could, and did, assume that the corps would always mirror the conservative tastes of the regime. The private correspondence of German diplomats often reflects differing opinions on political personalities or stratagems, but nowhere is there a suggestion that they believed that the Hohenzollern system, even under William II, should be significantly overhauled. In government, as in diplomacy, tradition was the watchword.

The social factor also favored aristocrats. The Foreign Office repeatedly emphasized the desirability of a diplomat's learning his graces and his languages in the nursery, a commonplace in noble households. Writing in 1925 to his friend, the journalist Theodor Wolff, Bernhard von Bülow declared with satisfaction that "from childhood, I have written and spoken French as fluently as my mother tongue."[41] The aristocratic hauteur with respect to languages was well illustrated in Philipp Eulenburg's exchange with his superior, Max von Philippsborn, a bourgeois Jewish counselor who had converted and acquired a title.

Philippsborn: Sie schreiben ja sehr nett Französisch. Wo haben Sie denn das gelernt?

---

und Caprivi: Erinnerungen eines deutschen Diplomaten aus den Jahren 1885–1894, 2d ed. (Berlin, 1939), p. 352.

[41] Wolff, *Marsch durch zwei Jahrzehnte* (Amsterdam, 1936), p. 128. See also the following for the conviction that there was no substitute for learning languages in childhood: Bülow, *Denkwürdigkeiten,* IV, 21–22, Richard von Kühlmann, *Die Diplomaten* (Berlin, 1939), p. 105; Busch, *Unser Reichskanzler,* I, 232.

Eulenburg: Seit meiner Kindheit spreche und schreibe ich Französisch.

Philippsborn: Soooo?—Ja der preussische Adel! Es ist doch etwas Merkwürdiges um den preussischen Adel.[42]

Assiduous imitation or diligent study as an adult might provide an approximation of such talents cultivated from infancy, but naturalness and ease would be lacking. Even the bourgeois diplomat, Moritz Busch, adhered to the proposition. "The education a wealthy nobleman receives," he wrote, "is undoubtedly better for the court circles in which an envoy is called to live and work than that which is provided for the children and half grown-up sons of the middle class."[43] What was essential for young diplomats, in the experience of those who had grown old in the service, was "*ein guter Kinderschule,*" "*usage du monde,*" "social culture," and so on.[44] The Foreign Office therefore felt no need to provide young diplomats with manuals of correct behavior, for the deft instinct which was the heritage of gentle birth would be sufficient to whatever a diplomat might encounter in the world.

Not all young aristocrats, to be sure, possessed these social virtues. Some spoke foreign tongues barbarously, if at all. Prince Hohenlohe as ambassador in Paris was forced to ask the Wilhelmstrasse to grant leave to his nephew, Prince

---

[42] Eulenburg, *Aus 50 Jahren: Erinnerungen, Tagebücher und Briefe* (Berlin, 1923), p. 51. Philippsborn's resentment of the old nobility was shared by another counselor, Karl Göring. Holstein diary, Apr. 29, 1884, HolN 3860/H195882.

[43] Busch, *Unser Reichskanzler*, I, 227–28. Walter Struve, *Elites against Democracy: Leadership Ideals in Bourgeois Political Thought in Germany, 1890–1933* (Princeton, 1973), pp. 26–27, contributes a valuable discussion of the German nobility's conception of its inherent superiority.

[44] Haller, *Aus dem Leben Eulenburg*, p. 13; Lichnowsky, *Abyss*, p. 87; Kühlmann, *Diplomaten*, p. 110; Reichstag, Mar. 16, 1910, pp. 2160–61 (Dirksen). Dirksen served in the Wilhelmstrasse, ultimately as a counselor, from 1880 to 1903.

Ratibor, a secretary in the embassy, so that he could take an intensive course in French. A few years later, Herbert von Bismarck was unable to assign Ratibor to London because he had no English whatsoever.[45] It is noteworthy that these linguistic deficiencies had not prevented the prince's entry into the service or his subsequent advancement. Other nobles had the gift of tongues but few traces of refinement. Count Maximilian Yorck von Wartenburg, a military attaché in St. Petersburg, was valued for his flawless Russian but deplored for his manners. He ate with unbecoming rapacity, devouring chicken with his fingers and then throwing the bones under the table.[46] Gentility and charm were not, as one diplomat pointed out, the exclusive property of aristocrats. But in the nobility these qualities were taken for granted, while in the bourgeoisie they were felt to be exceptional.[47]

The determination of the Foreign Office to preserve its noble character was successful in that up to the collapse of the empire in 1918 the aristocracy continued to supply the great majority of recruits to the service. But the German nobility had many geographical distinctions and ancestral gradations, and by 1914 the domination of the old Prussian nobles had given way in many areas to a new and different sort of diplomatic establishment.

From the 1870s on, Bismarck and others complained that the Wilhelmstrasse was not attracting a sufficient representation of aristocratic talent, especially from old Prussian noble families. The chancellor frequently lamented that he had only a thin reserve of distinguished ambassadors and ministers to move about the diplomatic chessboard, and not much in the way of young men who eventually would have

[45] Hohenlohe to BvB, Sept. 27, 1883, BüN 89; HvB to BvB, Oct. 11, 1887, ibid., 66.

[46] Adolf von Bülow to BvB, Nov. 24, 1884; BvB to Adolf von Bülow, Aug. 1, 1885, BüN 13.

[47] For an example of this attitude in a noble diplomat who had been born a bourgeois, see TN, XIII, 6–7.

to assume these positions. In Bismarck's opinion, the availability of eligible Prussian aristocrats had begun to decline as early as the 1840s and it had only worsened with time. In 1884, his son Herbert complained that there were too few Prussians and too many Saxons among the recruits enlisted by the Wilhelmstrasse, while a few years later, General Count Alfred von Waldersee, a Prussian with Hohenzollern ancestors, declared that "Prussians of good birth hardly enter [the diplomatic service], but on the other hand there are everywhere unknown people from the Reich and the Hanseatic cities."[48] This regrettable geographical shift alarmed the *altpreussisch* circle in the Foreign Office, and by the 1890s there was some concern there that an attempt had to be made to attract more aristocrats, and especially Prussians, into the service. In 1897, State Secretary Bülow noted the decline in the Prussian element and wondered, unfortunately without providing an answer, why this was so.[49] The Baroness Hildegarde Spitzemberg, a Württemberger with wide diplomatic connections in Berlin, reported three years later a conversation with Prince Lichnowsky, who at the time was in charge of diplomatic personnel. Lichnowsky, a Silesian, was "especially concerned" to increase the number of men of "good family," but such gentlemen, Spitzemberg noted with regret, represented a type that had recently shown a marked decline in the ranks of diplomats.[50]

An examination of the young men who entered the diplomatic service in junior positions from 1871 to 1914 indicates

[48] GW, XV, 7–8; HvB to FvH, Aug. 26, 1884, HolN 3853/H190-735; Heinrich O. Meisner, ed., *Denkwürdigkeiten des General-Feldmarschalls Alfred Grafen von Waldersee*, 3 vols. (Stuttgart and Berlin, 1923–25), II, 31. Bismarck's friend Eulenburg also disliked Saxon recruits. See his letters to HvB of Nov. 7, 1880, and July 19, 1882, BisN FC 2961/143–44, 1210.

[49] Memo from 1897, BüN 153, p. 331.

[50] Rudolf Vierhaus, ed., *Das Tagebuch der Baronin Spitzemberg: . . . Aufzeichnungen aus der Hofgesellschaft des Hohenzollernreiches*, 2d ed. (Göttingen, 1960), pp. 397–98.

the root of the Foreign Office's concern. It becomes clear that the percentage of recruits whose families bore titles awarded before 1800 and who often possessed landed estates east of the Elbe—a group denominated in Table 7 as "Old East Prussian"—declined between 1871 and 1914.[51]

TABLE 7

GEOGRAPHICAL ORIGIN OF
RECRUITS TO THE DIPLOMATIC SERVICE

	1871–1880		1881–1890		1891–1900		1901–1914		Total	
	#	%	#	%	#	%	#	%	#	%
Noble										
Old E. Prussian	15	29.41	15	22.39	26	29.21	28	14.81	84	21.21
Old W. Prussian	1	1.96	2	2.98	3	3.37	13	6.88	19	4.80
New E. Prussian	3	5.88	6	8.96	9	10.11	21	11.11	39	9.85
New W. Prussian	1	1.96	2	2.98	3	3.37	3	1.59	9	2.27
Other German	25	49.03	26	38.81	26	29.21	42	22.22	119	30.05
Non-German	2	3.92	—	—	1	1.12	2	1.06	5	1.26
Bourgeois	4	7.84	16	23.88	21	23.61	80	42.33	121	30.56
Total	51	100.00	67	100.00	89	100.00	189	100.00	396	100.00
Unknown (all noble)	9		3		1		5		18	
Grand total	60		70		90		194		414	

In the 1870s, Prussians from Junker families comprised about thirty percent of diplomatic recruits, while during the 1880s the percentage sank perceptibly. In both decades, old-family, East Prussian additions to the service were overwhelmed by those from elsewhere in Germany. The decline

[51] In constituting this table, diplomats are listed according to their places of birth except in those cases in which it is clear that this place was accidental or temporary. It includes only those recruited as attachés, assistants, or secretaries of legation. Those brought into the diplomatic service at higher ranks such as counselor or minister were middle-aged men whose appointments proceeded from their distinction in other fields.

in Junker recruits between 1871 and 1890 is probably due in part to the agricultural crisis in Germany which lasted from approximately 1880 to 1897 and which afflicted East Elbian proprietors with particular severity. It is significant that the Prussian groups whose progeny entering the diplomatic service in the period of the agricultural crisis did not decline are those who lived west of the Elbe, whose income if from agriculture was probably derived from viniculture and animals rather than from grain, and bourgeois, few of whom had any connections with the land.[52]

In the late 1890s, the agricultural depression lifted, and the number of Junkers recruited rose somewhat, although the percentage they represented among recruits declined. The return of Junkers to the diplomatic service after the mid-1890s was not due entirely to improving agricultural conditions. One factor was the determination of Pourtalès and Lichnowsky to arrest the drift toward non-Prussians which had set in during the 1880s. Another factor accounting for the increase in Prussians after 1890 may have been Bismarck's fall, for the chancellor was in some respects partial to non-Prussians as diplomats because of their attributes of personality and character, and because he believed that their inclusion in the service would promote the solidarity of the new empire.[53] The ascension in 1888 of William II, whose prejudices were clearly Prussian, may also have contributed to the increase in Prussian nobles after 1890. His confidant Philipp Eulenburg, who exercised considerable influence in recruiting diplomats after 1880, preferred fellow Prussians, especially if they had money, presence and good looks. At the same time, he was careful to note the value to the Hohenzollern cause of luring South German aristocrats into the diplomatic service.[54]

[52] The agricultural crisis and its effects on the diplomatic service are discussed more fully on pp. 176–84 below.

[53] Otto von Bülow to HvB, Nov. 25, 1879, BisN FC 2958/1145–47.

[54] See PzE to HvB, Nov. 7, 1880, July 19, 1882, and Oct. 9, 1887,

77

After the mid-1890s, the number of East Prussian recruits remained steady, but the percentage they represented among new diplomats was lower than it had been in the 1880s. In spite of the Wilhelmstrasse's efforts, Junker representation in the corps could not be increased. The reason is probably economic, for while agriculture, now protected by tariffs, was marginally profitable, the cost of becoming a diplomat had outpaced the improvement in aristocratic, agrarian fortunes. The decline in the percentage of diplomats recruited from East Elbian families in the twentieth century was not due to an upsurge of Prussian *Neuadel* or non-Prussian nobles in the ranks of Foreign Office officials but to the enormous increase—one which had been almost constant since 1871—in the number of bourgeois diplomats. This was a phenomenon related to the expansion of Germany's diplomatic network and did not represent a change in the Wilhelmstrasse's prejudice in favor of aristocrats. The creation of new posts, most of them in distant continents, required additional staff and increased the business of the personnel in the Wilhelmstrasse. Diplomatic assignments in these remote stations were disdained by nobles, but the Foreign Office considered them suitable posts for men of bourgeois origin. The same applied to positions in Berlin, where the aristocratic virtues of breeding, manners, and presence were not important. The proliferation of bourgeois in the service was thus one which affected only subsidiary positions and did not significantly alter the aristocratic hold on the higher reaches of the service.

✻

For aspiring diplomats, noble birth was the surest means of drawing on strategic connections. There were, however, other ways in which advantageous relationships could be more widely extended, or, in the case of bourgeois candi-

---

in ibid., FC 2961/1143–44, 1163–64, 1210, and Aug. 13, 1887, and May 20, 1888, in ibid., FC 2962/143–44, 158–59.

dates, initiated and assiduously cultivated. Especially important in this respect were membership in university fraternities, marriage to daughters of aristocratic houses, and commissions in elite regiments of the army.[55]

Membership in a fraternity was taken as a matter of course by the German nobility, and especially by those from Prussia.[56] There were altogether, at one time or another in the nineteenth century, 211 student fraternities in the German universities, but only three were of significance for the training of diplomats. These were the Borussen at Bonn, the Heidelberg Saxo-Borussen and, less important, the Göttingen Saxonia. These three were associated in the "white circle" of student organizations and were dominated by the Prussian aristocracy. The three fraternities prided themselves on their noble composition, and members were prone to engage in labyrinthine genealogical investigations to determine relationships between corps brothers.[57] The aristocratic preponderance in these three fraternities from 1871 to 1904, the last year for which membership rolls exist, is striking.

Fathers handed over their sons as legacies to their old corps or, if they were not themselves members, arranged the necessary introductions through connections.[58] Fraternity membership, like military service in a crack unit or a legal

[55] The connection of the military and the world of society is discussed on pp. 104–13 below.

[56] The indispensable listing of student corps members is Karl Rügemer, *Kösener Korpslisten 1789 bis 1904* (Starnberg/Munich, n.d. [1905]). Anyone entering the corps after about 1908 would not have finished the necessary legal training to enter the Foreign Office before 1914. Thus, except for those in the fraternities between about 1905 and 1908, Rügemer provides a complete listing of corpsmen in the diplomatic service between 1871 and 1914.

[57] Kurt von Stutterheim, *The Two Germanys*, trans. Moffat Freet (London, 1939), pp. 35–40; Hajo Holborn, ed., *Aufzeichnungen und Erinnerungen ans dem Leben des Botschafters Joseph Maria von Radowitz*, 2 vols. (Berlin, 1925), I, 26.

[58] TN, VI, 1; Herbert von Dirksen, *Moskau, Tokio, London: Erinnerungen und Betrachtungen zu 20 Jahre deutscher Aussenpolitik, 1919–1939* (Stuttgart, n.d. [1949]), pp. 11–12.

79

TABLE 8
SOCIAL CLASS OF FRATERNITY PLEDGES

Fraternity	# Pledges	# Noble	% Noble	% Bourgeois
Bonn, Borussen	308	304	98.70	1.30
Heidelberg, Saxo-Borussen	391	327	83.63	16.37
Göttingen, Saxonia	271	225	83.03	16.97
Total	970	856	88.25	11.75

education, was regarded as a prerequisite for a successful career in diplomacy. Prince Alexander Hohenlohe declared that "there was no better means to gain entry into the diplomatic career than if a young man had been a member of a fashionable fraternity during his stay at a university. For that reason the progeny of the wealthy bourgeoisie strove to get into the corps, seeing therein the first step on the ladder to the highest positions in the government."[59]

Fraternity membership was expensive, and the cost became inflated as the years went by. In 1877, Karl Georg von Treutler, a Saxo-Borussen, managed to get by on an annual allowance of 567 marks, which was among the most modest in his corps. Little more than a decade later the cost of membership in this fraternity had risen to about 375 marks per month, an expense which apparently was beginning to discourage the nobility from enrolling its sons. The charges continued to rise after the turn of the century, and members were expected to go into debt to keep up.[60] Whatever the expense, being enrolled in a corps was worth the price for those eager to enter the Foreign Office. While in the university, one established friendships with men who would

[59] Hohenlohe, *Meinem Leben*, pp. 28–30, 327–29.
[60] HvB to Wilhelm von Bismarck, Dec. 4, 1889, BisN FC 3011/596; TN, VI, 2; Stutterheim, *Two Germanys*, p. 36; John G. Williamson, *Karl Helfferich, 1872–1924: Economist, Financier, Politician* (Princeton, 1971), p. 25; Baron Magnus von Braun, *Von Ostpreussen bis Texas: Erlebnisse und zeitgeschichtliche Betrachtungen eines Ostdeutschen*, 2d ed. (Stollhamm, 1955), p. 35.

later be colleagues or valuable contacts outside the service. Consider, for example, part of the Borussen lists between 1882 and 1884. In the class of 1882 there were Count Unico von der Groeben, who rose to be first secretary in Paris before his premature retirement; Baron Ernst von Heintze-Weissenrode, who eventually became minister to Cuba; Count Botho von Wedel, who after serving as envoy in Weimar became the Political Division counselor in charge of personnel, a valuable contact for any young Borussen. The class of 1883 included Martin Rücker-Jenish of the Bülow clan, later minister in Stuttgart. One of his fraternity brothers in that year was Gottlieb von Jagow, destined to become ambassador to Italy and finally state secretary. Eighteen eighty-four saw the entry of no future diplomats but of several men who would be important contacts: Prince Max Egon zu Fürstenberg, later William II's most intimate friend, and two of the last kaiser's brothers-in-law. William II himself had been in the Borussen class of 1878, as had the heirs to the thrones of Baden and Oldenburg. Prince Carol of Rumania had been a Borussen pledge in the early 1860s, a fact which worked to the advantage of Joseph Maria von Radowitz, also a Borussen, when he was appointed consul general in Bucharest in 1869.[61]

Old members who had found positions in the Wilhelmstrasse looked after the career interests of young fraternity brothers, a bond which was annually renewed at the reunion of the three exclusive corps in Berlin. Radowitz, who eventually became an ambassador, declared that association after graduation between corps brothers provided, especially in diplomacy, a "quicker and more secure basis for identity and cooperation than would otherwise have been possible. From the start, one recognized that it was a particular recommendation, and indeed almost a guarantee, when one's opposite number was from the same corps."[62] Lesser fraternities were also ardent in keeping up old uni-

---

[61] Holborn, *Aufzeichnungen; Radowitz*, I, 187.
[62] Ibid., pp. 22–27; Hohenlohe, *Meinem Leben*, p. 327.

81

versity connections. Former members of the Tübingen Normannia, for example, maintained their social connections in Berlin throughout long and ascending bureaucratic careers. Otto von Glasenapp, a member of the Foreign Office's examination committee and vice president of the Reichsbank, was a pledge brother and lifelong friend of Alfred von Kiderlen-Wächter, who became state secretary in 1910. Glasenapp was a fanatical fraternity man and, after some disquieting doubts, he satisfied himself that Kiderlen had preserved his loyalty to the Normannia.[63]

Corps members, as well as others who had opportunity to observe them at close quarters, acknowledged that the fraternities had drawbacks. With their emphasis on dueling, carousing, and the pleasures of the hunt, they subverted whatever intellectual interest a young noble might have brought to the university.[64] At the same time, the corps were widely believed to inculcate character and polish manners. This was an important service, for some members of the Prussian nobility admitted that not all of their brethren were notable for their refinement or breadth of outlook.[65] Accounts of fraternity life almost uniformly attest to the corps' success in imparting some measure of these qualities to the raw material provided by the aristocracy.[66] One of the most perceptive analyses of the fraternities came

[63] Notes by Glasenapp entitled "Meine persönliche Beziehungen zu Alfred von Kiderlen-Wächter," in a letter by Glasenapp to Baron Hellmuth Lucius von Stoedten, Aug. 25, 1925, StoedtenN.

[64] Holborn, *Aufzeichnungen; Radowitz*, I, 20; Dirksen, *Moskau, Tokio, London*, pp. 11–12; Stutterheim, *Two Germanys*, pp. 39–40.

[65] PzE to BvB, Oct. 1, 1900, EN, LVI, 261–62; same to same, Mar. 1, 1901, ibid., LVII, 24; Mutius, *Abgeschlossene Zeiten*, pp. 62–63; Fedor von Zobeltitz, *Chronik der Gesellschaft unter dem letzten Kaiserreich*, 2 vols. (Hamburg, 1922), II, 319–29.

[66] Mutius, *Abgeschlossene Zeiten*, pp. 62–63; Braun, *Von Ostpreussen bis Texas*, pp. 33–41; Kessler, *Gesichter und Zeiten*, pp. 200–201; Bülow, *Denkwürdigkeiten*, I, 28; Count Karl Luxburg, *Nachdenkliche Erinnerungen* (Aschach/Saale, 1953), p. 6; Dirksen, *Moskau, Tokio, London*, pp. 11–12.

from a man who was never a pledge but who spent many of his university days with corps members. Count Harry Kessler's complimentary account may be regarded as fair because he was ordinarily hostile to the Prussian nobility. Describing his experience at Bonn among the Borussen, he acknowledged that the corps had succeeded in bestowing some degree of elegance on nobles who had arrived at the university with a lamentably short supply of that gloss. "Many were related to great families in Austria, Russia or England," he continued. "All were financially independent. Through them a small measure of self-criticism and European cosmopolitanism found their way into the higher reaches of the Prussian and German bureaucracy. Their prominence in the bureaucracy was not due only to their 'connections'—although these without question contributed to it—but just as much to their deportment [*Umgangsformen*], which in a preponderantly bourgeois and plebeian bureaucracy served them as a weapon with which they could strike down their middle-class competition."[67]

Given Chancellor Bismarck's indifference to formal education and his insistence on polish and tact, it is not surprising that he was an enthusiastic advocate of the corps. In his youth an exuberant member of the Göttingen Hannovera, he later developed reservations about the exaggerated superficiality of some corps members. Yet in his old age Bismarck declared that "the decent, dependable character, for which we Germans gladly praise our ruling class, is basically to be found only among officers and *Korpsstudenten*."[68] The chancellor's closest associate in the 1870s, State Secretary von Bülow, viewed the fraternities with distaste and forbade his sons to join. But one of these sons, later an eminent diplomat and finally chancellor, praised the corps for giving manners to those who had need of them.[69] Bismarck's

[67] Kessler, *Gesichter und Zeiten*, p. 201.

[68] GW, XIV(2), 925–26; Arthur von Brauer, *Im Dienste Bismarcks: persönliche Erinnerungen* (Berlin, 1936), p. 285.

[69] Bülow, *Denkwürdigkeiten*, I, 28; IV, 120–21.

Borussen son, Herbert, attended corps reunions with regularity and was notably susceptible to hiring and advancing corps members in the Foreign Office. Writing as under state secretary in 1884 to Holstein concerning a young Count Dönhoff who desired to become a diplomat, Herbert commented that "the only thing I know about him is that he was the chapter head of my old Bonn fraternity, and that makes me rather in his favor. Even so he may be a shiftless fellow, but I think that I'd nevertheless take him."[70] Herbert's good friend Bernhard Bülow, who was doubtless aware of his predilection for the fraternities, was careful, in appealing to Herbert to admit a cousin into the diplomatic service, to note that the young man in question had been a loyal member of the Borussen. Holstein, although not himself a member, recommended that Chancellor Hohenlohe have two of his sons join the corps.[71] The prejudice in the Wilhelmstrasse in favor of the fraternities was endorsed without reservation by William II, who as an adult liked to sport his Borussen jacket and who considered the corps a good training ground for future statesmen.[72]

Of the 548 Foreign Office officials of the minimal rank of attaché in the field or assistant in Berlin, 115 (20.99 percent) were fraternity men. Counting each of these persons in the highest position he held, the distribution of these 115 diplomats was: state secretary 4, under state secretary 2, ambassador/minister 44; director/counselor 21, legation secretary 29; assistant 9; attaché 2; miscellaneous 4. The desirability of membership for a diplomatic career is indicated by the fact that corps members tended to be found in the higher reaches of the service. Of the 187 men who served

[70] Letter of Aug. 26, 1884, HolN 3853/H190735.

[71] BvB to HvB, June 9, 1886, BisN FC 2958/573; Hohenlohe diary, Oct. 24, 1883, HohN, CC.X.11.

[72] Raschdau, *Unter Bismarck*, p. 215; Raschdau, *In Weimar*, p. 48; William II, *Aus meinem Leben, 1859–1888* (Berlin and Leipzig, 1927), pp. 163–64; Rupprecht Leppla, ed., *Carl Justi/Otto Hartwig: Briefwechsel, 1858–1903* (Bonn, 1968), pp. 272–73; memo by Prince Max von Ratibor und Corvey, May 4, 1901, HA, Rep. 53a, no. 44.

as envoys, forty-nine (26.20 percent) were pledges; twenty-nine of the 128 directors and counselors (or 22.66 percent) had a corps affiliation, while five of the eleven state secretaries and half of the eight under state secretaries belonged. The incidence of fraternity men was again evidence that in diplomacy connections, though by no means essential, were very helpful.

Marriage was a consideration of utmost importance to every German diplomat. Those who were single were expected to maintain a discreet bachelorhood, and flagrant violations of such a circumspect existence were rare. Kiderlen's twenty-year liaison with Frau Hedwig Kypke, his "housekeeper" in all his assignments abroad and in the Wilhelmstrasse 75 during his ultimate position as state secretary, was the only really notorious breach in the rule. Since marriage was professionally impossible, Kiderlen was unable to legalize the connection, but he had no intention of renouncing either his mistress or his career.[73] Kiderlen's long and untroubled passion for this handsome and judicious woman had an adverse effect on his career since it resulted in his ostracization at some German and foreign courts and in much of Berlin society. Three out of every ten diplomats were bachelors, and it would be interesting to know if their failure to marry was professional rather than physiological or emotional. An inability to find a consort

---

[73] Glasenapp, "Persönliche Beziehungen zu Kiderlen," StoedtenN; on Kiderlen's problems see Ernst Jäckh, ed., *Kiderlen-Wächter der Staatsmann und Mensch: Briefwechsel und Nachlass*, 2 vols. (Berlin, 1924), I, 15–17; Count Bogdan von Hutten-Czapski, *Sechzig Jahre Politik und Gesellschaft*, 2 vols. (Berlin, 1936), II, 30; Friedrich Rosen, *Aus einem diplomatischen Wanderleben*, 4 vols. in 3 (Berlin, 1931–59), II, 10. An interesting case is that of Baron Edmund von Heyking, who was married to the daughter of Count Alfred von Flemming, the Prussian minister to Baden. The countess had fallen in love with Heyking, a newspaperman, and divorced her first husband, who thereupon killed himself. See Elisabeth von Heyking, *Tagebücher aus vier Weltteilen, 1886/1904*, 2d ed. (Leipzig, 1926), pp. 9–11; GW, VIII, 371–72.

suitable for so exacting a role, the relatively modest expense of maintaining a celibate establishment, and the hardships of many foreign posts may all have been factors militating for the single life. An unmarried man may in some cases have enjoyed a tactical advantage. Military figures in St. Petersburg were of the opinion that, since bachelors spent much of their time idling in elegant clubs, they were in an especially good position to ferret out sensitive information.[74]

Diplomats who were married, or who elected to take brides while in the service, had to have wives who measured up to the Wilhelmstrasse's expectations. Consequently, they did not go to the altar with undiluted romantic thoughts.[75] With the exception of Holstein, a dyspeptic celibate who was incapable of realizing the importance of women in diplomatic colonies, the Foreign Office viewed the nuptial arrangements of its staff with considerable concern.[76] No diplomat, high or low, in Berlin or in the field, could marry without the permission of the chancellor and the emperor. This approval was usually readily given, but sometimes it was withheld. The unfortunate diplomat cast into such straits had to abandon either his betrothed or his calling. Ottomar von Mohl, whose title was very recent and not Prussian and whose means were slender, was anxious not to do anything to jeopardize his already shaky future as a diplomat. He therefore jettisoned an American girl with whom he had fallen in love, fearing that to marry her might displease Bismarck.[77] On the other hand, Count Lud-

[74] Count Gustav von Lambsdorff, *Die Militärbevollmächtigte Kaiser Wilhelms II. am Zarenhofe, 1904–1914* (Berlin, 1937), pp. 17, 120, 128. For a diplomat's appreciation of the clubs' usefulness see BvB to HvB, July 8, 1884, BisN FC 2958/374–75.

[75] For an involved example, see Alfred von Bülow's letters to BvB of Feb. 3 and 17, 1884, BüN 14; also same to same, Feb. 27, 1884 (2 letters) and BvB to Adolf von Bülow of Feb. 24, 1884, ibid., 13.

[76] Brauer, *Im Dienste Bismarcks*, pp. 111–12.

[77] Mohl, *Fünfzig Jahre Reichsdienst: Lebenserinnerungen* (Leipzig, 1921), p. 30.

wig von Arco-Valley, legation secretary at Vienna, tendered his resignation in 1873 on the eve of his marriage to an actress at the Burgtheater whom the Foreign Office believed once to have been the mistress of a Hamburg businessman. A year and a half later, Arco divorced her and, after providing Herbert Bismarck with a copy of the legal settlement, was then readmitted to the service.[78]

In the opinion of the Foreign Office, the qualities which made for a good diplomat were also desirable in his wife. The women, like the men, were to have grace, tact, and polish; they should be German-born and propertied. Aristocratic lineage was desirable but not essential, provided, as one diplomat outlined the necessities, a wife had a "patrician or cosmopolitan background and natural good manners, in addition to a lot of money."[79] Of the qualifications for wives, the one which occasioned the most difficulty, because it was the one which the Wilhelmstrasse was the least prepared to relax, concerned marriage to foreigners. The temptation for a bachelor diplomat to marry a lady indigenous to the land in which he served was great, and many young attachés and secretaries acquired foreign wives in the course of their first assignment abroad. In more advanced years, some unmarried envoys found brides among the widows or daughters of their diplomatic colleagues. Many wives proved useful because they were decorative adornments in their husbands' legations or because they had family connections in foreign capitals. Others were active in extracting information from courtiers and social figures with whom they associated. Countess Alvensleben, the wife of the innocuous ambassador in St. Petersburg from 1901 to 1905, was an invaluable adjunct to her rather dreary husband. She entertained elegantly, but also with premeditation, turning conversation in her salon into

[78] GN, 20–21; also Arco to HvB, July 6, 1875, BisN FC 2952/665–66; Monts to BvB, Nov. 16, 1891, BüN 106; Count Friedrich von Vitzthum to BvB, Apr. 12, 1890, ibid., 127.

[79] Alfred von Bülow to BvB, Feb. 27, 1884 (1st letter), BüN 13.

channels on which intelligence was needed, in order, as she put it, "to collect some honey."[80] Others, such as Bernhard Bülow's wife Marie, were less interested in foreign politics than in their husbands' careers and maintained an active diplomatic correspondence designed to further such ambitions.

No official was more concerned about diplomatic wives than Bismarck. He judged the distaff side of a partnership as sternly as the other, and some diplomats owed their promotions not to their own talents but to those of their wives. Bismarck fretted greatly about the marriages of his diplomats, finding little professional advantage in many alliances, and he was prepared to dismiss even his most competent servants if they made unsuitable marriages or insisted on staying with impossible wives. He once declared that it would perhaps be better if envoys had to take the priestly vows of celibacy.[81] One of the chancellor's objections was that married envoys became too involved in family life and consequently neglected their professional obligations. He wrote of General Lothar von Schweinitz, the ambassador in Vienna who married at fifty and proceeded to sire ten children, that as a bachelor Schweinitz had been a clever man, "but now one can see in every sentence that he has a child sitting on his knee."[82] Bismarck's principal reservation concerned wives who, like Frau von Schweinitz, were not Germans. The chancellor's objection to foreign marriages was that the hybrid establishments inhabited by mixed couples did not truly represent Germany and that such wives

[80] Prince Hugo von Radolin to FvH, Dec. 19, 1903, HolN 3860/H195381; Lambsdorff, *Militärbevollmächtigte*, pp. 28–29. On Ambassador Alvensleben's limited social gifts see Raschdau, *Unter Bismarck*, p. 138.

[81] Holstein diary, Feb. 15, 1883, HolN 3860/H195702; Bülow, *Denkwürdigkeiten*, I, 497. For a promotion due to a wife's abilities see HvB to KvR, Dec. 21, 1887, BisN FC 3014/1017.

[82] George Campbell, 8th Duke of Argyll, *Passages from the Past*, 2 vols. (London, 1907), I, 254; also HvB to FvH, Mar. 3, 1884, HolN 3853/H190680.

tended to influence their husbands in ways counter to the interests of the Fatherland. In 1868, he extracted from William I a royal edict prohibiting such marriages without the consent of both chancellor and king and making any violation grounds for instantaneous dismissal. At the same time, Bismarck characteristically reserved the right to allow exceptions, and more than one diplomatic romance was saved by his intervention with the crown.[83]

The rule against foreign marriages continued to be applied after Bismarck's fall. The bachelor chancellor, General Leo von Caprivi, was especially rigid on this point. Max von Brandt, the longtime and very able minister to China, was dismissed in 1893 when he insisted on marrying the daughter of the American minister to Korea. A similar fate, administered for the same reason, had fallen upon Heinrich von Kusserow, the Prussian minister to Hamburg, two years earlier on his marriage to an American. There seems to have been no objection to either woman other than her citizenship. Altogether, Caprivi dismissed at least five or six diplomats for nuptial reasons.[84] Under Bülow, the prohibition against foreign wives was applied with more elasticity. In 1886, as minister to Rumania, he had married a woman who was not only a Catholic and an Italian, but one who had been divorced under scandalous circumstances from his colleague, the minister to Saxony. Marie Bülow's great charm, fortified by the pleas of her friends,

[83] Reichstag, Mar. 19, 1903, pp. 8729–30 (Bülow); GW, VIa, 432–33.

[84] Max Ratibor to KvR, Dec. 30, 1891, BisN FC 2975/322. There is some evidence that Caprivi was aggravated at Brandt for other reasons and that he merely used the marriage as an excuse for dismissal. Brandt himself was convinced that his marriage was the cause. See Brandt, *Dreiunddreissig Jahre in Ost-Asien: Erinnerungen eines deutschen Diplomaten*, 3 vols. (Leipzig, 1901), III, 330–31; Mohl, *Fünfzig Jahre*, p. 255; Otto Franke, *Erinnerungen aus zwei Weltteilen: Randglossen zur eigenen Lebensgeschichte* (Berlin, 1954), p. 71; FvH to Hohenlohe, Apr. 16, 1895, HohN, XXII.A.4; Hohenlohe diary, Aug. 18, 1895, ibid., XXII.A.5.

89

the Prussian crown princess and Philipp Eulenburg, won the day, and Bismarck and William I agreed to allow the match.[85] There were many other exceptions, and some foreign wives proved to be among Germany's foremost diplomatic assets. There continued also to be casualties. William II preferred that his representatives abroad marry Germans, and some diplomats who failed to heed the sovereign's pleasure found that their careers did not prosper. The kaiser's position was not entirely capricious, for there were complaints abroad that the distaff side of his diplomatic establishments was too seldom German.[86]

If non-Germans were especially to be avoided as wives, so were women of uncompromisingly bourgeois origins. A mediatized prince, who had entered into a morganatic marriage with the daughter of a veterinarian, could not be allowed to pursue a diplomatic career.[87] Women with new wealth but without any offsetting social virtues were equally undesirable. An example of such an unfortunate match was that contracted in 1888 by Heinrich von Tschirschky und Bögendorff while he was serving as second secretary in Vienna. Tschirschky's bride was the daughter of an Austrian baron who was whispered to be Jewish and whose title had been awarded for his industrial entrepreneurship. On his marriage, Tschirschky was immediately reassigned to Athens. Twenty years later he returned to Vienna, this time as ambassador, but his appointment occasioned strong protests by some Foreign Office officials, who believed that Frau von Tschirschky would make her husband's position

---

[85] BvB to FvH, Apr. 19, 1884, HolN 3854/H191184–89; Nowak and Thimme, *Erinnerungen; Monts*, p. 154; Bülow, *Denkwürdigkeiten*, IV, 590–92; HP, II, 188–89; III, 112; Raschdau, *Unter Bismarck*, pp. 309–10.

[86] For such a complaint, see Count von Hatzfeldt-Wildenburg to FvH, Sept. 21, 1908, HolN 3818/E340340–43.

[87] Otto von Bülow to HvB, Nov. 25, 1879, BisN FC 2958/1145–47, concerning Prince Eberhard zu Erbach-Erbach. Prince Erbach's cousin, Prince Otto zu Stolberg-Wernigerode, a former ambassador in Vienna, admitted the difficulties but suggested that perhaps Erbach could be posted to an Asian capital.

impossible. She was in fact treated with disdain by Habsburg society, but Tschirschky was tolerated because of his admirable frankness, and he remained in the post until his death in 1916.[88] Divorced women, or those with compromised pasts, were personae non gratae at Catholic courts and with William II's consort, Auguste Victoria of Schleswig-Holstein, an inflexible believer in the sanctity and finality of marriage.[89]

Sometimes a foreign wife's national identity made her loyalties suspect. Such was the case of Frau von Radowitz, the Russian wife of the ambassador in Constantinople, whose allegiance was further complicated by the fact that her father had been the Russian envoy in the Ottoman capital while her sister was married to his successor. Holstein, who despised Radowitz, used this connection to hint at treachery within the embassy residence.[90] Some wives, while passable for the general run of posts, were unacceptable at courts with rarefied society. Since Vienna was particularly stringent in its social canons many a diplomat there had to be reassigned, or could not be considered for this station, because of his wife. Anna Jay, who as the daughter of the minister of the United States of America had to be tolerated by the Viennese haut monde, was, however, unacceptable in such quarters when she became the bride of the German ambassador, General von Schweinitz.[91] There was even such a thing as contracting too regal a marriage. Schweinitz' removal from the Habsburg capital was facilitated by the nuptials, a few years after the Jay-Schweinitz diplomatic merger, of Prince Heinrich VII

[88] Nowak and Thimme, *Erinnerungen; Monts*, p. 245; HP, IV, 499; Bülow, *Denkwürdigkeiten*, I, 406.

[89] FvH to PzE, Mar. 26, 1890, EN, X, 339–40; PzE to FvH, July 21, 1895, HolN 3856/H192432; Heyking, *Tagebücher*, pp. 135, 156, 161, 386.

[90] Raschdau, *Unter Bismarck*, pp. 222–23, 308–9; Meisner, *Denkwürdigkeiten; Waldersee*, II, 53; PzE to W2, Mar. 26, 1890, EN, X, 337–38; also Prince Heinrich VII Reuss to FvH, Mar. 30, 1887, HolN 3860/H195444.

[91] GW, VIc, 64–65.

Reuss, ambassador to Russia and a nephew of Tsar Alexander II, to a princess of Saxe-Weimar-Eisenach. The bride was herself a niece of the Russian sovereign as well as of the German emperor. Too great a degree of consanguinity between an envoy and the ruler to whom he was accredited was regarded as an undesirable encumbrance. But as the offspring of a reigning house, Vienna would give to the new Princess Reuss the welcome it would not extend to Anna Jay von Schweinitz. So the Wilhelmstrasse eventually had Schweinitz and Reuss exchange posts, to everyone's satisfaction.[92]

Of the 187 men serving as envoys between 1871 and 1914, 130 were married while in the diplomatic corps. Fifty-four (28.88 percent) were single, while marital information on the remaining three is unavailable. There were altogether 137 wives, and of these, ninety-two (67.15 percent) were Germans, eighty (58.39 percent) were of aristocratic lineage, and all but one of them married to noble envoys. The European embassies were seldom inhabited by a German ambassador with a bourgeois wife. Like General Schweinitz, Count Paul Hatzfeldt in London had a middle-class consort, but she was an English woman of good background and in any case they lived apart during most of his tour there. Besides these two, there was only Tschirschky's mésalliance. Many of the aristocratic wives in these high posts were of non-German origin, but this was allowed by Berlin doubtless because of the cosmopolitan nature of society in these capitals. The Prussian ministers were very likely to have German wives. This was natural enough for German

[92] Reuss to OvB, Oct. 4 and 13, 1875, BisN FC 2974/715–19; Hohenlohe diary, Nov. 3, 1875, HohN, XX.C.2; Wilhelm von Schweinitz, ed., *Briefwechsel des Botschafters General v. Schweinitz* (Berlin, 1928), pp. 105–06; Nowak and Thimme, *Erinnerungen; Monts*, p. 114; Holborn, *Aufzeichnungen; Radowitz*, I, 366–67. As a rule the Hohenzollerns did not approve of diplomatic careers for royal princes out of concern that their kinships would compromise their professional obligations. W2 to HvB, Aug. 17, 1886, BisN FC 2986/505–6.

TABLE 9
CITIZENSHIP AND SOCIAL CLASS OF ENVOYS' WIVES

	German		Non-German		Noble		Non-Noble		Single		Total	
	#	%	#	%	#	%	#	%	#	%	#	%
European embassies	20	57.14	10	28.57	25	71.42	5	14.29	5	14.29	35	100.00
Prussian ministries	32	57.14	7	12.50	33	58.93	6	10.71	17	30.36	56	100.00
European ministries	37	50.68	18	24.66	39	53.42	16	21.92	18	24.66	73	100.00
Major non-European ministries*	24	40.68	11	18.64	13	22.03	22	37.29	24	40.68	59	100.00
Other non-European ministries	21	42.86	3	6.12	8	16.33	16	32.65	25	51.02	49	100.00

* Argentina, Brazil, China, Japan, Morocco, Mexico, Persia, United States.

diplomats at German courts, and these ladies were for the most part aristocratic, though not to the extent that the châtelaines of the European embassies were. The wives of envoys of ministerial rank in European posts were neither so aristocratic nor so German, and those at the remaining assignments even less so. The pattern is clear: the more elevated the post, the more desirable it was to have an aristocratic envoy who had a wife of equal birth.

○

Finally, there was the question of religion. The Wilhelmstrasse imposed no confessional quotas on its staff and it never formulated an endorsement of Protestantism. But it was, nevertheless, critical of Catholics and implacably hostile to Jews.

William I, who took more than a casual interest in personnel matters, seems to have been unenthusiastic about having Catholics in high places in the Foreign Office.[93] Bismarck apparently had no prejudices against Catholic diplomats provided that they were not ultramontanes, but his son Herbert, who never bothered to conceal his distastes, informed Holstein in 1883 that "we have enough Catholics in the service." The Jesuits, Herbert declared three years later, "have made the high nobility so strongly clerical and for two generations rendered them so stupid that nowadays among the grand seigneurs there is not an ambassador to be found."[94] Under the cosmopolitan Hohenlohe, a Roman

[93] Holborn, *Aufzeichnungen; Radowitz,* II, 117; also Raschdau, *Unter Bismarck,* p. 10, for the scarcity of Catholics in the Foreign Office in the 1880s.

[94] HvB to BvB, July 17, 1885, BüN 65. Bismarck and others in the Wilhelmstrasse were very suspicious of the reputed ultramontane Pole, Count Bogdan von Hutten-Czapski, who had ambitions to become a diplomat. BvB to Hohenlohe, Feb. 12 and 25, 1883, HohN, XX.B.3; BvB to FvH, Feb. 4, 1883, HolN 3854/H191106–7. On Herbert's anti-Catholicism see Rudolf Morsey, *Die oberste Reichsverwaltung unter Bismarck, 1867–1890* (Münster, 1957), p. 248 note 39.

Catholic married to a Russian Protestant, and under Bülow, a Protestant wed to an Italian Catholic, the objection to Catholics became milder and they were made to feel more welcome in the service. This religious indulgence on the part of the leaders of the Wilhelmstrasse was offset, at least in part, by the animosity of William II to certain Catholic institutions, especially the Society of Jesus, and to all ultramontanes. The sovereign's reservations paled beside the Calvinist bigotry of his empress and her court ladies, the fervently Protestant "Hallelujah aunts."[95]

Because of this religious prejudice the percentage of Roman Catholics in the Foreign Office was considerably less than their share of the German or the Prussian population.[96] Of the 548 men serving in major positions in Berlin and/or in the field from 1871 to 1914, the religious identity of 445 (81.20 percent) is known. Of these 445, 363 (81.57 percent) were Protestants, seventy-seven (17.30 percent) were Catholics, while the five Jews constituted 1.12 percent of the sample. Table 10 indicates that the religious heritage of German diplomats as a group varied very little under the

[95] On William II and Catholics see Count Robert Zedlitz-Trützschler, *Zwölf Jahre am deutschen Kaiserhof: Aufzeichnungen* (Berlin, 1924), pp. 85–86; Bülow, *Denkwürdigkeiten*, II, 11; but cf. Princess Marie Radziwill, *Lettres de la Princesse Radziwill au Général de Robilant, 1889–1914: une grande dame d'avant guerre*, 4 vols. (Bologna, 1933–34), III, 94–95; Hutten-Czapski, *Sechzig Jahre*, I, 256; Holborn, *Aufzeichnungen; Radowitz*, II, 322. On Auguste Victoria see Baron Napoléon Beyens, *Germany before the War* (London, 1916), p. 59; Radziwill, *Lettres*, III, 59, 97; Bülow, *Denkwürdigkeiten*, I, 262; III, 73; Princess Louise of Coburg, *Throne die ich stürzen sah* (Zurich, 1927), p. 185. On the court, see Princess Victoria of Prussia, *My Memoirs* (New York, 1927), p. 51; Princess Evelyn Blücher, *An English Wife in Berlin* . . . (New York, n.d. [ca. 1920]), p. 220; Bülow, *Denkwürdigkeiten*, I, 246.

[96] The census of 1871 reckons the Catholic population of the empire at 36.21%, that of Prussia at 33.49%, while the corresponding figures for 1910 are 36.69% and 36.30%. Germany, Statistisches Amt, *Statistisches Jahrbuch für das deutsche Reich* (1880), p. 13; (1915), p. 9.

empire. The table considers noble diplomats only, since the religious identity of sixty percent of their bourgeois colleagues is unknown.

TABLE 10
RELIGIOUS IDENTITY OF NOBLE DIPLOMATS

	1871–1880		1881–1890		1891–1900		1901–1914	
	#	%	#	%	#	%	#	%
Protestant	87	80.56	105	81.40	126	81.29	187	78.57
Roman Catholic	21	19.44	24	18.60	29	18.71	50	21.01
Jewish*	—	—	—	—	—	—	1	.42
Total	108	100.00	129	100.00	155	100.00	238	100.00
Unknown	4		3		4		6	
Grand total	112		132		159		244	

* Of paternal Jewish descent and unbaptized
NOTE: Each diplomat is entered in the period in which he served.

The small number of Roman Catholics in the German diplomatic service does not seem to have been due to their rejection by foreign governments. Only St. Petersburg was known to prefer Protestant envoys, and the only Catholic to serve there as ambassador was Prince Radolin (1895–1900), an appointment which for confessional reasons caused some surprise among Foreign Office officials.[97] The Court of St. James, Europe's bastion of Protestantism, raised no objection to the fact that from 1885 to 1914 Germany's envoys in London were Catholics except during Marschall's brief tenure in 1912. The prejudice against Catholics was clearly internal, and the Wilhelmstrasse showed a pronounced reluctance to accredit Catholics to certain courts. The Prussian ministers to the German states were usually Protestants, and Prussia always sent men of

[97] Baron Egon von der Brincken (minister to the Netherlands) to FvH, Apr. 7, 1894, HolN 3916/E339235–36; also Schweinitz to BvB, Apr. 7, 1900, BüN 46; BvB to HvB, Mar. 17, 1887, BisN FC 2958/762–66.

that persuasion to the papacy, lest a Catholic appointment appear in Germany as a concession to the Pontiff.[98] Only seven of the fifty-six (12.50 percent) envoys accredited by Prussia were Catholics, while the corresponding percentage for the imperial ministers was 16.52 percent. At the highest level of diplomacy, slightly more than a quarter (27.27 percent) of the ambassadors were Catholics, a reflection of the fact that four of the seven European nations (France, Italy, Austria, and Spain) to whom Germany sent such dignitaries were heavily Catholic. Besides, cosmopolitanism was a virtue in such assignments, and many Roman Catholic envoys—such as Radolin, Hohenlohe, Hatzfeldt, and Metternich—possessed this advantage in abundance.

Jews were considered unsuitable for diplomacy and very few, whether baptized or unregenerate, were admitted to the service. The Foreign Office was not unusual in this respect, for neither the Prussian nor the imperial government allowed Jews any significant measure of entrée into bureaucratic service. The only exception was the judiciary, which Prussian aristocrats scorned, and in which Jews did win some prominence.[99] The prejudice erected against Jews by German society made it almost impossible for them to acquire the prerequisite antecedents considered desirable, if not necessary, for a diplomatic career. Only a handful of Jews played any role in Berlin society, very few acquired

[98] Monts to FvH, Aug. 7, 1886, HolN 3859/H194461–62 on the papacy. For the reservation of Prussian posts to Prussians see p. 173 below.

[99] Jules Huret, *En Allemagne: Berlin* (Paris, 1909), p. 344; Hohenlohe, *Meinem Leben*, p. 328; Ernst Hamburger, *Juden im öffentlichen Leben Deutschlands, 1848–1918* (Tübingen, 1968); Jacob Toury, *Die politischen Orientierung des Juden in Deutschland von Jena bis Weimar* (Tübingen, 1966), esp. p. 239; Jacob Segall, "Der Anteil der Juden in Deutschland an dem Beamtenstand," *Zeitschrift für Demographie und Statistik der Juden* (Berlin, 1912), pp. 54–55. For the dilemma of a young Jew in the restricted choice of professions in imperial Germany see Franz Oppenheimer, *Erlebtes, Erstrebtes, Erreichtes: Lebenserinnerungen* (Düsseldorf, 1964), pp. 67–69.

reserve commissions in the army and none were admitted to the elegant student fraternities.[100] Jews unfortunately were without connections.

Bismarck, like many of his colleagues among the East Elbian nobility and like several fellow diplomats, placed some of his business affairs in the hands of Jews and he used them as sources of information. But otherwise the aristocracy regarded almost all Jews as being beyond the pale of society. Bismarck's association with Gerson Bleichröder, the eminent Berlin banker who acquired a *von* in 1872, did not extend beyond financial affairs and diplomatic intelligence. The pompous and self-important financier, whom Herbert Bismarck loathed as a tiresome meddler, delighted in his association with the chancellor. He considered himself to be virtually an official of the Foreign Office, referring to Bismarck in conversations with German diplomats as *"unser hochverehrte Chef."*[101] The chancellor considered that Jews

[100] Huret, *En Allemagne*, pp. 343, 345; Zedlitz-Trützschler, *Zwölf Jahre*, pp. 187–88; Lord Edward Gleichen, *A Guardsman's Memoirs* (London, 1932), pp. 276–77; Werner T. Angress, "Prussia's Army and the Jewish Reserve Officer Controversy before World War I," Leo Baeck Institute, *Year Book*, XVII (London, 1972), pp. 19–42. On the role of Jews in Berlin society see Lamar Cecil, "Jew and Junker in Imperial Berlin," ibid., XX (London, 1975), pp. 47–58.

[101] On Otto Bismarck's relations with Bleichröder, see OvB to Bleichröder, Dec. 20, 1872, and Mar. 13, 1873, BisN FC 2955/123–24, 196–98; Count Friedrich zu Eulenburg to HvB, Mar. 8, 1872, ibid., FC 2961/793; FvH diary for Nov. 27, 1882, HolN 3860/H195674–75, for Mar. 30, 1885, ibid., 3861/H195977–78; for Jan. 14, 1884, ibid., 3860/H195749; also Fritz Stern, "Gold and Iron: The Collaboration and Friendship of Gerson Bleichröder and Otto von Bismarck," *American Historical Review*, LXXV, no. 1 (Oct. 1969), 37–46. On Herbert Bismarck's relations with Bleichröder see his letter to Franz von Rottenburg, Aug. 8, 1882, RottenburgN, II/2; HvB to KvR, July 4, 1889, BisN FC 3014/1208–9; Robert von Keudell, *Fürst und Fürstin Bismarck: Erinnerungen aus den Jahren 1846 bis 1872* (Berlin, 1902), pp. 194–95; HvB to FvH, Feb. 22, and Mar. 3, 1884, Oct. 7, 1884, HolN 3853/H190673, 190678, 190743; Holstein diary for Jan. 14, 1884, ibid., 3860/H195749; for Jan. 13, 1886, ibid., 3861/H196152–53; also Wilhelm von Bismarck to FvH, n.d. (Sept. 1884), ibid., 3854/H190984.

lacked the necessary inborn refinement and manners so requisite for a diplomat. Of Maximilian Harden, the acerbic editor of the *Zukunft*, Bismarck declared that he was in fact "a quiet, unpretentious man of great tact, not at all like a Jew." Any qualities which the chancellor deplored he tended to identify as Jewish or to single out Jews as victims of his singular gift for invective.[102] At the same time, he was prepared to admit that with respect to mixed marriages between Christians and Jews (as Chancellor Bülow later recalled his phrase) "the pairing of a German stallion and a Semitic mare occasionlly did not produce bad results." Bismarck was referring to Baron Max von Thielmann, who rose to become ambassador in Washington in the 1890s, and to Count Berchem, under state secretary from 1886 to 1890, both of whom had Jewish mothers. Holstein made a similar observation about Berchem, but attributed another diplomat's selfish manipulation of others and his lack of polish to his Jewish ancestry.[103]

Other Foreign Office officials shared Bismarck's critical attitude toward Jews. Herbert Bismarck did not want to admit them to the service because they were "always pushy" (*stets aufdringlich*), especially as they advanced to higher positions, and would create dissension in the ranks of their colleagues. Like his father, however, Herbert was only too happy to avail himself of information and hospitality Jews might provide.[104] Eulenburg was even more hostile to Jews, fearing that they were becoming too powerful in Germany. "I am no friend of the Jews," he baldly confessed

[102] Moritz Busch, *Bismarck: Some Secret Pages of His History*, 3 vols. (London, 1898), III, 383. For examples of Bismarck's anti-Semitism see Nowak and Thimme, *Erinnerungen; Monts*, p. 40; Brauer, *Im Dienste Bismarcks*, pp. 187, 196; GW, IX, 87.

[103] Bülow, *Denkwürdigkeiten*, IV, 484–85; Holstein diary, Apr. 8, and Oct. 18, 1885, HolN 3861/H195988–89, 196115.

[104] HvB to BvB, Nov. 22, 1884, BüN 65; HvB to OvB, Feb. 24, 1877, BisN FC 3003/192–93; HvB to FvH, Aug. 9, 1882, HolN 3824/E343486; HvB to Rottenburg, Sept. 25, 1887, RottenburgN, II/2, and the letters to Holstein in note 101 above.

to his sovereign, and he considered them for social reasons to be unsuitable as diplomats.[105] Kiderlen's correspondence is full of tasteless jokes about Jews, and he delighted in being able to withhold favors from Bleichröder.[106] The prejudice against Jews in the Wilhelmstrasse was mirrored at court by William I and by his grandson. The old Kaiser, according to Holstein, was a strong anti-Semite. William II, whose attitude toward Jews was ambivalent, was tolerant only to those who were wealthy and conservative, while his empress was resolutely opposed to anyone who was not fiercely Protestant.[107] Even had the Wilhelmstrasse and the crown had no prejudice against Jews, anti-Semitism at many foreign courts would have made them impossible as envoys. Thielmann's tour as minister at Munich, a court notorious for its decorum, lasted less than a year. Thielmann's

[105] PzE to W2, Dec. 17, 1892, EN, XXII, 795. See also ibid., XVIII, 201a–d; XXII, 791–92; Eulenburg, *Mit dem Kaiser als Staatsmann und Freund auf Nordlandsreisen*, 2 vols. (Dresden, 1931), I, 162; Eulenburg, *50 Jahren*, p. 113, for other examples of Eulenburg's pronounced anti-Semitism. For social unsuitability of Jews as diplomats see PzE to FvH, Feb. 9, 1892, EN, XVII, 65–67, and PzE to W2, Mar. 7, 1894, ibid., XXVIII, 217.

[106] Kiderlen to Hedwig Kypke, May 24, 1892, KWN, MS 312, no. 11. For the prejudice of other diplomats against Jews see Münster to FvH, June 18, 1896, HolN 3859/H194759; Radolinski to FvH, Feb. 23, 1888, ibid., H195029; Holstein diary for Mar. 22, 1884, ibid., 3860/H195844–47; diary for Apr. 8, 1885, ibid., 3861/H195988–89; KvR to HvB, Aug. 28, 1882, BisN FC 3028; Eisendecher to HvB, Oct. 18, 1873, ibid., FC 2961/419–20.

[107] On William I, see Holstein diary for Feb. 7–8, 1884, HolN 3860/H195784–88. On William II's attitude toward Jews see Cecil, *Ballin*, pp. 100–101, as well as the following: Nicholas Murray Butler, *Across the Busy Years: Recollections and Reflections*, 2 vols. (New York, 1930–40), II, 302; Arthur N. Davis, *The Kaiser as I Know Him* (New York, 1918), pp. 161, 167; Maurice V. Brett, ed., *Letters and Journals of Reginald, Viscount Esher*, 4 vols. (London, 1934–38), II, 255. For an example of William II's prejudice against a partially Jewish official, Otto von Mühlberg, see a letter by the Austro-Hungarian ambassador in Berlin, Ladislaus von Szögyényi-Marich to Foreign Minister Count Agenor von Goluchowski, Jan. 23, 1906, HHStA, 162–V.

tactlessness was partially responsible for his abrupt recall, but another factor was Wittelsbach's disdain for his Jewish extraction.[108] Even the most illustrious Jewish families could not prevail against the barriers erected in the Foreign Office. Holstein was opposed to Jewish candidates, even if they happened to be Bleichröders. "I heard a few days ago," his diary for February 12, 1884, reported with accuracy, "that Bleichröder wants to get his youngest son into the diplomatic service. He will not succeed."[109] Baron Albert von Goldschmidt-Rothschild, whose title was more recent than Bleichröder's but whose background and whose refinement put him on an altogether more lofty plane, had all of the advantages of wealth and background. William II greatly admired his Jewish grandmother for her philanthropies and Edward VII singled out Rothschild for special attention. Nevertheless, it seems that Rothschild was made to feel an outsider during his service as attaché in the London embassy. The First World War interrupted his career, but there is nothing to indicate that he had a promising future as a diplomat.[110]

Rothschild was the only Jew the Foreign Office ever admitted to the service and assigned abroad. Other Jews of distinguished families attempted to win entry, but, like Bleichröder's son, found themselves frustrated. One unsuccessful candidate was a wealthy Baron von Oppenheim from Cologne.[111] In 1887, Herbert Bismarck had prevented

[108] Monts to BvB, June 20, 1895, BüN 106.

[109] HolN 3860/H195797–98.

[110] Zedlitz-Trützschler, *Zwölf Jahre*, pp. 187–88; Bülow, *Denkwürdigkeiten*, IV, 28–29; Wilhelm Widenmann, *Marine-Attaché an der kaiserlich-deutschen Botschaft in London, 1907–1912* (Göttingen, 1952), p. 38.

[111] On the Oppenheim case see HvB to Rottenburg, Sept. 25, 1887, RottenburgN, II/2; undated and unsigned memo, probably by Hohenlohe and probably ca. 1896, HohN, XXII.D.5; FvH to PzE, July 21, 1898, EN, LI, 168–70; Alexander Hohenlohe to Hohenlohe, May 13, 1897, HohN, XXII.A.11.

his entry into the diplomatic corps, arguing that Jews in general were tactless, that their admission would offend their gentile colleagues, and that Oppenheim's name was so prominently Jewish that he would be ridiculed. Oppenheim did not give up easily, and four years later, this time backed by Ambassador Hatzfeldt in London, he tried again, once more in vain. In 1896, Oppenheim finally wrested a consular position in Cairo. The Wilhelmstrasse was fearful that he would try to use this foothold to transfer into diplomacy, and in 1898 Oppenheim did make just such a request. No reasonable case could be made against his professional qualifications, for he was an experienced man with wide connections in Africa and the Near East. Socially the picture was perhaps clouded (though Hatzfeldt had noted pointedly that his mother was a Christian), but Oppenheim's Jewish extraction was atoned for by the fact that he spent grandiosely on race horses and was therefore a member in good standing of Berlin's aristocratic Union Club. His princely colleagues there backed his application to the Wilhelmstrasse, but to no avail. Oppenheim's candidacy was complicated by the fact that another Jewish member of the Union, an unnamed man of relatively modest wealth and a title from a minor German court but a horseman of note, was also seeking admission. Holstein, commenting on this other person, rendered the negative verdict on both Jewish candidates. "I am absolutely persuaded," he wrote to Eulenburg, "that what we have here is not a question of *one* Jew but of his numerous correligionists who will press through the breach which he makes. . . . If one is let in, a cry of lamentation [*Zetergeschrei*] will ensue if others are refused."[112] Neither aspirant was admitted.

The Foreign Office was also opposed to appointing Jews to positions in the Wilhelmstrasse. Only two unbaptized Jews can be identified, but they occupied posts of importance. Rudolf Lindau was the Political Division counselor in charge of press affairs from 1880 to 1892, and Wilhelm

[112] FvH to PzE, July 21, 1898, EN, LI, 168–70.

Cahn was for many years an influential assistant in the commercial section. Both men seem to have been quiet and unobtrusive, and their premature departures from the Foreign Office were apparently not due to anti-Semitism. There were also three bureaucrats of Jewish ancestry who had submitted to the rite of baptism. Paul Kayser and Bernhard Dernburg were both directors of the Colonial Division. Kayser was a very determined, and therefore unwelcome, personality. He eventually quit the service because of differences of opinion on policy but also because of the callous way in which he was treated by his colleagues.[113] Dernburg was a commanding financial figure when he entered the Foreign Office and he was not trifled with during his tour, which lasted only a year. The other baptized Jew, Max von Phillipsborn, who became minister to Denmark in the 1880s, got much the same treatment Kayser had experienced, as did those in the Wilhelmstrasse who were suspected of trying to hide their Jewish maternal descent.[114] In all the ranks of the Foreign Office, only one man, Otto Hammann, a Protestant counselor who succeeded Lindau in the press section, is reported as having tried to bring more Jews into the diplomatic service.[115] He found no response among his colleagues.

[113] Vierhaus, *Tagebuch; Spitzemberg*, p. 365; Helmuth Rogge, ed., *Holstein und Hohenlohe . . .* (Stuttgart, 1957), p. 328; Eulenburg, "Eine Erinnerungen an den 'kleinen Kayser,'" EN, IX, 225–32; Walther Frank, "Der Geheime Rat Paul Kayser: neues Material aus seinem Nachlass," *Historische Zeitschrift*, CLXVIII (1943), 302–35, 541–63. See also HvB to KvR, Oct. 21, 1886, BisN FC 3014/897.

[114] Münster to FvH, June 18, 1896, HolN 3859/H194759; Brauer, *Im Dienste Bismarcks*, p. 37; Rogge, *Holstein und Hohenlohe*, pp. 346–47; Bülow, *Denkwürdigkeiten*, IV, 485.

[115] FvH memo, Apr. 29, 1908, HolN 3852/H197027–28.

## CHAPTER IV

Diplomats and Soldiers

The Foreign Office, with its elaborate selection procedures and aristocratic code, not only passively awaited the application of men who aspired to diplomatic careers, but also actively sought to persuade persons with suitable endowments to join the service. Sons, nephews, and family friends constituted an always fertile source of supply, but the Wilhelmstrasse's primary hunting ground was the officer corps of the Prussian army.

No institution was more like the Foreign Office in its personnel or in its prescriptions for service than the Prussian army, and the connection between the Wilhelmstrasse 76 and the Königsplatz, the headquarters of the General Staff, was very close. Symptomatic of the liaison was the fact that the Iron Chancellor's assistants in the Foreign Office were popularly referred to as "Prince Bismarck's General Staff." Moritz Busch, Bismarck's foremost mouthpiece, pointed out that a diplomat was like a general in that his purpose was constantly to maintain the advantage and finally win over his opponent. The very language of diplomacy, with its talk of "diplomatic strategy, diplomatic tactics, and diplomatic campaigns," was that employed by soldiers at war. Busch, like his chief, meant such comparisons as compliments.[1]

The similarity between German diplomats and Prussian soldiers extended from the prerequisites insisted upon for

[1] Heinrich von Poschinger, *Stunden bei Bismarck* (Vienna, 1910), pp. 173–74; Busch, *Unser Reichskanzler: Studien zu einem Charakterbilde*, 2 vols. (Leipzig, 1884), I, 223–24, 252–53. See also Stresemann's remarks before the Reichstag on Mar. 29 and 31, 1909, pp. 7812, 7907–9, and those of Müller-Meiningen on Apr. 15, 1913, p. 4779.

entering either service to many of the intricate qualifications which determined who would succeed and who would be relegated to mediocre assignments without hope for advancement. It is therefore to be expected that both services competed for the same sort of young men and that in both a similar type rose to prominence.

Like the Foreign Office, the army put no great store in formal education. Candidates for military commissions also had to take qualifying examinations, to prepare for which many first repaired to cram schools. These interrogations do not appear to have been very rigorous, however, for the army, like the Wilhelmstrasse, in its measurement of candidates placed more emphasis on character and practical talent than on intellectual accomplishments. Army officers, like diplomats, were expected to have private means, for military service, like diplomacy, was costly, and salaries did not equal the professional demands placed on men in either occupation. As in the foreign service, certain assignments were especially expensive and therefore had to be reserved to men of affluence. Officers were required to furnish their own uniforms, pay their share of mess charges, and in some cases assume the expense of their quarters, take care of the wages of their body servants, and, in the cavalry, maintain a pair of horses.

Service in the cavalry, the most socially elite branch of the army, could be ruinous, for two steeds might cost as much as 7,000 marks. The chief of the General Staff, General Count Alfred von Waldersee, wrote in 1889 to the Prussian War Minister, Julius von Verdy de Vernois, that "the purchase of horses has frequently begun to ruin the modest wealth of our officers."[2] An officer's annual expenses might run as high as 16,000 marks per year, and the army

[2] Baron Otto von Dungern, *Unter Kaiser und Kanzlern: Erinnerungen* (Coburg, 1953), pp. 9–10; Heinrich O. Meisner, ed., *Aus dem Briefwechsel des Generalfeldmarschalls Alfred Grafen von Waldersee* (Berlin, 1928), p. 228.

assumed that he would be in a position to shoulder most of this burden. Estimates of the private income required of officers ranged between 3,600 and 16,000 marks annually, figures falling in the same reach as the private income requirement applied by the Foreign Office for diplomatic candidates.[3] Impecunious military gentlemen, like their insolvent brethren in the diplomatic corps, were expected to go into debt to maintain themselves in a manner proper to their station and profession. Before he became chancellor, General von Caprivi was reduced to selling his foreign decorations to a Berlin jeweler.[4] Military assignments, like those in the diplomatic service, were often made on the basis of wealth. The Züllichau Ulans, for example, were popularly referred to as the *arme Grafen Regiment*.[5] Fiscal requirements made military service prohibitively expensive for many nobles whose families had traditionally supplied the Prussian crown with its military muscle, and as a result, the army, like the Foreign Office, encountered increasing difficulty after 1871 in recruiting officers from the old nobility.[6] The General Staff was therefore confronted with the necessity of opening the officer corps to the sons of the Ger-

[3] General Gerold von Gleich, *Die alte Armee und ihre Verirrungen: eine kritische Studie* (Leipzig, 1919), p. 53; Dungern, *Kaiser und Kanzlern*, p. 12; Prince Heinrich von Schönburg-Waldenburg, *Erinnerungen aus kaiserlicher Zeit* (Leipzig, 1929), pp. 11, 47–48; Jules Huret, *En Allemagne: Berlin* (Paris, 1909), p. 276. See also Major Kurt Ernst von Bülow, *Preussischer Militarismus zur Zeit Wilhelms II.: aus meiner Dienstzeit im Heer* (Schweidnitz, 1930), p. 38, and F. von Schulte, "Adel im deutschen Offizier- und Beamtenstand: eine soziale Betrachtung," *Deutsche Revue*, XXI, no. 1 (1896), 189–90.

[4] General August Keim, *Erlebtes und Erstrebtes: Lebenserinnerungen* (Hanover, 1925), pp. 71–72; Gleich, *Alte Armee*, pp. 48–49.

[5] Fedor von Zobeltitz, *Ich hab so gern gelebt: Lebenserinnerungen* (Berlin, 1934), p. 49; General Hermann von Stein, *Erlebnisse und Betrachtungen aus der Zeit des Weltkrieges* (Leipzig, 1919), pp. 140–41.

[6] General Friedrich von Bernhardi, *Denkwürdigkeiten aus meinem Leben: nach gleichzeitigen Aufzeichnungen und im Lichte der Erinnerungen* (Berlin, 1927), p. 263.

man plutocracy, a development viewed with distaste but accepted as necessary. Just as there were *Diplomatenadel* so were there *Geldoffiziere*. A French journalist, visiting a regiment of ulans at Saarbrücken composed largely of sons of industrialists, declared that "for each of its lieutenants there are ten smokestacks ablaze."[7]

In selecting candidates for admission, the army was disposed, as was the Wilhelmstrasse, to give preference to nobles, for the warrior's art, like diplomacy, was to the nobility a *standesgemäss* profession. Accustomed to military duty because of generations of family service, the fearless, equestrian Prussian noble was the proper arm for the defense of the Fatherland. "Aristocrats," as one noble commanding officer put it, "pledge themselves first and foremost to an ironclad devotion to duty."[8] Although the exigencies of military preparedness had demanded the employment of middle-class officers, the army was free to discriminate against them. Bourgeois officers tended to be gazetted to inelegant regiments in out-of-the-way places, where they performed unpleasant or technical services considered unsuitable for Junkers. These physically remote units represented the army's equivalent of the consular service or of the South American ministries; expenses were low but so was prestige. Some regiments were exclusively noble, and the few bourgeois admitted were often at once given titles so that the aristocratic purity of the outfit could be maintained. Moreover, the loftier ranks of the Prussian army, like the choicest diplomatic posts in the gift of the Wilhelmstrasse, were reserved for the nobility. Of Prussia's

[7] Huret, *En Allemagne*, pp. 275, 280; Gleich, *Alte Armee*, pp. 48–49; Stein, *Erlebnisse und Betrachtungen*, pp. 140–41; Prince Alexander von Hohenlohe, *Aus meinem Leben* (Frankfurt/Main, 1925), pp. 327–28. See also the interesting observations by Fedor von Zobeltitz in his *Chronik der Gesellschaft unter dem letzten Kaiserreich*, 2 vols. (Hamburg, 1922), II, 319–29.

[8] General Baron Paul von Schoenaich, *Mein Damaskus: Erlebnisse und Bekenntnisse* (Berlin, 1926), p. 129.

numerous supply of field marshals, only Anton von Mackensen was of common birth. As with ambassadors and ministers, generals without aristocratic prefixes did not abound.[9]

The army placed constraints on the personal lives of its officers similar to those imposed in the diplomatic service. Approval was required for marriage; an officer was expected to entertain in an appropriate fashion, to acquit himself with distinction in society, and to cut a properly elegant figure in public, an increasingly expensive duty as tastes became more sumptuous.[10] Indeed, the social roles of diplomats and soldiers were virtually identical, and they regularly rubbed shoulders in aristocratic salons and royal palaces in the fulfillment of their duties. Hostesses, like royalty, cherished the glamorous uniforms of the hussars, Garde du Corps, and cuirassiers, who, like diplomats, were celebrated for their tact, grace, and terpsichorean accomplishments. One noble fixture of Berlin society, Marie von Bunsen, described very precisely the social attraction of the soigné officer. Herself the daughter of a diplomat, she recalled that in the society of the 1880s "the regiment was the important thing, not only for the individual immediately concerned, but also for the prestige of the family with whom the regiment was known to be on a friendly social footing. If people said of a family: 'The place is simply swarming with Second Dragoon Guards,' that meant a lot, but if it were 'with Garde du Corps' it fairly took one's breath away."[11] Count Georg von Werthern, minister to

[9] Lamar Cecil, "The Creation of Nobles in Prussia, 1871–1918," *American Historical Review*, LXXV, no. 3 (Feb. 1970), 794. See also Gleich, *Alte Armee*, pp. 54–55; General Karl von Einem, *Erinnerungen eines Soldaten: 1853–1933* (Leipzig, 1933), pp. 72–74; Schoenaich, *Damaskus*, pp. 71–72.

[10] General Baron Hugo von Freytag-Loringhoven, *Menschen und Dinge wie ich sie in meinem Leben sah* (Berlin, 1923), pp. 41–42; Schulte, "Adel," 190–91; Marquis Francisco de Reynoso, *50 Jahre Diplomat in der grossen Welt: Erinnerungen* (Dresden, 1935), p. 164.

[11] Bunsen, *Lost Courts of Europe: The World I Used to Know,*

Bavaria, wrote admiringly to Herbert von Bismarck in 1882 of the social triumphs of the military members of his staff. Young Baron von Gerstenberg, a lieutenant attached to the ministry, was a *beau de société*, while the military attaché, Major von Pannwitz, also prominent in the social life of the city, had won over the Bavarian military leaders by inviting them to small dinners.[12] Especially important in an officer's social life was his casino or military club. The mother of one young lieutenant expressed no regret at the hundred-mark bill her son ran up month after month in the Berlin casino, for, she noted, "it is greatly to Lothar's social advantage if he is regularly seen at the officers' table, where in addition to the military a whole file of diplomats, princes, and foreigners are present."[13]

The close social connection between diplomats and army officers only intensified the already narrow social perspectives of the diplomatic services. The army's prejudices—against religious minorities, liberal institutions, and the lower social orders—were its own. The army's position with regard to Jewish officers, for example, was as fixedly hostile as that of the Wilhelmstrasse to Jewish diplomats, and for the same reason. Jews would not mix easily with the social element of which the two services were traditionally com-

---

1860–1912 (New York, 1930), pp. 58–59. Bleichröder, for example, had only Garde officers to his parties. See Hans Fürstenberg, ed., *Carl Fürstenberg: die Lebensgeschichte eines deutschen Bankiers* (Wiesbaden, n.d. [1961]), p. 90. On the army's role in society see Schoenaich, *Damaskus*, pp. 48–49; Lillie de Hegermann-Lindencrone, *The Sunny Side of Diplomatic Life* (New York, 1914), p. 288; Herbert von Hindenburg, *Am Rande zweier Jahrhunderte: Momentbilder aus einem Diplomatenleben* (Berlin, 1938), pp. 61–62.

[12] Werthern to HvB, Mar. 24, 1882, BisN FC 2982/1029.

[13] Rudolf Vierhaus, ed., *Das Tagebuch der Baronin Spitzemberg . . .: Aufzeichnungen aus der Hofgesellschaft des Hohenzollernreiches*, 2d ed. (Göttingen, 1960), p. 282. On the casinos see especially Schönburg-Waldenburg, *Erinnerungen*, p. 59; Bernhard von Bülow, *Denkwürdigkeiten*, 4 vols. (Berlin, 1930–31), IV, 288–89.

posed.[14] A few Jews did succeed in making their way into the army, but as in diplomacy they were kept in the lower ranks and given inferior assignments. The prejudice was equally strong in the reserves.[15] Catholics were also underrepresented in the Prussian army, for as in diplomacy, the preference was for Protestants.

Given the social homogeneity of the officer and the diplomatic corps, it is natural that their professional as well as their social association was very close. Young aristocrats moved from the army to diplomacy (and then usually back to the army), while a few older officers were sometimes called into ambassadorial or ministerial positions. The significant diplomatic missions always had a weighty complement of officers assigned to their staffs. There was nothing accidental about this development. Among Foreign Office officials, Bismarck in particular stressed the desirability of recruiting military figures for the diplomatic service, since he believed that civilian candidates lacked distinction. In his opinion, the especial virtue of officers was their dependability, for they were industrious, financially prudent, balanced in judgment, skilled in negotiation, and in all things truthful.[16] Given the chancellor's suspicion of formal educa-

[14] Count Kuno von Westarp, *Konservative Politik im letzten Jahrzehnt des Kaiserreiches*, 2 vols. (Berlin, 1935), I, 298–99; Stein, *Erlebnisse*, pp. 165–67; Count Bogdan von Hutten-Czapski, *Sechzig Jahre Politik und Gesellschaft*, 2 vols. (Berlin, 1936), I, 63–64.

[15] Huret, *En Allemagne*, pp. 343, 370 and cf. p. 280; Werner T. Angress, "Prussia's Army and the Jewish Reserve Officer Controversy," Leo Baeck Institute *Year Book*, XVII (London, 1972), pp. 19–42.

[16] HvB to KvR, Apr. 18, and Aug. 23, 1881, BisN FC 3014/679–80, 701; Arthur von Brauer, "Die deutsche Diplomatie unter Bismarck," *Deutsche Revue*, XXI, no. 2 (Apr. 1906), 72–73; Brauer, *Im Dienste Bismarcks: persönliche Erinnerungen* (Berlin, 1936), p. 285; Baron Oskar von der Lancken Wakenitz, *Meine dreissig Dienstjahre, 1888–1918: Potsdam—Paris—Brüssel* (Berlin, 1931), pp. 27–28; Count Johann-Heinrich von Bernstorff, *Memoirs*, trans. Eric Sutton (New York, 1936), pp. 29–30.

tion, it is not surprising to encounter him arguing that for diplomacy the practical talents of an officer were more desirable than the resources of "ponderous specialists" (*bedächtige Fachleute*).[17] Prussian diplomats without some leaven of military training were too querulous for the chancellor's tastes. "As a minister," he wrote in his memoirs, "I always had the good will of a native son for genuine Prussian diplomats, but I was rarely able to act officially on such feelings, and in fact [could do so] only when the person in question transferred to the diplomatic service from a position in the military. In the case of a purely civil diplomat, who had never, or only insufficiently, been exposed to military discipline, I usually encountered a strong inclination to criticism, to *Besserwissen*, to opposition and to personal finickiness. All this was bolstered by the dissatisfaction which a Prussian from the old nobility, with his notions of equality, feels when a social peer moves beyond him or becomes his superior in relationships other than those of a military nature."[18] Bismarck therefore deliberately recruited new blood for the Foreign Office from the ranks of the Prussian army or preferred men who in their youth had served with the colors. Table 11 indicates that the chancellor's successors shared his inclination on this point.

All of the German chancellors after 1890 were Prussian officers with the exception of Prince Hohenlohe, who had never borne arms but who insisted on being given a uniform when he became *Statthalter* of Alsace-Lorraine in 1885. Hohenlohe's successor, Bernhard von Bülow, was proud of his own, as well as his family's, military accomplishments, and he wistfully observed after the collapse of the empire in 1918 that "all things considered, the army was the best of what we had."[19]

[17] Brauer, "Deutsche Diplomatie," pp. 72–73; Brauer, *Im Dienste Bismarcks*, p. 302; Reichstag, Mar. 14, 1877, p. 159 (Bismarck).

[18] GW, XV, 7; Brauer, "Deutsche Diplomatie," p. 72. See also GW, VIII, 385.

[19] Theodor Wolff, *Der Marsch durch zwei Jahrzehnte* (Amsterdam,

TABLE 11

MILITARY SERVICE OF FOREIGN OFFICE RECRUITS

	Noble		Bourgeois		Total	
	#	%	#	%	#	%
Recruited by Bismarck, 1871–1890						
With military service	54	58.06	4	50.00	57	57.00
Without military service	39	41.94	4	50.00	43	43.00
Total	93	100.00	8	100.00	100	100.00
Military service unknown	17		12		30	
Grand total	110		20		130	
Recruited, 1890–1914						
With military service	100	57.14	18	56.25	118	57.00
Without military service	75	42.86	14	43.75	89	43.00
Total	175	100.00	32	100.00	207	100.00
Military service unknown	8				77	
Grand total	183		32		284	

From 1871 to 1914, of the 6,615 German or Prussian diplomatic *positions*, military figures filled 1,325 (20.03 percent). The number of such positions and the percentage they represented in the diplomatic corps as a whole rose steadily in the period.

The seven European embassies always claimed the lion's share of military personnel, never dropping much below forty percent of the total. The German ministries to the European states were also substantially represented, while the Prussian ministries declined in importance as depots for the military. The concentration of military positions in Europe accounted for sixty percent of the total, and the balance of such positions was distributed between the other conti-

1936), p. 128; for Bülow's love of wearing his hussar's uniform as a diplomat see HvB to BvB, June 17, 1885, BüN 65. For Lichnowsky's appreciation of the virtues of military training for diplomats see his *Heading for the Abyss: Reminiscenses* (New York, 1928), pp. 85–86.

TABLE 12

MILITARY PERSONNEL IN FOREIGN OFFICE POSITIONS, 1871–1914

	1871– 1880	1881– 1890	1891– 1900	1901–1914*	Total
# Positions filled by army/navy officers	104	200	365	656 (469)	1325
# Positions filled by civilians	588	981	1336	2385 (1704)	5290
Total	692	1181	1701	3041 (2173)	6615
% Positions filled by army/navy officers	15.03	16.94	21.46	21.57	20.03
# Positions filled by navy officers	—	14	38	83	135
Navy officers as % of all officers in positions	—	7.00	10.41	12.65	10.19

* Figures in parentheses for 1901–1914 are prorations for a ten-year period.

nents and the central offices in the Wilhelmstrasse, in which after 1889 a significant number of positions were created. The total number of military *figures* holding diplomatic appointments between 1871 and 1914 was 487, of whom 441 (90.55 percent) were drawn from the army and of whom 362 (74.33 percent) bore titles of nobility.

*

Military personnel serving in diplomatic posts can be divided into five categories: (1) ambassadors or ministers, (2) military plenipotentiaries (*Militärbevollmächtigte*), (3) military and naval attachés, (4) officers *kommandirt* to legations or to the Foreign Office, and (5) officers serving as attachés in legations or in the Wilhelmstrasse. In addition, there were a handful of military figures who served under miscellaneous titles such as agricultural or legal expert, translator, and the like. The 487 military personnel constituted 47.05 percent of the 1,035 civil and military figures serving in Berlin or in the field between 1871 and 1914.

TABLE 13
MILITARY PERSONNEL IN FOREIGN OFFICE POSITIONS, 1871–1914

Position	Army Officers	Navy Officers	Noble Officers	Bourgeois Officers	Total
Envoy	8	—	8	—	8
Military Plenipotentiary	7	1	7	1	8
Military Attaché	94	5*	87	12	99
Naval Attaché	—	36	15	21	36
Kommandirt Personnel	302	4	221	85	306
Attaché	18	—	17	1	18
Miscellaneous Personnel	12	—	7	5	12
Total	441	46	362	125	487

* From 1883 to 1897 the military attaché in London was a naval officer.

NOTE: Each person is ranked in highest position achieved.

Of these military figures, the *kommandirt* officers and the attachés (as opposed to the military and naval attachés) were similar to the bulk of civilian recruits to the foreign service, for they also were young and had only probationary status. Like some of their civilian counterparts, some of these officers wanted only to see the world, but others hoped eventually to resign their commissions and become full-fledged diplomats.

Kommandirt officers were posted to legations or assigned to the Wilhelmstrasse, with a few occasionally being attached to consulates. Their selection and assignment were apparently made by the Foreign Office on the recommendation of the army or at the behest of diplomats or other patrons.[20] Between 1871 and 1914, the number of such posi-

[20] The evidence on this point is murky. See letters to HvB by Limburg-Stirum, Nov. 17, 1880, BisN FC 2370/389–90; Solms, Nov. 15, 1887, ibid., FC 2980/1091–93; and Prince Heinrich XI Pless, Sept. 22, 1885, ibid., FC 2973/20.

tions assigned to Italy (forty-nine) exceeded that of any other post, an attest not of Rome's marked importance but of its popularity as a social paradise. Next came France with forty, while Turkey received thirty-six, probably because of the Prussian army's participation in the professionalization of the Ottoman armed forces.[21] The reason for the substantial representation of *kommandirt* officers in certain foreign posts, in addition to introducing them to a diplomatic regimen, was to enable Berlin to follow military affairs in nations in which Germany had a strategic interest or, in the case of Washington and Tokyo, in which technical observation of modern means of warfare might best be conducted. Of the German states, the ministry in Munich claimed the overwhelming share of such officers, for next to Prussia, Bavaria contributed the most substantial element to the unified German army. Three officers were even commanded to the Vatican, an assignment which presumably was to provide the Pontiff with a decorative complement to the Swiss Guard. In addition to those officers sent abroad, another forty-eight were assigned to the Foreign Office to serve as liaisons between military and diplomatic officials and to prepare for later assignments abroad. One diplomat complained that there were so many lieutenants milling about in the corridors of the Wilhelmstrasse that it seemed as though a mobilization of the army had been ordered.[22]

The *kommandirt* officers, invariably lieutenants, captains, or majors, were still on active military duty and were thus regarded as only temporarily assigned for diplomatic work. The period of service was usually only one or two years, but

[21] Other nations to which officers were *kommandirt* were Bavaria (35), the United States (33), Japan (29), Belgium (26), the Netherlands (26), China (25), Austria-Hungary (25), Great Britain (23), Spain (22), Sweden (19), Switzerland (16), Persia (15), Rumania (12), Mexico (10), Denmark (9), Portugal (8), Saxon states (8), Brazil (6), Greece (6), Argentina (5), Norway (5), Chile (3), La Plata states (3), Papal states (3), Abyssinia (2).

[22] Brauer, "Deutsche Diplomatie," p. 73.

occasionally the term might be extended to as long as seven. These officers were officially subordinates of the heads of mission and took their orders from them rather than from military authorities in Berlin or from the military attachés at posts having such a figure. When it suited William II's purposes, however, he ordered that they follow the commands of the military attachés, who in turn were responsible to the kaiser.[23] Unlike military and naval attachés, the *kommandirt* officers were accredited members of the diplomatic colony. From 1871 to 1914, there were 556 such positions, 529 of them filled by army officers and twenty-seven by naval figures. Of these 556 positions, forty-seven (8.45 percent) were in the Wilhelmstrasse and the remainder in the field. The increase in the number of *kommandirt* positions is quite striking, especially in the 1880s and 1890s, and it was much greater than the proliferation of civil diplomatic personnel. Clearly, this military element was steadily becoming a much more pronounced part of German diplomatic stations.

Of the 306 army and navy officers filling these posts, 221 (72.22 percent) bore titles and at least sixty-one (19.93 percent) were members of families who held or had held prominent diplomatic positions. There were, for example, four Bülows, three Wedels and Arnims, as well as a sprinkling of Bernstorffs, Richthofens, Radowitzes, and Radolins. The parental or avuncular nepotism noted among diplomats is no less apparent in the case of such young officers, for not a few were sons or nephews of ambassadors or high officials in the Wilhelmstrasse.

There were two ways in which a young officer could find his way, however temporarily, into the diplomatic service. One was to bring himself to the attention of dignitaries in the Foreign Office; the other was by being nominated by

[23] W2 to PzE, Jan. 11, 1894, BüN 75. For an example of such subordination see Heinrich O. Meisner, *Militärattachés und Militärbevollmächtigte in Preussen und im deutschen Reich: ein Beitrag zur Geschichte der Militärdiplomatie* (Berlin, 1957), p. 18.

TABLE 14
KOMMANDIRT POSITIONS

	1871– 1880	1881– 1890	1891– 1900	1901–1914*	Total
Field positions (army officers)	20	70	149	262 (187)	501
Field positions (navy officers)	—	2	6	—	8
Foreign Office (army officers)	—	—	27	1 (1)	28
Foreign Office (navy officers)	—	—	—	19 (14)	19
Total Positions	20	72	182	282 (202)	556
Total Civilian Positions	588	981	1336	2385 (1704)	5290
Kommandirt Positions as % of civil positions	3.40	7.34	13.62	11.82	10.51

* Figures in parentheses for 1901–1914 are prorations for a ten-year period.

the army for such reassignment of duty. The Wilhelm-strasse was ready to make use of suitable candidates, and it is clear that many young officers were eager to acquire diplomatic experience in order to weigh the possibility, or desirability, of an eventual transfer to the foreign service. But other, and probably most, officers were looking for a chance to travel, to improve their gentlemanly polish, or to learn languages. Only thirty-seven of the 306 (12.09 percent) officers *kommandirt* to the Wilhelmstrasse eventually left the military to pursue diplomatic careers. Their motivation was as nonprofessional as that which led some young civilian aristocrats to enter the diplomatic service. Some officers, bored by military service in remote border backwaters or exasperated by the routine in Potsdam and Berlin, yearned to see the world. There was hardly a better way to visit exotic places, and to do so in the company of refined compatriots with the social distinction of official

117

status, than as a member of the diplomatic establishment. Prince Heinrich XI of Pless, however, wanted his eldest son, who had lived abroad for almost a decade, assigned to the Foreign Office so that he would spend some time in Germany.[24] Sometimes an officer would request being sent to a specific post for highly personal reasons which had nothing to do with diplomacy. In 1895, for example, Count Wilhelm von Hohenau, whose rheumatism had made the performance of his military duties impossible, was sent to the Prussian legation in Dresden in order to be near his doctor, whose practice was in the Saxon capital.[25] On the other side of the coin, the Wilhelmstrasse saw an advantage in posting to foreign capitals elegant, wealthy, and sociable young officers, resplendent in their elaborate uniforms. They were bound to impress society and win Germany friends in high places. Military dress, one diplomat noted, enhanced one's social position and thereby made work easier.[26] In the early 1890s, regimental commanders were instructed periodically to recommend lieutenants who might be suitable for assignment to diplomatic posts. Perhaps as a result of this encouragement, after about 1890 more *kommandirt* officers tended to transfer permanently to the diplomatic service. The candidates thus sent forward were often men of talent, but the order was also used to rid units of unpopular officers.[27]

Army officers assigned to diplomatic service were usually members of socially elite units. Of the 221 such officers bearing titles of nobility, about a quarter served in the four most exclusive and expensive guards units: the Garde du Corps, the 1. Garde-Kürassiere, the 1. Garde Regiment zu Fuss, and the 1. Garde Husaren. Prussian noble families

[24] Pless to HvB, Sept. 22 and 26, 1885, BisN FC 2973/20–22.

[25] Hohenlohe to W2, Sept. 19, 1895, HohN, XXII.A.5; see also Reichstag, Mar. 15, 1910, pp. 2160–61 (Dirksen).

[26] BvB to HvB, June 7, 1885, BisN FC 2958/450.

[27] TN, IX, 6; Count Karl von Pückler, *Aus meinem Diplomatenleben* (Schweidnitz, 1934), p. 7.

prided themselves on their representation generation after generation in these units. A third belonged to lesser guards regiments, and a quarter to miscellaneous Prussian regiments of scant distinction. About one in eight were officers in armies of various other German states. The eighty-five bourgeois *kommandirt* officers reveal an entirely different profile. Only about ten percent served in the crack units, seventy percent in lesser Prussian regiments, and the remainder in the other German armies. Considering both noble and bourgeois officers as a group, about twenty percent were in crack regiments, a quarter in other guards regiments, forty percent in lesser Prussian units, and the rest for the most part in other German armies. The pattern is again evident. When the Foreign Office selected young officers for temporary diplomatic service it preferred men of noble birth, ample means, good manners, and family connections, men distinguishable from civilian diplomats only because of their martial uniforms. The custom of attaching young officers to embassies and legations in this way only reinforced the aristocratic mentality, with all its prejudices as well as its gifts, which prevailed in the diplomatic service.

Similar to the *kommandirt* officers in their youthfulness and inexperience were the eighteen military figures, who, unlike the *Kommandirte*, had been formally, although provisionally, admitted to the diplomatic corps and who were described as attachés. Beginning in 1899, eight (44.44 percent) were assigned to the Wilhelmstrasse in order to acquaint them with the central organs of the ministry, while the rest were given foreign assignments. All were allowed to retain their active commissions until such time as their apprenticeship expired, whereupon the great majority (77.77 percent) became full-fledged diplomats. There is no indication that, once in the service, they were given preferential positions or more rapid advancement. All but one of the attachés were nobles, all of them from the army, and most had entered the diplomatic lists as *kommandirt* officers. Like the *kommandirt* officers, the attachés were accredited and fell under the jurisdiction of the heads of mission.

In addition to these young military recruits to the diplomatic service, more mature military officers were from time to time appointed envoys or given appointments as military plenipotentiaries, military attachés, or naval attachés.

Military officers rarely served as heads of mission, and in the period from 1871 to 1914 only eight of the 187 ambassadors and ministers accredited by Germany or Prussia were officers on active service. With the exception of Enzenberg and Wedel, these officer-envoys had held appointments in the diplomatic service for some years before being named to their initial ministerial or ambassadorial posts. They had, however, retained their active military status, and their promotion in the diplomatic corps was accompanied by advances in their military rank.

St. Petersburg and Vienna were the only posts in which there was a strong preference for military figures, especially

TABLE 15

MILITARY ENVOYS

Name	Highest Military Rank	Post	Date
Karl von Eisendecher	Vice-Admiral	Japan	1876–1883
		USA	1883–1884
		Baden	1884–1914
Count Gustav von Enzenberg	Major	Mexico	1873–1874
Prince Heinrich VII Reuss	General	Russia	1867–1876
		Austria	1878–1894
Heinrich von Roeder	General	Switzerland	1867–1883
Lothar von Schweinitz	General	Austria	1869–1876
		Russia	1876–1892
Count Carl von Wedel	General	Sweden	1893–1894
		Italy	1899–1902
		Austria	1902–1907
Bernhard von Werder	General	Russia	1892–1895
Prince Gustav zu Ysenburg und Büdingen	Lt. General	Oldenburg	1871–1883

those who were aides-de-camp of the emperor.[28] From 1867 to 1895, the heyday of Russo-German relations, a general served as ambassador in St. Petersburg, while generals occupied the Austro-Hungarian embassy almost continuously from 1869 to 1907. At the other ideological extreme, the French were suspicious of any concentration of military figures in the German embassy in the Rue de Lille, and no general ever served as ambassador in Paris. In 1892, when rumors began to circulate that General Carl von Wedel might be appointed German envoy in the French capital, Ambassador Jules Herbette sought out Holstein and warned him that Wedel's presence would seriously complicate Franco-German relations.[29] The French were even touchy about too many officers being assigned to the German embassy, and the Wilhelmstrasse was careful not to appoint veterans of the Franco-Prussian war to vacant consular posts in France.[30]

The practice of naming high-ranking officers as envoys was particularly congenial to William I, who appointed six of the eight to their initial posts. The first German kaiser was himself a soldier and it is not surprising that he was inclined to draw upon his trusted lieutenants to fill diplomatic slots. Bismarck's appreciation for military qualities in diplomats led him to approve or perhaps even to encourage the sovereign's predilection. In addition to General von Werder, the only general William II named to an envoyship was Count von Wedel, who managed to embrace a career which

[28] Wilhelm von Schweinitz, ed., *Denkwürdigkeiten des Botschafters General v. Schweinitz*, 2 vols. (Berlin, 1927), I, 256; Count Erhard von Wedel, ed., *Zwischen Kaiser und Kanzler: Aufzeichnungen des General-adjutanten Grafen Carl von Wedel aus den Jahren 1890–1894* . . . (Leipzig, 1943), p. 176; Bülow, *Denkwürdigkeiten*, I, 407–8.

[29] FvH to PzE, Apr. 16, 1892, EN, LXIV; BvB to PzE, July 20, 1898, ibid., LI, 158–60; Wedel, *Zwischen Kaiser und Kanzler*, p. 180.

[30] TN, X, 4; J. Lepsius et al., eds., *Die grosse Politik der europäischen Kabinette, 1871–1914*, 40 vols. (Berlin, 1922–27), VII, 296–98.

alternated military and bureaucratic service. However, on at least three occasions between 1890 and 1914, William wanted to name officers as envoys but either changed his mind or retreated before objections by the Foreign Office.[31] The position of military plenipotentiary was restricted to St. Petersburg except in 1871 and 1872, when such an official was posted to Munich, and in 1877 and 1878, when Saxony and Württemberg were both staffed with one. The intention behind the St. Petersburg appointment, one made by the emperor personally, was that it would promote closer relations between the German and Russian rulers, and it was successful in effecting this aim until Nicholas II came to the throne in 1894. Thereafter the post seems to have done little to ameliorate the dynastic connection of the two powers. The military plenipotentiary, usually a general, envoyed a unique position in that he was the personal emissary of the sovereign, attached not to the embassy but to the person of the tsar. The plenipotentiaries were without exception aides-de-camp of the German emperor, which gave them additional luster as well as the prerogative of writing directly to the sovereign. William II pointed out to the Wilhelmstrasse that "when your ruler offers you one of his aides, he is proposing to you the best that he has in the army."[32]

There was no bureaucratic connection between the plenipotentiary and the ambassador, who used different codes for dispatches. The plenipotentiary was not required to

[31] In 1890 William promised an embassy to General Adolf von Bülow, and in 1891 he favored General Carl von Wedel to replace Münster in Paris. See Wedel, *Zwischen Kaiser und Kanzler*, pp. 97–98, and John C.G. Röhl, *Germany without Bismarck: The Crisis of Government in the Second Reich* (Berkeley, 1967), p. 60; Lepsius et al., *Grosse Politik*, VII, 295–96. In 1913, he tried unsuccessfully to make his favorite, General Oskar von Chelius, ambassador in Rome. See General Count Gustav von Lambsdorff, *Die Militärbevollmächtigte Kaiser Wilhelms II. am Zarenhofe, 1904–1914* (Berlin, 1937), p. 209; Hutten-Czapski, *Sechzig Jahre*, II, 107.

[32] FvH to BvB, Nov. 23, 1896, BüN 90.

show his reports to the envoy, although he sometimes did so, and he, like the ambassador, might on occasion write to the chancellor.[33] Usually the dispatches were addressed directly to the kaiser, who often kept their contents to himself. Bismarck complained that William I regarded the plenipotentiaries as his *Spezialgesandter* and that they were therefore entrusted with more significant negotiations than were the German envoys in St. Petersburg. The plenipotentiaries' reports were stale when, and if, William granted Bismarck access to them.[34] The chancellor held that the plenipotentiary in Munich, and presumably the one at the Romanov court, was subordinate to the civilian staff of the legation, and he made an unsuccessful attempt to have the Russian plenipotentiary report to the Foreign Office as well as to the German emperor.[35] Bismarck's aggravation at the independent position of the St. Petersburg plenipotentiary continued almost at the end of his chancellorship, for both Alexander II and Alexander III, as well as William I, had the highest regard for General Bernhard von Werder, who held the post uninterruptedly from 1869 to 1887 and who from 1892 to 1895 served as ambassador to the tsar. In the 1840s, Werder had been a comrade of Ambassador von Schweinitz in the l. Garde Regiment zu Fuss, and the two men got on well, even though Werder often pursued an independent policy, to the irritation of both Schweinitz and Bismarck.[36] One of the casualties of the cooling of Russo-German relations following Berlin's failure in 1890 to renew the Reinsurance Treaty was the termination in 1891 of the German plenipotentiary post, which was not revived until

[33] Lambsdorff, *Militärbevollmächtigte*, pp. 31, 180; GW, XV, 389.

[34] Baron Robert Lucius von Ballhausen, *Bismarck-Erinnerungen* (Stuttgart, 1921), p. 381; GW, XV, 389.

[35] Bismarck in the Abgeordneten Haus, Jan. 15, 1872, printed in GW, XI, 224; Limburg-Stirum to KvR, Oct. 21, 1880, BisN FC 2370/312.

[36] GW, XV, 389; Gordon A. Craig, *The Politics of the Prussian Army, 1640–1945* (New York, 1956), pp. 264–65.

1906; no Russian plenipotentiary was sent to Berlin after 1892.

The tension between the Wilhelmstrasse and the military plenipotentiaries did not improve under William II. The plenipotentiary forwarded his reports to the kaiser, who sent them to the chief of the military cabinet with a list of the persons to whom they should be distributed.[37] The Foreign Office was not always included or sometimes was put at the tail of the list. In 1910, a dispatch by the plenipotentiary, Captain Paul von Hintze, was almost a month old before the Foreign Office could obtain it and send it on to Ambassador Pourtalès with a notation that the chancellor did not approve of what Hintze had related concerning his diplomatic activities.[38] As a result of this lack of communication, both the Foreign Office and its ambassadors in Russia were often undermined.

The position of the military attaché in the German diplomatic service is considerably more complex than that of the military plenipotentiary, for it had a longer history and its incumbents were both more numerous and farther flung. From the posting of the first Prussian military attaché to Louis Philippe's court in 1830, the number of attachés grew steadily, as did the number of posts to which they were assigned. The chief of the military cabinet designated both the officers and the states to which they would be accredited. From 1871 to 1914, 443 military attaché positions in German or Prussian legations were filled, all of which were located in Europe except for a handful assigned to Washington, Peking, or Tokyo.[39] The seven great European embassies were of course the most handsomely represented,

[37] Lambsdorff, *Militärbevollmächtigte*, p. 219.

[38] State Secretary Baron von Schoen to Pourtalès, May 16, 1910, PourtalèsN, 00645–46.

[39] Military attachés were assigned to the following nations (unless otherwise specified they served continuously from the date given until 1914). Bavaria (1871), Great Britain (1871), Württemberg (1871–72), France (1872), Austria (1873), Belgium (1873), Swit-

124

for most were powers with large standing armies on or near Germany's borders. France, presumably Germany's most formidable neighbor as well as the power athirst for revenge, was assigned two military attachés from 1873 to 1893, after which the second became a naval attaché. In Europe, attachés assigned to other than the great powers were sent to the strategically located neighboring states of Belgium and Switzerland. Rumania, a key military state because of its proximity to both Russia and the Habsburg domains, acquired a military attaché in 1895 and thereafter one was regularly assigned to Bucharest.

The duties of the military attachés were succinctly prescribed in an order of 1890, which declared that they should "make themselves familiar with all important developments in the army . . . of the power in question and steep themselves in its character and organization, observing personnel, matériel, regulations, education, and technical developments."[40] Military attachés were differentiated from military plenipotentiaries in a number of respects, and to the attachés one of the more irritating distinctions was that of rank. Plenipotentiaries, as noted, were not a part of the diplomatic complement in St. Petersburg but were attached instead to the person of the tsar. As such, they were regarded as part of the court entourage and therefore enjoyed precedence over all diplomats. Military attachés were assigned to diplomatic missions and were accordingly under the jurisdiction of the envoy and ultimately of the Foreign Office. They were, however, not formally accredited, and the Wilhelmstrasse ranked them below the accredited staff of the legation, with the exception of the

---

zerland (1875), Italy (1876–77, 1880), Spain (1878), Turkey (1878, 1897), Russia (1892), Rumania (1895), China (1901), Japan (1902), United States (1902), Sweden (1911), Serbia (1913).

[40] The document can be found in Dd 149, vol. 2, 280/00092–96, and is printed in Meisner, *Militärattachés und Militärbevollmächtigte*, pp. 73–75.

resident clergyman and physician. Consequently, on ceremonial occasions the military attachés straggled in behind a number of young *kommandirt* officers or attachés of inferior military rank, who took precedence because they were accredited members of the staff while the military attachés were not. Military and naval attachés were listed below the plenipotentiaries and *kommandirt* officers in the official publications of the Prussian and imperial governments. These slights, which could only be regarded as intentional, were factors in the hostility felt by the military attachés toward the Foreign Office and the German diplomatic corps at large.[41] In 1896, the attaché at Vienna tried unsuccessfully to have his position ranked second to that of the ambassador, an attempt which Holstein interpreted as part of a wider campaign by the military to acquire envoyships.[42]

A matter of considerably more importance than rank and precedence was the nature of the military attachés' dispatches. The army argued that political affairs should properly come within the scope of the reports, and the Wilhelmstrasse did not object to the inclusion of political material provided that the dispatches were shown to the envoy.[43] A related question was the determination of to whom the military attachés should report. This was a subject of very acrimonious debate between the Foreign Office and the military establishment and one in which the chancellor and the sovereign were continuously involved. Since the organization of the Foreign Ministry of the North German Confederation in 1869, military attachés had been subservient to the Prussian Minister President, who in 1871 became the *Chef* of the imperial Foreign Office. It was he

[41] Lambsdorff, *Militärbevollmächtigte*, p. 31.

[42] FvH to BvB, June 10, 1896, BüN 90.

[43] When an attaché's report was political in character the Foreign Office retained the document, although it allowed the War Ministry to see it. Memo by HvB, Mar. 8, 1889, Gen 1 AA.a.61, vol. 1, 280/00035–37.

to whom their reports were forwarded unless they con-- tained only information of a purely technical nature, in which case they went directly to the War Ministry. At- tachés were expected to present their dispatches to the head of mission, who was permitted to comment on them in his own separate report but who could not alter what the attachés had written nor block the forwarding of their dis- patches to Bismarck. The envoy, of course, might agree with what the attachés reported, but he might also point out what he considered to be errors or exaggerations.[44] To the Foreign Office, the envoy's prerogative mitigated against an independent diplomatic policy by the military, but to the army it represented an unwarranted interference in mili- tary affairs by nonprofessional men of questionable judg- ment.

There was, however, a loophole through which an attaché could be enabled to counteract the ambassador's rein. This was by being designated, as every military plenipotentiary had been, an aide-de-camp of the Prussian sovereign, for such officers enjoyed the right of royal access both in per- son and in writing. An example of the privileged nature of the position, as well as of the attitude that led to its being employed, is revealed in a letter written in English in 1904 by William II to Tsar Nicholas II.

I have selected major Count Lamsdorf [*sic*], my personal aide-de-camp, as milit. Attaché. He is instructed by me to consider himself as attached to your person solely, as it was in the days of Nicolai I and Alexander II. He is only responsible in his reports to me personally and is forbidden once and for all to communicate with anybody

[44] Heinrich O. Meisner, ed., *Denkwürdigkeiten des General-Feld- marschalls Alfred Grafen von Waldersee*, 3 vols. (Stuttgart, 1923– 25), I, 67–68; Meisner, *Militärattachés und Militärbevollmächtigte*, p. 53. The attaché in St. Petersburg had no official connection with the plenipotentiary, but since the latter was the higher ranking officer, the attaché often consulted him. See HvB to KvR, Feb. 27, 1884, BisN FC 3014/1122.

else either Gen. Staff, or Foreign Office, or Chancellor. So you may entrust him with any message, enquiry, letter etc. for me and make use of him in every respect as a direct link between us two. Should you like to send me one of your suite who enjoys your full confidence, I will receive him with pleasure, for I think it highly necessary during these grave events [the Russo-Japanese war], that you should be able to quickly communicate with me "le cas écheant," without the lumbering and indiscreet apparatus of Chancelleries, Embassies, etc.[45]

Fourteen of the ninety-nine men serving as military attachés between 1871 and 1914 were aides-de-camp. All were assigned to the European embassies and all but four were appointed by William II.

The Foreign Office and the heads of mission were determined that the military attachés be placed as firmly as possible under their jurisdiction. Unless all members of a mission worked for the same goal, Germany's diplomatic efforts would be characterized by internal contradictions and confusion, which would provide the opposite power with an undesirable advantage. Even generals who were diplomats admitted that, for this reason, military figures serving in legations should be made answerable to civilian personnel.[46] Consequently an important consideration in selecting an envoy was whether he could assert himself against an independent-minded military attaché.[47] Bismarck left it to the heads of mission to determine the degree to which they would keep their military attachés informed on political matters.[48] As long as Bismarck was in office, the

---

[45] Walter Goetz, ed., *Briefe Wilhelms II. an den Zaren, 1894–1914* (Berlin, n.c. [ca. 1920]), pp. 341–42.

[46] Hutten-Czapski, *Sechzig Jahre*, I, 176–78.

[47] FvH to Hohenlohe, Nov. 11, 1894, HohN, XXII.A.1.

[48] Count Friedrich von Vitzthum (second secretary, St. Petersburg) to BvB, n.d. (ca. Apr. 1887), BüN 127. For a quarrel between a military attaché and an envoy which was resolved by the attaché's reassignment see Holstein's undated (ca. 1885) memo in HolN 3859/H194912–14.

army did not contest the Wilhelmstrasse's control of political affairs in foreign posts. In 1875, the war minister, General Georg von Kameke, wrote explicitly to Captain Count von Keller, who was shortly to take up the post of military attaché in Vienna, instructing him that in political matters he was not to traffic privately with Austrian officials and that he was to lay all reports containing political information before the ambassador, General von Schweinitz. Keller did not heed these instructions, and two years later he was dismissed for indulging in questionable political activities without the knowledge or consent of the embassy. In the wake of this difficulty, Bismarck had State Secretary Bülow inform Kameke that in the future any orders the army might have for the military attachés were to be communicated to them only through the Foreign Office.[49]

The Wilhelmstrasse secured the dismissal of other military attachés for failing to realize that certain ostensibly military acts on their part were fraught with unfortunate political implications. Captain Morgen, the military attaché at Constantinople from 1897 to 1901, was an aide-de-camp in favor with William II, whom he inflamed with alarmist reports that Russia had predatory designs in the Near East. In 1901, Morgen, without consulting the ambassador, Baron Adolf Marschall von Bieberstein, agreed to the sultan's request that he conduct a maneuver with Turkish troops designed to repulse a would-be invader coming from the Black Sea. Eulenburg, to whom fell the task of defusing the monarch, denounced Morgen as an *"intriguanter Confusionsrat"* and persuaded him that the attaché's behavior had been very unwise. William thereupon transferred Morgen to a battalion command in the German forces then being sent to China to suppress the Boxer rebellion, in order that the former attaché might, in Chancellor Bülow's words,

[49] HvB to State Secretary Bülow, Sept. 12, 1877, BisN FC 2958/56; also his letter to same of Nov. 2, 1877, in Gen 1 AA.a.68, 280/00599–600; Bülow to War Minister Kameke and Chief of the General Staff Moltke, Nov. 15, 1877, ibid., 00602–5; Kameke to Keller, Nov. 12, 1895, 00610–11.

"give vent to his military enthusiasm in a more suitable place."[50]

Certainly there were some military attachés who were superior in talent to the ministers or ambassadors under whom they served. One example would be the disparity between Count Eberhard zu Solms-Sonnenwald, the German representative at the Quirinal from 1887 to 1893, a lackluster personality of no great diplomatic adroitness, and his military attaché, Colonel Karl von Engelbrecht. Engelbrecht was aggressive and ambitious and he did not get on well with Solms, but he was considerably more knowledgeable about Italy than was his chief and, unlike the envoy, he was fluent in Italian.[51] Other attachés, however, had Engelbrecht's drive without his ability and, like Morgen in Constantinople, they were notable only for their ability to make trouble. Their presence in a legation did much to make an ambassador's position very difficult.

A number of military dignitaries were steadfast in their determination to acquire a maximum influence for their attachés and to encourage them not to shrink from challenging their heads of mission, openly or behind their backs. The most conspicuous, and the least attractive, spokesman for this point of view was Count von Waldersee, the chief of the General Staff from 1888 to 1891. As with his every move, Waldersee's concern with the independence of the military attachés was related to the advancement of his own career. Fortified by the considerable but short-lived goodwill of William II, Waldersee had ambitions to succeed Bismarck. Should that have come to pass, it would of course have been very desirable to detach the military attachés from any connection with the heads of mission and make

[50] On Morgen's service in Constantinople see Marschall to the Foreign Office, July 6, 1901, and BvB to same, July 25, 1901, Dd 135, vol. 3, 345; PzE to BvB, July 10, 1899, EN, LIV, 158; Lepsius et al., *Grosse Politik*, XII, 573–74; also Monts to FvH, Dec. 14, 1899, HolN 3859/H194633–37, for Morgen's influence on the kaiser.

[51] Meisner, *Denkwürdigkeiten; Waldersee*, II, 30, 42, 355; also ibid., 37–41, 136.

them directly answerable to the chancellor. When Walder-see failed in 1890 to win the chancellorship, he reasoned that an alternate way of preventing the Foreign Office from controlling the military attachés would be to place them under the personal supervision of the kaiser, through whom Waldersee would in turn be able to exert influence. The general's argument proceeded from his conviction that the mental powers of the military attachés were superior to those of their diplomatic associates, who were, he declared, nothing but "professional liars." Besides, the attachés were *echt preussisch*, while more and more the diplomatic corps seemed to Waldersee to be composed of alien and inferior types. The general also believed that Bismarck had suc-ceeded in reducing German envoys to personal satellites, that consequently they reported only what the chancellor wanted to hear, and that the unfortunate result was that William II was prevented from receiving diverse opinions from his diplomats. If the attachés were given independence from the heads of mission, the crown would be bet-ter served. "This is another case," Waldersee concluded, "in which dividing and ruling would work."[52]

Bismarck's successor, General von Caprivi, was opposed to Waldersee's schemes, as was the newly appointed state secretary at the Foreign Office, Baron Marschall von Bie-berstein.[53] At the end of 1890 William II, anxious to avoid a chancellor-crisis so soon after Bismarck's resignation, con-sented to an order drawn up by Caprivi designed to regu-late the matter.[54] This edict, issued on December 11, 1890, began by declaring that the military attachés, insofar as

[52] FvH to Münster, Dec. 20, 1893, MünsterN 10; Hutten-Czapski, *Sechzig Jahre*, I, 176; FvH to Max von Brandt, Dec. 26, 1890, HolN 3847/E359684–86; Meisner, *Denkwürdigkeiten; Waldersee*, II, 170–71. Solms admitted to Holstein that Engelbrecht was well informed. See his letter to FvH of Jan. 2, 1888, HolN 3860/H195540–41.

[53] Meisner, *Denkwürdigkeiten; Waldersee*, II, 136, 139; FvH to Brandt, Dec. 26, 1890, HolN 3847/E359684–86.

[54] The document is in Gen 1 AA.a.61, vol. 1, 280/00092–96, and is printed in Meisner, *Militärattachés und Militärbevollmächtigte*, pp. 73–75.

their activities in their posts were concerned, were subordinate to the head of mission and were to do his bidding. Furthermore, the attachés were to eschew "independent political activity," and if they felt that some trespass into nonmilitary matters was necessary they were to consult the envoy. The order confirmed the traditional disposition of the dispatches. The military attaché was to give them to the head of mission, to whom was reserved the privilege of adding comments. The envoy would then forward the reports to the chancellor, who in turn would hand them over to the kaiser and to the Prussian war minister.

To Waldersee, Caprivi's order was a piece of treachery, for the chancellor was first an army officer and only secondly a bureaucrat. Had the order been strictly adhered to it might have been effective in preventing the army from maintaining an independent existence within embassy walls. As it was, William II at once began to impair its effectiveness. The military attachés who were aides-de-camp—at the time of the crisis those in Paris, Rome, St. Petersburg, and Vienna—were to continue to enjoy the right of corresponding directly with the sovereign. Less than a week after the publication of the order, William announced that he intended to remind these officers of their prerogative.[55] Some attachés paid scant attention to Caprivi's order, continuing to report on political as well as military matters. In May 1891, State Secretary Marschall called to the chancellor's attention the fact that the attachés in St. Petersburg and Paris were still addressing some of their reports to the chief of the General Staff.[56]

It seems very likely that the military's continuing involvement in political affairs in foreign posts was due to the emperor's encouragement. Not only did he order his aides in the field to correspond with him, but in the late 1890s he

[55] Meisner, *Denkwürdigkeiten; Waldersee*, II, 165–67. There is, however, no indication that the Kaiser in fact issued this reminder.
[56] Marschall to Caprivi, May 8, 1891, Gen 1 AA.a.61, vol. 2, 280/00109–10.

commissioned several of those who were attached to his retinue in Berlin to report to him on developments in specific European nations. One was the former attaché at the Quirinal, von Engelbrecht, who was to advise the kaiser on Italy. Although these officers had no formal connection with the Foreign Office, they were apparently given access to diplomatic correspondence for the execution of their assignment, one which occasioned considerable resentment in the Wilhelmstrasse.[57] At the turn of the century, William II took still another step to tighten the connection between the military attachés and the crown. In February 1900, Chancellor Hohenlohe, undoubtedly on the sovereign's demand, issued a directive revising Caprivi's regulation of December 11, 1890. According to the new order, military and naval attachés would in the future be subservient, not to the chancellor, but to the kaiser.[58] While the heads of mission could continue to comment on the dispatches of their service attachés, who were still to stick to military matters, the chancellor could no longer exercise any control as to who saw these reports nor could he even be certain that he himself would be allowed access to them. The procedure followed for the transmission of the attachés' reports after the 1900 order went into effect was now the same as that which governed information coming from the military plenipotentiary in St. Petersburg. The reports went first to the kaiser, who listed the persons to whom he wished copies sent, and the documents were then sent to the chief of the Military Cabinet, who made the distribution.[59]

After 1900, relations between the Foreign Office and the military attachés seem to have worsened. Protected now by

[57] FvH to Münster, Mar. 14, 1896, MünsterN 10; to Radolin, Mar. 22, 1896, HP, III, 601; Münster to FvH, Mar. 19, 1896, HolN 3859/H194750.

[58] Gen 1 AA.a.61, vol. 4, 280/00225–28, partially printed in Meisner, *Militärattachés und Militärbevollmächtigte*, pp. 73–75.

[59] Foreign Office memo, Mar. 15, 1901, Gen 1 AA.a.61, vol. 4, 280/00269; Lambsdorff, *Militärbevollmächtigte*, p. 219.

the *Immediatstellung* to William II, the attachés often did not bother to show their reports to the heads of mission before placing them in the dispatch pouches destined for Berlin. Bülow, who succeeded Hohenlohe in 1900, was not inclined to deal firmly with the problem and he did not protest the fact that the kaiser showed him only the more important of the attaché reports.[60] The chancellor's relationship to the military attachés was compromised by the fact that his brother Karl served in that capacity in Vienna from 1899 to 1906. Eulenburg, the ambassador to Austria-Hungary from 1894 to 1902, had considerable difficulty with Colonel von Bülow and complained that William II invested his attachés with such a nimbus that they behaved as though they were a law unto themselves, feeling superior to the envoys and conspiring tirelessly against them.[61] In 1911, State Secretary Kiderlen-Wächter sent a memorandum to all envoys warning that the military attachés were reporting more and more on political affairs and reminding the ministers and ambassadors of their right to read and comment on these dispatches before sending them on to the kaiser.[62]

Naval attachés were neither so numerous nor so widely dispersed as military attachés. The first was Karl von Eisendecher, posted to Washington from 1873 to 1876, but it was not until late in the following decade that Berlin, at William II's order, began to send a steady stream of naval attachés to the leading maritime powers.[63] The nations other than the United States receiving such officers, with the date of

[60] Foreign Office memo, Mar. 15, 1901, Gen 1 AA.a.61, vol. 4, 280/00269; Johannes Haller, *Aus dem Leben des Fürsten Philipp zu Eulenburg-Hertefeld* (Berlin, 1924), p. 247.

[61] Eulenburg's undated notes (ca. 1897), EN, XL, 126, and LVI, 241. In 1891, while minister in Bucharest, Bülow had made overtures to Berlin about obtaining a military attaché slot for another of his brothers. See BvB to Lindenau, June 15, 1891, BüN 99.

[62] Kiderlen to Pourtalès, Feb. 1, 1911, PourtalèsN, 00665–66.

[63] On William's role in the proliferation of naval attachés see Meisner, *Militärattachés und Militärbevollmächtigte*, pp. 11, 13, 21.

original appointment, were Russia (1886), Great Britain (1888), France (1894), Italy (1897), Japan (1898) and Austria-Hungary (1911).

Naval attachés were identical to military attachés in their low rank within the embassy or ministry staffs and in that their dispatches were also governed by Caprivi's order of 1890, as amended in 1900 by the kaiser. Like their counterparts in the army, naval attachés had their share of quarrels with the heads of mission. Otherwise there were few similarities. For one thing, only a single naval attaché was an aide-de-camp of the sovereign. This was Paul von Hintze, né Hintze, a particular favorite of William II, who served at St. Petersburg from 1903 to 1908. The rarity of this distinction is perhaps due to another difference between military and naval attachés. Of the ninety-nine men who served as military attachés, eighty-seven (87.88 percent) were of noble birth, while of a total of thirty-six naval attachés only fifteen (41.67 percent) were aristocratic.

The naval attachés had a very persistent and usually very effective ally in the head of the Imperial Naval Office, Admiral Alfred von Tirpitz, and his insistence on an independent role for the naval attachés was grounded in much the same judgment already indicated for the army. War and defense were professional arts which should be entrusted to experts, not civilians, Tirpitz' thinking on this issue had another dimension which one does not find is so widespread or dogmatic a form in military circles. This was his view—at first merely an opinion but later a paranoic obsession—that England was bent on Germany's destruction and that the kaiser's diplomatic representatives in London as well as his servants in the Wilhelmstrasse 76 were too dense, or too perverse, to realize or acknowledge this threat. Therefore, to Tirpitz the naval attachés' right to report their views, which invariably coincided with his own, had to be upheld, not out of personal ambition or even for the navy's interest, but for the very preservation of the Fatherland. Since the naval attachés, excepting von Hintze in remote St. Petersburg, were not aides-de-camp, they had no access to the kaiser save through the envoys. But in Tirpitz' view, the German representatives in London, especially Ambassador Count Paul Wolff Metternich, in office from 1901 to 1912, were hopelessly obtuse to the danger England represented. To circumvent this unfortunate state of affairs, in or about 1907 Tirpitz began to encourage the naval attaché in London, Captain Wilhelm Widenmann, to send private letters directly to him on any and all developments in England not covered in Widenmann's official reports. Though not specifically prevented by the orders of 1890 and 1900, such secret communications violated their spirit. Widenmann, an unquestioning disciple of Tirpitz, hastened to comply.[64] The language in these private letters was much more pungent and much more political in nature than that in Widenmann's official dispatches, which were forwarded to Berlin after being reviewed by the ambassador. One of the naval attaché's letters, for example, concluded "If only Metternich were out of here. He is a national misfortune for us."[65] Tirpitz saw that the kaiser read at least some, and perhaps all, of Widenmann's letters, and in this way he managed to provide William II with a view of the naval situation without its being contradicted by Metternich. Tirpitz also arranged for the naval attachés in London to see the kaiser on their frequent trips to Berlin.[66]

Shortly after 1900, a disagreement erupted in the London embassy which was so violent that it almost led to a duel between Widenmann and the first secretary, Richard von Kühlmann. Widenmann held Tirpitz' view that the increasing antipathy of England was due to trade rivalry, while

[64] Widenmann, *Marine-Attaché an der kaiserlich-deutschen Botschaft in London, 1907–1912* (Göttingen, 1952), esp. pp. 19–20, 23, 33, 36–40.

[65] Admiral Alfred von Tirpitz, *Politische Dokumente*, 2 vols. (Stuttgart, 1924–26), I, 322; see also ibid., p. 356, for similar language by Widenmann's successor.

[66] See ibid., I, 188–89, as an example of William II's being shown Widenmann's communications with Tirpitz; Widenmann, *Marine-Attaché*, p. 65.

Kühlmann argued equally vehemently that Germany's intransigeant navalism was in fact the cause of discord. Metternich, whose sympathies were entirely with his secretary, refused to allow political observations to appear in Widenmann's reports. The orders of 1890 and 1900 justified Metternich's disapproval of the political content of Widenmann's reports, but they also prohibited his interfering with their being forwarded. In Tirpitz' opinion, reports without political intelligence were useless and he therefore protested the ambassador's action. The quarrel was not limited to Kühlmann and Widenmann, for other military and civilian members of Metternich's staff were reluctant to share information with one another. Chancellor Theobald von Bethmann-Hollweg supported Metternich in the dispute, writing in unusually strong language to William II that "unity in the conduct of imperial foreign policy is very seriously put in jeopardy if the military agents attached to foreign missions encroach without authority upon the orders which Your Majesty entrusts to those responsible for [the execution of] such policy. . . ."[67] Early in 1913, Kühlmann declared groundless the argument in a report by the military attaché, Major Ostertag, that the British fleet was likely to "Copenhagen" the German navy. William II's notes in the margin of Kühlmann's dispatch reveal where he stood on this division between his diplomatic and military servants. He wrote that "The disparity in the diplomatic reports of civil and military personnel is historic. . . . The civilians are never able to perceive or admit the extent of the danger to which the military point. As soon as relations between two nations begin to have to be taken into reckoning by the military, the military point of view is always criticized and ridiculed out of pique by the civilians. Ostertag is entirely correct and we must act accordingly."[68]

The antagonism between Metternich and Tirpitz made

[67] Tirpitz, *Politische Dokumente*, I, 294.
[68] Ibid., p. 367 note 1. For another example of William II's siding with the naval attaché in London see Heinrich von Tschirschky und Bögendorff, minister in Hamburg, to BvB, Aug. 2, 1903, BüN 23.

the ambassador's continuation in London impossible. "Poor Metternich," William had written in 1909, "he can neither understand nor tolerate the navy."[69] In May 1912, he was replaced by Marschall von Bieberstein, the former state secretary who was then serving as envoy in Constantinople. Marschall, however, was felled by apoplexy shortly after taking office and his successor, Prince Karl Max von Lichnowsky, proved to be as determined a foe of Admiral Tirpitz as Metternich had been. As a result, the naval attachés and the ambassador and his staff continued to work at cross purposes. The naval attachés kept up their correspondence with Tirpitz, criticizing the attitude of the envoy on naval questions. Lichnowsky, in retaliation, wrote strong criticisms on the attachés' official reports and, like Metternich, refused to send to Berlin naval and military dispatches which he felt to be politically misleading.

❋

No matter at what level—from the novice *kommandirt* lieutenants to ambassadorial generals—military officers were introduced into the diplomatic service, the Foreign Office viewed them with distaste and envy. The only exceptions were the military plenipotentiaries in St. Petersburg, who got on tolerably well with the German ambassadors. From 1867 to 1895, the envoy himself was a general, which doubtless helped.

The Wilhelmstrasse was particularly opposed to the appointment of generals as envoys, a procedure which did much to lower morale by frustrating expectations nurtured by seniority. To many diplomats, generals removed from the battlefield or parade ground had few talents other than an ability to ingratiate themselves with royalty. They suspected, besides, that such appointments were inspired, not by the crown, but by the army in order to rid itself of un-

[69] Tirpitz, *Politische Dokumente*, I, 128.

desirable generals.[70] Bismarck, however, did not share his colleagues' hostility. As already noted, he was disposed to employ military figures in diplomatic offices, an inclination of which the army took full advantage. Herbert von Bismarck, minister at The Hague, deplored his father's inclination and noted in 1884 that the chancellor was under considerable pressure from General Emil von Albedyll, the chief of the Military Cabinet, to use the diplomatic corps as a "dumping ground" for senior generals. This was a disturbing admission, since Herbert as well as his friend Bernhard von Bülow believed that a number of generals, including Albedyll, thirsted for ambassadorships. "It is really remarkable," Bülow complained a few years later, "how many officers, courtiers, parliamentarians and grand seigneurs believe that the diplomatic profession . . . can be practised by any outsider. Why give Waldersee an embassy when no one would think of entrusting [State Secretary] Hatzfeldt with an army corps?"[71]

An object of particular vituperation from the Foreign Office was General Count Carl von Wedel, whose intermittent diplomatic career began in 1877 as military attaché in Vienna, where he served for ten years. Wedel was a follower of Bismarck, an intimate adviser and aide-de-camp of William II, and a man fussily concerned with his military and diplomatic status.[72] In 1892, the kaiser decided to name Wedel minister to Sweden, the first time a military figure had been appointed as envoy since Prince Reuss' nomination to Vienna in 1878. Bismarck, in exile at Friedrichsruh, acidly observed that one could not make an envoy out of a

---

[70] Brauer, *Im Dienste Bismarcks*, p. 46; Helmuth Rogge, ed., *Holstein und Hohenlohe* . . . (Stuttgart, 1957), p. 366; Meisner, *Denkwürdigkeiten; Waldersee*, II, 340; HvB to BvB, Aug. 27, 1884, BüN 65.

[71] HvB to FvH, Aug. 26, 1884, HolN 3853/H190733; BvB to HvB, Sept. 6, 1884, BisN FC 2958/389–90, and Mar. 17, 1887, ibid., 762–66.

[72] See Wedel, *Zwischen Kaiser und Kanzler*, pp. 186–99.

piece of wood.[73] Few diplomats begrudged Wedel icy Stockholm but many resented the preference given to a man outside the service and feared that Wedel's nomination would be the beginning of a series of military appointments.[74] Bülow wrote from his post in Rumania to a friend in the Wilhelmstrasse that "if the numerous generals and aides-de-camp . . . see that Wedel, without any distinguished diplomatic qualifications, with his stiff, military manner and his poor command of French, becomes an envoy, they will run all over the diplomatic checkerboard like a pack of hungry dogs." Furthermore, the Wilhelmstrasse would be damaged because these officers could avail themselves of their privilege as aides to write directly to the sovereign. The next step would be to appoint a general as state secretary, one who would then make diplomatic appointments from the ranks of his military colleagues. Civil diplomats would therefore have to stop sniping at one another lest William II replace the victims with military figures.[75]

Chancellor Caprivi, although himself a general, took the position after Wedel's appointment that no more high-ranking officers were to be appointed to envoyships.[76] He reckoned, however, without William II and Alexander III. When General von Schweinitz decided in 1892 to retire as ambassador in St. Petersburg, Caprivi asked that the post go to the senior minister, Count Johann Friedrich von Alvensleben, minister in Brussels. The kaiser, who disliked Alvensleben's bland personality, did not concur and instead yielded to the tsar's entreaty that General von Werder, the former military plenipotentiary in Russia, be given the post.[77] The nomination of Werder, whose single but impor-

[73] GW, IX, 256.

[74] Vierhaus, *Tagebuch; Spitzemberg*, p. 385.

[75] BvB to Lindenau, Oct. 6 and 13, 1892, BüN 99.

[76] PzE to BvB, Feb. 28, 1893, ibid., 75.

[77] Schweinitz to BvB, Apr. 7, 1900, ibid., 46; BvB to Lindenau, Oct. 17, 1892, ibid., 99; PzE to BvB, Feb. 28, 1893, ibid., 75; Alfred von Bülow to BvB, Nov. 6, 1892, ibid., 14. Alvensleben himself did not want to be transferred to Russia.

tant qualification was his intimacy with the tsar and various other Romanovs, created much resentment in the Wilhelm-strasse, especially among younger diplomats who were anxious to have the vacancy filled by a professional diplomat so that they in turn could move on up the ladder.[78] Under Chancellor Hohenlohe, the only general to be named an envoy was William II's protégé, General von Wedel, who in 1899 was posted to Italy. His candidacy was also backed by Hermann von Lucanus, the chief of the Civil Cabinet, who enjoyed great influence with the kaiser. Lucanus, according to Kiderlen, was favorably disposed to diplomat-generals and believed that Colonel von Engelbrecht, whom he declared to be more a diplomat than a soldier, was also qualified for such a position.[79]

After the turn of the century, Chancellor Bülow, although generally in favor of recruiting fledgling diplomats from the army, was vigorously opposed to making ambassadors or ministers out of generals. As a professional diplomat, he wished to see men promoted from the ranks of the Foreign Office and he feared that the accreditation of one general as envoy might lead to an avalanche of such appointments. Bülow's only nomination of a military figure occurred in 1902, but this was only a shift of Wedel from Rome to Vienna. This move was probably accomplished only at the insistence of William II, whose partiality for Wedel was made very obvious on this occasion. The kaiser awarded the general the Black Eagle, the highest of Prussian decorations, conspicuously failing to bestow this distinction on two much more senior, and able, career diplomats, Joseph Maria von Radowitz at Madrid and Marschall von Bieberstein in Constantinople.[80]

[78] See BvB's letters to Lindenau of Oct. 13, 1892, and Jan. 2, and Mar. 27, 1893, in ibid., 99, and PzE's letter to BvB of Feb. 28, 1893, ibid., 75. On Werder's relations with the Romanovs see Brauer, *Im Dienste Bismarcks*, p. 52.

[79] Kiderlen to FvH, July 3, 1897, BüN 92.

[80] Vierhaus, *Tagebuch; Spitzemberg*, p. 421.

141

The Foreign Office's objection to military attachés proceeded from several grounds. The most important, already discussed above, was that sometimes they pursued policies counter to those represented by diplomats. Another objection to the attachés was the suspicion on the part of some heads of mission that they were engaged in clandestine operations bordering on spying. Diplomats considered such behavior an intolerable breach of propriety and resented the way in which such activity compromised Germany's position as well as their own reputations.[81] They received little support on this point from William II. When Ambassador Münster complained that the military attaché in his embassy in Paris was engaged in espionage the kaiser retorted in the margin of Münster's report: "Donnerwetter! Wozu sind denn meine Militärattachés da!?"[82] Envoys were also concerned that the attachés serving in their legations were not only impairing their attempts to promote cordial relations with other powers but were also eager to have their positions. Ambassador Monts, no admirer of the military, declared that military attachés regarded their assignments as a "springboard" (*Sprungbrett*) for ministerial or ambassadorial posts, an opinion shared by his friend Philipp Eulenburg.[83]

A case of particular interest in 1893 and 1894 was that of Colonel von Engelbrecht, the military attaché at Rome, whose ambition was to supplant the aging ambassador, Count Solms-Sonnewald, who seemed ripe for retirement.

[81] Herbert von Nostitz, *Bismarcks unbotmässiger Botschafter, Fürst Münster von Derneburg (1820–1902)* (Göttingen, 1968), pp. 224–29; undated notes by PzE (ca. 1897), EN, XL, 126; Münster to FvH, Nov. 12, 1894, HolN 3859/H194720; Hutten-Czapski, *Sechzig Jahre*, I, 373–74. The injunction against "independent political activity" contained in both the 1890 and the 1900 orders is interpreted by Meisner (*Militärattachés und Militärbevollmächtigte*, p. 59) as referring to spying.

[82] Nostitz, *Münster*, pp. 224–29.

[83] Karl F. Nowak and Friedrich Thimme, eds., *Erinnerungen und Gedanken des Botschafters Anton Graf Monts* (Berlin, 1932), p. 46.

William II was responsive to Engelbrecht's plan but the Foreign Office was resolutely opposed. Holstein, Kiderlen, Eulenburg, and Bülow embarked on a campaign to prevent the post from going to any military figure but especially to Engelbrecht. The opposition had not decided on a specific civilian candidate for the post, but Bülow very much hoped that he would be selected. His mother-in-law, the celebrated Donna Laura Minghetti, aristocratic widow of a distinguished minister of King Humbert, attempted to persuade the Italian ruler that he should tell William II, who had been bombarding Humbert with names of potential military candidates, that he preferred a civilian diplomat as Solms' successor. The king, however, was unwilling to do so because Engelbrecht's own intimate relationship with the kaiser and Solms' very distant one indicated to him that an ambassador from the ranks of the Prussian army would have more entrée with William II. Besides, if he told William he wanted a civilian the military establishment in Berlin, of whose influence Engelbrecht was a good example, would turn against him and also against Italy.[84]

By May 1893, the matter had come to a standstill. Humbert refused to ask for a civilian ambassador and William II was not yet prepared to recall Solms and insist on Engelbrecht or some other officer as his replacement.[85] In the summer of 1893, Engelbrecht began to sense that if Solms left Rome at this juncture he might not receive the embassy because he was not yet a general, and, moreover, he had reports from Berlin that it was likely that Bülow would be designated ambassador if Solms retired in the immediate future. In Engelbrecht's opinion, Solms was "un asino" but a convenient one, since the military attaché, as Humbert realized, could be the leading German authority in Rome

[84] See BvB to Lindenau, Mar. 27, and May 7, 1893, BüN 99. General Count Wedel, named to Stockholm in 1893, also wanted Rome but his candidacy got nowhere. BvB to Lindenau, Mar. 27, 1893, ibid.

[85] BvB to Lindenau, May 7, 1893, ibid.

as long as the ambassador was weak. But if Bülow succeeded to the Quirinal this would no longer be the case, for he was strong-willed and ambitious. Engelbrecht therefore began to urge William II not to replace Solms, at least not for the moment. Finally, in December, 1893, yielding to the united front put up by the Wilhelmstrasse, the kaiser decided to appoint Bülow. But later he warned the Foreign Office that he would not tolerate any attacks on Engelbrecht. "I must have *Ruhe im Schiff*," the kaiser declared.[86]

Even before Bülow took over as ambassador, he declared that as far as Engelbrecht was concerned he was determined to "press him against the wall." The new envoy arrived in Rome in the spring of 1894 and almost at once reported to Holstein that "of all the difficulties with which I have to contend Engelbrecht is the most serious and disagreeable." Engelbrecht in turn complained to the kaiser that he was being persecuted by Bülow and the Wilhelmstrasse.[87] In 1895, William II was finally prevailed upon to remove Engelbrecht and appoint a less troublesome military attaché, and Bülow reported later that Engelbrecht's successor behaved himself in a "correct and loyal" fashion.[88] Even as late as 1897, however, the Foreign Office continued to speculate that William might at some point try to send Engelbrecht to Rome as ambassador.[89]

The young officers *kommandirt* to legations and those who served as probationary attachés posed less of a problem to more seasoned diplomats, for they were directly under the control of the heads of mission. They were of course much too young and inexperienced to be competitors for high positions. Nevertheless, these officers were

[86] W2 to PzE, Jan. 11, 1894, ibid., 75.

[87] BvB to Lindenau, Dec. 13, 1893, ibid., 99; BvB to FvH, June 7 and Dec. 9, 1894, Feb. 20, 1896, HolN 3854/H191292, H191301–2, H191377.

[88] BvB to FvH, Feb. 20, 1896, HolN 3854/H191377.

[89] Kiderlen to FvH, July 3, 1897, BüN 92; Monts to FvH, July 8, 1897, HolN 3859/H194565.

criticized by some Wilhelmstrasse personnel as well as by others outside the government, who felt that they consumed places in the diplomatic service which properly should go to civilians in possession of the requisite talent and training. Moreover, the Foreign Office paid these officers salaries which exceeded those given to civilian personnel in the same, or even higher, categories.[90] What compounded the injury was the fact that many of these subaltern officers entered diplomacy only to enjoy a temporary fling at seeing the world before returning to their chosen profession at arms. They were in fact dilettantes, not diplomats.[91] Bismarck had in his day disapproved of this cavalier attitude. "The custom of using officers as attachés," he wrote in 1855, "is doubtless very pleasing to a mission, but it is useful only if one employs such positions to determine whether there is a kernel of a future diplomat in the young man in question. Otherwise it is merely a *Bummel-Commando.*"[92]

Ambassador Solms in Rome, who would later have his difficulties with Colonel von Engelbrecht, was crossed by young Second Lieutenant Count Robert Zedlitz-Trützschler, who was assigned to his staff in 1887.[93] At the end of a year, Zedlitz declared to Solms that he wished to extend his service. The envoy at once informed State Secretary Bismarck that this was by no means to be allowed, for Zedlitz was merely playing and making himself generally disliked at the embassy. He strutted about, Solms declared, because he was a member of the l. Garde zu Fuss, which made him superior to all the other personnel in the legation, in particular the second secretary, Herr Milburg-Godeffroy. Godef-

[90] Meisner, *Militärattachés und Militärbevollmächtigte*, p. 49.

[91] Pückler, *Diplomatischen Leben*, p. 7; Reichstag, Mar. 16, 1910, pp. 2160–61 (Dirksen); pp. 2168–69 (Schoen).

[92] GW, XIV(1), 412.

[93] Solms to HvB, Nov. 15, 1887, BisN FC 2980/1091–93; Zedlitz-Trützschler, *Zwölf Jahre am deutschen Kaiserhof: Aufzeichnungen* (Berlin, 1924), p. 15. For two other unserviceable officers see W2 to HvB, Aug. 25, 1886, BisN FC 2986/509–11.

froy, the scion of a patrician Hamburg shipping dynasty, had money to spare but no title and no reserve commission. Zedlitz apparently baited Godeffroy to exasperation and the secretary challenged him to a duel. A timely intervention kept the two parties from meeting on the field of honor and Zedlitz was shortly removed from Rome. He eventually entered the court service of William II, his fellow officer in the Garde zu Fuss. For military gentlemen of noble birth, the Prussian crown could always provide shelter.

## CHAPTER V

Careers

The real beginning of every young diplomat's career came with the announcement of accreditation to his first post. His status was now official; his wages, however meager, provided for in the budget. Entry into the service had come by successfully meeting a series of qualifications which had exposed him to the subjective as well as the objective criteria of the Foreign Office. Although the abilities of young diplomats just posted would be measured by a less impressionistic standard than that applied during their training, the caprice, inclination, or prejudices of men in higher positions remained fundamental determinants in the Wilhelmstrasse's assessment as to who should be advanced, to what posts, and with what speed. Contacts, personal relationships and family continued, as with admission to the service, to be of utmost importance.

The decision as to where to post a fledgling diplomat lay with the Political Division, for only rarely did the state secretary or the chancellor become involved in low-level appointments. The Foreign Office tried to match the man with his first post. Candidates whose means were slender or those with unworldly wives were assigned to less expensive, quieter legations; those in frail health were sent to sunny climates. One well known example was Gottlieb von Jagow, who in 1913 very reluctantly gave up his ambassadorship in Italy to become state secretary. Jagow began his career in Rome and spent virtually the rest of his service in various positions in the embassy there because of his allegedly enfeebled constitution.[1] After the initial appointment, a can-

---

[1] Alfred von Bülow to BvB, Nov. 9, 1888, BüN 14; Count Anton Monts, "Unsere Diplomatie," *Politische Aufsätze* (Berlin, n.d.), p.

didate's merits usually played a greater role than his circumstances, and diplomats with modest means and poor health might even find themselves in St. Petersburg, the costliest and most mortal of all assignments.

For a novice diplomat, nothing was more vital than an ability to ingratiate himself with his initial chief of mission. The personality and character of this envoy were decisive in many ways. If he was generous, he might personally train a tyro in the arts of intelligence-gathering and report writing. Indeed, one important factor in many a young secretary's estimation of a post was the degree to which his future head of mission would be qualified to teach him something of diplomacy.[2] If the relationship prospered, the younger man might become a protégé of the senior official. As the envoy moved ahead in the service, it was not unusual for him to request the Foreign Office to send him a young secretary whose intelligence, behavior, or personality he had found pleasing in the course of an earlier assignment.[3] Many a young diplomat could draw on the helpful assistance of senior friends or kinsmen who might influence a head of mission to ask for, or a Wilhelmstrasse counselor to propose, that he be added to a legation's complement.[4]

On the other hand, the Foreign Office was swift to recall

84; Bernhard von Bülow, *Denkwürdigkeiten*, 4 vols. (Berlin, 1930–31), III, 33–34.

[2] Count Friedrich von Pourtalès to HvB, Oct. 17, 1885, BisN FC 2974/377–78; Florian von Thielau to HvB, Aug. 8, 1877, ibid., FC 2982/1020.

[3] Herbert von Hindenburg, *Am Rande zweier Jahrhunderte: Momentbilder aus einem Diplomatenleben* (Berlin, 1938), p. 221; Arthur von Brauer, *Im Dienste Bismarcks: persönliche Erinnerungen* (Berlin, 1936), p. 51; Helmuth Rogge, ed., *Holstein und Hohenlohe* . . . (Stuttgart, 1957), p. 231; Hohenlohe to OvB, Nov. 19, 1882, HohN, XX.B.3.

[4] FvH to Münster, June 8, 1895, MünsterN 10; Joseph Maria von Radowitz to BvB, Nov. 11, and Dec. 31, 1882, BüN 114; BvB to Karl von Lindenau, July 7, 1888, ibid., 99.

an underling who had displeased his chief, who in turn was often ready to nominate a more suitable successor. One reason for recall was improper behavior. In 1877, Count Andreas Bernstorff, secretary of legation at Washington and son of a former ambassador, made an impolitic speech without first clearing the contents with Minister Kurd von Schlözer. Both Schlözer and Bismarck were enraged, and Bernstorff was recalled and then dismissed from the diplomatic service.[5] A more frequent problem lay in the inability of some members of a legation to get along comfortably with their brethren. Amicability was especially necessary in posts located in primitive countries, for in such circumstances the personnel both lived and worked within embassy walls. Some legations were composed almost exclusively of bachelors, all of whom took up residence in the embassy or ministry. Prince Heinrich VII Reuss presided over such an establishment in St. Petersburg in the 1870s and he declared that his staff lived "like brothers in a cloister." A reason for this solidarity which eluded Reuss was the common aggravation of his underlings at the ambassador's regal pretensions.[6] When trouble broke out, the offender had to be packed off, no matter how remarkable his talents might be. In 1900, Ambassador Münster in Paris, for example, wrote to State Secretary Bülow that he could no longer put up with his second secretary and cousin, Count Unico von der Groeben. According to Münster's indictment, Groeben had irritated the military contingent of the embassy and also deliberately created friction between the first and third secretaries and their wives. Groeben was

[5] OvB to Schlözer, Mar. 24, 1877, SchlözerN, 00731–33. See also Hohenlohe to OvB, Nov. 19, 1882, HohN, XX.B.3.

[6] Holstein diary, Feb. 15, 1884, HolN 3860/H195801; Brauer, *Im Dienste Bismarcks*, pp. 46–47; Karl F. Nowak and Friedrich Thimme, eds., *Erinnerungen und Gedanken des Botschafters Anton Graf Monts* (Berlin, 1932), p. 117. Even those who had not served under Reuss disliked his airs. See HvB to Wilhelm von Bismarck, June 18, 1885, BisN FC 3010/436.

promptly reassigned to Madrid, later moving on to St. Petersburg, where he quickly alienated the ambassador's wife.[7] Frequently the difficulties were between the envoy himself and a member of his staff. In 1876, Count Münster, always a notoriously critical superior, tried to have a secretary in his London embassy removed because he fraternized excessively with the Prince of Wales, of whose wayward character the ambassador thoroughly disapproved. Münster also disliked Kiderlen, who served briefly under him in Paris, because he was crude, secretive, and not very deft in his relationship with the prickly ambassador.[8] Some envoys were jealous of their junior associates. Heinrich von Tschirschky und Bögendorff, ambassador in Vienna, whose bourgeois wife was unacceptable to Viennese society, complained in 1910 of the "burning ambition" of Count Ulrich von Brockdorff-Rantzau, the elegant general consul in Budapest. The envoy was miffed because Brockdorff had gone to a "rout" given by a prominent Habsburg dignitary who had pointedly left the embassy staff uninvited. Secretaries, on the other hand, were frequently irritated by the long absences of their heads of mission.[9]

As junior diplomats advanced in their careers, they had to be careful to avoid certain pitfalls. One was to escape being classified by the Foreign Office as a specialist in Asian or African matters, for once a diplomat was so typed, European posts might be forever beyond his reach. Even too

[7] Münster to BvB, Sept. 2, 1900, BüN 46; Radolin to FvH, Dec. 19, 1903, HolN 3860/H195381. For another staff quarrel under Münster, see BisN FC 2954/204–5, 211–12.

[8] GN, 1150, concerning Count Wilhelm von Redern; Pourtalès to HvB, Apr. 18, 1886, BisN FC 2974/389–90.

[9] GN, 203. A similar social jealousy apparently existed between the wives of the ambassador and the first secretary in St. Petersburg in the 1880s. See BvB to HvB, Apr. 14, 1886, BisN FC 2958/642–43. Also Baron Egon von der Brincken to HvB, May 1, 1886, ibid., FC 2957/248–50; BvB to HvB, Dec. 9, 1884 and Sept. 23, 1885, ibid., FC 2958/406, 479.

long a sojourn in an obscure European capital could be dangerous, for the important thing, as Herbert Bismarck noted, was always to keep oneself *en vue* and in the mainstream of European politics. In 1887, Bismarck advised his friend Bernhard von Bülow that it would be a mistake to exchange his position as second secretary in St. Petersburg for a minor envoyship such as Darmstadt or Sofia.[10] Although Bülow was ambitious to become a head of mission and was thoroughly weary of Ambassador Schweinitz, Russian weather, and the financial drain of St. Petersburg society, he stayed on in the Russian capital until two years later the important ministership in Bucharest became available. The same reasoning led some diplomats destined for overseas assignments to accept transfers to the consular service if such a change would result in receiving a post on the continent.

At the same time, circumstances could arise which made it inadvisable to decline a post which was essentially undesirable. Bismarck and his successors were usually careful to consult all diplomats before making their assignments, but turning down a prospective appointment might irritate the state secretary or the chancellor.[11] Considerations of seniority, which was based on a time-in-rank formula, were also a complicating factor. A first secretary, for example, could not continue to decline appointments as minister, even if the post in question were mediocre, lest the position, and consequently seniority, go to another first secretary. The Foreign Office's rule of thumb seems to have been that a diplomat might decline an initial offer, but with a second refusal he lost his claim to seniority.[12] The Wilhelmstrasse

[10] HvB to BvB, Apr. 13, 1887, BüN 66; HvB to OvB, Apr. 14, 1887, BisN FC 3004/400; TN, X, 3–4; Redern to HvB, Oct. 17, 1881, BisN FC 2975/418–19. On the desirability of a general consulship see HvB to KvR, Mar. 8, 1883, ibid., FC 3014/1082.

[11] For Bismarck's habit of consulting his diplomats and for an example, see Brincken to HvB, Mar. 8, 1880, BisN FC 2957/258–59.

[12] Hohenlohe to Münster, Nov. 29, 1895, MünsterN 9; HvB to FvH, Oct. 8, 1881, HolN 3853/H190407–9.

devised a way to get around this in that it occasionally transferred a first secretary to Berlin as a counselor and simultaneously conferred on him the dignity as minister. This kept the person warm for a desirable ministerial post as soon as one developed.[13] Some counselors in the personnel section adhered strictly to considerations of seniority in recommending appointments. Others, especially Herbert Bismarck and Kiderlen, took a more elastic view and preferred to measure candidates by some standard other than their longevity.[14]

A diplomat who had been in the service for a number of years became eligible for review for appointment as minister. Prince Lichnowsky, who controlled personnel matters for several years at the turn of the century, confessed that "at forty or so, a German diplomat who does not happen to have a black mark against his name and who possesses the necessary pliability will as a rule have attained the rank of minister, often without any extraordinary exertions on his part, most of his feats having been achieved at the festive board or in the ballrooms and drawing-rooms of society."[15] Promotion to one of the seven ambassadorships, however, entailed a more demanding scrutiny. Bismarck's opinion, expressed in 1873 to Count Wilhelm von Perponcher-Sedlnitzky, minister to Belgium who sought in vain an embassy, was that for most diplomats a ministry was the extent of

[13] For example see FvH to Hohenlohe, n.d. (ca. Apr. 16, 1885), HohN, XXII.A.5; Ludwig Raschdau, *In Weimar als preussischer Gesandter: ein Buch der Erinnerungen an deutsche Fürstenhöfe, 1894–1897* (Berlin, 1939), p. 29; Rudolf Vierhaus, ed., *Das Tagebuch der Baronin Spitzemberg . . . : Aufzeichnungen aus der Hofgesellschaft des Hohenzollernreiches,* 2d ed. (Göttingen, 1960), p. 437.

[14] HvB to OvB, Apr. 14, 1887, and Oct. 5, 1888, BisN FC 3004/400, 473; HvB to KvR, Oct. 28, 1879, ibid., FC 3014/586–87; Alfred von Bülow to BvB, Aug. 13, 1892, BüN 14; PzE to BvB, Mar. 9, 1894, ibid., 75; Monts, "Unsere Diplomatie," pp. 78–79.

[15] Prince Karl Max Lichnowsky, *Heading for the Abyss: Reminiscenses* (New York, 1928), pp. 84–85.

legitimate expectations and that for ambassadorships uncommon talents were essential.[16]

Once installed as an envoy, a diplomat could expect to serve until he reached seventy or seventy-five, provided that his behavior continued to be judicious. Some diplomats, however, wilted prematurely or insisted on clinging to offices for which they no longer had sufficient prowess. Radolin and Münster, for example, had to be retired as ambassadors to France at sixty-nine and seventy-nine respectively because their energies and abilities were perceptibly declining. Others were released after committing faux pas that the Wilhelmstrasse found intolerable. At a dinner honoring Sarah Bernhardt in 1879 in Copenhagen, the German minister, Johannes Emil von Wagner, generously praised "la belle France," to which the divine Sarah archly replied by referring to "la belle France entière." Bismarck was beside himself that Wagner had provided an opening for this insulting reference to Alsace-Lorraine and he dismissed the envoy, a veteran of forty years in the service.[17] Holstein commented curtly on the performance of the envoy, who was rumored to be of Jewish extraction: "Magnus und Sarah . . . internationales Judenthum."[18]

For appointment to an envoyship, a variety of factors came into play to determine who would get what post. Approval by the state to which a diplomat was to be accredited was requested and usually obtained with little difficulty. The calculations of the Foreign Office were very elaborate, for it had not only to discover whether a particular candidate would accept a post in question but also to ascertain whether this diplomat would be acceptable to the kaiser. Royal approval could not always be counted on, and

---

[16] GN, 1027; also HvB to State Secretary Bernhard Ernst von Bülow, May 25, 1875, BisN FC 2957/32.

[17] Count Friedrich zu Limburg-Stirum to OvB, Sept. 9, and 20, 1880; Wagner to OvB, Aug. 21, 1880, RichthofenN 1/2. See also FvH to Clemens Busch, July 8 [1876], HolN 3851/H188970.

[18] FvH to HvB, Aug. 25, 1880, BisN FC 2966/497.

often the Wilhelmstrasse's proposals for filling vacancies were rejected or swept aside by the sovereign. As in most matters, in the appointment of envoys the crown, not the government, was decisive.

As far as the diplomat's own preferences were concerned, the Wilhelmstrasse was generally scrupulous in consulting candidates for posts as to whether they would be prepared to accept them. The prospective envoy had to weigh a number of factors: the location, cost, and salary of the position; the identity of the Political Division counselor in whose bailiwick it fell; the nature of German relations with the power in question; and especially the effect accepting or rejecting the assignment would play in his future career. As a result, diplomats had very strong preferences for certain assignments.

Of all posts, none was so scrupulously avoided as the state secretaryship, and a long file of Foreign Office dignitaries—among them Alvensleben, Hatzfeldt, Hohenlohe, Holstein, Jagow, Monts, Radowitz, and Werthern—at one time or another declined the post or resisted its being thrust upon them.[19] Bismarck himself admitted that it was a thank-

[19] For Bismarck see Hajo Holborn, ed., *Aufzeichnungen und Erinnerungen aus dem Leben des Botschafters Joseph Maria von Radowitz*, 2 vols. (Berlin and Leipzig, 1925), II, 105. For resistance to the state secretaryship see the following: Hohenlohe diary, Oct. 28, 1879, HohN, CC.X.7; diary for Feb. 22, 1880, ibid., CC.X.8; FvH to Hohenlohe, Feb. 8, 1880; Hohenlohe to FvH, Feb. 8, 1880, Hohenlohe to Prince Otto zu Stolberg-Wernigerode, Feb. 3, 1880, ibid., XX.H.1, dealing with Hohenlohe's distaste for the position; on Alvensleben, Wilhelm von Schweinitz, ed., *Denkwürdigkeiten des Botschafters General v. Schweinitz*, 2 vols. (Berlin, 1927), II, 403; Brauer, *Im Dienste Bismarcks*, p. 330; Count Erhard von Wedel, ed., *Zwischen Kaiser und Kanzler: Aufzeichnungen des Generaladjutanten Grafen Carl von Wedel aus den Jahren 1890–1894 . . .* (Leipzig, 1943), pp. 60–61; Holborn, *Aufzeichnungen; Radowitz*, II, 323; Heinrich O. Meisner, ed., *Denkwürdigkeiten des General-Feldmarschalls Alfred Grafen von Waldersee*, 3 vols. (Stuttgart, 1923–25), II, 122; on Holstein's objection to the post, see Prince

less job. The state secretary was allowed considerable latitude in administration, but in diplomatic matters he was only the chancellor's spokesman. Herbert Bismarck, who served in the position from 1885 to 1890, exerted an enormous influence on policy, but this was due not to the office itself, which he loathed and in which he served only at the chancellor's insistence, but to his intimate relationship with his father.[20]

Candidates for the state secretaryship, most of whom were envoys, were very explicit about their reasons for not wanting to exchange their posts for the Wilhelmstrasse 76. To highly placed ambassadors, one factor was money. The office paid considerably less than their positions yet it also entailed considerable entertaining as well as constant attendance at court. To some the post seemed a demotion from which the only exit would likely be a premature retirement. An objection to the state secretaryship made not only by ambassadors but also by less exalted nominees was that the position did not have the prestige of an ambassadorship or ministership, for the state secretary was really

---

Alexander von Hohenlohe, *Aus meinem Leben* (Frankfurt/Main, 1925), p. 312, and Helmuth Rogge, ed., *Friedrich von Holsteins Lebensbekenntnis in Briefen an eine Frau* (Berlin, 1932), p. 168; on Jagow, see his note to BvB of Jan. 5, 1913, in BüN 46, and Hindenburg, *Am Rande*, p. 261. On Monts, see Nowak and Thimme, *Erinnerungen; Monts*, pp. 155, 360, and Monts, "Unsere Diplomatie," p. 77; for Radowitz, see Holborn, *Aufzeichnungen; Radowitz*, II, 115, but cf. Limburg-Stirum to Hohenlohe of Nov. 13, 1880, in HohN, XX.H.2, which declares that Radowitz preferred being state secretary to returning to Athens; on Werthern, see Heinrich von Poschinger, *Bismarck-Portfeuille*, 5 vols. (Stuttgart, 1898–1900), II, 186. At least two Foreign Office officials, Count Limburg-Stirum and Clemens Busch, wanted the post but were frustrated in their attempts to obtain it. See Hohenlohe's diary for June 18, 1881, HohN, CC.X.9, and for Nov. 4, 1882, ibid., XX.C.10; Hohenlohe to Alexander Hohenlohe, Mar. 27, 1890, Alexander Hohenlohe *Nachlass*, Bundesarchiv, Koblenz, 4.

[20] BvB to Lindenau, Sept. 17, 1890, BüN 99.

only a functionary of the state, while an envoy was the personal representative of the sovereign. Moreover, he was outranked by the least of the ministers in the Prussian cabinet, since an imperial state secretaryship was not an *Immediatstelle*, and the person holding one could therefore approach the sovereign only through the imperial chancellor.[21]

Too often policies were dictated by the chancellor or emperor, with the state secretary expected merely to implement these directives and to defend them from critics. In 1898, State Secretary Bülow declared that his position had so many drawbacks—especially low pay and long hours— that he would not have taken it under any chancellor other than Hohenlohe. His reasoning was entirely negative. Hohenlohe was "old, sick, indolent and utterly passive," and the complete freedom the state secretary therefore enjoyed

[21] On the financial burdens of the post see FvH to HvB, July 22, 1882, BisN FC 2966/245; BvB to PzE, July 20, 1898, EN, LI, 158–60; PzE to BvB, July 25, 1898, ibid., 177; Hohenlohe diary for Oct. 28, 1879, HohN, CC.X.7; Baron Wilhelm von Schoen, *Erlebtes: Beiträge zur politischen Geschichte der neuesten Zeit* (Stuttgart, 1921), pp. 121–22; Monts, "Unsere Diplomatie," 77–78; Rogge, *Holstein und Hohenlohe*, pp. 102–3; Heinrich von Poschinger, *Stunden bei Bismarck* (Vienna, 1910), pp. 173–74. On qualms about the rank of the state secretaryship see BvB to FvH, Jan. 3, 1896, HolN 3854/H191367–69; Holborn, *Aufzeichnungen; Radowitz*, II, 115; Rogge, *Holstein und Hohenlohe*, pp. 102–3; FvH to HvB, Aug. 25, 1880, BisN FC 2966/497. For the prestige factor see Schoen, *Erlebtes*, pp. 51–52; Rogge, *Holstein und Hohenlohe*, pp. 125–26; Rudolf Morsey, *Die oberste Reichsverwaltung unter Bismarck, 1867–1890* (Münster, 1957), p. 256, note 28; Karl A. von Müller, ed., *Fürst Chlodwig zu Hohenlohe-Schillingsfürst: Denkwürdigkeiten der Reichskanzlerzeit* (Stuttgart, 1931), p. 279. Three state secretaries were made Prussian ministers without portfolio, which enabled them to have direct access to the crown. But two of these appointments —to Baron Marschall von Bieberstein in 1895 and to Baron Oswald von Richthofen in 1905—came at the end of their service as state secretary. Bülow, who became state secretary in 1897, was introduced into the Prussian ministry in the following year.

was the compensating factor which made the office tolerable. Yet when in 1900 Bülow succeeded to the chancellorship, he treated his new state secretary, Baron von Richthofen, in a condescending manner.[22]

Until 1890, the figure of whom state secretaries had to be most wary was Bismarck; after his fall William II proved an even more vexatious master. In 1893 Philipp Eulenburg spurned overtures by his friends that he succeed Marschall von Bieberstein as state secretary in the event that the post should fall vacant. The reason he gave was that the contact with William II which the position would require would harm the cordial relationship which Eulenburg had succeeded in establishing with his sovereign.[23] In the following year, Eulenburg was again approached about assuming the post and again he turned it down because, he declared, "the *constant* opposition between aides-de-camp and *Militär- und Kabinettspolitik* on one side and on the other the civilian organization and professional outlook of the Foreign Office, which can never prevail over an ascendant military group that regards the Kaiser as a 'comrade,' would pulverize me between two millstones."[24] Another distinct reason for which many diplomats avoided becoming state secretary was to escape the frequent interrogations required before the Reichstag, a prospect as unpalatable to an aristo-

[22] BvB to PzE, July 20, 1898, EN, LI, 158–60; BvB to Lindenau, July 18, 1897, Apr. 9, 1890, May 6, 1891, BüN 99; Lichnowsky to BvB, Oct. 18, 1900, and BvB to Lichnowsky, Oct. 19, 1900, ibid., 98.

[23] On Bismarck see Holborn, *Aufzeichnungen; Radowitz*, II, 116; on William II and Eulenburg see Johannes Haller, *Aus dem Leben des Fürsten Philipp zu Eulenburg-Hertefeld* (Berlin, 1924), pp. 129–30, and Friedrich Curtius, ed., *Denkwürdigkeiten des Fürsten Choldwig zu Hohenlohe-Schillingsfürst*, 2 vols. (Stuttgart, 1907), II, 497–98. For the general difficulties of the state secretary see Schoen, *Erlebtes*, pp. 51–52; Otto Hammann, *Zur Vorgeschichte des Weltkrieges: Erinnerungen aus den Jahren 1897–1906* (Berlin, 1919), p. 1; Monts, "Unsere Diplomatie," pp. 77–78.

[24] Haller, *Leben Eulenburg*, pp. 129–30.

cratic envoy as it was unfamiliar to one trained in the gentlemanly art of diplomatic negotiation.[25]

The under state secretary was completely subservient to the state secretary and it was therefore a post to be avoided. Bernhard von Bülow, in 1887 a much discussed candidate for the office, declared that he would take any ministry or even remain first secretary in St. Petersburg rather than accept such an "odious" assignment.[26] The only advantage of the position was that it usually led to an advance in the service. Of the eight incumbents, only two found it a terminal post. Two others were elevated to state secretary, three became ministers in foreign capitals, and one had the misfortune to die in office.

Diplomats differentiated carefully between assignments in the field. Even among the seven great embassies there was a clear ranking. London, St. Petersburg, Paris, and Vienna, all politically vital and socially attractive as well as endowed with high salaries, were the crowning of a career.[27] The Foreign Office as well as the diplomatic corps made little distinction between the four posts. The importance of Constantinople rose and fell with the fluctuating barometer of the Eastern Question, while appointments to Rome or Madrid were matters of relatively small concern. Bismarck regarded St. Petersburg as the most important assignment, since most of the other capitals lay in the toils of republicans or parliamentarians, a deplorable state of affairs which in his opinion made both governments and public opinion less susceptible to manipulation by diplomatic

[25] See Ludwig Raschdau, *Unter Bismarck und Caprivi: Erinnerungen eines deutschen Diplomaten aus den Jahren 1885–1894*, 2d ed. (Berlin, 1939), p. 301; Nowak and Thimme, *Erinnerungen; Monts*, p. 155; Hindenburg, *Am Rande*, p. 261; Holborn, *Aufzeichnungen; Radowitz*, II, 323; Schoen, *Erlebtes*, pp. 51–52; Hammann, *Vorgeschichte*, p. 1; Monts, "Unsere Diplomatie," pp. 77–78.

[26] Ernst Jäckh, ed., *Kiderlen-Wächter der Staatsmann und Mensch: Briefwechsel und Nachlass*, 2 vols. (Berlin, 1924), II, 91.

[27] Washington received embassy status in 1893, Tokyo in 1906.

talent.[28] After Bismarck's fall in 1890 and the subsequent failure to renew the Reinsurance Treaty with Russia, St. Petersburg suffered a decline in importance. William II declared in 1892 that the Russian post was inferior to Constantinople and that who filled it was consequently a matter of no great concern.[29] London, and especially Vienna, became after 1890 the leading diplomatic assignments.

To diplomats, Constantinople had both good and bad features. The dependence of the Ottoman Empire on German diplomatic and military officials made even the lesser positions in the embassy at Pera appear to be of critical importance, and the result, in the opinion of one attaché stationed there in the early 1880s, was that service in Turkey engendered an excess of self-esteem. After Pera, a secretary of legation felt himself ready for an ambassadorship.[30] On the other hand, the heat, squalor, and remote location of the Ottoman capital made it unhealthy and inaccessible to Germany, a disadvantage for an ambassador concerned to maintain a close connection with the powers in the Wilhelmstrasse or to keep his business affairs in order. The ambassador to the Porte, Marschall von Bieberstein, lamented in 1909 that he would "under no circumstances remain here more than a year longer. I have been ambassador in Constantinople for twelve years. I no longer enjoy the climate, I am too far from my estates, and I can't have my children with me. This cannot continue."[31] The Ottoman position changed hands almost twice as frequently as any of the four

[28] OvB to William I, July 5, 1885, BisN FC 2986/87–90; HvB to Wilhelm von Bismarck, Aug. 25, 1884, ibid., FC 3010/407; Nowak and Thimme, *Erinnerungen; Monts*, p. 222.

[29] PzE to FvH, Oct. 2, 1892, HolN 3855/H192343–44; Radolin to FvH, June 25, 1895, HolN 3859/H195151–52.

[30] Alfred von Bülow to BvB, Mar. 4, 1883, BüN 14.

[31] Jäckh, *Kiderlen-Wächter*, II, 35; MiquelN, 00245–46; Radolinski to FvH, July 20, 1883, HolN 3859/H195083–84. Eulenburg declined Constantinople in 1888 because of family considerations. See HvB to OvB, Oct. 5, 1888, BisN FC 3004/473. For another diplomat's rejection of the post see ibid., FC 2958/99–101.

leading European embassies, and of all the men who served as ambassador to one or another of these seven capitals or as state secretary no one ended his career languishing in exile on the Bosporus.

Rome was more attractive. It was relatively stagnant politically and almost the least handsomely paid of the European embassies but it was to many diplomats the choicest of assignments because of Rome's engaging society and the splendor of the German embassy in the Palazzo Caffarelli. The Italian capital was infinitely more desirable than Madrid, the worst paid, socially most desperate, and politically least significant of the European ambassadorships. Herbert Bismarck thought it inferior even to the first secretaryship in St. Petersburg.[32] The only advantage of the Spanish assignment was that it conferred ambassadorial rank and was on the same continent as Berlin. Otherwise it was, as one incumbent complained, an "exile," and as often as not the only avenue of departure from Madrid was death or retirement. Even novice diplomats tried to avoid secretarial positions in Spain.[33]

Diplomats due for promotion from the lower ranks to ministerships almost invariably sought assignments in Europe. In most cases, an imperial post was preferred to a Prussian ministry within Germany or at the Vatican. Many of the imperial ministries in Europe were very desirable assignments, quite apart from the fact that they trained men for more exalted embassies. Some were sought after because the country in question was sensitive and the work therefore was more exciting than the routine diplomacy conducted in settled capitals. Kiderlen, for example, preferred Bucharest to Copenhagen for that reason, while

[32] Count Friedrich von Vitzthum to BvB, n.d. (ca. Apr. 1887), BüN 127.

[33] Count Bogdan von Hutten-Czapski, *Sechzig Jahre Politik und Gesellschaft*, 2 vols. (Berlin, 1936), I, 272; Wedel, *Zwischen Kaiser und Kanzler*, p. 199; BvB to Lindenau, May 6, 1891, BüN 99; Vitzthum to BvB, Apr. 20, 1890, ibid., 127.

Bülow, who found Rumania politically interesting but easy enough to allow him to catch up on his reading, refused to leave Bucharest until Berlin was ready to offer him an embassy or the ministry in Brussels or at the Vatican.[34] Often, however, diplomats prized the European ministries for the very fact that they were dull, unexacting posts. To some envoys, the minor European posts were desirable assignments because service there would afford them a needed rest following service in a demanding capital or allow them to recover from illness, or because they were simply unambitious and measured the attractiveness of posts in terms of their tranquility and proximity to Germany.[35]

In the case of some diplomats, there was a more positive reason for wanting a somnolent post, for assignments to languid European capitals would enable envoys to take long leaves, which could in part be spent in fence-mending at the Political Division. Athens, in particular, was widely regarded by diplomats as a sinecure, one which would provide the person holding it with a substantial income with which to defray the expense of living in Berlin.[36] This was the reason for the appointment to Greece of Joseph Maria von Radowitz. He arrived at Athens on August 1, 1875, left

[34] Bülow, Denkwürdigkeiten, I, 395; BvB to Lindenau, June 12, 1888. Dec. 16. 1889. June 1, 1890, BüN 99. He also preferred Rumania to Washington. See BvB to HvB, Feb. 17, 1888, BisN FC 2958/827–28, 833–34.

[35] Rudolf Le Maistre (minister in Darmstadt) to FvH, July 19, 1886, HolN 3820/E341190–91; Monts to Marie von Bülow, Nov. 6, 1902, BüN 106; BvB to Lindenau, July 20, 1887, and Oct. 6, 1892, ibid., 99; Alfred von Bülow to BvB, n.d. [1885], ibid., 14, p. 147. Alfred asked his brother for Berne. Bernhard passed the request on to Herbert Bismarck, who arranged for Alfred to have the post. See BvB to HvB, July 7, 1885, BisN FC 2958/465.

[36] Arthur von Brauer et al., eds., Erinnerungen an Bismarck: Aufzeichnungen von Mitarbeitern und Freunden des Fürsten . . . , 4th ed. (Stuttgart, 1915), p. 320; Holborn, Aufzeichnungen; Radowitz, I, 343; Ludwig Raschdau, "Fürst Bismarck als Leiter der Politischen Abteilung: aus dem schriftlichen Nachlass des Unterstaatssekretärs Dr. Busch," Deutsche Rundschau, CLI (1912), 47–54.

three weeks later, not to return until the very end of the year. For the next six years, this absenteeism was the rule in the minister's life. During this period, Radowitz entrenched himself in Berlin as the virtual head of the Political Division, served as chief of protocol at the Congress of Berlin in 1878, and represented Ambassador Hohenlohe during his absence from Paris for several months in 1880 and 1881. The Greeks got whatever time Radowitz could spare, a slight which did not pass unnoticed in Athens.[37] The Reichstag occasionally raised questions concerning envoys' extended absences, even in time of crisis, from their posts, but its interpellations were brushed aside by the state secretary as impertinent.[38] The liberal press also kept track of absentee ambassadors and ministers. Eulenburg, whose extended withdrawals from Vienna made him an apt target, complained that this sort of picayune reckoning directed at an envoy demeaned him to the level of a "slovenly functionary."[39]

Among the European ministries, Belgrade was avoided because, along with Sofia, it was the most primitive capital in Europe and was impossible for ministers with small children because of the unavailability of foodstuffs and the difficulty of finding suitable housing.[40] Besides, the ministership there seemed often to lead only to Lisbon, a post held

[37] Radowitz to BvB, June 27, and Oct. 31, 1877, BüN 114; Holborn, *Aufzeichnungen; Radowitz,* I, 288–343. For Bismarck's comments on Radowitz' absence from Athens see Reichstag, Dec. 15, 1884, pp. 359–60.

[38] Reichstag, Feb. 14, 1896, especially Marschall's curt answer to August Bebel, pp. 956–57. Bismarck had Radowitz return to Athens in 1880 in order to avoid such questions being raised in the Reichstag. Limburg-Stirum to HvB, Oct. 21, 1880, BisN FC 2370/120; OvB to Radowitz, Oct. 31, 1880, ibid., FC 2974/1166–71.

[39] PzE to Count Agenor von Goluchowski (Austro-Hungarian foreign minister), Sept. 5, 1901, and to W2, Sept. 7, EN, LVIII, 167, 170–71; see also Prince Max von Ratibor und Corvey (first secretary, Vienna), to FvH, Oct. 22, 1894, HolN 3821/E341989–90; Hohenlohe to Ratibor, Nov. 5, 1895, HohN, XXII.A.6.

[40] Alfred von Bülow to BvB, May 22, 1888, BüN 14.

in particular contempt. The Portuguese capital was, at best, only a warming pan for Madrid and it was avoided by diplomats at all levels of the service. Count Harry von Arnim once declared that he would rather dwell in a hut in Germany than in a palace on the Tagus. Lisbon's undesirability was, however, useful to the Foreign Office, since when it wished to separate a diplomat from the service, the offer of the post in Portugal was usually enough to secure the desired resignation.[41]

The Prussian ministries to the German states and to the Vatican were pleasant assignments for the most part but posts of little consequence. Even Munich, after Berlin the most distinguished of German capitals, made few demands on the Prussian envoy, a fact given considerable attest by the career of Baron (later Count) Georg von Werthern, minister there from 1867 to 1888. This able but eccentric official, who periodically took extended cures at Bad Kissingen, invariably spent the months of June through October managing his ancestral estates in Thuringia.[42] Karl Georg von Treutler, who served as minister in Munich from 1912 to 1917, was often absent from his post for five or six weeks at a time in order to accompany William II on cruises in Norwegian waters, leaves which the Bavarian government did not find flattering.[43] Even when the envoys in such posts stayed at their desks, they sometimes were very casual

[41] Brauer et al., *Erinnerungen an Bismarck*, p. 320; Raschdau, *In Weimar*, pp. 164–78; Baron Robert Lucius von Ballhausen, *Bismarck-Erinnerungen* (Stuttgart, 1921), p. 66; memo by HvB, Dec. 18, 1887, BisN FC 3004/441–43. The tender of Athens was also used to force resignations. See HvB to KvR, Dec. 20, 1887, BisN FC 3014/1015.

[42] Prince Philipp zu Eulenburg-Hertefeld, *Aus 50 Jahren: Erinnerungen, Tagebücher und Briefe* (Berlin, 1923), p. 112.

[43] TN, XVIII, passim. See also Count Johann-Heinrich Bernstorff, *Memoirs*, trans. Eric Sutton (New York, 1936), pp. 54–55. On the triviality of the ministry in Württemberg see Hindenburg, *Am Rande*, p. 177; see also Raschdau's *In Weimar*, and Radolin to FvH, Jan. 28, 1894, HolN 3859/H194892, for similar experiences elsewhere.

in the execution of their duties. The Prussian minister in Stuttgart, who regarded his posting there as a sign from the Foreign Office that he had no future as a diplomat, had a member of the clerical staff write his reports. Karl von Schlözer, minister in Munich from 1907 to 1910, did the same, declaring that since the Bavarians were *Bundesbrüder* the Prussian envoy should not in fact report on them at all.[44]

Bismarck considered the Prussian ministries to be of minor significance and under his chancellorship Berlin's relations with the German states were largely handled by his own Reichskanzlei or in the Bundesrat, not in the Wilhelmstrasse.[45] Prior to 1871, the task of the Prussian ministers at the German courts and at Hamburg had been to propagandize Prussia's leadership in Germany's unification. Bismarck therefore had permitted these envoys to take an active role in pursuing such an end. With the formation of the empire, which increased the animosity toward Prussia in many quarters, Bismarck ordered the Prussian ministers to become inconspicuous and avoid becoming embroiled in the internal affairs of the German states. "The less one *feels* the effectiveness and the influence of an envoy," he wrote in April, 1871, to Werthern in Munich, "the more he will be able to accomplish the task which now stands before him of keeping the course of national development free from opposition in the Reichstag or Bundesrat and in particular of winning the confidence of the [Bavarian] government." Werthern, a Protestant, was especially to avoid becoming too closely identified with his Catholic separatist friends such as Ignaz von Döllinger.[46] In similar fashion, in 1882 the chancellor advised Kurd von Schlözer, the first Prussian minister to the Vatican, that modesty was to be his watch-

[44] Hindenburg, *Am Rande*, pp. 177, 210.
[45] Walter Bussmann, ed., *Staatssekretär Graf Herbert von Bismarck: aus seiner politischen Privatkorrespondenz* (Göttingen, 1964), pp. 525–26.
[46] GW, VIc, 4–6, 12–13.

word. He was not expected to secure a definitive accommodation between Berlin and the Holy See but merely to maintain the status quo. Schlözer, whose forte was society and literature rather than negotiation, was delighted to comply and he became a notably successful envoy.[47] Nevertheless, to Bismarck as well as to his subordinates, the German ministries were useful as way stations for aspiring diplomats in which they could sharpen their diplomatic finesse while waiting for a position in an embassy to fall vacant. In 1888, the chancellor wrote to his son Herbert, then state secretary, that "the little posts [in Germany] are schools and depots, without which we could not properly fill the great ones."[48] The subsequent careers of the sixty men who held Prussian ministries to the German states between 1871 and 1914 indicate the validity of Bismarck's observation. Ten proceeded in the course of their service to European embassies, another twenty-one became ministers in Europe, six went to envoyships in the western hemisphere, while the remaining twenty-three spent their entire careers in the Prussian posts.

Of all the Prussian ministries, Munich was the one from which great careers were most likely to be launched. Next came the positions in Württemberg; Hamburg-Bremen-Mecklenburg, the ministry embracing Oldenburg, Brunswick, and the Lippes; and then Baden. Saxony, the Thuringian states and Hesse appear to have been of reduced importance. "Minister in Weimar," Bismarck sneered, was merely a *Reisetitel.*[49] Oldenburg's significance is curious, for it was of considerably less political consequence than many other German states. Nevertheless, of the nine Prussian emissaries to Oldenburg who moved on from that post be-

[47] Ibid., p. 268.

[48] Bussmann, *Herbert von Bismarck*, pp. 525–26. Herbert agreed. See his letter to his father of Apr. 14, 1887, BisN FC 3004/400.

[49] Holstein diary, May 14, 1884, HolN 3860/H195915. To Herbert Bismarck Oldenburg was nothing—"Oldenburg ist ja kein diplomatischer Posten." HvB to KvR, Jan. 27, 1888, BisN FC 3014/1163.

fore 1914, six rose to important Prussian or imperial assignments. Oldenburg, unlike Dresden or Darmstadt, seems to have been a post the Foreign Office reserved for promising young diplomats such as Eulenburg or Count Anton Monts. It was a dreary and lifeless place; one incumbent referred to his position as *Konsul-Oldenburg*. But this was in fact the very advantage which the Wilhelmstrasse saw in assigning its favorites to this post. Since there was so little work to be performed in Oldenburg, the minister was often free to make the short trip to Berlin to serve as a consultant in the Political Division. Bernhard von Bülow, ever fertile in plotting careers (especially his own), congratulated Eulenburg on his appointment to Oldenburg in 1888 by noting that

> Wie fruchtbar ist der kleinste Kreis
> Wenn man ihn recht zu pflegen weiss![50]

Eulenburg's assignment to Oldenburg was designed to keep him occupied until Munich, the post for which William II had destined him, could be made free. His duties in the Grand Duchy did not prevent his traveling with the kaiser for much of the summer or from making extended consultative trips to the Wilhelmstrasse.[51]

Only in exceptional cases did diplomats regard an assignment beyond Europe with pleasure. Kiderlen expressed himself on the point with his customary tactless forthrightness. Once, when state secretary, he observed to Count Bernstorff, ambassador in Washington, and to the American

[50] Eulenburg, *50 Jahren*, pp. 199–200; Nowak and Thimme, *Erinnerungen; Monts*, p. 327.

[51] HvB to OvB, Oct. 5, 1888, BisN FC 3004/473; W2 to PzE, Oct. 31, 1888, EN, IV, 161. For Eulenburg's repeated presence in Berlin and his travels with the kaiser while minister in Oldenburg see Eulenburg, *50 Jahren*, p. 218, and his *Mit dem Kaiser als Staatsmann und Freund auf Nordlandsreisen*, 2 vols. (Dresden, 1931), I, 29–136. Bismarck considered appointing his son to Oldenburg so that he could come frequently to Berlin. Holstein diary, May 4, 1884, HolN 3860/H195895–96.

envoy to Germany that he had never been outside Europe. Bernstorff expressed surprise, to which Kiderlen candidly replied, "No, thank God, never."[52] Even within Europe, one did well to concentrate on the embassies. Treutler, a favorite of William II, reminiscing about a career which finally led to Munich, decided that as a young diplomat he had erred in accepting the invitation of Count Friedrich von Alvensleben, minister to Belgium, to join his staff. He should instead have gone to Italy, which the kaiser had promised him, "because one could all too easily be shunted off into the '*kleine Karrière*' if one did not from the beginning cultivate good relations with the *big* missions."[53] Baroness Edmund von Heyking, whose aspirations for her husband would have been satisfied only if he were to have become ambassador to France and then *Statthalter* of Alsace-Lorraine, was consequently very disappointed when he received instead a number of ministries scattered around the world. First there was China ("Death would look good if, from the grave, one thought of Peking"), and then Mexico ("What have we done to deserve this!"). But finally Heyking managed to acquire the lowly post of minister to Serbia, to his wife's boundless joy ("It is ours—a European ministry.").[54]

The disadvantages of overseas duty in the nineteenth century were numerous. The capitals, to Germans, were socially primitive and hygienically impossible. It was consequently not safe in many places for wives or children to

[52] Bernstorff, *Memoirs*, pp. 105–6.

[53] TN, X, 3–4; Hindenburg, *Am Rande*, p. 206.

[54] Elisabeth von Heyking, *Tagebücher aus vier Weltteilen, 1886/1904*, 2d ed. (Leipzig, 1926), pp. 154, 161, 206, 214, 288–89, 401. The baroness, whose father was Prussian minister to Baden, was regarded as pushy. See Monts to BvB, Dec. 9, 1895, BüN 106. For an outburst at the mere prospect of being offered an Asian post see HvB to Franz von Rottenburg, Sept. 2, 1882, BisN FC 2977/410; also HvB to Wilhelm von Bismarck, Sept. 16, 1882, ibid., FC 3011/345.

accompany a diplomat, one reason why the service had a high percentage of bachelors in its ranks.[55] Treutler, minister to Brazil from 1901 to 1907, was the only member of his legation to take his wife overseas. He grumbled that his existence was bearable only because he and his family lived the year around in the summer capital of Petropolis and imported literally everything from Europe.[56] Asia was worse. On his arrival in Peking as minister in 1875, Max von Brandt declared that the ministry was unfit for human habitation and moved the entire staff to a rented dwelling until such time as the building could be refurbished.[57] The trip home from such distant posts was long and the cost was met by the Foreign Office only if the journey came at the termination of an assignment. Vacations, which in remote legations such as China might amount only to a few months every five years, were paid out of one's own pocket. It is therefore hardly surprising that a diplomat who had served for several years in an overseas post felt entitled to a European assignment as a reward for his exile, a claim which the Wilhelmstrasse was usually prepared to honor.[58] Seldom would a diplomat accredited to a European legation exchange his post for one in Asia or America, although some counselors in Berlin, anxious to acquire experience in the field or ministerial dignity, were happy to accept even the least attractive of Caribbean posts.[59]

[55] Married diplomats tried to fob off hardship posts on bachelors. See Prince Max Ratibor to Alexander Hohenlohe, Apr. 26, 1896, HohN, XXII.A.8.

[56] TN, XIIIe, 1.

[57] Brandt, *Dreiunddreissig Jahre in Ost-Asien: Erinnerungen eines deutschen Diplomaten*, 3 vols. (Leipzig, 1901), II, 28–29.

[58] TN, XIIIf, 1; Alvensleben to HvB, July 28, 1875, BisN FC 2952/594–96; KvR to HvB, Oct. 7, 1882, ibid., FC 3028.

[59] MichahellesN, p. 79. For the occasional diplomat who saw an advantage in an Asian rather than a European post see Gerhard von Mutius, *Abgeschlossene Zeiten* (Hermannstadt, n.d. [ca. 1929]), p. 203, and Count Karl Luxburg, *Nachdenkliche Erinnerungen* (Aschach/Saale, 1953), p. 46.

Of all non-European posts, Washington was the most important and, although quite expensive, the most desirable. Otto Bismarck thought it equal in significance to Rome and also more arduous, while Herbert Bismarck ranked it just behind the great European embassies.[60] The possibility of travel on the Indian frontier made America attractive duty in the 1870s and 1880s, a point emphasized by Baron Max von Thielmann, from 1874 to 1878 a secretary of legation in Washington and twenty years later ambassador there, in an aphorism which enjoyed some currency among diplomats: "In Amerika ist viel Urwald, daher auch viel Urlaub."[61] By the end of the century, the badlands had been cleansed of red warriors but there were now East Coast heiresses to be plundered. Washington offered fruitful opportunities for aristocratic fortune hunters who were prepared to regild their lusterless coronets with New World doweries. Emil Witte, a German newspaperman in America about 1900, declared that "The real staff of the [German] embassy, that is secretaries and attachés, was composed of blue-blooded aristocrats who looked upon it rather as an insult to live for a while in a democratic republic. Truth demands that I should here state that the influenial circles in Washington for the most part looked with derision and scorn on the representative European noblemen, as they usually see in them fortune hunters and seekers for the hands of rich American heiresses. . . . The Americans have a scale for the worth of European titles, but in this case the Germans appear quite at the bottom."[62]

America was altogether a tolerable place, but one in which an envoy's thoughts were concentrated on the pros-

[60] GW, XIV/2, 840; HvB to BvB, Feb. 4, and 13, 1888, BüN 66.

[61] Kurd von Schlözer, *Amerikanische Briefe, Mexikanische Briefe 1869–1871, Briefe aus Washington 1871–1881* (Berlin, 1927), pp. 142–43.

[62] Witte, *Revelations of a German Attaché: Ten Years of German-American Diplomacy* (New York, 1916), pp. 77, 80. The title is misleading, for Witte had no official diplomatic status.

pects of an eventual transfer to Europe. The plaintive tone of the German emissaries in the United States was well expressed by Kurd von Schlözer on his reassignment to Washington from Mexico in 1871. "I'm quite happy," he wrote, "that I'll no longer have to wander about under palm trees. . . . Now I must wait to see whether I will have to remain forever in America or whether one fine day Europe will again beckon to me. . . ."[63] In 1882, Schlözer was delighted to leave Washington to become minister at the Vatican. With the increasing importance of the United States, the ambassadorship there became a more demanding post, which to some diplomats did not add to its attractiveness.[64]

Of the other non-European legations, diplomats regarded some as more desirable than others. In terms of importance, Japan headed the list, followed at some distance by China, which, unlike Japan, was never accorded embassy rank.[65] German diplomats in China escaped to Japan for vacations, and reassignment from Peking to Tokyo was regarded as an advance. An indication of the low status China enjoyed as late as 1895 lies in the rejection of Peking by Count Christian von Tattenbach, minister resident in Morocco, and his subsequent acceptance of the humdrum ministry in Berne.[66] Persia was significant in that it was a training post for China, which in turn often prepared envoys for Japan. Mexico, Argentina, and Brazil usually proved temporary assignments for men who would later have careers in Europe, but these South American capitals were nonetheless very unpopular. Rio de Janeiro was not only far away but also very expensive. Count Monts, who in his youth had served there and who in 1894 feared that he was destined

[63] Schlözer to OvB, Dec. 5, 1872, BisN FC 2978/622; Schlözer, *Amerikanische Briefe*, p. 91.

[64] Theodor von Holleben (ambassador in Washington) to PzE, Feb. 4, 1900, EN, LV, 46; HvB to Wilhelm von Bismarck, Feb. 6, 1888, BisN FC 3011/559.

[65] Tokyo was raised to an ambassadorship in 1906, while Washington had received that status in 1893.

[66] Monts to BvB, Dec. 9, 1895, BüN 106.

to be transferred from the general consulship in Budapest to become minister to Brazil, declared that he would rather resign. Instead, the envoy in Argentina was moved to Rio, and Monts, after a brief intermission in Oldenburg, became Prussian minister in Munich.[67] Diplomats generally disdained the lesser South American ministries, and the remaining posts in Africa and Asia were considered fit only for refugees from the consular service.

In making assignments the Foreign Office had to take into consideration not only the preferences of its diplomats but also those of the governments to which they were to be accredited. The Wilhelmstrasse's candidates were almost always accepted without demur, a reflection of the care with which they were chosen. Occasionally a head of state was asked to make a choice between candidates under consideration but ordinarily only a single name was proffered.[68] There is only one instance between 1871 and 1914 in which a foreign government insisted on a specific diplomat, even though the person in question was not one the Wilhelmstrasse desired. This occurred in 1892, when the tsar asked that General Bernhard von Werder, the former military plenipotentiary in St. Petersburg, be made ambassador. Although William II preferred another candidate he agreed rather than offend Alexander III.[69]

Although foreign governments were usually complacent about accepting the nominees preferred by Berlin, they did not hesitate to ask for the recall of unsatisfactory envoys. In spite of the Wilhelmstrasse's precautions, some diplomats proved to be ill-suited to their assignments and a few, heretofore regarded as men of some talent, suddenly revealed a deplorable lack of judgment or refinement which necessitated their swift removal. As long as Bismarck was in pow-

[67] Monts to BvB, Mar. 26, 1894, ibid.; see also HvB to BvB, Feb. 3, 1885, ibid., 65.

[68] Schoen, *Erlebtes*, p. 93.

[69] Raschdau, *Unter Bismarck und Caprivi*, p. 265; PzE to Marschall von Bieberstein, Nov. 13, 1892, Asseverat 45.

er, foreign governments sometimes suggested but never insisted on the recall of a German diplomat, an indication either of his watchfulness over the behavior of his envoys or of the fear which foreign statesmen had of annoying him.[70] Even after Bismarck's fall, the removal of a German diplomat at the demand of a foreign government was a rare occurrence. The Chinese, with some assistance from German naval officers, secured the dismissal of the arrogant Baron von Heyking and his meddlesome wife.[71] A few years earlier, and then only after a protracted struggle with Berlin, the Japanese and the German colony in Japan succeeded in obtaining the transfer of Baron Felix von Gutschmid, an unattractive and rough-mannered Saxon. William II delayed Gutschmid's recall for a year, declaring that he was unwilling to do Tokyo such an admitted favor.[72] Gutschmid's lack of polish paled beside the bumptiousness of the minister to Switzerland, Count von Tattenbach, who in the course of an earlier assignment as secretary of legation in Peking had already given an indication of his unsuitability as a diplomat. Tattenbach had the temerity to conclude an overly inquisitive interrogation of the president of the Confederation regarding his recent visit to Paris by declaring that "Ich glaube, alte Junge, du willst mich beschwindeln." The Swiss government immediately indicated to Berlin that Tattenbach's recall would be welcome. The revelation of such lack of diplomatic grace made it necessary for the Wilhelmstrasse to consign Tattenbach to the darkest corner of Europe. For the next eleven years he rusticated in Lisbon, finally moving to Madrid in 1908, where his undistinguished career was ended by his death two years later.[73]

[70] See Holstein's diary for Oct. 18, 1885, and Mar. 14, 1887, HolN 3861/H196115, H196246–47.

[71] Hugo Jacobi to BvB, Aug. 3, 1900, BüN 108.

[72] Heyking, *Tagebücher*, pp. 166–67.

[73] FvH to Paul Kayser, Dec. 6, 1897, Kl. Erwb. 458F, 10. For Tattenbach's career in China, see Holstein diary, Jan. 28, 1884, HolN 3860/H195775.

In attempting to match a man with a post, the Foreign Office had to make a number of calculations which were far more complex than satisfying the preferences of envoys or the pleasure of another government. The assessment of what diplomat to send to what post required consideration of the candidate's antecedents, connections, personality, means, and ability. Even if the man seemed in respect to his personal qualities a natural choice for a vacancy, the Wilhelmstrasse had also to measure carefully the ramifications his appointment would have in the service.

Birth, first of all, was a factor which had to be weighed. The disposition of the Wilhelmstrasse to pick young men of Prussian origin as recruits for the diplomatic service has been indicated in Chapter III. Prussian-born diplomats were given similar preferment in the promotion to high positions. Some specific posts were regarded as suitable only for diplomats of Prussian lineage. This was especially true of the embassy in St. Petersburg. On his retirement as ambassador in 1892, after sixteen years of service in the Romanov capital, General Lothar von Schweinitz pleaded with Chancellor Caprivi and other officials in the Foreign Office that his successor, like Schweinitz himself, be a Prussian. The envoy argued that the ties that bound the Spree to the Neva were Prussian, not German, and that an ill-bred Saxon, a liberal Badener, or a Bavarian Catholic would only alienate the Russians.[74] Schweinitz's successor was General von Werder, a Prussian of old family. Only in 1905, long after Russo-German amity had turned to ashes, was the chain of Prussian ambassadors to St. Petersburg broken with the appointment of the Hessian Wilhelm von Schoen. Bismarck and other officials in the Wilhelmstrasse felt that the state secretary and the heads of Prussian ministries to the German states, like the ambassador to Russia, whenever

---

[74] Schweinitz to BvB, Apr. 7, 1900, BüN 46; Schweinitz, *Denkwürdigkeiten*, II, 442. His first secretary, Bernhard von Bülow, also thought that the envoy in St. Petersburg should be a Prussian. BvB to HvB, Mar. 17, 1887, BisN FC 2958/762–66.

possible should be Prussian citizens. Subaltern posts in the German capitals should also be withheld from South Germans.[75]

Of the 187 men who served as envoys from 1871 to 1914, 105 (56.14 percent) were Prussian-born. Of these, ninety were aristocrats. The Prussians received the better positions. Their claim to the choice posts in Europe was slightly higher than their strength in the service, while they were underrepresented in the less desirable assignments in American, Asian, and African capitals. A chronological breakdown of the figures reveals, however, a very discernible decrease between 1871 and 1914 in the control of high offices by Prussians. In the first decade of the empire, Prussians held slightly more than seven of every ten envoyships; in the 1880s this hold fell to 65 percent, while in the 1890s less than half of the envoys accredited were Prussians (Table 16. Table 17 indicates origins of *new* envoys.)

The retreat of Prussian nobles from diplomatic posts did not equally affect all levels of appointments. The European embassies, the most sublime among the posts, stayed solidly in their hands. Here the percentage of Prussian *Uradel* actually rose very slightly from 1871 to 1914 (from 49.05 percent to 51.93 percent). In the Prussian ministries to the other German states, which the Foreign Office tried to reserve to Prussians, there was up and down movement in the Prussian/non-Prussian percentages, but the Prussians showed an overall decline, their places being assumed by aristocrats from elsewhere in Germany. Prussian nobles tended to increase in the more important non-European posts (which were often cheaper, though otherwise less desirable, than those in Europe), but this gain was canceled out by a fall of about the same percentage in the minor non-

[75] Memo, probably by Pourtalès, to Hohenlohe, Apr. 13, 1895, HohN, XXII.A.4; Holstein diary, May 4, 1884, HolN 3860/H195895; Wedel, *Zwischen Kaiser und Kanzler*, p. 59; FvH to BvB, Feb. 21, 1895, BüN 90; FvH to HvB, July 31, 1880, BisN FC 2966/457; GN, 790.

TABLE 16
GEOGRAPHICAL ORIGIN OF ENVOYS

	1871–1880 #	1871–1880 %	1881–1890 #	1881–1890 %	1891–1900 #	1891–1900 %	1901–1914 #	1901–1914 %
E. Prussian noble	28	58.34	32	53.33	23	30.26	40	39.22
W. Prussian noble	3	6.25	3	5.00	7	9.21	6	5.88
Non-Prussian noble	10	20.83	15	25.00	33	43.42	44	43.14
Unknown noble	1	2.08	—	—	—	—	—	—
Total noble	42	87.50	50	83.33	63	82.89	90	88.24
E. Prussian bourgeois	3	6.25	4	6.67	3	3.95	5	4.90
W. Prussian bourgeois	—	—	—	—	3	3.95	1	.98
Non-Prussian bourgeois	3	6.25	6	10.00	7	9.21	6	5.88
Unknown bourgeois	—	—	—	—	—	—	—	—
Total bourgeois	6	12.50	10	16.67	13	17.11	12	11.76
Total all envoys	48	100.00	60	100.00	76	100.00	102	100.00
Total all E. Prussians	31	64.59	36	60.00	26	34.21	45	44.12
Total all W. Prussians	3	6.25	3	5.00	10	13.16	7	6.86
Total all Prussians	34	70.84	39	65.00	36	47.37	52	50.98
Total all non-Prussians	13	27.08	21	35.00	40	52.63	50	49.02
Total unknown	1	2.08	—	—	—	—	—	—

NOTE: Each envoy is entered in each decade in which he served.

TABLE 17
GEOGRAPHICAL ORIGIN OF ENVOYS

	1871–1880 #	1871–1880 %	1881–1890 #	1881–1890 %	1891–1900 #	1891–1900 %	1901–1914 #	1901–1914 %
E. Prussian noble	28	58.34	16	47.06	6	15.00	29	44.62
W. Prussian noble	3	6.25	2	5.88	4	10.00	2	3.08
Non-Prussian noble	10	20.83	9	26.47	23	57.50	25	38.46
Unknown noble	1	2.08	—	—	—	—	—	—
Total noble	42	87.50	27	79.41	33	82.50	56	86.16
E. Prussian bourgeois	3	6.25	3	8.83	1	2.50	4	6.15
W. Prussian bourgeois	—	—	2	5.88	1	2.50	1	1.54
Non-Prussian bourgeois	3	6.25	2	5.88	5	12.50	4	6.15
Unknown bourgeois	—	—	—	—	—	—	—	—
Total bourgeois	6	12.50	7	20.59	7	17.50	9	13.84
Total all envoys	48	100.00	34	100.00	40	100.00	65	100.00
Total E. Prussian	31	64.59	19	55.89	7	17.50	33	50.77
Total W. Prussian	3	6.25	4	11.76	5	12.50	3	4.62
Total all Prussian	34	70.84	23	67.65	12	30.00	36	55.39
Total all non-Prussian	13	27.08	11	32.35	28	70.00	29	44.61
Unknown	1	2.08	—	—	—	—	—	—

NOTE: Each envoy entered in decade in which he received his first envoyship.
Those receiving such posts before 1871 are listed under 1871–1880.

European ministries. The striking decline in Prussian envoys occurred in the European posts other than the seven ambassadorships and the positions within Germany. In the first decade of the empire, no less than 92.86 percent of the diplomats filling such posts were Prussian nobles, but thereafter the percentage fell steadily until from 1901 to 1914 they accounted for only 40.54 percent. European ministries were expensive courts and some were highly self-conscious of their dignity. It was therefore desirable to fill them with men of distinguished lineage and comfortable means. In these posts, Prussian nobles were usually replaced by non-Prussian *Uradel*, who apparently had the money as well as the aristocratic antecedents necessary to maintain German honor.

Confronted by a decline in the availability of Prussian aristocrats for envoyships, the Foreign Office's insistence on qualities it held to be essentially aristocratic led it to look for replacements not among the bourgeoisie but among the nobility of the other German states. Although the number of bourgeois in the diplomatic service increased greatly from 1871 to 1914, middle-class diplomats tended to fill subaltern posts in Berlin rather than positions, both high and low, in the field. The tenuous claim of bourgeois diplomats to envoyships showed no appreciable variation between 1871 and 1914, while the non-Prussian nobles in such posts increased strikingly in the 1880s and 1890s. The Foreign Office's determination to preserve the aristocratic stripe of its ambassadors and ministers was successful, for from 1901 to 1914, 88.24 percent of the Prussian-imperial envoys were nobles, a figure which compared favorably with 87.50 percent for the period from 1871 to 1880.

These figures pose two questions. First, why did the representation of Prussian aristocrats in the ranks of envoys decline so markedly between 1871 and 1900? Second, why was there a recovery after 1900?

Bismarck's hostility to the arrogant *Besserwissen* of some Junker diplomats may account in part for the decline in

Prussian envoys up to 1890, but the fact that the shrinkage continued during the decade following his retirement would indicate that there were reasons for the withdrawal of Prussian nobles from envoyships which had nothing to do with the Iron Chancellor.[76] It seems likely that the primary cause for the retreat from 1871 to 1900 of Prussian aristocrats as envoys and for their departure from the diplomatic corps at large was the agricultural depression which became perceptible in the early 1870s and critical by the beginning of the following decade. The depression affected landowners in the East Elbian provinces of Prussia with particular severity. Encouraged by the rising grain prices which had prevailed from 1830 to 1870, they had become convinced that this favorable trend was one which would prove permanent. Farm land, which therefore was in great demand, rose in cost, and the result was that farmers had to borrow increasing sums of money, on which interest was rising. Wages for agricultural labor also increased. The system was tolerable only so long as grain prices continued their ascent, but, beginning about 1872, the market began to show some weakening because of the importation of cheaper foreign grains. The downward turn was temporarily stemmed at the end of the decade because of food shortages, but after 1881 grain prices began a decline which was not arrested until the end of the century. As prices fell, farmers were often unable to meet their mortgage payments. Some were forced to dispose of their estates; others managed to get by through practicing severe economies.[77] It was a situation in which the financial de-

[76] See pp. 77, 111 above for the chancellor's reservations about Prussians as bureaucrats.

[77] The late nineteenth-century agricultural depression in Germany has an extensive and distinguished bibliography. See especially Karl W. Hardach, *Die Bedeutung wirtschaftlicher Faktoren bei der Wiedereinführung der Eisen- und Getreidezölle in Deutschland* (Berlin, 1967), esp. pp. 80–100; Wilhelm Abel, *Agrarkrisen und Agrarkonjunktur: eine Geschichte der Land- und Ernährungswirtschaft Mitteleuropas seit dem hohen Mittelalter* (Hamburg, 1966), esp. pp.

mands of the diplomatic service became increasingly insupportable.

The extent to which East Elbian farmers may have rescued themselves through diversification is difficult to measure. Adverse grain prices did not result in a reduction of the hectarage under cultivation in such crops. Intensity of farming declined slightly from the late 1870s until about 1896, after which the yield per hectare planted in rye, wheat, and oats showed extraordinary increases. Some landowners profited by a timely conversion to, or intensification of, animal husbandry, for beef rose noticeably in value, while pork commanded a steady price in the marketplace from 1870 to 1914. There is a marked increase in cattle and pig raising east of the Elbe in the 1880s, and much of the profit acquired from this investment undoubtedly flowed to noble accounts. Some aristocrats may also have won an advantage from the formidable chicken culture which emerged in East Prussia at the end of the century. The government did not keep statistics on fowl until shortly after 1900, and the 1907 report showed some 30,000,000 chickens east of the Elbe.

The involvement of the German diplomatic corps in agriculture is difficult to substantiate with exactitude because the data on the financial position of German diplomats, apart from their salaries, is very thin. The service was preponderantly aristocratic and the pursuit of agriculture was the business of many nobles. Diplomatic fortunes were therefore often connected with the land. The nature of this

---

253–61; Heinz Haushofer, *Die deutsche Landwirtschaft im technischen Zeitalter* (Stuttgart, 1963), pp. 205–8. Hans Rosenberg, "Die Demokratisierung der Rittergutsbesitzerklasse," in Wilhelm Berges and Carl Hinrichs, eds., *Zur Geschichte und Problematik der Demokratie: Festgabe für Hans Herzfeld* (Berlin, 1958), pp. 459–86, is of considerable interest on the fortunes of the aristocracy in this period. Prices for agricultural products are conveniently summarized in Alfred Jacobs and Hans Richter, *Die Grosshandelspreise in Deutschland von 1792 bis 1934* (Berlin, 1935).

TABLE 18

CROP AREAS IN EAST ELBIAN PRUSSIA IN HECTARES

Date	Rye	Wheat	Oats
1878	3,058,409	566,226	1,538,918
1896	3,167,942	607,720	1,620,879
1913	3,474,914	628,512	1,879,900
	Crop Yields in kgs.		
1878	3,354,695	846,467	2,023,810
1896	3,386,771	893,495	1,660,800
1913	6,333,331	1,518,515	4,114,634
	Crop Yields in kgs. per hectare		
1878	1.10	1.50	1.32
1896	1.07	1.47	1.02
1913	1.82	2.42	2.19

SOURCE: Germany, Imperial Statistical Office, *Statistisches Jahrbuch für das deutsche Reich* (Berlin, 1880–1919), 1880 ed., pp. 23, 25; 1898 ed., pp. 22–23; 1914 ed., pp. 42–43.

TABLE 19

ANIMAL HUSBANDRY IN EAST ELBIAN PRUSSIA

Date	Cattle	Pigs
1873	5,669,236	2,913,029
1883	5,852,615	3,970,629
1897	7,058,200	6,010,700
1907	8,090,547	9,635,026

NOTE: Figures are from the *Statistisches Jahrbuch*, 1881 ed., p. 28; 1890 ed., p. 20; 1900 ed., p. 27; 1910 ed., p. 46. For beef and pork retail prices in Prussia, see Ashok V. Desai, *Real Wages in Germany, 1871–1913* (Oxford, 1968), p. 70.

relationship can be illuminated by an analysis of the 187 men appointed to envoyships between 1871 and 1914. Of these 187, fifty-two (27.81 percent) can be identified as landowners. Another forty-one (21.93 percent) were sons of landlords, and for these it is probable that their patrimony, if there was any, was based on agriculture. Thus at least ninety-three (49.74 percent) of all envoys had some connection with the land, and it is possible that some of those for whom biographical data is minimal were also landowners or sons of landowners. Since fifty of the fifty-two landowning diplomats and all but two of those with landlord fathers were nobles, the concentration of landowning or land-based fortunes was higher among the aristocratic envoys. Of the 158 *noble* envoys, eighty-nine (56.33 percent) are known to have been personally associated with the land or had such a connection through their fathers.

TABLE 20

AGRICULTURAL PROFILE OF ENVOYS

# Diplomats appointed to first envoyship	1871–1880		1881–1890		1891–1900		1901–1914	
	48		34		40		65	
	Noble envoys from East Elbian Prussia							
	#	%	#	%	#	%	#	%
Landowning envoys	8	16.67	4	11.76	1	2.50	11	16.92
Non-landowning sons of landowners	7	14.58	6	17.65	2	5.00	7	10.77
Total	15	31.25	10	29.41	3	7.50	18	27.69
	Other Prussian noble envoys							
Landowning envoys	4	8.33	2	5.88	1	2.50	2	3.08
Non-landowning sons of landowners	1	2.08	1	2.94	—	—	—	—
Total	5	10.41	3	8.82	1	2.50	2	3.08
Total of all landowning envoys and non-landowning sons of landowners	20	41.66	13	38.23	4	10.00	20	30.77
	Non-Prussian noble envoys							
Landowning envoys	4	8.33	2	5.88	7	17.50	4	6.15
Non-landowning sons of landowners	1	2.08	4	11.76	5	12.50	5	7.69
Total	5	10.41	6	17.64	12	30.00	9	13.84
	Bourgeois envoys							
Landowning envoys	—	—	—	—	1	2.50	1	1.54
Non-landowning sons of landowners	1	2.08	1	2.94	—	—	—	—
Total	1	2.08	1	2.94	1	2.50	1	1.54
Grand Total	26	54.15	20	58.81	17	42.50	30	46.15

NOTE: Each diplomat is entered in the decade in which he was first appointed as envoy. Those receiving such posts before 1871 are tabulated under 1871–1880.

TABLE 21
AGRICULTURAL PROFILE OF ENVOYS

	1871–1880		1881–1890		1891–1900		1901–1914	
# Envoys in service	48		60		76		102	
	Noble envoys from East Elbian Prussia							
	#	%	#	%	#	%	#	%
Landowning envoys	8	16.67	8	13.33	7	9.21	14	13.73
Non-landowning sons of landowners	7	14.58	9	15.00	4	5.26	9	8.82
Total	15	31.25	17	28.33	11	14.47	23	22.55
	Other Prussian noble envoys							
Landowning envoys	4	8.33	5	8.34	4	5.26	5	4.90
Non-landowning sons of landowners	1	2.08	2	3.33	2	2.63	1	.98
Total	5	10.41	7	11.67	6	7.89	6	5.88
Total of all landowning envoys and non-landowning sons of landowners	20	41.66	24	40.00	17	22.36	29	28.43
	Non-Prussian noble envoys							
Landowning envoys	4	8.33	4	6.66	9	11.84	9	8.82
Non-landowning sons of landowners	1	2.08	5	8.34	10	13.16	9	8.82
Total	5	10.41	9	15.00	19	25.00	18	17.64
	Bourgeois envoys							
Landowning envoys	—	—	—	—	1	1.32	1	.98
Non-landowning sons of landowners	1	2.08	2	3.33	1	1.32	—	—
Total	1	2.08	2	3.33	2	2.64	1	.98
Grand Total	26	54.15	35	58.33	38	50.00	48	47.05

NOTE: Each diplomat is entered in each decade in which he served as envoy.

The chronological and geographical distribution of the eighty-nine noble landowning or land-based envoys is suggestive. The percentage of all noble envoys who owned land declined from 33.33 percent in the period from 1871 to 1880 to 26.31 percent in the 1890s, then staged a recovery to 27.45 percent in the period from 1901 to 1914 (Table 21. Table 20 indicates profile of *new* envoys.)

181

Since there was certainly no prejudice in the Wilhelm-strasse against landed envoys and since the posts which went begging for East Elbian aristocrats, whether land-owners or not, were the socially and professionally desirable European ministries, there was clearly no negative change in the process of selection or in the conditions of service that would have led them to retire. This suggests that an exogenous factor accounts for their retreat, and it is likely that this was the fact that the operation of estates had become less compatible with service as a diplomat.

The geographical differentiation of those envoys having some connection with the land provides a sharper focus on the location of Germany's agricultural difficulties. Tables 20 and 21 indicate that during the period from 1871 to 1900, while *Prussian* noble landlords and landlord sons among envoys declined with increased force, noble envoys from elsewhere in Germany who had agricultural interests show an increase in this period. What is the reason for this difference? It would seem likely that the fall of Prussian landed envoys up to 1900 and their rise thereafter was related to the fact that the agricultural depression was a misfortune which especially affected the sort of one-crop grain estate typical of the Prussian nobility. In some cases the scale of the disaster was enormous. Count Hugo von Radolinski, a diplomat-landowner from Posen, complained in 1884 to Holstein that as a result of an incompetent agent—one hired on the Bismarcks' recommendation—and a bad harvest he had lost no less than 250,000 marks in one year.[78] Radolinski was very wealthy and could absorb the loss, but many landlords, and especially those in the east, undoubtedly discovered that diplomatic careers for their sons or for themselves were now simply beyond their means. On the other hand, the south-central agricultural estates, at least some of which were smaller, less dependent on one-crop farming or more

[78] Radolinski to FvH, June 5, 1884, HolN 3859/H194897–99; Radolinski to HvB, Nov. 3, 1879, and Apr. 9, 1881, BisN FC 2974/ 1119–22.

susceptible to viniculture or metallurgy, and less encumbered by debt, were perhaps more resilient in the throes of agricultural depression.

All German farmers, however, felt some form of hardship during the crisis, and that meant that the management of estates could no longer be handled in cavalier fashion. Determination, ingenuity, and improvement were now essential, and landowners could no longer afford to be away from their property for extended periods. But this sort of absenteeism was of course very often demanded of diplomats. Some Foreign Office officials, such as Lichnowsky, had to forsake their diplomatic careers in order to look after their property. Still other landlord-diplomats found that the performance of their duties as envoys inevitably entailed neglect of their estates.[79] The agricultural depression did not affect only the ranks of ministers and ambassadors; it also complicated the lives of subordinate officials. Some, like the Posener Count Bogdan von Hutten-Czapski, felt compelled to leave the service in the opening stages of their careers in order to deal with the decline of their agricultural incomes. Several others, such as Count Wilhelm von Redern, first secretary in St. Petersburg in 1883, had to retire on the eve of their appointments as envoys because of agricultural difficulties—in Redern's case, his estates in Brandenburg—which required their immediate and total attention.[80] There continued to be a number of prominent East Elbian landlords among German diplomats on into the twentieth century. But economic exigencies probably led much of the nobility of Prussia, and especially those who resided east of the Elbe, to avoid expensive offices and to seek instead positions in branches of the bureaucracy that were finan-

[79] Radolinski to FvH, July 30, 1883, HolN 3859/H195083–84; Otto von Bülow to HvB, Nov. 30, 1879, BisN FC 2958/1147–48; Vitzthum to HvB, June 12, 1883, ibid., FC 2983/844; Hohenlohe to Max Ratibor, Apr. 19, 1884, HohN, XX.E.6; Reichstag, Feb. 25, 1878, pp. 202–3 (Bismarck).

[80] Hutten-Czapski, Sechzig Jahre, I, 27.

cially less demanding, or to resign themselves to eking out a living from their estates. Since diplomatic salaries were deliberately set below the cost of service, envoys and lesser officials had to rely on their private incomes. When these evaporated, diplomatic careers were no longer possible, unless, as was sometimes the case, the lure of office overcame a reluctance to go into debt.

The recovery after 1900 of the Prussian landed interest among the envoys, one which was rather modest (Tables 20 and 21), is perhaps related to the lifting of the agricultural depression at the end of the century and to the protectionist tariff adopted in 1902. Agricultural prices rose after 1896, but they failed to return to predepression levels.[81] The increase in East Elbians after 1900 is also doubtless due in part to the awareness and concern of the Foreign Office at the decline of Prussian nobles in the diplomatic service and to its determination to do something about it. In the 1890s the Wilhelmstrasse, although it introduced no provision for making the service financially more attractive, made a determined effort to enlist Prussian nobles. As a result, by the period from 1901 to 1914, these recruits were beginning to appear in the ranks of envoys (Tables 16 and 17).[82]

A diplomat's means, like the circumstances of his birth, were a factor in his career. Because of the enormous demands the service placed on an envoy's income, the Wilhelmstrasse made some attempt to see to it that its less wealthy senior diplomats were not accredited to expensive capitals.[83] The Foreign Office believed that the relationship between states was affected by the impression which an envoy's style and that of his establishment made on a foreign court or government, as well as on the country's press and public opinion. A shabby embassy could be regarded

[81] See note 77 above.

[82] See pp. 74–78 above for the incidence of Prussians among recruits to the diplomatic service.

[83] Monts, "Unsere Diplomatie," p. 84.

as a sign of German indifference to the nation concerned or as an indication that Germany was not a power of the first magnitude. If the legation of one great power was notable as a particularly brilliant center of society, it became necessary for the other powers to try to keep up. This required riches, political grace, and socially adept châtelaines. Eulenburg, always attuned to the social factor, warned William II in 1894 that the elegant Austrian ministry in Munich would entice the Bavarians into the Habsburg camp if Prussia did not succeed in maintaining an equally impressive representation. In similar fashion, Schweinitz advised Chancellor Caprivi in 1892 that his replacement as ambassador in St. Petersburg should have a wife whose éclat could match that of the Marquise de Montebello at the French embassy.[84]

Among other factors, a prospective envoy's social rank and his age had to be considered. The Foreign Office maintained the embassies as the exclusive preserve of noblemen, while bourgeois diplomats usually found haven only in the lesser ministries on distant continents.

TABLE 22

DIPLOMATIC POSITIONS OF NOBLE AND BOURGEOIS DIPLOMATS

	Noble		Bourgeois		Total	
	#	%	#	%	#	%
Embassies	33	100.00	—	—	33	100.00
Prussian Ministries	55	96.49	2	3.51	57	100.00
European Ministries	66	92.96	5	7.04	71	100.00
American Ministries	57	76.00	18	24.00	75	100.00
Asian Ministries	23	85.19	4	14.81	27	100.00
African Ministries	6	50.00	6	50.00	12	100.00

NOTE: Each diplomat is entered in highest post achieved.

[84] PzE to W2, Mar. 7, 1894, EN, XXVIII, 217; Schweinitz to BvB, Apr. 7, 1900, BüN 46; Alfred von Bülow to BvB, Nov. 6, 1892, ibid., 14; see also HvB to Wilhelm von Bismarck, June 18, 1885, BisN FC 3011/346; Jäckh, *Kiderlen-Wächter*, II, 173; Meisner, *Denkwürdigkeiten; Waldersee*, II, 52.

The more important assignments were entrusted by and large to more mature men, a development which in any case was usually effected by the rules of seniority. But occasionally a diplomat had to be delayed in the assumption of a post until such time as he was considered to be old enough for it.[85] Diplomatic polish, which came in various degrees of patination, was also a factor which the Wilhelmstrasse had to keep in mind. In some capitals, social grace was more useful than an enthusiasm for furthering Germany's interests, but in others the complicated nature of diplomacy required something more than a elegant mannequin.[86] Any suggestion of crudity of manners was unthinkable in Munich, Vienna, or London, but not necessarily ruinous in a New World capital such as Washington or in a semibarbarous outpost such as Sofia. A high degree of refinement was necessary in the Political Division but not particularly essential in the other branches of the Foreign Office.[87] Wit, like that forever titillating all who knew Count Monts, was suitable in Rome's permissive society but out of place at more staid courts. The Quirinal might also tolerate a degree of social abrasiveness in a German envoy which would be entirely unthinkable in the other European embassies. Diplomats without gifts for entertaining were useless in St. Petersburg, while there was no point in wasting in a back-

[85] Hohenlohe diary, Oct. 26, 1883, HohN, CC.X.11; Lichnowsky, *Abyss*, p. 2; Raschdau, *Unter Bismarck und Caprivi*, pp. 309–10.

[86] On this distinction see BvB to HvB, Mar. 17, 1887, BisN FC 2958/762–66; Hohenlohe to BvB, May 7, 1885, ibid., FC 2965/396.

[87] Count Max von Berchem to HvB, June 28, 1886, BisN FC 2953/137; BvB to HvB, Apr. 27, 1886, ibid., FC 2958/564; HvB to KvR, June 26, 1880, ibid., FC 3014/624; PzE to W2, Mar. 7, 1894, EN, XXVIII, 217; Monts to FvH, July 8, 1897, HolN 3859/ H194565; Vierhaus, *Tagebuch; Spitzemberg*, p. 547. There is only a single case, one involving Kiderlen, in which an unpolished secretary was posted to a European embassy in the hope that it would teach him some manners. Limburg-Stirum to HvB, Nov. 13, 1880, BisN FC 2370/373–74.

water post an envoy who was particularly dashing in appearance.[88]

Just as German envoys had to compete socially with representatives of other states, so had they to be able to hold their own with foreign statesmen of special talent. Schweinitz, writing to State Secretary Bülow in April 1900, noted that the primary attribute desirable in the German ambassador to St. Petersburg was not, as it had been under Schweinitz's tenure from 1876 to 1892, an ability to get on well with the tsar but to equal in adroitness Alexander III's remarkable minister of finance, Count Sergei Witte. For that reason, a seasoned diplomat was more serviceable in Russia than a Prussian general, a type for which the Romanovs had a strong inclination.[89] If, on the other hand, a foreign government accredited a particularly competent envoy in Berlin through whom negotiations could proceed, it was not vital for Germany to place a strong figure at that post.[90]

The Foreign Office also had to take into consideration how well a diplomat would suit the existing structure of a post to which he might be assigned as well as how his advancement would fit in with the composition of the service at large. In order to preserve some measure of continuity, the Wilhelmstrasse considered it undesirable to accredit new envoys or to name new division heads in Berlin when the state secretary himself was a recent appointee. Similarly, a head of mission and a first secretary should not be

---

[88] Bülow, *Denkwürdigkeiten*, I, 606; Monts to BvB, Mar. 20, 1895, BüN 106; BvB to PzE, Sept. 27, 1902, EN, LIX, 93–94; Berchem to HvB, Sept. 13, 1889, BisN FC 2954/285–86; KvR to HvB, Oct. 7, and Nov. 28, 1882, May 12, 1883, ibid., FC 3028. See also Theodor Wolff, *Der Marsch durch zwei Jahrzehnte* (Amsterdam, 1936), pp. 52–53.

[89] Schweinitz to BvB, Apr. 7, 1900, BüN 46. Bülow, Schweinitz's first secretary, also believed that the time for a general was past. BvB to HvB, Mar. 17, 1887, BisN FC 2958/762–66.

[90] Memo by HvB, Dec. 18, 1887, BisN FC 3004/441–43.

simultaneously accredited to the same post.[91] Weakness or strength in certain officials in a legation could be offset by adding to the staff a man with countervailing characteristics. Herbert Bismarck was content to let the competent but very old-fashioned Schweinitz remain in St. Petersburg as long as Bernhard Bülow, who was young and energetic, served as first secretary.[92] The shuffling of men in posts—or *revirements*, the word used in the Wilhelmstrasse—also forced the Foreign Office to weigh factors which often had little to do with the man or the post to which he was to be assigned. Sometimes an envoy was shuffled from one legation to another only because the Wilhelmstrasse's decision to forward the career of some other diplomat made the change necessary. Some diplomats won appointments not on their own merits but in order to keep the position warm for a future incumbent on whom Berlin had already settled but who was as yet unable to take up the position. The appointment of the aging Marschall von Bieberstein to London in 1912 was due, according to Lichnowsky, to the fact that Wilhelm von Stumm, the forty-three-year-old director of the Political Division, was not yet old enough to assume the embassy.[93]

Advancement in the service was thus very often related less to a diplomat's capacities for negotiation than it was to his birth, his command of riches, his sociability, or the tastes and attractiveness of his wife. If one had all, or even some, of these attributes or possessions, promotion could be expected and usually was forthcoming without complication or delay. But in the course of his career, every diplomat had to be careful not only to maintain good relations at foreign courts but also to ingratiate himself with officialdom in Berlin. The greatest asset any diplomat could possess was the

[91] TN, XIIId, 2; FvH to Kayser, Dec. 6, 1897, Kl. Erwb. 458F, 10.

[92] HvB to BvB, Aug. 27, 1884, BüN 65; same to same, Apr. 13, 1887, ibid., 66. For another similar case see HvB to FvH, May 14, 1884, HolN 3853/H190698.

[93] Lichnowsky, *Abyss*, p. 2.

good opinion of his superiors, and young men in the Wilhelmstrasse had to be wary of elder counselors, directors, and state secretaries. Diplomats in the field had to appease these luminaries and their heads of mission and, at the same time, keep on the right side of kings and chancellors and their satellites, civil and military, none of whom hesitated to involve themselves in the careers of the men who served the state as diplomats.

## CHAPTER VI

The Crown

The prerogatives of the Prussian-German sovereign insofar as they affected diplomacy were set forth in the Prussian constitution of 1851 and in that of the empire, promulgated in April 1871. Articles 47 and 48 of the Prussian charter reserved to the crown the right to make all appointments and to conclude treaties. The imperial constitution in article 11 declared that the emperor would represent the empire in foreign affairs, conclude treaties and accredit and receive envoys. Article 18 extended the same general appointive powers the sovereign enjoyed in Prussia.[1] The crown's authority in matters of personnel was thus absolute. Furthermore, neither the constitution of Prussia nor that of the empire reserved any policy-making functions to the federal states, with the exception of a Bundesrat committee on foreign affairs under the chairmanship of Bavaria. Bismarck never allowed this body any power, however, and in 1879 it was permitted to lapse. The commission was revived in 1908 but it never acquired any meaningful authority.

The sovereign was therefore in a position to exercise complete control over the Foreign Office, its personnel and its policies. In practice, however, only one of the three Prussian king-emperors elected to make full use of his extraordinary prerogatives. William I was disposed to leave many, though by no means all, diplomatic matters to Bismarck, and during his brief reign Frederick III was too ill to exercise any direction over the Wilhelmstrasse. William II was much more inclined than his father or grandfather to assert his position and he interferred frequently in the Foreign Office, insisting on having his way concerning men as well

---

[1] Ernst R. Huber, *Dokumente zur deutschen Verfassungsgeschichte,* 3 vols. (Stuttgart, 1961–66), I, 406; II, 293.

as measures. After Bismarck's dismissal in 1890 the kaiser encountered no effective bureaucratic obstacles. During his reign, German diplomacy was usually regarded, and for good reason, as a reflection of the sovereign rather than of the chancellor or the Wilhelmstrasse.

The crown's exercise of its prerogatives in all three reigns was almost exclusively devoted to matters of diplomatic policy and senior appointments. It played a negligible role in enlisting men in the diplomatic service. William I and his successors were generally content to sign diplomatic commissions presented to them by the Foreign Office. Occasionally, however, the ruler might intervene to facilitate the entry of a novice or an old friend into the service. Friedrich von Holstein was a case in point. In 1861, eager to join the corps but rejected by the Prussian Minister of Foreign Affairs because he lacked sufficient legal training, he appealed to the regent. Prince William acknowledged Holstein's plea and he was admitted at once.[2] On the other hand, the Wilhelmstrasse was not always willing to accommodate royal protégés. In 1880, the Prussian crown princess enlisted the aid of the acting state secretary, Ambassador Hohenlohe, to support the entry of a son of the celebrated mythologist, Wilhelm Grimm. Herbert Bismarck, to whom the matter was entrusted, protested that he knew nothing about Grimm, whose candidacy got no further.[3]

Rulers of other German states enjoyed some influence in the Wilhelmstrasse but they seem rarely to have applied it to obtain their subjects' entry into the service.[4] The satellite entourages at the various German courts similarly played

[2] Helmuth Rogge, ed., *Friedrich von Holstein: Lebensbekenntnis in Briefen an eine Frau* (Berlin, 1932), pp. 17–23.

[3] Memo by Hohenlohe, July 11, 1881, HohN, XX.H.3; FvH to HvB, July 29, 1880, BisN FC 2966/451–52.

[4] Only two cases of such influence are recorded. See Hajo Holborn, ed., *Aufzeichnungen und Erinnerungen aus dem Leben des Botschafters Joseph Maria von Radowitz*, 2 vols. (Berlin, 1925), I, 352, and a letter by Kiderlen of Oct. 12, 1879, in Georg Cleinow, "Diplomaten-Erziehung: eine Erinnerungen zu Bismarcks Geburtstag," *Die Grenzboten*, LXXII, no. 13 (1913), 589–90.

almost no role in influencing admissions, assignments, or promotions. The Civil Cabinet and the retinue of the Prussian crown did, however, occasionally prevent patents of nobility or diplomatic positions being awarded to bourgeois or *Neuadel* who aspired to diplomatic careers. One example of such interference concerned Captain Karl Grumme, a naval adjutant to William II. In 1900, Grumme married the daughter of the kaiser's industrialist friend, Count Hugo Douglas, and the wedding was marked by the bestowal of a patent of nobility on the groom. Herr von Grumme now hoped to become a diplomat, but the court in Berlin was opposed because he was the son of a merchant. Grumme's application did not prosper, and William II had to prevail upon his friend, Albert Ballin, the managing director of the Hamburg-American Line, to offer Grumme a position.[5]

The first of Germany's three emperors, William I (1871–1888), was exceptional only in his longevity. He had, however, a number of attractive attributes, among which were an appropriate sense of his position, a redoubtable energy, and some awareness of his intellectual limitations. He was quiet, agreeable, prosaic, and also somewhat reluctant to act forcefully. In his old age—he was almost seventy-four when proclaimed emperor—he took no interest in arts or letters, had no cosmopolitan tastes, and was content to attend to affairs of state and be mindful of his health. The king-emperor cared little for society save for a mild interest in the theater and a more pronounced attraction to the pleasures of the hunt. Neither diversion was allowed to interfere with work, and in the execution of his duty William was very methodical and thorough. Only as he approached ninety did his energy begin to fade.

It would be difficult to imagine two men who were as unlike as Otto von Bismarck and his royal master. The Iron Chancellor was volcanic, abusive, and vindictive. Morose

---

[5] Baron Robert Lucius von Ballhausen, *Bismarck-Erinnerungen* (Stuttgart, 1921), p. 373; Rogge, *Holstein: Lebensbekenntnis*, p. 334.

where William was pleasant, Bismarck was self-indulgent, adventurous, petty, and careless. The two men did share personal fearlessness and a distaste for society, although both could be charming if they chose. William's withdrawn nature was born of shyness and modesty, while Bismarck's proceeded from misanthropy. If William was punctilious in insisting that his authority be respected, the chancellor was imperious in his conduct of affairs. Occasions arose on which royal prerogative clashed with Bismarck's autocratic temperament. The king and the chancellor were a strange and unsettling combination, and it surprised no one that their relations were often tempestuous. Not long after William's death Bismarck confided to a friend that "in my long ministerial career I have always found that the most difficult problems of diplomacy are the relations with one's own court."[6]

Bismarck regarded William, to whom he usually referred as "*der alte Herr*," with more than respect but less than veneration. The chancellor appreciated the sturdy personal qualities of his sovereign but he found his insistence on prerogative annoying, his manner a trifle flat and dry, and some of his notions concerning foreign affairs dead wrong. Their relationship was that of master and servant, not that of friends, and both kept the other at a distance. The chancellor, by his own admission, often let State Secretary Bernhard Ernst von Bülow, a master of the sonorous flattery and unctuous parlance to which William was susceptible and for which Bismarck himself had little talent, deal with the ruler.[7]

An always disturbing element in Bismarck's relationship with his sovereign was the redoubtable Queen-Empress Augusta. Married to William in 1828, this headstrong princess of Saxe-Weimar had grown increasingly temperamental with advancing years and declining health. Long before the 1870s, their marriage had settled into a formal ritual. Augusta had not been the passion of William's youth and she was not destined to be the solace of his old age. Rouged and ringletted, she was a torrent of frenetic energy. She did not talk, she lectured, an affliction derived from her childhood lessons in rhetoric addressed to empty chairs. She meddled incessantly in state affairs, kept a busy salon in her celebrated *bonbonnière* in the Unter den Linden palace and made herself generally tiresome and sometimes quite obnoxious. No one other than William I suffered from her whims and caprices so much as Bismarck, and no one was so capable of enraging her as was the chancellor.

Their rivalry was of long standing, for from almost their first acquaintance in the 1840s they had discovered an antipathy which was to become deep and enduring. Augusta never forgot that in 1848 Bismarck had tried to dispossess William of his claim to the Prussian throne, and as a cosmopolitan princess of Weimar she identified in Bismarck, quite incorrectly, the eponym of the narrow, pedestrian, unlettered Prussian Junker. Her love was France, and throughout her life she surrounded herself with French readers and French servants, making transparent her inclination for France, Roman Catholicism, and Poles. Augusta's defective patriotism, as the chancellor characterized these wayward tastes, was not the worst of her faults. He was even prepared to admit that she was intelligent. What he could not excuse was her interference in diplomacy. Augusta corresponded with foreign sovereigns, inferring that she did so on behalf of her consort. She gossiped with ambassadors, and one prominent member of her circle in the 1870s was the royalist French envoy, Baron Elie de Gontaut. Although the German ambassador in Paris considered Gontaut to be a harmless tittletattler, Bismarck insisted that he was dangerous and had to be removed. In 1877 Gontaut was replaced by Count St. Vallier, a republican who steered clear of Augusta.[8]

[8] Hohenlohe diary, May 18, Sept. 8, and Dec. 8, 1875, HohN, XX.C.3; diary for Mar. 19, 1877, ibid., XX.C.4; Hans Goldschmidt,

If Bismarck could not bear opposition from a king whom he respected, it is not surprising that he was even more determined to reduce an opponent he neither liked nor admired. William's notions of policy at least proceeded from principle, whereas the chancellor believed that Augusta's opposition was often grounded in prejudice. If he was for something, she led the opposition against it. She was, Bismarck believed, the rallying point for all his other enemies. The unfortunate king, subjected to the incessant barrages of his *"Feuerkopf,"* yielded to her so as not to have to endure more. There was nothing quite like her, and Augusta, like Ludwig Windthorst, was one of the few enemies Bismarck never succeeded in pulverizing. "She made more trouble for me than all the foreign powers put together," he confessed. "The struggle against her upset me more than all my other difficulties."[9]

William I almost always dealt openly with Bismarck. Although he was inclined, to Bismarck's irritation, to keep reports from military attachés to himself for as long as several weeks before forwarding them, he was not one to go behind the chancellor's back in diplomacy. Bismarck himself admitted that William always kept him fully informed and was receptive to his arguments when they disagreed.[10] The only exception to this open relationship was the special privilege William accorded to Count Harry von Arnim, ambassador in Paris from 1871 to 1874, and later to Count Georg Herbert zu Münster, while envoy in London from 1873 to 1885, to send reports directly to the ruler rather than to the Wilhelmstrasse. As far as the chancellor was concerned the problem with Arnim, which largely centered on Bismarck's fear that the ambassador was conspiring to succeed him, was resolved in 1874, when Ar-

"Mitarbeiter Bismarcks im aussenpolitischen Kampf," *Preussiche Jahrbücher,* CCXXV (Jan. 1934), 43–44.

[9] GW, XV, 432–35; Lucius von Ballhausen, *Bismarck-Erinnerungen,* p. 110; Hermann Hoffmann, *Fürst Bismarck, 1890–1898 . . . ,* 3 vols. (Stuttgart, 1913–14), I, 183–84.

[10] GW, IX, 88.

nim fled abroad after criminal charges had been leveled against him following the discovery that documents from the embassy files were missing.[11] State Secretary Bülow, like Bismarck, disapproved of ambassadorial circumvention of the Foreign Office and in 1876 persuaded the kaiser to agree that, in the future when the sovereign was in Berlin, Münster's reports would go first to the Wilhelmstrasse but that when William was not in the capital the ambassador could write to him directly.[12] Bismarck, who had a high regard for Münster ("the best horse in my diplomatic stall"), wrote to the envoy pointing out that for ambassadors to send reports directly to the ruler was a violation of diplomatic tradition. He concluded by noting that "we are too old friends to take such things in a pointed way (*pointilliös*), but if Bülow were here [in Berlin] he would probably make a *Cabinetsfrage* out of it."[13] Münster did not comply at once with Bismarck's request, but eventually he ceased to correspond with the kaiser.

Bismarck did not treat his sovereign with the same frankness. His compromising negotiations with Marshal Prim on the eve of the Franco-Prussian war are the most significant example of his devious diplomacy. Even in the more mundane daily conduct of business, Bismarck was reluctant to keep William informed, less out of fear of royal opposition or obstruction than because the more the kaiser knew the more bothersome he was likely to be. Senility was not the grounds for the chancellor's evasiveness, for his complaints about the time and trouble William I took long antedated the ruler's dotage. The root of the problem lay in William's tirelessness in the execution of his responsibilities, and for-

[11] Johannes Penzler, ed., *Kaiser- und Kanzler-Briefe: Briefwechsel zwischen Kaiser Wilhelm I. und Fürst Bismarck* (Leipzig, 1900), p. 115.

[12] BvB to Radowitz, July 1, 1876, Gen 1 AA.a.61, vol. 2, 279/00608–10.

[13] Letter of July 6, 1876, MünsterN 4. A draft of the letter in HvB's hand is in BisN FC 2973/585–87. See also Lother Bucher to HvB, July 19, 1875, ibid., FC 2957/632.

eign affairs were a particular object of his attention. Bismarck ruefully declared in May 1876 that William was more and more showing signs of being his own foreign minister.[14] The ruler required that diplomatic dispatches, and not merely Wilhelmstrasse resumés of incoming correspondence, be laid before him. These documents then prompted a stream of royal questions and comments, which, to the chancellor's irritation, had to be answered.[15] If the reports submitted to William referred by number to earlier dispatches, he often would want to reread the older material as well. In William's old age the problem was compounded by his failing memory, for he could no longer always remember what he had read and consequently was prone to claim that Bismarck was keeping things from him.[16] Besides, if Bismarck felt that the views expressed in the sovereign's marginalia were wrong, to say so and to steer William back into the approved course of action required an elaborate exercise in courtly grandiloquence. To forestall the kaiser's questions, Bismarck instructed envoys not to refer to earlier dispatches, an order which put the ruler off the scent but which made it difficult for the Wilhelmstrasse to note the proper sequence of reports. The chancellor concluded that it would have been altogether better had William spent his hours at his desk playing solitaire.[17]

The issue of prerogative was only one of the divisions between William I and Bismarck. Differing ambitions had been the cause of their difficulties before 1871, for the sovereign had by no means shared the statesman's obsession with German unification nor had he always approved of Bismarck's maneuvers to realize his goal. William also viewed with distaste the chancellor's predilection for politi-

[14] Lucius von Ballhausen, *Bismarck-Erinnerungen*, p. 90.

[15] Ibid., p. 70; memo by FvH, July 2, 1900, BüN 91; see also GW, VIII, 384–85; XV, 431.

[16] Hohenlohe diary, Jan. 20, 1880, HohN, CC.X.8; diary for Oct. 22, 1881, ibid., CC.X.9.

[17] Lucius von Ballhausen, *Bismarck-Erinnerungen*, p. 70.

cal innovation, especially if—as in the broad Reichstag franchise devised by Bismarck—it appeared liberal, if not radical. He felt ideologically more comfortable with Moltke, Roon, and other superannuated stalwarts of his magnificent army. The conservative Roon was an especially close associate, and he could usually be found in the kaiser's anteroom, leafing through documents. Roon also disapproved of the chancellor's liberalism, and Bismarck for his part thought the old field marshal senile and narrowminded.[18]

There were also differences of policy between William and Bismarck after 1871. In the first decade of the empire's existence, the chancellor's diplomacy in both the East and the West seemed to William to be moving onto dangerous ground. Although both men agreed that France thirsted for revenge, they were at odds as to how the danger should be handled. In Bismarck's view, as long as the monarchical faction in France was in control, France would be more likely to attack Germany because she would find support at foreign courts. The purpose of German diplomacy therefore should be to support the republicans, who were also revanchist but who, for the moment at least, seemed less likely to undertake an attack across the Rhine. Germany consequently had to be ever vigilant. The chancellor feared that William, too much under the influence of the royal sympathist Arnim, did not fully share either his policy or his sense of alarm. The kaiser, who was ideologically suspicious of republicans, declared that he was too old to fight another war. He believed that the chancellor's conviction that France was determined on revenge was exaggerated and concluded that it was in fact Bismarck who was provoking Paris rather than the reverse. The disagreement be-

[18] HepkeN 2, entry of July 6, 1871; Erich Marks, *Kaiser Wilhelm I*, 8th ed. (Munich, 1918), pp. 355–56. Ambassador Schweinitz also did not approve of Bismarck's liberalism. See Arthur von Brauer, *Im Dienste Bismarcks: persönliche Erinnerungen* (Berlin, 1936), pp. 48–49.

tween the two became particularly marked in 1874 and 1875 during the "war in sight" crisis manufactured by Bismarck. The recently appointed ambassador in Paris, Prince Hohenlohe, fortunately enjoyed excellent relations with both king and chancellor, and he managed after several trips to Berlin and to Bismarck's Pomeranian estate at Varzin to calm the situation.[19] The electoral victory of the republicans in France in May, 1877, and the subsequent elimination of the royalist faction as a serious contender for power finally dispelled the differences between Bismarck and his chief on this point.[20]

The disagreement between the two men regarding eastern policy was even more acute. William I believed that Germany's orientation lay toward the East, to St. Petersburg. The neighboring monarchies were drawn to one another by a common appreciation for conservative statecraft, religion, and by a suspicion of the modern West. The Romanovs and Hohenzollerns were dynastically related and William had a particular affection for his nephew, Alexander II. The Prussian sovereign believed that the ties, especially those of a military nature, between the Neva and the Spree should be cultivated and strengthened.

The maintenance of the Russian connection became an acute point of controversy between Bismarck and William I at the end of the 1870s. While the chancellor was prepared to accept the inconvenience that the ruler's insistence on prerogative sometimes occasioned in the conduct of official business, on questions of *grosse Politik* he was unwilling to compromise. Bismarck's growing suspicion of Russia, which was based in part on what he believed to be the inordinate territorial appetite St. Petersburg had revealed in the Russo-Turkish war of 1877 and 1878, his anger at having

[19] Hohenlohe diary for Aug. 31, Oct. 24–25, Nov. 9, 1874, HohN, XX.C.1.

[20] For Bismarck's difficulties with William I concerning France in 1876–77 see OvB to State Secretary von Bülow, Oct. 11, 1876, and May 15, 1877, in BisN FC 2957/1065–70, 1023–28.

become an object of pan-Slav vituperation, and his resentment that the tsar had criticized the settlement he had forged at the Congress of Berlin, led him more and more to the notion of an alliance with Vienna, and specifically a defensive one with Russia as the putative troublemaker. The kaiser was absolutely determined to frustrate Bismarck's plan, and he was also plainly upset. "I cannot tell you," he wrote to the chancellor on September 10, 1879, "how painful this incident has been to me inasmuch as it is the first time in seventeen years that we appear unable to agree."[21] Bismarck was no less distressed; it was, he declared, as though a dearly beloved wife had been found unfaithful. At the same time, he was obdurate. Bathetic scenes ensued in which threats of resignation were countered by intimations of abdication.[22] The emperor, whose tenacity did not equal Bismarck's, eventually abandoned the struggle and in October, 1879, very reluctantly accepted the Austrian pact. He was provoked with the chancellor, but once the document had been signed he ceased to complain about it. Roon's death in the same year removed a complicating factor in the emperor's relations with Bismarck, and in the last nine years of William's reign there were no further serious disagreements between the two men concerning matters of policy.

William I had distinct preferences on matters of diplomatic personnel and these did not always coincide with Bismarck's. The sovereign usually let the chancellor have his way, but on occasion, such as the struggle in 1885 to have Herbert Bismarck appointed state secretary, Bismarck had to break down the kaiser's resistance.[23] As far as Wil-

[21] Ibid., FC 2985/751–58.

[22] Hohenlohe diary, Sept. 14 and 22, 1879, HohN, CC.X.7; Lucius von Ballhausen, *Bismarck-Erinnerungen*, pp. 172, 180. Radowitz, who as acting state secretary had many dealings with the kaiser, noted that firmness was the way to bring William around. See BisN, FC 2975/54–56.

[23] Heinrich O. Meisner, ed., *Denkwürdigkeiten des General-Feldmarschalls Alfred Grafen von Waldersee*, 3 vols. (Stuttgart, 1923–25), I, 292.

liam was concerned, diplomats were a species to be avoided. He did not care much for the foreign colony in Berlin and he was not close to very many of his own envoys.[24] But he had a serious interest in the careers of civil servants of high rank. Even when recovering his equilibrium following two assassination attempts in the summer of 1878, he interfered constantly in diplomatic appointments arranged by Bismarck and by the regent, Crown Prince Frederick William.[25] Once attracted to anyone, a body servant or a lofty bureaucrat, the ruler was loath to let him go, for he liked things and people to be familiar. This is why he persisted, over Bismarck's objections, in retaining Count Arnim in Paris and Count Albrecht von Bernstorff in London, and in appointing his old friend Baron Karl von Werther minister to Constantinople in 1874.[26] Werther was known as the *Kriegs-Botschafter* since he had served in Copenhagen in 1864, in Vienna in 1866, in Paris in 1870, and in Constantinople in 1878. Being himself an elderly man, William I was inclined to prefer middle-aged men for distinguished appointments or elevations in bureaucratic titles. He would sometimes reject names submitted to him for ambassadorial or ministerial posts because the candidates in his opinion were not yet ripe.[27] William was partic-

---

[24] Ludwig Raschdau, *Unter Bismarck und Caprivi: Erinnerungen eines deutschen Diplomaten aus den Jahren 1885–1894* (Berlin, 1939), p. 174.

[25] Hohenlohe diary, Nov. 16, 1878, HohN, CC.X.5; Lucius von Ballhausen, *Bismarck-Erinnerungen*, p. 147.

[26] Penzler, *Kaiser- und Kanzler-Briefe*, pp. 110, 115; Lucius von Ballhausen, *Bismarck-Erinnerungen*, pp. 62–63; Paul Knaplund, ed., *Letters from the Berlin Embassy: Selections from the Private Correspondence of British Representatives at Berlin and Foreign Secretary Granville, 1871–1874, 1880–1885* (Washington, 1944), pp. 96–97; Holborn, *Aufzeichnungen; Radowitz*, I, 290. For Bismarck's negative opinion of Werther see HvB to State Secretary Bülow, BisN FC 2958/45–46.

[27] Lucius von Ballhausen, *Bismarck-Erinnerungen*, p. 86; Holborn, *Aufzeichnungen; Radowitz*, I, 262. He declined Bismarck's request to make the thirty-five-year-old Herbert von Bismarck a *Wirklicher*

ularly concerned that diplomats named to ambassadorships be well into middle age. In 1876, he rejected the chancellor's proposal to name fifty-two-year-old Robert von Keudell, minister to Italy, to the embassy in Vienna because William believed him to be unsuitably young. Bismarck lost on Keudell, but he did overcome the ruler's objection to youthful ambassadors, for the man who got the Habsburg post was Prince Otto zu Stolberg-Wernigerode, who was in fact not quite forty but whose youth was doubtless offset by the fact that he was a mediatized aristocrat of impeccable lineage whom Bismarck considered as a likely successor as chancellor.[28]

Keudell's rejection for the post in Vienna may also have been due to the fact that his family was undistinguished and its title was created as recently as 1789. William preferred to fill the more illustrious diplomatic assignments with aristocrats of pedigree, and it was not until the end of the reign that Bismarck managed to overcome this prejudice.[29] Of the twelve ambassadors William appointed, four were members of royal or mediatized houses, while five were *Uradel*. Slightly more than one out of every three envoys of all grades whom he accredited were derived from such ancient and exalted lineage. At the same time, bourgeois and *Neuadel* elements were conspicuous among his envoys, especially those in lesser posts.

William I was determined to deny preferment to men whose pasts were compromised by incendiary or merely

---

Geheimer Rat when he assumed the state secretaryship in 1885. OvB to William I, Oct. 22, 1887, BisN FC 3004/417–20.

[28] The average age of William I's ambassadorial appointees was 51.89, compared to 55.09 for those of William II. The ages of Frederick III's three envoys averaged 42.33. For an example of Bismarck's persuasive recommendations for shifts of personnel see his letter to the emperor of July 5, 1885 in BisN FC 2986/87–90.

[29] Karl F. Nowak and Friedrich Thimme, eds., *Erinnerungen und Gedanken des Botschafters Anton Graf Monts* (Berlin, 1932), p. 50; HvB to KvR, Nov. 30, 1887, BisN FC 3014/1000.

TABLE 23
ANCESTRY OF ENVOYS

Antiquity of Title	William I #	William I %	Frederick III #	Frederick III %	William II #	William II %	Total #	Total %
Royal or mediatized	6	8.11	—	—	8	7.27	14	7.49
Uradel	20	27.02	3	100.00	45	40.91	68	36.36
15th–17th century	11	14.86	—	—	8	7.27	19	10.16
18th century	4	5.41	—	—	10	9.09	14	7.49
19th–20th century	16	21.62	—	—	19	17.27	35	18.71
Date of title unknown	5	6.76	—	—	3	2.73	8	4.28
Bourgeois	12	16.22	—	—	17	15.46	29	15.51
Total	74	100.00	3	100.00	110	100.00	187	100.00

NOTE: Each envoy is listed under the ruler who appointed him to his initial envoyship.

liberal political behavior. He never succeeded in overcoming a suspicion of Lothar Bucher, a counselor who enjoyed Bismarck's particular favor and who was a friend of both Mazzini and Kossuth, because of his revolutionary activities in 1848.[30] In the 1880s the chancellor toyed with the idea of securing an envoyship for the National Liberal leader, Rudolf von Bennigsen, a Hanoverian. The kaiser would have none of it, however, because of Bennigsen's opposition to the Prussian state during the unification crisis between 1862 and 1866.[31] Sometimes William I's hostility to certain diplomats was as unfathomable as it was absolute. In 1872, for example, he refused to permit Hermann von Balan, a capable Prussian Protestant of long diplomatic experience who had taken leave as minister to Belgium to serve quite satisfactorily as acting state secretary, to be made the permanent incumbent of that office. Bismarck was surprised and embarrassed that he therefore could not reward the innocent Balan. But, he noted, he had too many other wor-

[30] Holborn, *Aufzeichnungen; Radowitz*, II, 80; GW, IX, 87; undated Holstein memo, HolN 3862/H196831–32.
[31] Lucius von Ballhausen, *Bismarck-Erinnerungen*, pp. 188, 304.

ries to make a *Cabinetsfrage* out of William's opposition. Balan returned to Brussels and shortly thereafter died.[32]

When William I expired on March 9, 1888, after a brief illness, the crown prince ascended as Frederick III. The new monarch had for some years shown an interest, one which cannot be characterized as vital, in diplomatic affairs, occasionally corresponding with Bismarck about policies and appointments and maintaining contact with various envoys and counselors.[33] William I did not have a high opinion of his heir's judgment, and neither he nor Bismarck had done much to educate Frederick in the diplomatic complexities through which Germany had to find its way.[34] In the last year of the old kaiser's life, the crown prince's German physicians discovered that he had been stricken with a malignant growth on the larynx. By the early fall it was clear to everyone (except the crown princess, who pathetically insisted that English doctors could cure what she and they believed to be a much less serious malady) that Frederick was a dying man. His mortality greatly weakened his position in the Wilhelmstrasse. To Bismarck, the heir apparent's illness was an occasion for calculation rather than sympathy. He was not above reminding the crown prince's protégés, whom Frederick attempted to advance while he was still in line for the throne, that it was the prince and not the chancellor who would soon be laid in a grave. Frederick, for example, had been anxious in 1887 to secure the

---

[32] Balan to OvB, July 28, 1875, BisN FC 2953/139; GW, XIV/2, 852–53; Holborn, *Aufzeichnungen; Radowitz*, I, 277–78. For another example of William I's prejudice see GW, IX, 87.

[33] See, for example, Frederick's letters to OvB of Jan. 25, 1878, Sept. 22, 1881, and May 14, 1884, BisN FC 2962/934–36, 1022–23, 1031.

[34] HvB to OvB, Nov. 9, 1886, ibid., FC 3004/386–91; Prince Philipp zu Eulenburg-Hertefeld, *Aus 50 Jahren: Erinnerungen, Tagebücher und Briefe* (Berlin, 1923), pp. 187–88. It appears that in 1880 the crown prince tried to win a greater role for himself in diplomatic affairs but the attempt came to nothing. See FvH to HvB, July 29, 1880, BisN FC 2966/451–52.

under state secretaryship for Karl von Normann, minister to Oldenburg, who had been brought into the diplomatic service in 1884 at the crown prince's insistence. The chancellor, getting wind of the project, summoned Normann and pointedly advised him that if he was offered and took the position he would be hounded out of the service as soon as Frederick died. If, however, he remained in Oldenburg (which Bismarck conceived of as his terminal post), a change in rulers would not affect his tenure. Normann heeded Bismarck's warning.[35]

By the time Frederick came to the throne, he was barely able to perform even the ceremonial duties of his office. The Foreign Office came to a standstill awaiting the death of the sovereign. To Bismarck, such an intermission was not unwelcome. "In my entire ministerial career," he wrote with ill-concealed satisfaction in his memoirs, "the conduct of business was never so pleasant or so lacking in friction as it was during the ninety-nine days of the Emperor Frederick."[36] On earlier occasions, when William I's illnesses or advancing age had made Frederick's ascension appear imminent, the chancellor had certainly not anticipated so smooth a course of affairs. The crown prince and his English consort were both moderately liberal and very Anglophile, and their relations with the chancellor, never easy, had been punctuated over the years by a number of serious differences as well as a succession of petty quarrels. Many Germans probably shared the belief of Gerson von Bleichröder, Bismarck's financial advisor and a man of limitless connections, that Frederick would get rid of the chancellor when he came to the throne.[37] But when he finally did succeed his father it was too late. Realizing the helplessness of his position, Frederick treated the Bismarcks with defer-

[35] Holstein diary, May 14 and 22, 1884, HolN 3860/H195913–14, H195920; Brauer, *Im Dienste Bismarcks*, p. 246.

[36] Hoffmann, *Bismarck*, I, 185.

[37] Hohenlohe diary, June 8, 1883, HohN, CC.X.11; Holstein diary, Mar. 22, 1883, HolN 3860/H195710.

ence and made no changes in policy and few in personnel. He did not attempt to sack diplomats, such as Prince Heinrich VII Reuss at Vienna, whom he disliked, and he refrained from making appointments, such as accrediting Normann to Stockholm, to which Bismarck was opposed. On the other hand, he accepted with equanimity the nomination of the chancellor's son-in-law, Count Kuno von Rantzau, to become minister to Bavaria.[38] Frederick survived his father by little more than three months and on June 15, 1888, was succeeded by his twenty-nine-year-old son, William II.

*

Like any royal princeling, the new kaiser had been exposed in his youth to diplomatic society both at home and in foreign capitals. He thereby learned something of the form of diplomacy but little of its principles, for he never received any systematic instruction in the conduct of foreign affairs nor was he allowed to read any diplomatic dispatches until shortly before he ascended the throne. William's first exposure to the exercise of diplomacy came in 1884, when Bismarck suggested to William I that he send his grandson to St. Petersburg to represent the kaiser at the coming of age ceremonies for the Russian heir apparent, the later ill-fated Nicholas II. During his mission, William made a good impression on Alexander III, who was notoriously difficult to please.[39] In the course of his visit to St. Petersburg, William was taken in tow by Herbert von Bismarck, then the first secretary of the German embassy. The two began a lively correspondence while the prince was still in Russia, and this initial contact matured into a friend-

[38] HvB to BvB, Mar. 21 and 29, 1888, BüN 66.

[39] OvB to William I, May 23, 1884, HA, Rep. 54a, no. 31. See also William II's correspondence with Alexander III in ibid., Rep. 43a, no. 5; and Meisner, *Denkwürdigkeiten; Waldersee*, I, 239.

ship.[40] In August 1886, the kaiser invited his grandson to be present at a meeting at Bad Gastein with the Emperor Franz Josef, with whom William had been congenial since their first meeting in 1873. With footholds thus established both at Vienna and St. Petersburg, in September, 1886, William decided to entrust his grandson with his first real exercise in diplomacy. The prince was sent to Brest Litovsk to inform Alexander III of what had transpired at Gastein and to discuss with him the current Bulgarian crisis involving Prince Alexander of Battenberg.[41] Once again, William conducted himself circumspectly and his behavior pleased both the tsar and the kaiser.

Not long after Prince William's return from Russia, Herbert Bismarck requested that he be initiated into the workings of the Foreign Office. Because of William I's satisfaction with his grandson's diplomatic talent, he was happy to agree, for he was as attracted to his deferential and adoring grandson as he was distressed by the remote and taciturn manner of the crown prince. Furthermore, the kaiser considered Frederick to be immature and overly dependent on his English wife.[42] The crown prince, already aggravated because he had hoped to be sent to Russia to

[40] The correspondence is in BisN FC 2986/480–553. See also HvB to Wilhelm von Bismarck, May 13, 1884, ibid., FC 3011/389; HvB to FvH, May 18, 1884, HolN 3853/H190699; Meisner, *Denkwür-digkeiten; Waldersee*, I, 238–39, 281–82, 299. William II's account of the trip is in his *Aus meinem Leben, 1859–1888* (Leipzig, 1927), pp. 292–305, and in his *Ereignisse und Gestalten: aus den Jahren 1878–1918* (Leipzig, 1922), pp. 11–12.

[41] William's notes of his conversation with the tsar, a copy of which he sent to Herbert Bismarck, are in BisN FC 2986/342–45. See also his *Ereignisse und Gestalten*, pp. 12–14 and *Aus meinem Leben*, pp. 320–25.

[42] On Herbert's role see his letter to OvB, Nov. 9, 1886, BisN FC 3004/385–88; Holstein diary for Sept. 18, 1896, HolN 3861/H196201–3. On William's I's relations with his son and grandson see Eulenburg, *50 Jahren*, pp. 187–88, and also HvB to KvR, Dec. 18, 1886, BisN FC 3014/936.

represent the kaiser, was very displeased, for he himself, although in his mid-fifties, had never been granted more than partial and temporary access to diplomatic materials. He protested the fact that he had not been consulted in the matter and warned that because of his son's ignorance and impetuosity an exposure to diplomatic affairs would in fact be dangerous.[43] Nevertheless, in the fall of 1886 and on into the spring of the following year Prince William came once or twice a week to the Wilhelmstrasse, where he was shown selected documents. Herbert Bismarck, now state secretary, himself dispensed instruction in European politics, a task necessitated by Holstein's refusal to do so because of his reservations about William's discretion and because of the crown prince's objections.[44] Ludwig Raschdau, a young counselor in the *Handelspolitische Abteilung*, was put in charge of introducing William into colonial and non-European affairs. Raschdau remembered the prince as an inquisitive, though shallow, student, one whose interest in Russia was great but who showed no inclination to bother with more distant lands.[45]

William's introduction to diplomacy and to the operations of the Foreign Office gave Bismarck an opportunity to observe the Hohenzollern heir at close range. The chancellor's association with William had begun in the early 1880s, when the young and impressionable prince fell under the spell of both the chancellor and his son. Both Bismarcks were mindful of the advantage to which William's adulation

[43] HvB to OvB, Nov. 9, 1886, BisN FC 3004/386–91; Crown Prince Frederick William to OvB, Sept. 28, 1886, ibid., FC 2962/1067–69; W2 to HvB, Aug. 17, 1886, ibid., FC 2986/504–5; HvB to KvR, Nov. 2, Dec. 13 and 20, 1886, ibid., FC 3014/882, 930, 937–38; OvB to the crown prince, Oct. 2, 1887, ibid., 917. See also William II, *Aus meinem Leben*, p. 320; and GW, VIc, 347–48.

[44] Holstein diary, Sept. 18, and Dec. 1, 1886, HolN 3861/H196201–3, H196215–16.

[45] Raschdau, *Unter Bismarck und Caprivi*, pp. 15, 17; William II, *Ereignisse und Gestalten*, pp. 10–11; Meisner, *Denkwürdigkeiten; Waldersee*, I, 281–82, 299.

might eventually be put. At the same time, the prince's apprenticeship in the Wilhelmstrasse indicated to the chancellor the eagerness but also the superficiality with which William approached matters of state.

William's tour in the Wilhelmstrasse left him impressed at the total control which Bismarck exercised over the Foreign Office and only reinforced the admiration he felt for the architect of the empire over which he one day would rule. But even before he ascended the throne, William had declared that Bismarck would eventually have to retire and that the crown would then assume some of the authority accumulated by the Iron Chancellor.[46] Shortly before William II became kaiser, the first sign of the forthcoming differences between the two men appeared. The occasion was William's attraction in 1887 to the Christian Social movement of Adolf Stoecker, whose program and personality were equally repugnant to Bismarck. Neither the chancellor nor the prince, who knew that his succession to the throne was now imminent, wanted to precipitate a break, and the prince eventually disassociated himself from Stoecker. By 1889 a number of well-placed observers were noting that the chancellor's standing with the young kaiser had begun a decline likely to be permanent.[47]

The enormous difference in age between the two men— Bismarck was four years older than William II's maternal grandfather, Prince Albert—was always in the background. The kaiser was increasingly troubled by the fact that he and

[46] William II, *Ereignisse und Gestalten*, p. 3; *Aus meinem Leben*, pp. 241–42; Lucius von Ballhausen, *Bismarck-Erinnerungen*, p. 413; Adolf von Scholz, *Erlebnisse und Gespräche mit Bismarck* (Stuttgart, 1922), pp. 81–83.

[47] W2 to OvB, Dec. 21, 1887, and Jan. 14, 1888, BisN FC 2986/359–63, 386–87; two notes by PzE, one dated Dec. 29, 1887, the other undated, EN, II, 110, 113; Holborn, *Aufzeichnungen; Radowitz*, II, 295; Meisner, *Denkwürdigkeiten; Waldersee*, II, 76; Rogge, *Holstein: Lebensbekenntnis*, p. 152; Eulenburg, *50 Jahren*, pp. 224–28; FvH to Karl von Eisendecher (minister to Baden), July 5, 1889, HolN 3847/E359788–92.

Bismarck were clearly of different minds on almost all matters and that the chancellor was not in the least inclined to abandon or even to alter his view of how Germany's domestic and diplomatic affairs should be arranged. Bismarck believed that turmoil at home, especially if created by organized labor or Social Democrats, should be repressed, if necessary by arms or even by a coup d'état. Appeasement would be a sign only of weakness or dissolution. In diplomacy, he was insistent that Germany's destiny lay with the conservative monarchies, and in 1887 he had overcome his hostility to Russia sufficiently to negotiate a secret defensive alliance with the tsar. By the time William II came to the throne, Bismarck's Germany, at home and abroad, was solidly aligned with the right.

A young ruler such as William II, although conservative by instinct, was nevertheless anxious to perpetuate in himself the popularity which both his grandfather and his father had enjoyed. To do so he was convinced that he would have to be a modern ruler, compassionate, enlightened, and cautiously liberal. This would require binding the working class to the monarchy through reform rather than by trying to reduce it by force. It would also entail a less firm orientation of German diplomacy to the reactionary East.[48] In such a scheme, the chancellor's domestic and diplomatic policies were grotesquely out of place. Early in 1890 it became apparent to both men that their positions were irreconcilable and that neither was prepared to make effective compromises. When, in addition to these differences, the kaiser began to suspect that Bismarck was contesting his authority he allowed the chancellor to resign on March 22, 1890. Herbert Bismarck surrendered the state secretaryship a few days later.

With the fall of the Bismarcks, the kaiser was free to assume the direction of German diplomacy. The new chancel-

[48] As early as May, 1888, Bismarck had suspected that the kaiser did not share his views on foreign policy. W2 to OvB, May 10, 1888, BisN FC 2986/391–96.

lor, General Leo von Caprivi, had no experience in foreign relations. Herbert's successor as state secretary, Baron Adolf Marschall von Bieberstein, was a lawyer who in middle age had become minister of Baden at Berlin. He was thus virtually ignorant of *grosse Politik* and of the regimen of the Foreign Office. The young monarch, in his own opinion, had the training for diplomacy that both Caprivi and Marschall lacked and he therefore was determined to manage Germany's relations with the other powers himself. Even before coming to the throne William had declared that personal contact between sovereigns was the most effective form of diplomacy. In 1887 he crowed to Raschdau à propos of a problem in Russo-German relations: "Just send me to St. Petersburg. I know the tsar and within twenty-four hours I'll have things in order."[49] Shortly after becoming kaiser he gave an indication of his distaste for diplomats and of his own striking lack of sensitivity by observing to the Italian ambassador in Berlin that "next to the French, the people I hate most are diplomats and parliamentarians."[50] The kaiser's dislike of diplomats, German and foreign, and his conception of the efficacy of personal diplomacy increased as he grew older. He was accustomed to say that he could best resolve diplomatic matters by dealing directly with his "colleagues" among Europe's sovereigns.[51]

Moreover, when he did entrust diplomatic affairs to diplomats, William II intended that they would perform their functions as mirrors of the imperial will. The reign began with the royal pronouncement of *sic volo sic jubeo.* "He just talks himself into an opinion," Kiderlen complained to Hol-

[49] Raschdau, *Unter Bismarck und Caprivi*, p. 17.

[50] Holstein diary, Nov. 11, 1888, HolN 3861/H196323. On another occasion he declared to an English friend that diplomats were "freaks." See Gen. W. H-H. Waters, *Potsdam and Doorn* (London, 1935), pp. 129–30.

[51] Bernhard von Bülow, *Denkwürdigkeiten*, 4 vols. (Berlin, 1930–31), I, 80 and II, 62, 397.

stein in 1891. "Anyone in favor of it is then quoted as an authority; anyone who differs from it 'is being fooled.' "[52] The tone did not change in the next twenty-five years of William's reign. If anything, the monarch's determination to be the director of Germany's destiny only increased, and the language in which he clothed his pretensions became more strident. William's insistence on retaining the direction of affairs in his own hands proceeded, as it had with Bismarck, from his dissatisfaction with—and eventually his contempt for—the Foreign Office and its staff. His complaints were often capricious and often unjustified, for many of the Wilhelmstrasse's problems, as well as those endured by its envoys, were products of the sovereign's antic behavior. William's language respecting the Foreign Office was often abusive. Its officials were "swine"; it lacked both keenness and confidence; it was the department of his government for which he had the least respect; it did nothing but raise objections. "I will tell you something," he declared in 1912 to Wilhelm von Stumm, the director of the Political Division. "You diplomats are full of shit and the whole Wilhelmstrasse stinks."[53] Holstein's characterization made a few years earlier of the kaiser's attitude toward the Foreign Office as "pathological" does not seem overdrawn.[54]

In William's judgment of diplomats, professional considerations might dictate sending a certain man to a certain

---

[52] Kiderlen to FvH, Aug. 3, 1891, HolN 3858/H194199–200.

[53] Walter Görlitz, ed., *Der Kaiser . . . : Aufzeichnungen des Chefs der Marinekabinetts Admiral Georg Alexander v. Müller über die Ära Wilhelms II* (Berlin, 1965), p. 109. For other imperial attacks on the Foreign Office see TN, XV(6), 6 and XV(9), 1; HP, IV, 289–96; Ernst Jäckh, *Kiderlen-Wächter der Staatsmann und Mensch: Briefwechsel und Nachlass*, 2 vols. (Berlin, 1924), II, 35–36; PzE to BvB, Mar. 8, 1897, BüN 76; FvH to BvB, Jan. 11, 1906, ibid., 91; Arthur Zimmermann to Kiderlen, Aug. 25, 1900, KWN, box 5, drawer 71, no. 73. After his abdication in 1918, the former kaiser continued his diatribes. See for example an account of a visit to Doorn in about 1926 in the StoedtenN, 3/2.

[54] Memo by FvH dated Feb. 1, 1909, HP, I, 173.

post, and he was prepared to admit that some diplomats for whom he entertained no great liking were nevertheless talented envoys. There were, however, other diplomats whom the kaiser liked and who therefore enjoyed a special advantage. His favorites were Philipp Eulenburg, Bernhard von Bülow, Wilhelm von Schoen, Heinrich von Tschirschky und Bögendorff, Count Friedrich von Pourtalès, Karl Georg von Treutler, and, for a while, Kiderlen. To these he gave nicknames—Treutler'schen, Purzelchen (Pourtalès), Phili—or addressed in the familiar form of address. These minions differed with respect to their talent as diplomats but all had in common a compliant vein which made them very accommodating to the vagaries of their imperial master. Bülow, for good reason, was known around the Wilhelmstrasse as the "eel." Eulenburg was a legendary sycophant, whose gushy adulation of William II knew no bounds, while Schoen was notable for the equivocation with which he approached not only his royal master but diplomatic confrontations of every sort. "Safe Schoen," as he was sometimes called, allegedly evaded a question regarding the identity of a statuary group in the gardens of the German embassy in Paris by responding that "peut-être c'est la guerre, ou peut-être c'est la paix."[55] These diplomats rarely confronted the kaiser with objections or contradictions. Moreover, he found most of them diverting and amusing, and therefore he frequently had them accompany him on trips. He saw to it that they were swiftly advanced in the service and received the choicest appointments at his disposal. On the other hand, there were a number of diplomats the kaiser could not abide because they were either dull (such as Ambassador Solms or State Secretary Richthofen) or egotistical and inclined to argue with him. State Secretary Marschall, Herbert Bismarck, and Kiderlen, who rivalled one another in both arrogance and candor, eventually found themselves in disfavor.

[55] Herbert von Nostitz, *Bismarcks unbotmässiger Botschafter, Fürst Münster von Derneburg (1820–1902)* (Göttingen, 1968), p. 163.

A diplomat who wanted to advance his career found it advisable to make his views coincide with those of his royal master and not, as under Bismarck, with those of the chancellor. It was therefore especially important that envoys fashion their dispatches to correspond not to the reality of the situation but to what they, or their friends in the Foreign Office, believed to be the kaiser's point of view on the matters in question. What William liked were short reports specializing in narrative accounts of people. Accuracy was not important, for he did not discriminate between gossip and fact. Critical language, personal vituperation, or scandalous inferences about foreign personnages—all tendencies much deplored by Bismarck and forbidden during his chancellorship—were grist for William's mill, especially if the barbs were directed against states or personalities entered in his extensive demonology. At the palace, spice was always more valued in a report than substance, and it was therefore essential for a diplomat to be careful, in Holstein's telling phrase, "to put raisins in the cake."[56] William frequently had no patience with a diplomat whose reports ran on at too great length. He would read three or four pages, scribble a notation to signify that he had digested the contents, and then lay the rest of the dispatch aside.

An envoy who failed to draw his material from a variety of sources, at least some of which could presumably provide human interest material, found himself reprimanded. Count Paul von Hatzfeldt-Wildenburg, the capable ambassador in London at the end of the century, suffered from emphysema and rarely appeared in society. He was, however, on excellent terms with the equally reclusive Lord Salisbury, and his reports were copious if rather dry analyses of what the prime minister told him. Such arrid reportage displeased the kaiser, and he preferred the more broadly collected intelligence contained in the reports of the first secretary, Count Paul Wolff Metternich. In 1901, Metternich

[56] HP, IV, 241; Bülow, *Denkwürdigkeiten*, II, 164.

succeeded Hatzfeldt, but in time William complained that Metternich himself had dried up as a source of information and that he therefore had to depend on the first secretary, Count Johann-Heinrich von Bernstorff, a fixture of London society, to find out what was going on.[57]

The kaiser's predilection for highly colored, gossipy, and abbreviated reports was well known to his diplomats. This placed them in an unfortunate position, for if they did not report on consequential matters in an accurate manner, the Wilhelmstrasse could not determine what policies should be adopted. But such detailed, businesslike reports would bore and annoy William II, on whose goodwill every envoy had to rely if he wanted to advance in the service. Confronted by this dilemma, some diplomats capitulated wholly to the royal whim, writing only what was certain to please the sovereign, regardless of the effect which such twisted information might have on German diplomacy.[58] Diplomats who had a more professional sense of their responsibilities learned to dissimulate their views or to write private letters to the kaiser in the vein he appreciated, while utilizing a more accurate approach in their dispatches. But this hedge was not without danger, for no diplomat either in Berlin or in the field could tell what official documents might eventually find their way into William's hands. Envoys therefore had to be careful in their language. "Every word of a report," Kurd von Schlözer, the Prussian minister at the Vatican, warned in 1891, "must be weighed with respect not to the facts but to the receiver." In such circumstances, Schlözer argued that the best procedure for a diplomat was to work hard but seldom report.[59]

William II, like his grandfather, had only a nominal interest in the recruitment of young men for diplomatic careers,

[57] FvH to Countess Hatzfeldt, May 1, 1900, HolN 3818/E340276–84; Bernstorff, *Memoirs*, trans. Eric Sutton (New York, 1936), p. 93.

[58] TN, XV(9), 3; Kurd von Schlözer, *Letzte Römische Briefe* (Stuttgart, 1924), pp. 149–50; Bülow, *Denkwürdigkeiten*, II, 163–64.

[59] Schlözer, *Römische Briefe*, pp. 163, 168.

and only rarely did he intervene with the Wilhelmstrasse to have a favorite admitted. The one example of any subsequent significance was Karl Georg von Treutler, whose military career had been terminated by a riding accident and whom the kaiser then had assigned to the Wilhelmstrasse.[60] William II, however, frequently took a positive role in diplomatic *revirements*. Unlike William I, who often perfunctorily acquiesced in the candidates proposed by Bismarck, William II's involvement in personnel questions was an always prominent and sometimes disturbing factor with which all diplomats had to reckon. An envoy who knew how to write what the ruler wanted to hear found that the kaiser would intervene to further his career.[61] Others whose reports were undistinguished found William's favor because they were rich or handsome, or because of their wit, their wealth, or their vulgarity. The sovereign had the habit of promising diplomats future advancements to specific posts. The Foreign Office had no choice but to accommodate itself to the royal inspiration.[62] The emperor's intrusion into questions of appointments placed the personnel counselors and the state secretary in a vexatious position. On the one hand they had to appease the royal will, while on the other the legitimate expectations of a professional corps had also to be considered. What the kaiser wanted did not always correspond with what the Foreign Office considered a satisfactory solution.

When William had a man in mind for a post, he declined to be bound by the standards by which advancement had traditionally been measured. Seniority, usually an impor-

---

[60] TN, X, passim.

[61] Elisabeth von Heyking, *Tagebücher aus vier Weltteilen, 1886/1904*, 2d ed. (Leipzig, 1926), pp. 127, 136.

[62] W2 to Bethmann, n.d. (ca. Apr. 16, 1912), Dd 135, vol. 1, reel 345; Jäckh, *Kiderlen-Wächter*, II, 173; Eulenburg, *50 Jahren*, p. 197; Count Erhard von Wedel, *Zwischen Kaiser und Kanzler: Aufzeichnungen des General-adjutanten Grafen Carl von Wedel aus den Jahren 1890–1894* (Leipzig, 1943), pp. 97–98, 187–88; Bülow, *Denkwürdigkeiten*, II, 301.

tant ingredient in the assignment of places, could not be allowed to interfere. In October, 1888, for example, he was determined to secure a ministerial appointment for one of his close friends, Philipp Eulenburg, even though Eulenburg had entered the service only nine years previously. Eulenburg, then the senior secretary in the Prussian ministry in Munich, was seventh in line to be given envoy rank. William ordered him jumped ahead of all his seniors, defending the decision on the grounds that Eulenburg was older than the others since he had come into diplomacy only after extended military service.[63] William did not calculate a diplomat's utility in terms of his dutiful peregrination from third to second to first secretary, then to minister and at last to ambassador. All this was secondary to the ruler's intuitive judgment of the man. To the consternation of some Foreign Office officials, on three occasions the kaiser plucked for ambassadorships relatively young men who had had no experience as ministers plenipotentiary but whom he liked personally and believed were well qualified. Baron Hermann Speck von Sternburg, the consul general in Calcutta, was chosen in 1903 to become envoy in Washington, and when he died in 1908, his handpicked successor was the consul general in Cairo, Count Bernstorff. Bernstorff proved more capable and popular than "Specki," but both men were departures from the previous, virtually inviolate rule that only men who had served as ministers were to be awarded with ambassadorships. In 1912 William II personally selected Prince Lichnowsky, a retired counselor whose last position in the field had been as first secretary in Vienna, to become ambassador at the Court of St. James. Chancellor Bethmann Hollweg was not enthralled at the kaiser's choice and wrote a long memorandum discussing the pros and cons of the appointment. William found Bethmann's missive tiresome and unattractively weighted on the negative side of the proposition. He replied with considerable exasperation that "I send only *my* ambassador to Lon-

[63] OvB to HvB, Oct. 5, 1888, BisN FC 3004/473.

don, who has *my* confidence, obeys *my* will, fulfills *my* orders with *my* instructions."[64] This was language which would not have been used by William I and an attitude which Bismarck would not have tolerated. The preferment given to Sternburg, Bernstorff, and Lichnowsky meant that the promotion schedules in the Foreign Office had to be revised to take William's pleasure into account. The result inevitably was the retardation of ministerial or ambassadorial rank for other diplomats, and this left a residue of resentment toward the sovereign and his favorites.

Once William II had decided on an appointment there was little that could be done to resist it. "The Kaiser wishes," according to Bernhard Bülow, "that everyone takes what he is offered. [The diplomatic corps] is to be like the army."[65] Similarly, when a diplomat fell from favor, or when the kaiser needed his post in order to make it available for someone in greater favor, he peremptorily called for the diplomat's resignation and retirement.[66] The willingness of the kaiser to dispense with the services of some diplomats was often a convenience to the Foreign Office, for there were no retirement age regulations and there were envoys who went on serving after their minds or bodies had become inequal to their tasks. William II, however, did not always pick the superannuated for his victims, and often those whom he forced from office were guilty, not of being old, but of being contrary. Often the royal demand for a resignation might come without warning and be tersely, al-

[64] Hans-Günter Zmarzlik, *Bethmann Hollweg als Reichskanzler, 1909–1914* (Düsseldorf, 1957), p. 28.

[65] Ludwig Raschdau, *In Weimar als preussischer Gesandter: ein Buch der Erinnerungen an deutsche Fürstenhöfe, 1894–1897* (Berlin, 1939), p. 166.

[66] Rudolf Vierhaus, ed., *Das Tagebuch der Baronin Spitzemberg . . .: Aufzeichnungen aus der Hofgesellschaft des Hohenzollernreiches* (Göttingen, 1960), p. 424; Tschirschky to BvB, Oct. 12, 1900, BüN 46.

most rudely, worded. This did much to exacerbate the wounds of those removed from the service in this way.[67]

Although William II's interference in matters of appointments was constant and very bothersome to the Wilhelmstrasse, it should not be exaggerated. For every case of royal interposition there were scores of appointments sent up to the palace and there routinely approved. The kaiser's flamboyance in both gesture and language made his presence appear more pervasive than it actually was. Sometimes he insisted on his favorites, but more often he blustered at Foreign Office nominations and then acquiesced. Some officials went so far as to argue that the kaiser never insisted on diplomatic appointments and never rejected recommendations made to him. Prince Lichnowsky, who was *Personalreferent* in the Political Division from 1899 to 1904, and Count Botho von Wedel, who held the same office from 1910 to 1917, both declared after the war that there was not a single case in which the kaiser doggedly insisted, over Wilhelmstrasse objections, in placing a man in a position. Similar testimony was given by State Secretary Schoen.[68]

Such evidence is perhaps a case of postwar wistfulness for the exiled monarch; it is certainly an example of the faulty or selective memory of Wilhelmine diplomats when they came to write about their service. Their accounts are not to be taken at face value, however, for we know from other sources that William II caused Lichnowsky and Schoen considerable difficulty in several appointments. One of Lichnowsky's initial problems as personnel counselor was in fact the kaiser's insistence that Schoen be given a suitable post. In 1896 Schoen had left the corps to accept a position

[67] GW, IX, 247.

[68] Friedrich Thimme, ed., *Front wider Bülow: Staatsmänner, Diplomaten und Forscher zu seinen Denkwürdigkeiten* (Munich, 1931), pp. 268–69; Lichnowsky, *Heading for the Abyss: Reminiscences* (New York, 1928), p. 90; Schoen, *Erlebtes: Beiträge zur politischen Geschichte der neuesten Zeit* (Stuttgart, 1921), pp. 125–26.

in the service of the grand duke of Saxe-Coburg and Gotha, but William II, who liked Schoen immensely, was determined to retrieve him for diplomacy. Lichnowsky consequently in 1900 was forced to make an extensive *revirement* so that Schoen could be inserted as minister to Denmark. Even Schoen, towards whom William was always very accommodating, could not always overcome the kaiser's resistance in personnel questions.[69]

The last kaiser's role in the formulation and execution of foreign policy was even more pervasive than that in personnel matters. From the beginning of his reign he took a very lively interest in diplomatic affairs and, since he believed that he himself was Germany's most effective envoy, personnel questions were therefore subsidiary to those of policy. His reign opened not with a tour of his own empire but with a series of visits to foreign sovereigns. Bismarck soon found that he and his new chief had serious disagreements about foreign as well as domestic affairs, and their differences as to the relationship Germany should have with Russia contributed significantly to the chancellor's fall in 1890. From 1890 to 1914, William's involvement in German diplomacy steadily increased. He did and said what he pleased, and unlike his grandfather, he was not scrupulous in consulting or informing the Wilhelmstrasse, which was expected to align itself to the kaiser's views as best it could.[70]

A disagreement over policy between a headstrong young autocrat and a professional Foreign Office would have greatly complicated Germany's diplomacy. After Bismarck's fall, however, this was not a major problem in Berlin. In general, the Wilhelmstrasse shared the kaiser's basic notion of what German policy should be: the preservation of the Triple Alliance, the balancing of Austrian and Russian interests in the Balkans, an active colonial program, vigilance against France, and some form of accommodation with Eng-

[69] Heyking, *Tagebücher*, p. 301; Jäckh, *Kiderlen*, II, 109. See also Bülow, *Denkwürdigkeiten*, II, 301.

[70] Münster to FvH, Mar. 19, 1896, HolN 3859/H194750.

land provided this did not encompass any diminuation of Germany's strength. The Foreign Office's problem with William II lay less in the emperor's position than it did in his personality. Even though the sovereign expressed a line of argument with which the Wilhelmstrasse was in general agreement, his behavior in expressing his views often seemed perversely calculated to alienate the very audience whose sympathies he was trying to enlist. Any interview or speech by the kaiser, any imperial journey, even the most seemingly innocuous conversation or letter became a prospective embarrassment and headache for the Foreign Office. To give William his due, it must be said that occasionally he acquitted himself handsomely, his tactful behavior at the deathbed of his English garndmother being the most familiar example. Performances which succeeded were, alas, exceptional.

William II's indelicate diplomatic manner first began seriously to alarm the Foreign Office in the mid-1890s. On New Year's Day, 1895, Holstein wrote to Eulenburg noting how smoothly Germany's foreign relations had been conducted since Bismarck's fall. But then, he pointed out, the kaiser recently had indicated to St. Petersburg that he might support Russia's age-old ambition to acquire the Dardanelles, a sensational disclosure which had immediately upset Berlin's relations with all the other European capitals.[71] The following year brought, in Holstein's phrase, the first of William's diplomatic "pranks," the Kruger telegram.[72] This unfortunate episode, which served to set England and Germany on a poisonous course for the next two

[71] The letter is in BüN 92; FvH to PzE, Dec. 13, 1894, EN, XXXIII, 968–70. See also PzE's notes for Sept. 10 and 11, 1895, ibid., XXXVII, 596–600.

[72] FvH memo, Jan. 13, 1909, HolN 3842/H197063; for the Krüger episode see Norman Rich, *Friedrich von Holstein: Politics and Diplomacy in the Era of Bismarck and Wilhelm II*, 2 vols. (Cambridge, England, 1965), 466–72, and John C. G. Röhl, *Germany without Bismarck: The Crisis of Government in the Second Reich* (Berkeley, 1967), pp. 164–66.

decades, illustrates the complications created by William's personality. The Foreign Office and the sovereign were agreed that a British incursion into the Transvaal could not be tolerated and were prepared to countenance the use of force to prevent such a development. The crisis reached a climax in December, 1895, with the unsuccessful raid on Johannesburg by Dr. Leander Starr Jameson. The kaiser ordered Ambassador Hatzfeldt to make a strong protest, one to which Lord Salisbury replied in a conciliatory fashion, noting that the British government had had no hand in Jameson's action and had ordered his immediate recall. The Foreign Office considered that the prime minister's statement had settled the immediate crisis and that a definitive resolution of Great Britain's interest in South Africa could be left to subsequent negotiations. The Wilhelmstrasse, however, had reckoned without the kaiser, who was determined that the failure of the Jameson expedition be the occasion for a humiliation of Great Britain as well as the tool for securing funds from a reluctant Reichstag for an increase in the German navy. In pursuit of these aims he entertained a number of schemes, including the dispatch of German troops to Africa, all of which the Foreign Office regarded as dangerous and unnecessary. State Secretary Marschall finally persuaded William to content himself with addressing a telegram to Paul Kruger, the president of the Transvaal republic, congratulating him on the repulsion of the English invaders. The British reaction was instant and extraordinarily hostile, and it was largely directed against the kaiser personally. The Foreign Office was appalled by William's action, and both Chancellor Hohenlohe and State Secretary Marschall explained that they had agreed to the telegram, which Marschall himself had composed following the kaiser's outline, only in the hope that it would restrain him from some more belligerent act. But, in an autocracy, there was little for diplomats to do in the wake of such a faux pas except to express the hope, as Marschall did to the Austro-Hungarian ambassador, that the matter would blow over without any lasting enmity between England and Germany.[73] Unfortunately the affair would leave a residue of animosity which subsequent efforts at conciliation never succeeded in entirely overcoming.

Even when the emperor's maladroit and impetuous behavior did not result in serious impairment of Germany's diplomatic position, it often caused the Foreign Office concern and embarrassment. William II, for example, was fond of giving unsolicited advice to his brother sovereigns. In doing so, he was doubtless well meaning and sometimes his opinions were quite sound. Some rulers, usually those of lesser states, tolerated his gratuitous counsel with a remarkably even temper. King Oscar II of Sweden, for example, does not seem to have resented William's recommendations as to how the king should deal with his unruly Norwegian subjects.[74] But Tsar Nicholas II, the victim of the so-called Willy-Nicky exchange, found William's continuous injunctions obnoxious, which they were, and also an intrusion on his prerogative. The kaiser's meddlesome inclination contributed to the cooling of relations between the two sovereigns and to the drifting apart of their empires.[75]

William II also suffered from a trait which was intolerable in a professional diplomat: he was indiscreet. Always inclined to say what was on his mind, he regarded his tendency to do so as one of his virtues. "I have to *say* what I want to," he declared in 1899, "in order that the intelligent elements will know how and whom they should follow. If I'm silent, the utterly incompetent middle class would have no idea what it should do."[76] Loquacity before his own subjects was one matter; a wandering tongue with foreigners

[73] Ladislaus von Szögyényi-Marich to Count Agenor von Goluchowski, Jan. 5, 1896 (2B), HHStA, 147–B.

[74] W2 to Crown Prince Gustav of Sweden, July 25, 1895, HohN, XXII.A.6.

[75] See Bülow, *Denkwürdigkeiten*, II, 86. The correspondence is printed in Hermann Bernstein, ed., *The Willy-Nicky Correspondence: Being the Secret and Intimate Telegrams Exchanged between the Kaiser and the Tsar* (New York, 1918) and in Walter Goetz, ed., *Briefe Wilhelms II. an den Zaren, 1894–1914* (Berlin, n.d. [ca. 1920]).

[76] Bülow, *Denkwürdigkeiten*, I, 448.

opened the possibility that secrets of state might be revealed or, at the least, that feelings might be bruised. Chancellor Bülow observed that William more often treated non-Germans to his volubility since he found them more interesting than his own subjects.[77] An example of the kaiser's indiscretion, one which also illustrates the fact that he learned nothing from mistakes even when recently committed, occurred a year after the Kruger dispatch crisis. At a court ball in Berlin he observed to the Transvaal plenipotentiary, in an unmistakable reference to the British, that he knew "how hard it was to struggle honorably against dishonorable means." Holstein at once had an assistant point out to the diplomat that for the kaiser's remark to make its way into the press would be "unloyal." The envoy got the message and William's gaffe was buried.[78] The Foreign Office unfortunately had no way of controlling the access which foreigners had to the kaiser. It could only try to restore what could be salvaged from a verbal foray by the emperor. In 1897, for example, Holstein quivered when he learned that Professor Paul Güssfeldt, an intimate of the emperor's, had invited the Italian ambassador to a small luncheon at which William was to be present. As Holstein feared, the envoy, recognizing his splendid opportunity, posed to the kaiser a number of questions which the Wilhelmstrasse clearly would not have answered. William, however, at once provided the ambassador with what he wanted to know.[79]

From 1871 to 1914, every German diplomat—from the chancellor to the counselors and secretaries of legation—had to reconcile obedience to the crown with the maintenance of a professional sense of diplomacy. Under William I and Bismarck this had occasioned almost no problems, for the Iron Chancellor had prevailed over the emperor, determined what policy would be, and saw to it that German

[77] Ibid., I, 453.
[78] FvH to BvB, Feb. 5, 1897, BüN 90.
[79] FvH to BvB, Mar. 10, 1897, ibid., 92.

diplomats in the field and in Berlin carried out his will. With the ascension of William II, an entirely different situation emerged, for the young emperor was determined from the beginning of his reign to be his own man. What had been under the grandfather an essentially passive role on the part of the crown in the affairs of the Foreign Office and German diplomacy became under his grandson a *persönliches Regiment*.[80] William's possessive involvement in diplomatic matters, whether in the Wilhelmstrasse or in Germany's relations with other nations, was very emphatic but only spasmodic in application. But even in those interludes when the sovereign was quiescent, German diplomats had prudently to anticipate what the ruler's pleasure might be. Both appointments and policy therefore had to be assessed, not only in their diplomatic contours, but also in the reaction they might produce at some point in the future with the crown. Thus, in person, William II constituted an unpredictable and turbulent intrusion into the work of the Foreign Office, while even at a distance his personality could promote considerable anxiety. Unfortunately, few of Bismarck's successors were equal to coping with the "new course" of a vainglorious and erratic ruler.

[80] The question of whether Wilhelmine Germany labored under a *persönliches Regiment* and, if so, what was its nature and extent, has not itself been the subject of definitive analysis. But historians who have tackled the question as a byproduct of their investigations of various aspects of the reign have disagreed. Recent treatments arguing for a *persönliches Regiment* are Volker R. Berghahn, *Der Tirpitz-Plan: Genesis und Verfall einer innenpolitischen Krisenstrategie unter Wilhelm II.* (Düsseldorf, 1971), esp. pp. 34, 43–45; John C. G. Röhl, *Germany without Bismarck: the crisis of government in the Second Reich* (Berkeley, 1967); and Michael Stürmer, "Bismarcks Deutschland als Problem der Forschung," p. 20, in Stürmer, ed., *Das kaiserliche Deutschland: Politik und Gesellschaft, 1870–1918* (Düsseldorf, 1970). This view has been contested by Dirk Stegmann in his "Wirtschaft und Politik nach Bismarcks Sturz: zur Genesis der Miquelschen Sammlungspolitik, 1890–1897," p. 183, in Immanuel Geiss and Bernd Jürgen Wendt, eds., *Deutschland in der Weltpolitik des 19. und 20. Jahrhunderts* (Düsseldorf, 1973).

## CHAPTER VII

Bismarck, the Succession, and the Foreign Office

Bismarck considered the Foreign Office to be his *speziale Aufgabe* and, as chancellor, he was officially designated its *Chef*. His emotional predilection was always for foreign rather than internal affairs, and certainly his success in the former was as spectacular as his failure in the other. Bismarck was self-confident, overbearing, and hypercritical by nature, and he was therefore inclined to manage the Wilhelmstrasse dictatorially, both because his estimation of his own talents was boundless and because he had scant regard for a great many of his diplomatic servants.

It may be that the aristocratic nature of the Foreign Office personnel made him chary of the staff, for the chancellor, although paternally of *Uradel* Junker extraction was never entirely at home with his Prussian social equals. The entourage with which he surrounded himself at Friedrichsruh or Varzin or Schönhausen was not composed of neighboring gentry but rather of doctors, journalists, and relatives. Ambassadors Münster and Keudell were probably closer to him than any other envoys, but even their relationships with the chancellor were based on business. It was not from the aristocratic establishment that Bismarck's single intimate (if one excepts his son Herbert) within the Foreign Office was drawn. This was the taciturn and indefatigable Lothar Bucher, forty-eighter, journalist, and from 1864 to 1886 a counselor and Bismarck's confidential secretary. "To me," the chancellor declared after Bucher's death, "he was like an organ. You had only to note the registration and it would play all the chords and notes by itself."[1] Bismarck complained time and again that he had

[1] GW, IX, 87.

few first-rate envoys or officials on whom he could draw. Some, he admitted, were so inept that they had to be hustled off to insignificant posts until they could be forced into retirement.[2] Strong leadership had therefore to atone for such a meager following. Bismarck was in earnest when he expressed his oft repeated maxim: "At my command, and without knowing why, my diplomats must fall into rank like soliders."[3] This was the case in the Wilhelmstrasse and equally true for his servants in the field.

With very few exceptions, Bismarck treated officials in Berlin with indifference and had a limited regard for their abilities. "Prince Bismarck received me today," the British ambassador reported in 1881, "and after his usual complaints about the weary work imposed upon him by the obstinacy of his Imperial Master, the incapacity of his Colleagues, the ignorance of Parliament and the imbecility of mankind, he said that he was glad to rest his weary brain by talking over foreign affairs, which constituted the only recreation left him, in his overworked existence."[4] Almost no one other than the state secretary had steady access to him, and none, according to one official, had any influence.[5] Prior to the mid-1870s Bismarck had often consulted the counselors, perhaps because he did not care for Hermann

[2] Ottomar von Mohl, *Fünfzig Jahre Reichsdienst: Lebenserinnerungen* (Leipzig, 1921), p. 141; Moritz Busch, *Unser Reichskanzler: Studien zu einem Charakterbilde*, 2 vols. (Leipzig, 1884), I, 277–78; Baron Robert Lucius von Ballhausen, *Bismarck-Erinnerungen* (Stuttgart, 1921), p. 188; Friedrich Curtius, ed., *Denkwürdigkeiten des Fürsten Chlodwig zu Hohenlohe-Schillingsfürst*, 2 vols. (Stuttgart, 1907), II, 106; GW, VIII, 377.

[3] Busch, *Unser Reichskanzler*, I, 250; Heinrich von Poschinger, *Fürst Bismarck und die Parlamentarier*, 3 vols. (Breslau, 1894–96), II, 210.

[4] Paul Knaplund, ed., *Letters from the Berlin Embassy: Selections from the Private Correspondence of British Representatives at Berlin and Foreign Secretary Lord Granville, 1871–1874, 1880–1885* (Washington, 1944), p. 188.

[5] Richard Krauel, *Persönliche Erinnerungen an den Fürsten Bismarck* (Stuttgart, 1915), p. 23.

von Thile, the state secretary, whose dismissal he finally secured in 1872 after Thile had acted without the chancellor's approval during his absence.[6] Thile's removal was part of a wider purge by Bismarck between 1872 and 1875 of a number of officials in the Wilhelmstrasse. Three senior counselors who had run afoul of the chancellor—Robert Hepke, Moritz Busch, and Bernhard König—were forced out.

For replacements, Bismarck did not turn to other members of his diplomatic staff but instead recruited new counselors from outside the service. One was Ludwig Aegidi, a notably effective propagandist in the employ of the Prussian government. Clemens Busch, consul in St. Petersburg, was another, and both he and Aegidi construed their duty to be the strict fulfillment of the chancellor's wishes.[7] Similarly, when Thile was dismissed, Bismarck found a successor outside the ranks of the service. His choice fell on Bernhard Ernst von Bülow, the minister of Mecklenburg in Berlin. Bülow, as Bismarck described him, was an *"Aktentiger,"* and he was a determined and formidable, if piously tiresome, official. Nothing escaped the state secretary's attention, and unlike some of his successors he kept a steady

[6] Von Dietz-Daber, *Bismarck und Bleichröder: das Rechtsbewusstsein und Gleichheit vor dem Gesetze* (Munich, 1897), pp. 98–100, a copy of which is in BisN FC 2959/756–864; Johann Sass, "Hermann von Thile und Bismarck," *Preussische Jahrbücher,* CCXVII (1929), 257–79; Hajo Holborn, ed., *Aufzeichnungen und Erinnerungen aus dem Leben des Botschafters Joseph Maria von Radowitz,* 2 vols. (Berlin, 1925), I, 249; Hepke diary for Mar. 30, Oct. 15 and 29, 1871, and Sept. 15, 1872, Oct. 13, 1875, Jan. 16, and Feb. 14, 1876, HepkeN 2; Arthur von Brauer, "Die deutsche Diplomatie unter Bismarck," *Deutsche Revue,* XXI (Apr. 1906), 70–71; undated Holstein memo, HolN 3842/H196850–53.

[7] Holstein diary for Mar. 12, and Nov. 28, 1882, HolN 3860/H195665–66, H195675–76; FvH to HvB, Mar. 12, 1884, BisN FC 2966/745. Holstein noted that Bismarck had a predilection in diplomacy for employing people he knew only slightly. Holstein diary, Jan. 28, 1884, HolN 3860/H195776.

hand on the legal and trade sections of the Foreign Office as well as on the more important Political Division. "*Die heilige Kraft*," the nickname Bülow bore in the Wilhelmstrasse, was acutely disliked for his domineering manner, but the chancellor valued him highly. Like Aegidi and Busch, the state secretary did not consider the Foreign Office an arena for discussion but rather the instrument for carrying out Bismarck's instructions to the letter.[8] Bülow feared that unless all communications from the Wilhelmstrasse to the chancellor were made through him, the counselors might be tempted to pursue an independent policy. He therefore asked and got Bismarck's consent that all papers would be presented through the state secretary. The chancellor agreed to the alteration because he had great confidence in Bülow and because this arrangement made it possible for him to see as few officials as possible. The result of this system was a reduction in the position of the counselors. They now saw the chancellor only when an especially complex matter, one beyond the state secretary's competence, required clarification.[9]

On Bülow's death late in 1879, Bismarck was unsuccessful in finding someone willing to assume the post. Prince Hohenlohe therefore temporarily left Paris to fill in until finally in 1881 Count Paul von Hatzfeldt-Wildenburg, ambassador in Constantinople, reluctantly agreed to take over. It was, Hatzfeldt complained, like becoming a donkey after one had been a horse, and, having no enthusiasm for his new office, he allowed a degree of laxity unthinkable under

[8] KvR, "Autobiographische und andere Aufzeichnungen, 1903–1909," BisN FC 3030/621–23, 714–15. For OvB's appreciation of Bülow see his letter to him of Dec. 31, 1877, ibid., FC 2957/1132–36.

[9] Heinrich von Poschinger, *Stunden bei Bismarck* (Vienna, 1910), pp. 71–72; Holborn, *Aufzeichnungen; Radowitz*, I, 263–64; Brauer, "Deutsche Diplomatie," p. 71; on Bülow's dictatorial manner see Holstein's undated memo, HolN 3842/H196906–7.

Bülow to penetrate the Wilhelmstrasse.[10] But neither Hatzfeldt nor his colleagues questioned Bismarck's authority. The British envoy described Hatzfeldt as a "shrewd, cautious man, without convictions, who does what he is told intelligently and diligently and that is what Bismarck likes in his agents. . . . Any attempt at independence of initiative he stamps out at once."[11] Meanwhile, Bismarck was grooming his elder son Herbert for the state secretaryship, for Hatzfeldt had no intention of remaining long in Berlin. Herbert, who was only thirty-two when Hatzfeldt became state secretary, was moved about from post to post to acquire the requisite experience. In 1885, Hatzfeldt went to London to replace Münster, who translated to Paris, recently vacated by Hohenlohe, who had become *Statthalter* of Alsace-Lorraine. Herbert then succeeded as state secretary.

Herbert was, down to his handwriting, a copy, usually exaggerated and sometimes grotesque, of his famous sire. The father drank copiously, the son stupendously; Otto was ironic, while Herbert specialized in sarcasm; the elder man was olympian, the younger merely arrogant. Like his father, Herbert had a pronounced contempt for his fellow man. Bernhard Bülow, who enjoyed Herbert's company and admired his intellectual gifts, regretted that he assumed a priori that all men were canaille.[12] Some German diplomats thoroughly disliked Bismarck *fils*, others found him crude but entertaining; a few were terrified of him. No one seems to have doubted that Herbert had a quick and fine intelligence, but most were in agreement that his appointment as state secretary created an undesirable tension in the Wilhelmstrasse. Herbert, however, had to assert himself force-

[10] KvR, "Autobiographische Aufzeichnungen," BisN FC 3030/688-89; FvH to HvB, July 22, 1882, ibid., FC 2966/245.

[11] Knaplund, ed., *Letters from the British Embassy*, p. 208.

[12] BvB to PzE, Mar. 2, 1890, BüN 75; Holstein diary, Jan. 10, 1884, and Oct. 15, 1885, HolN 3860/H195745, 3861/H196110-11. For an example of one of Herbert's broadsides against German diplomats see his letter to BvB of Aug. 15, 1884, BüN 65.

fully in order to redress the disorder which had set in under Hatzfeldt.[13] He possessed without reservation his father's confidence, and he came in time to be the alter ego of the aging chancellor. The two men worked well together, but the chancellor was no less demanding of his son than he was of the rest of his staff. In 1886, Herbert fell seriously ill, a misfortune which provoked his father to annoyance as well as sympathy. Paul Kayser, a counselor singular in his frankness with the chancellor, told Bismarck that the decline in Herbert's health was due to the demands which the chancellor placed on him. Bismarck's curt rejoinder was that "in every great state there must be people who overwork themselves."[14]

In the early years of Bismarck's chancellorship, the counselors would survey all incoming documents, denote the appropriate person or department for handling such matters, and send them on to the state secretary. The secretary and the chancellor would reserve some of these documents for their own attention and refer the rest back to the counselors, sometimes noting how the problems the dispatches raised were to be handled. On occasion, a counselor might be called for in person, but if his presentation failed to accommodate the chancellor's taste for brevity and clarity, he might never see Bismarck again. Under State Secretary Busch provided counselors with guidelines for their conferences with the chief: they would do well to be quick, ask no questions, never interrupt Bismarck's fragile train of thought, and leave promptly.[15]

By the late 1880s, as the volume of Foreign Office business greatly increased, Bismarck had to become selective.

[13] Holstein diary, Nov. 27, 1885, HolN 3861/H196133; see also diary for Aug. 25, 1885, ibid., H196084–85, and for Dec. 1, 1886, H196217; and Holstein's undated memo, ibid., 3842/H196844–45; KvR's "Autobiographische Aufzeichnungen," BisN FC 3030/688–89.

[14] Krauel, *Erinnerungen an Bismarck*, pp. 20–21; HvB to KvR, Oct. 21, 1881, BisN FC 3014/142–43.

[15] Holborn, *Aufzeichnungen; Radowitz*, I, 263–64; Krauel, *Erinnerungen an Bismarck*, p. 2.

In July, 1884, a memo went out to all missions ordering a reduction in the volume of reports in order to spare the chancellor, who, it was noted, read them all. This was an exaggeration, for in December of the same year Bismarck declared to the Reichstag that with the annual crop of dispatches running to some 70,000 pieces he could not even make his way through all those directed to the Political Division.[16] The practice came to be that the counselors would draw up a daily abstract of incoming correspondence and forward it to the state secretary for transmission through the Reichskanzlei to the chancellor. Foreign Office memoranda recommending a course of action were presented in a similar fashion, but by the 1880s the counselors transmitted only what they considered to be the most important of the *Konzepte*.[17] This was a development not without risks, for officials could never be sure that what they considered significant would also strike Bismarck in the same way. If the counselor brought forward something the chancellor considered beneath his notice, he would complain that nothing could be settled without his approval. On the other hand, if a document was not presented to him, and he later discovered it as he leafed through the *Akten*, he might greatly resent not having been consulted. Radowitz, who for years worked closely with Bismarck in the Wilhelmstrasse, declared that the problem with the chancellor was that one could never be certain of his favor or of his confidence.[18]

[16] Memo of July 20, 1884, Gen 1 AA.a.61, vol. 5, 279/00770–72; Reichstag, Dec. 15, 1884 (Bismarck), pp. 359–60; GW, VIc, 304; Hohenlohe to BvB, Apr. 6, 1884, BüN 89.

[17] Ludwig Raschdau, "Fürst Bismarck als Leiter der Politischen Abteilung: aus der schriftlichen Nachlass des Unter Staatssekretärs Dr. Busch," *Deutsche Rundschau*, CLI (1912), 47–49; LoebellN 27, II, 10–11; Krauel, *Erinnerungen an Bismarck*, p. 19.

[18] Krauel, *Erinnerungen an Bismarck*, p. 10; Julius von Eckardt, *Lebenserinnerungen*, 2 vols. (Leipzig, 1910), II, 113; also Knaplund, *Letters from the British Embassy*, p. 272; Holborn, *Aufzeichnungen; Radowitz*, II, 116.

In 1883 Bismarck's health began to decline very markedly, which led to an increase in his irritability and to his retreat from Berlin to his estates, from which, he said, he could run the Foreign Office.[19] Thereafter he rarely ever put foot in Number 76, and even the faithful Bucher complained that weeks would sometimes go by without his seeing the chancellor. Bismarck's interest in inferior diplomatic appointments, which he had once followed closely, began to abate. He now concerned himself only with the most important positions, always being careful to consult candidates for high posts before recommending their names to William I.[20] He did not, however, relax his grasp on matters of policy. When, late in 1882, State Secretary Hatzfeldt suggested that Bismarck husband his strength by leaving mere details to others, the chancellor's reaction was one of suspicion and he thereafter entrusted fewer decisions to the state secretary.[21] The only counselors who met with Bismarck with any regularity were Friedrich von Holstein, whose entrée proceeded from his close friendship with Herbert, and Rudolf Lindau, whose literary style the chancellor especially admired.[22] Because of Bismarck's remoteness, a counselor's work was conducted by reports and memoranda, but even at this distance the chancellor's chilling presence could be felt. If a counselor converted Bismarck's notes literally in composing an official dispatch, the chancellor would complain that he might as well have dictated the note. If, on the other hand, an official made more free use of Bismarck's memoranda, he might be abused for having an inelegant style. Radowitz asserted that probably never had a draft come back from Bismarck's office without some alteration. The chief asked for clarity, not embellishment.

[19] Holstein diary, Jan. 10, 1886, HolN 3861/H196418.

[20] Brauer, "Deutsche Diplomatie," p. 71; Ludwig Raschdau, *In Weimar als preussischer Gesandter: ein Buch der Erinnerungen an deutsche Fürstenhöfe, 1894–1897* (Berlin, 1939), pp. 167–68.

[21] Holstein diary, Jan. 2, 1883, HolN 3860/H195688; also for Feb. 11, and Apr. 17, 1884, ibid., H195794, H195866–67.

[22] Eckardt, *Lebenserinnerungen*, II, 113–14.

"What I want is a good scaffolding," he declared. "I will take care of the polishing myself."[23] The counselors, in turn, exercised the same stringent supervision over the junior assistants. Julius von Eckardt, a young underling in the mid-1880s before moving on to a career in the consular service, was assigned to a subsection in the *Handelspolitische Abteilung* in charge of retrieving articles lost by German travelers and other inconsequential matters. Even reports dealing with such trivia would be returned with copious editorial comment by the counselors. Baron Eugen von Buddenbrock, the official under whom Eckardt worked, declared that the Foreign Office had its "own very definite style, one which is concerned with the flourishes and fine ornamentation of a sort as traditional as those in a Saxon porcelain manufacture. I can assure you that even *Goethe* would have to put up with corrections if he came to work here."[24]

Bismarck's principal concern in the Wilhelmstrasse was not his counselors and their treatment of daily business, for few of them caused him any difficulties and many served loyally for decades. Prussian and German representatives abroad, from the greatest ambassadors to the most insignificant ministers-resident, were the chancellor's special interest and his major problem. Bismarck treated his diplomats in the field no better than his staff in Berlin. Some diplomats, especially the younger ones, he knew less by personal contact than by the quality of their reports, but sometimes he could remember neither their names nor the positions they held.[25] Envoys whom he did know but whom he considered unimportant or dull, or with whom he was pro-

---

[23] Holborn, *Aufzeichnungen; Radowitz*, I, 263–64; Krauel, *Erinnerungen an Bismarck*, p. 11; Holstein diary, Mar. 12, 1882, HolN 3860/H195665–66; undated Holstein memo, ibid., 3842/H196837; FvH to HvB, Mar. 12, 1884, BisN FC 2966/745.

[24] Eckardt, *Lebenserinnerungen*, II, 117.

[25] Brauer, "Deutsche Diplomatie," p. 71.

voked, found that Bismarck would not see them on their trips to Berlin. Others were kept waiting, often with insultingly trifling excuses. When envoys or secretaries were finally ushered into the presence, or when they received a letter from the chancellor, Bismarck often made his displeasure with their behavior unmistakable.[26] A false step by an envoy or a secretary could result in immediate recall and, in some cases, dismissal. In professional matters, Bismarck was a demanding chief, quick to condemn and stingy with praise.

To Bismarck, many diplomats were no more than liveried letter carriers who consumed stately dinners and purveyed malicious gossip. The Prussian ministers to the German states were merely emissaries of good will—"installment payments," he said of these assignments, on more brilliant posts in the future.[27] In the chancellor's opinion, too many of his envoys were attracted to diplomacy by its glamour and consequently they emphasized the social aspects of their positions. German diplomats especially delighted in the great European embassies and more important ministries, in part for the important business to be transacted there, but also for the gala fêtes and impressive ceremonies which were their daily fare.[28] This enthusiasm for society diminished the diplomat's energy for affairs of state, and some envoys were decorative social fixtures who were inattentive to their duties. Many diplomats, according to the chancellor, promptly fell in love with the land in which they served. This was an attraction for which Bismarck was par-

[26] Holstein diary, Mar. 5, 1882, HolN 3861/H195661; Eckardt, *Lebenserinnerungen*, II, 114; GW, VIc, 30–32, 308. See also Ludwig Raschdau, *Wie ich Diplomat wurde: aus dem Leben erzählt* (Berlin, 1938), p. 72.

[27] Busch, *Unser Reichskanzler*, I, 231–32; Baron Egon von der Brincken to FvH, Jan. 1, 1882, HolN 3816/E339148–50.

[28] Baron Hermann von Mittnacht, *Erinnerungen an Bismarck*, 4th ed., 2 vols. (Stuttgart, 1904), I, 55; Busch, *Unser Reichskanzler*, I, 233–37.

tially responsible, for he was inclined to allow envoys to stay for years in the same post.[29] Some diplomats were unequal to such a temptation and degenerated into incompetency. A case in point, and one quite painful to Bismarck, was Baron Carl von Canitz und Dallwitz, a friend of the chancellor's from childhood, whom Bismarck had to dismiss in 1882 as minister at The Hague because he was no longer able to perform his duties to the chancellor's satisfaction.[30]

Bismarck denied many of his diplomats any appreciable measure of independence, and he once declared that "if an ambassador can obey, more is not required."[31] Even those envoys, such as Hatzfeldt, whom he trusted most, were kept on fairly short leash. The chancellor probably inspired, and most certainly would have approved, a statement by Lothar Bucher, referring to Bismarck's position as president of the Prussian State Ministry, that "envoys are not colleagues of the minister but his agents."[32] On appointing an envoy to a post, Bismarck was careful to provide him with a general charge which would serve as an outline for the policy he was to pursue. Hohenlohe, for example, on being entrusted with Paris was informed that he was to create good relations with France and prevent her from forming any alliances. He was also to make the French press aware that the chancellor would not tolerate any attacks on Germany.[33] While envoys could express their own ideas in their reports, they were expected to carry out with precision the instructions they received from Berlin. After 1877, only in exceptional circumstances was an ambassador or minister allowed to give a written communication to a foreign government unless it had previously been presented verbatim to

[29] Bernhard von Bülow, *Denkwürdigkeiten*, 4 vols. (Berlin, 1930–31), II, 114–15; GW, XIV/2, 840 and VIII, 148.

[30] GW, VIc, 232.

[31] Holstein diary, Feb. 11, 1884, HolN 3860/H195794.

[32] Busch, *Unser Reichskanzler*, I, 245–46.

[33] Undated instructions (1873), HohN, XX.A.1.

the Foreign Office.[34] Most envoys were faithful in adhering to this edict. There were very few instances in which an ambassador exceeded his orders or otherwise failed to do Bismarck's will, and when he did so he lost his position. One such victim was Friedrich von Eichmann, who as minister in Constantinople in 1873 had been instructed to regard his post as that of a general consul and involve himself only in commercial affairs. Instead, he meddled in politics and therefore had to be demoted to Dresden.[35] Bismarck, moreover, considered it neither desirable nor necessary to keep his envoys fully informed of his own role in the diplomatic relations between Germany and foreign powers. According to Holstein, the chancellor once replied negatively to a question as to whether an envoy should be let in on a piece of information by declaring, "We would not want to deprive the man of his naïveté."[36] Bismarck sometimes entrusted junior officials with diplomatic negotiations which properly belonged to the heads of mission. One of the chancellor's agents was his son Herbert, who later as state secretary would pass intelligence on to underlings while withholding it from envoys.[37]

Bismarck's dissatisfaction with the limited abilities among his envoys led him to look beyond the Prussian-imperial diplomatic corps for his ambassadors and ministers, just as he had for his associates in the Wilhelmstrasse. As has already been indicated, he was particularly susceptible to the recruitment of generals. Schweinitz, for example, was promoted from military attaché in Vienna to the ambassadorial position there. Prince Hohenlohe, who in 1873 became the envoy in Paris, had previously been minister-president of

[34] Memo by State Secretary Bülow, Oct. 22, 1877, Gen 1 AA.a.61, vol. 2, 279/00657–58.

[35] GW, VIII, 114.

[36] Friedrich Rosen, *Aus einem diplomatischen Wanderleben*, 4 vols. in 3 (Berlin, 1931–59), I, 79–80.

[37] MiquelN, 00188; GW, XV, 396–97; HvB to BvB, Sept. 23, 1886, BüN 66.

Bavaria as well as a member of the Reichstag. Three years later, Bismarck persuaded Prince Otto zu Stolberg-Wernigerode to resign as *Ober-Präsident* of Hanover to take the embassy in Vienna. Stolberg held this position until 1878, when he returned to the Prussian bureaucracy. The chancellor then handed the post to Stolberg's brother-in-law, Prince Heinrich VII Reuss, a general who had earlier served as ambassador in St. Petersburg. Count Münster, appointed to London in 1873, was a Hanoverian diplomat who had fought against Prussia at Langensalza in 1866. An interesting case on the fringes of the chancellor's network was that of Colonel Count Gustav von Enzenberg, who as Hessian minister to Paris in the late 1860s had divulged to Bismarck certain military secrets regarding the mitrailleuse. In 1872, the grateful chancellor had the informant made a *major à la suite der Infanterie* in the Prussian army and then persuaded William I to appoint him minister to Mexico.[38]

To Bismarck, the compleat diplomat was one whose ability to win effortless entrée to the right places was unquestioned, one who possessed a deft appreciation of how the chancellor's directives were best to be carried out, and one who could report on his activities with clarity and precision. Diplomacy was not logic and method so much as it was intuition and discretion. "The educated German," he argued, "has too much training in logic. As a methodical thinker, he makes up his mind on the basis of the evidence presented. This is not enough in political affairs, even less so in diplomacy."[39] Bismarck therefore was inclined to recruit young men, not on the basis of examination performance, but by the impression they made, and he stressed social as well as intellectual qualifications in the appointment of envoys. His prescription for an accomplished diplomat balanced both factors. In social terms, an ambassador had to be able to communicate easily in French or, in the

[38] Mohl, *Fünfzig Jahre Reichsdienst*, p. 32.
[39] Raschdau, *In Weimar*, pp. 145–46.

case of the envoy to the Court of St. James, in English. He had to establish rapport with the right people, which to Bismarck meant more than upper-class society. In many places, governments were reflections of the popular will rather than the whim of the sovereign. Envoys should be familiar with all ranks, for by the late nineteenth century, diplomacy had become—it was a development the chancellor deplored but accepted—a matter of economics as well as politics.[40]

Once a diplomat had established his contacts, he had with few exceptions simply to follow instructions from Berlin. What bound Bismarck to his men in the field was less their conduct, for which he provided them blueprints, than their reports. The chancellor knew beforehand what his envoys were to do; what he wanted was a description of the reaction his directives had produced. A diplomat's reports, therefore, were to Bismarck a matter of utmost importance, and there was no aspect of diplomacy on which he lavished so much attention and for which he laid down such a body of regulations. Bismarck had a generally low opinion of diplomats' reports, and he did not hesitate to criticize the dispatches of even the most senior of his ambassadors. On the other hand, if he liked a man's style, he might single him out for transfer to a more desirable post.[41] The chancellor's fundamental belief was that a diplomat's reports were to be narrative, not interpretative. He should relay what he had heard or observed and let the state secretary and the chancellor make of this information what they would.[42] In doing

---

[40] Hermann Hoffmann, *Fürst Bismarck, 1890–1898*, 3 vols. (Stuttgart, 1913–14), I, 124–25; Brauer, "Deutsche Diplomatie," p. 74. Cf. Raschdau, "Fürst Bismarck," p. 50.

[41] Busch, *Unser Reichskanzler*, I, 280–81; OvB to Münster, Jan. 16, 1881, Gen 1 AA.a.40, vol. 4, 279/00472–74; Bülow to heads of mission, Jan. 14, 1875, ibid., vol. 2, 279/00447–48; GW, XV, 396–97; Ludwig Raschdau, *Unter Bismarck und Caprivi: Erinnerungen eines deutschen Diplomaten aus den Jahren 1885–1894*, 2d ed. (Berlin, 1939), pp. 1–2.

[42] GW, XV, 396–97.

so, an envoy should avoid a number of pitfalls through which his dispatches could lose much of their value. First and foremost, they should not be too long—nor should they be unnecessarily frequent. Some dispatches ran on to such length that Bismarck claimed that he had to read them diagonally. Reports which attempted to deal with more than one problem were partly responsible for such wordiness, but even more destructive to brevity was the unfortunate tendency of some envoys to fall into gratuitous descriptions of local geography or to retail useless *Klatsch*. Count Max von Berchem, chargé in Stockholm in 1884, sent in almost daily reports dealing with the landscape and its monuments, which led the chancellor to observe tartly, "Berchem seems to believe that he has discovered Sweden."[43] Shortly thereafter Berchem was removed from his post and subsequently had assignments only in Berlin. The only area in which the chancellor would tolerate longwindedness was in economic affairs, which he liked to have clothed in statistics. "Foreign policy and economic matters," he declared, "should never be mixed up. They are in fact neatly balanced, and if the one is burdened by the other the balance is lost."[44]

The correctly fashioned communiqué should avoid rumors and excessively piquant or critical remarks about another country, its statesmen, or its rulers, for these negative observations might make their way back, with disastrous results, to the capital from which they had emanated. Moreover, if an envoy collected nothing but critical comments about a nation, he might contribute to poisoning Berlin's attitude to it. The habit of German diplomats to

[43] Bülow, *Denkwürdigkeiten*, IV, 485; GW, VIb, 247–48 and IX, 304; OvB to Münster, Jan. 16, 1881, Gen 1 AA.a.40, vol. 4, 279/00472–74; Brauer, "Deutsche Diplomatie," pp. 73–74; Holborn, *Aufzeichnungen; Radowitz*, I, 35; Busch, *Unser Reichskanzler*, I, 279–80; Hohenlohe diary, Oct. 24, 1883, HohN, CC.X.11.

[44] Brauer, "Deutsche Diplomatie," p. 74; Hoffmann, *Bismarck*, I, 124–25.

employ exaggerated language became so prevalent that in 1875 State Secretary Bülow dispatched to all heads of mission a circular which noted Bismarck's displeasure and ordered that, in future reports, the verbiage be no more pointed than was necessary for the comprehension of the material. Finally, dispatches were to have some literary quality. As Bülow put it, they were to be to the point without being dull, while the chancellor himself observed that "style was not the man, but it was certainly a part of his make-up."[45]

All of Bismarck's staff, whether stationed in Berlin or in the field, had to endure his small side. The chancellor was not only an autocrat, he was also a martinet. From 1871 to 1890, he bombarded the Foreign Office with countless memoranda specifying in the most minute detail exactly how he wanted the daily work of the Wilhelmstrasse conducted. On some matters he was obsessive. One anathema was Latin orthography, which Robert von Puttkamer, the Prussian minister of interior, tried to introduce in the early 1880s. Bismarck at once declared that he would make a *Cabinetsfrage* of the matter and threatened to subject to official punishment any diplomat who followed Puttkamer's practice. Akin to Bismarck's detestation of Latin characters was his insistence that German words of Latin derivation were to bear their *German* gender. Diplomats would kindly make reference to *das*, not *der*, *Episkopat*. German, not French, was to be the Wilhelmstrasse's language of diplomacy. The chancellor decreed that all correspondence written in Berlin was to be in the mother tongue except for answers to communications addressed in French to Berlin.

[45] Bülow to heads of mission, Jan. 14, 1875, Gen 1 AA.a.40, vol. 2, 279/00447–48; Bülow to Roeder (minister to Switzerland), Mar. 31, 1875, ibid., 00460–63; Bülow to Count von Bray-Steinberg (consul general, Belgrade), Oct. 28, 1876, ibid., vol. 3, 00464–65; GW, VIc, 30–31. The quotation by Bismarck is from Raschdau, *In Weimar*, p. 147. See also Holstein diary, Jan. 10, and Apr. 18, 1884, HolN 3860/H195741–42, H195873.

In such cases, the responses were to be in French, unless the correspondence originated in Paris, in which event the replies were to be *auf deutsch*.[46] Diplomats were to stifle their predilection for polite phrases such as *ergebenst*, for too much courtly folderol tended to obscure the meaning of a communication. And they would kindly not exaggerate the capital letter in their signatures. A diplomat who wanted to make an impression on the chancellor would also do well to have a scribe whose handwriting pleased him.[47] Even the color of ink and the quality of letterheads fell under the chancellor's scrutiny.[48]

Stern, distant, and demanding as Bismarck was, he seems to have been worshipped by his staff. There were, of course, some exceptions, but by and large in the Wilhelmstrasse adulation was the order of the day. The thrall which the chancellor exercised did not proceed from affection, for too few of his subordinates knew him well enough for such warmth of feeling to have developed. The junior staff were reverential and referred to their chief as the "great bowwow" (*grosser Wauwau*), while to some older diplomats he was the "great uncle."[49] Young assistants or secretaries of legation treasured the rare invitations issued by the great man and seldom failed to record every detail of a dinner at Friedrichsruh or a talk in the chancellor's office. Older servants were equally awed by his presence. Ludwig Aegidi, after his first conversation with Bismarck following his appointment as a counselor, described the chancellor's

[46] Bismarck to all envoys and consuls, Mar. 5, 1890, Gen 1 AA.a.61, vol. 1, 280/00068–69; Richard von Kühlmann, *Die Diplomaten* (Berlin, 1939), p. 105.

[47] Lucius von Ballhausen, *Bismarck-Erinnerungen*, pp. 83–84; GW, VIII, 378; Raschdau, "Fürst Bismarck," pp. 51–52; Hohenlohe diary, Nov. 7, 1882, HohN, CC.X.10.

[48] GW, VIc, 276; Eckardt, *Lebenserinnerungen*, II, 113–114; Raschdau, "Fürst Bismarck," pp. 51–52; Holstein diary, Mar. 7, 1885, HolN 3861/H195963.

[49] Count Robert Zedlitz-Trützschler, *Zwölf Jahre am deutschen Kaiserhof: Aufzeichnungen* (Berlin, 1924), p. 17; Winfried Sühlo, *Georg Herbert Graf zu Münster* . . . (Hildesheim, 1968), p. 144.

spell in a letter to his wife. "Oh, I will do everything to win his satisfaction; that is my goal. If I succeed, nothing in the world will ever separate me from [the execution of] my responsibilities."[50] Not a few officials were terrified of Bismarck. Max von Philippsborn, who served the chancellor as a counselor for over twenty years and of whom Bismarck sarcastically observed that he had much *Lippe* and little *Born*, was a shy man who never overcame his fright.[51] Everyone fulfilled Bismarck's will without question. A senior counselor declared that "wax would be a hard metal if compared to our pliancy toward the chancellor's will."[52] The veneration which Bismarck's staff felt for him was derived from the olympian nimbus which surrounded the chancellor after the wars of unification, one which only increased with his subsequent diplomatic triumphs. There was an obvious satisfaction in serving Europe's preeminent statesman, for every German diplomat could feel that he shared the reflection of Bismarck's glory. "We German diplomats," wrote Kurd von Schlözer, longtime minister at the Vatican, "who were merely the modest agents of Bismarck's will at foreign courts, matured under him and felt very bound up in the service that we thereby rendered to the most powerful of statesmen and to our Fatherland."[53]

✻

After William's accession in 1888 and then more precipitously following Bismarck's resignation in 1890, the Wilhelmstrasse's morale began to deteriorate, confidence gave

[50] Aegidi, "Eintritt ins Auswärtigen Amt und erster Besuch in Varzin," *Deutsche Revue*, XXIII, part 1, no. 4 (Oct. 1898), 109 note 3.

[51] Karl F. Nowak and Friedrich Thimme, eds., *Erinnerungen und Gedanken des Botschafters Anton Graf Monts* (Berlin, 1932), p. 40; Arthur von Brauer, *Im Dienste Bismarcks: persönliche Erinnerungen* (Berlin, 1936), p. 37.

[52] Eckardt, *Lebenserinnerungen*, II, 114–15.

[53] Schlözer, *Letzte Römische Briefe* (Stuttgart, 1924), pp. 149–50.

way to despair. The cause was the increasingly bizarre behavior of William II, the procession of chancellors and state secretaries who, however well intentioned, did not seem to measure up to the standards realized in Bismarck's day. As a result, German diplomacy was discredited and the nation encircled by enemies. Much of the authority which before 1890 had been held tightly by the chancellor now reposed in the hands of the sovereign or with the vengeful and paranoid Friedrich von Holstein, the senior counselor of the Political Division, of whose good will even his friends could not be certain.

Unfortunately, as the trust which envoys had in Berlin declined they became less and less able to resist the encroachments made on their prerogatives. The introduction of the telegraph reduced the independence of an envoy and threatened to convert him into a mouthpiece for stratagems devised in Berlin.[54] In addition to this drawback, the conditions of a diplomat's routine were changed. As Europe became more and more democratized, the business of diplomacy no longer consisted of the decorous waiting upon kings in porphyry halls; instead ambassadors were plunged into the hurly-burly world of parliamentarians and press lords. No longer were reports devoted to analyses of the corporeal and psychological state of royalty but to trade, industry, and the convolutions of legislatures and political parties. Count Anton Monts, who entered the service in 1878 and retired in 1909 as ambassador to Italy, wrote wistfully after the World War, "We diplomats of the old days who were trained by Bismarck lived by the maxim that the relations of courts to one another was of decisive importance. . . . Nowadays it is different. One usually obtains influence through the press, and that costs money, lots of money, or through the purchase of prominent . . . parlia-

---

[54] Baron Wilhelm von Schoen, *Erlebtes: Beiträge zur politischen Geschichte der neuesten Zeit* (Stuttgart, 1921), pp. 114–15; Busch, *Unser Reichskanzler*, I, 241.

mentarians, for which one also needs a great deal of cash."[55] Diplomacy, once a preserve of refinement, had become proletarianized. Moreover, there were similar problems in a Germany infected with liberalism. Herbert Bismarck declared in 1890 that even German diplomats could no longer avoid the demands of a meddlesome Reichstag and, that being the case, he had no further taste for the service.[56]

Bernhard von Bülow, who was responsible for some of the difficulties under which German diplomats had to labor, once jotted down in his journal the dictum of a Russian envoy to the effect that "a diplomat must be more a diplomat with his own government than with foreign regimes."[57] This was certainly the experience of German emissaries after 1890, for if the diplomatic service was an aristocratic club it was not one whose membership worked in harmony when deprived of a strong leader. The foreign states to which German envoys were accredited often pursued aims counter to those which they had to represent, but these were fair differences which could be resolved or compromised by the exercise of careful negotiation and persuasion. After 1890 the principal problems in these diplomatic exchanges were created not by foreign cabinets but by Berlin. It is therefore not surprising that following Bismarck's fall diplomats felt little warmth for the Wilhelmstrasse, a disposition revealed by the epithet they coined for it: the poisonous den (*Giftbude*).[58] The fastidious Philipp Eulen-

[55] Nowak and Thimme, *Erinnerungen; Monts*, p. 222; also Busch, *Unser Reichskanzler*, I, 241.

[56] Raschdau, *Unter Bismarck und Caprivi*, pp. 134–35.

[57] BüN 151, Book C, p. 83.

[58] TN, XI, 1 and XIIId 2–3; Philipp Eulenburg, *Erlebnisse an deutschen und fremden Höfen* (Leipzig, 1934), p. 89; Johannes Haller, *Aus dem Leben des Fürsten Philipp zu Eulenburg-Hertefeld* (Berlin, 1924), p. 106; Bülow, *Denkwürdigkeiten*, I, 12. See also Count Erhard von Wedel, ed., *Zwischen Kaiser und Kanzler: Aufzeichnungen des General-adjutanten Grafen Carl von Wedel aus den Jahren 1890–1894* . . . (Leipzig, 1943), pp. 193–94; PzE to BvB, May 16 [1894], BüN 75.

burg castigated the Foreign Office as a *timbale à la surprise* and an ant hill, but he confessed that even under Bismarck he had found the fortification of a schnapps necessary before presenting himself at number 76.[59] The objections of Eulenburg and other diplomats to the Wilhelmstrasse was that it made their work unnecessarily difficult, that it disregarded their advice, and that it treated them unfairly.

The charge that the Foreign Office was responsible for placing obstacles in the envoy's execution of his duty was based on the fact that the Wilhelmstrasse did not always provide its representatives in the field with sufficient information. This meant that ambassadors and ministers had to protest their ignorance or be evasive when questioned. If foreign statesmen or rulers believed these avowals they had to assume that Berlin did not trust the envoy; if the denials of knøwledgeability were unconvincing, then the envoy lost his credibility and as a result much of his effectiveness. In either case it was not a welcome position. While Bismarck kept some things to himself, his envoys had had no serious cause for complaint on this score. But after 1890 what under Bismarck had been an occasional practice became much more frequent, and much of the blame was attributed to Holstein, who used his authority in the Political Division to withhold information from envoys who had fallen from his favor.[60]

One was Ludwig Raschdau, Prussian minister to the Saxon states from 1894 to 1897 and an implacable enemy of Holstein, who in turn detested Raschdau. The envoy complained that Holstein would send him no information on political and diplomatic affairs, to which the grand duke of Saxe-Coburg and Gotha felt entitled. The disclosure of sensitive material to the German princes admittedly involved risks, since their kinships often embraced foreign sovereigns

[59] PzE to W2, Feb. 27, 1896, EN, XL, 101–7; Haller, *Leben Eulenburgs*, p. 106.
[60] Rosen, *Wanderleben*, I, 80.

who were not on good terms with Germany.[61] The grand
duke was not a case in point, however, for he was an uncle
of William II and one who—unlike his brother, the Prince
of Wales—was in good standing in Berlin. There was therefore no diplomatic reason to deny the ruler the information he wanted. In withholding documents from Raschdau,
Holstein was trying to undermine the envoy's credibility
and ultimately to force his retirement.[62] Raschdau appealed
in vain to Holstein, then to State Secretary Marschall and,
after Marschall's reassignment to Constantinople in 1897,
to State Secretary Bülow. Bülow claimed that the matter
was one which Chancellor Hohenlohe would have to resolve, but when Raschdau turned to the chancellor, Hohenlohe's response was that *he* would determine what the
grand duke should be told. According to Raschdau, the
whole affair, which contributed to his decision to retire, had
the effect of converting the grand duke from an ally of the
regime in Berlin into an opponent.[63]

While Holstein was battling Raschdau, he also began to
prevent information from reaching the ambassador in
Vienna, Philipp Eulenburg, a diplomat whose influence on
William he feared. When Eulenburg realized Holstein's
maneuver he became infuriated and appealed to Bülow,
who apparently did nothing to help him. Holstein explained the matter away to Bülow by declaring that Eulenburg was excessively sensitive (which was certainly true)
and that the basis of the envoy's complaints actually lay in
the fact that the Austrian government was trying to stir up
trouble between the Foreign Office and Eulenburg (which
was probably false).[64] The exclusion of information from

[61] TN, XI, 2–3.
[62] Ludwig Raschdau, "Zum Kapitel Holstein," *Deutsche Rundschau*, LI (1924), 237–47.
[63] Nowak and Thimme, *Erinnerungen; Monts*, p. 349; Raschdau,
In Weimar, pp. 28, 161–62, 166.
[64] FvH to BvB, Mar. 24, 1897, BüN 90; FvH to PzE, Feb. 27,
1897, ibid., 92. For another example see FvH to BvB, July 25, 1898,
ibid., 91.

envoys who were not in Holstein's favor continued until his retirement in 1906. Thereafter, because of the efforts of Otto von Mühlberg, under state secretary from 1900 to 1907, Wilhelm von Stumm, a Political Division counselor in 1910 and director of the division after 1912, and State Secretary Gottlieb von Jagow, envoys were given wider access to materials, although some documents continued to be withheld lest the sources on which their revelations were based be compromised.[65]

Another complaint frequently lodged by diplomats was that the Foreign Office frequently disregarded their advice. There were no objections during Bismarck's chancellorship that envoys' representations on any subject were wantonly consigned to the *Akten* without being carefully weighed. After 1890, however, the Wilhelmstrasse, now more independent of the chancellor, began to display an omniscence which soon alarmed German diplomats in the field.[66] Some envoys did not let the change pass unnoticed. Prince Radolin, the ambassador to France from 1900 to 1910, wrote to his friend Princess Marie Radziwill in the heat of the first Moroccan crisis to decry the "shabbiness" (*mesquinerie*) of the Foreign Office. "You can have no idea of the narrowness of their outlook. When I remonstrate with them, black on white, that matters are not as they think they are, they give me an ironical look and say: 'You talk as though you've practically become French yourself, but we see things more clearly than you and we know perfectly well that things are otherwise.'"[67] Even on more mundane affairs, the Wilhelmstrasse was fixed in its belief that its understanding was superior to that of its agents abroad.

[65] MiquelN, 00190; ThimmeN 24, p. 16; TN, XI, 2–3.

[66] See in general Nowak and Thimme, *Erinnerungen; Monts*, p. 455, and General Count Gustav von Lambsdorff, *Die Militärbevollmächtigte Kaiser Wilhelms II. am Zarenhofe, 1904–1914* (Berlin, 1937), p. 28.

[67] Radziwill, *Letters de la Princesse Radziwill au Général de Robilant, 1889–1914: une grande dame d'avant guerre*, 4 vols. (Bologna, 1933–34), III, 206.

Karl Georg von Treutler, minister to Brazil from 1900 to 1907, doggedly tried to point out to Berlin the disastrous financial hardship imposed on German diplomats by the rate of exchange then prevailing in Rio de Janeiro and Petropolis. The answer he was vouchsafed by the Foreign Office was that "Ambassador XYZ imagines that he understands things better only because he is on the spot."[68] As Holstein pointed out to Chancellor Bülow, if an envoy reported something contrary to the Wilhelmstrasse's wisdom on the subject it had merely to affix a covering letter to the dispatch pointing out to the kaiser what, in its opinion, were the errors in the envoy's interpretation.[69]

Ambassadors and ministers who hoped that, once in Berlin on leave, they could have more success representing their views to officials in the Wilhelmstrasse often returned to their posts in disappointment. Bismarck had occasionally declined to see envoys at whom he was piqued, but after 1890 this isolation became a much more common feature. A particularly flagrant example occurred in 1903, a year in which the Foreign Office's concern focused on France's ambitions in Morocco. The minister to the sultanate, Baron Friedrich von Mentzingen, languished in Berlin for ten days and returned to Tangier without having been able to secure an audience with State Secretary Richthofen, Chancellor Bülow, or William II.[70] Since envoys had to obtain prior permission to come to Berlin, the Wilhelmstrasse could forestall any unwelcome appearance by declining, as it frequently did, the envoy's request for leave.[71]

The resentment felt by diplomats in the field against the Foreign Office had to be concealed unless one was, like

[68] TN, XIIIe, 5. Münster registered a similar complaint in a letter to Holstein of May 31, 1899, HolN 3859/H194794.

[69] Unaddressed letter by FvH, dated July 21, 1901, almost certainly to BvB, BüN 91.

[70] Rudolf Vierhaus, ed., *Das Tagebuch der Baronin Spitzemberg* . . . : *Aufzeichnungen aus der Hofgesellschaft des Hohenzollernreiches,* 2d ed. (Göttingen, 1960), p. 435.

[71] Raschdau, *In Weimar,* pp. 95–98.

Radolin, a grandee secure in the imperial favor and safely ensconced in an ambassadorship from which no further advance was possible, or, like Raschdau, wealthy enough to be prepared to resign rather than be mistreated by Berlin. But most diplomats were in mid-passage in their careers, eager for advancement, and often not sufficiently rich or independent minded to be willing to risk the consequences of overt criticism. The run of German diplomats treated the Political Division with caution, for they knew that it would review their reports and recommend future assignments. They were therefore careful to make discreet inquiries as to whether their dispatches were being favorably received or whether any revelation might be made of what their next posts would be.[72] Even senior ambassadors were suspicious that Wilhelmstrasse officials, especially Holstein, were conspiring to rob them of their places.[73]

Some of the ill will between diplomats in Berlin and those in the field was caused by the latter group. If the Wilhelmstrasse offended envoys by frequently disregarding them, the patronizing and even abusive tone employed by some diplomats to characterize their less aristocratic and less affluent brethren in the Wilhelmstrasse did little to create smooth relations between the two arms of the diplomatic establishment. Of all the critics of the "poisonous den," Count (later Prince) Münster, successively ambassador in London and Paris from 1873 to 1900, was the most devastating. This snobbish peer, who despised experts of every sort, usually referred to the Foreign Office as the *Zentralrindvieh* and to its officials as the "little blockheads" (*Kleinvieh*). Once driving down the Wilhelmstrasse he observed, drawing abreast of number 76, that "the counselors

[72] BvB to Karl von Lindenau, May 9, 1890, May 6, 1891, BüN 99; Alfred von Bülow to BvB, Aug. 13, 1892, ibid., 14; Alvensleben (minister in Darmstadt) to Under State Secretary Busch, Oct. 19, 1880, and Holleben (minister to Argentina) to Busch, Nov. 29, 1881, in BuschN, 00007–10, 00285–86.

[73] Raschdau, *Unter Bismarck und Caprivi*, p. 207.

are all swine."[74] Since Foreign Office personnel serving in Berlin were for the most part of a social status inferior to envoys, observations such as Münster's were probably considered social as well as professional slights. The arrogance of some envoys was reflected in the highhanded manner they took in dealing with the Wilhelmstrasse. Prince Lichnowsky, the ambassador in London from 1912 to 1914, was a particularly aggravating example. Rich, imperious in manner, and dramatic in gesture, on being named envoy to the Court of St. James he immediately upset State Secretary Kiderlen by announcing to the press what *his* policy toward England would be and then further alarmed the Political Division by refusing to listen to its instructions for the strategy he was to represent in London. Once installed in Carlton Terrace, Lichnowsky plunged into a private correspondence with the kaiser, much to the Foreign Office's irritation, but it finally had to resign itself to treating the ambassador as an "obstinate and spoiled child."[75]

The friction between Berlin and the field by no means was the extent of the rivalries and discord which beset the German diplomatic service, for the staff in Berlin was rent by internal differences, and diplomats on foreign assignment were even less able to avoid quarrels with one another. In Bismarck's day, these problems had surfaced in the early 1880s, when the ailing chancellor began to retire for extended periods to his estates. Following State Secretary Bülow's death at the end of 1879, the Wilhelmstrasse fell into disorder and the counselors were left without much direction. In 1885, with the appointment of Herbert Bismarck as state secretary, the firm direction of number 76 was restored. The fall of the Bismarcks in 1890 consequently occasioned misgivings as to whether the Foreign Office

---

[74] Münster to FvH, Apr. 22, and May 8, 1899, HolN 3859/ H194787, H194790; Baron Hermann von Eckardstein, *Lebenserinnerungen u. politische Denkwürdigkeiten*, 3 vols. (Leipzig, 1919– 21), I, 90–91; Raschdau, *In Weimar*, pp. 145–46.

[75] ThimmeN 24, pp. 7–17.

would revert to the sort of personal scramble for power which had characterized it ten years earlier.[76]

These fears were more than realized in the 1890s as Holstein, now firmly in charge of the Political Division, began to assert himself against the rest of the Wilhelmstrasse in a way that soon wrecked the unity achieved under the Bismarcks. Holstein was hostile to the other departments in the Foreign Office, jealous of competitors, and he forced out those who, like Ernst von Bothmer in the legal section or Paul Kayser in the *Kolonial Abteilung*, opposed him openly. Kayser was a difficult personality and a man of great ambition, and it is easy to understand why he and Holstein did not get along. But Kayser's differences with Holstein were not entirely personal, for if he wanted to see colonial affairs handled by a separate office with himself as state secretary, he did so not solely out of personal gratification but because he believed that Holstein and the Political Division knew nothing and cared nothing about non-European affairs.[77] Kayser eventually resigned from the diplomatic service, but Holstein's persecution of the Colonial Division continued.[78] The struggle between the Political Division and the *Kolonial Abteilung* was not resolved until 1906, when Holstein resigned and shortly thereafter an independent Colonial Office was established.

The relationship of diplomats in the field was often very unfortunate, and part of the hostility of one diplomat for another was the work of officials in Berlin. Even under Bismarck, diplomats had used their connections in the Wilhelmstrasse as a means of undermining their heads of mis-

[76] BvB to Lindenau, Apr. 9, 1890, BüN 99. Holstein had expressed curiosity on this point as early as 1884. Holstein diary, Jan. 28, 1884, HolN 3860/H195768.

[77] Raschdau, *In Weimar*, p. 78.

[78] In 1900, Dr. Georg Irmer, a counselor in the Colonial Division, requested and was granted transfer to the consular service because Holstein withheld documents from him. See Irmer to BvB, May 25, 1900, BüN 61.

sion in order to get rid of them—to demolish (*demolieren*) them, as the expression went. Bismarck did not like for legation secretaries to write to counselors (though they might communicate with Herbert) since this sort of correspondence lent itself precisely to such intrigue. As a result, the efforts by diplomats to demolish one another became pronounced only after Bismarck's resignation as chancellor in 1890.[79] Some diplomats attempted to have their chiefs removed, not in order that they might themselves succeed, but in order that a more palatable envoy—one who would recommend them to Berlin in more positive terms—be appointed.[80] More frequently, however, their campaigns were directed against other envoys whose posts they were themselves anxious to obtain. In such cases, the method employed was to send knowledgeable reports to Berlin on the country to which one aspired to be accredited. Count Anton Monts, minister to Bavaria, longed for the ambassadorship in Rome and repeatedly sent Holstein detailed dispatches on Italian affairs. Monts was soon transferred to Italy.[81] A final type of demolition was the attempt occasionally made by ambassadors in superior positions to damage more lowly placed envoys, not of course because they wanted their posts themselves, but because they disliked them and perhaps envisioned that if these enemies could be ruined their places might be taken over by protégés. Eulenburg, for example, as ambassador in Vienna, complained to Chancellor Hohenlohe that Count Monts, minister in Munich, alas could not fathom the Bavarians, while at the same time Monts advised Holstein that Count Otto von Dönhoff at Darmstadt was more disliked there than anyone save the

[79] KvR, "Autobiographische Aufzeichnungen," BisN FC 3030/628–29; Eckardstein, *Lebenserinnerungen*, I, 170–71.

[80] See for example Radolin to Holstein, Apr. 2, 1895, HolN 3859/H195145–46.

[81] Monts to FvH, Nov. 3, 1899, ibid., H194620–23, and Radolin to FvH, Mar. 11, 1900, ibid., 3860/H195317.

reactionary grand duke.[82] It would seem that the Political Division must have found such machinations acceptable (and perhaps even desirable), for it did nothing to stop the appeals or accusations addressed to Berlin by diplomats eager to improve their positions at the expense of their colleagues.

Bernhard von Bülow was an active participant in careerist maneuvers, not only against his own head of mission but against other diplomats as well. Ambassador von Schweinitz, under whom Bülow served in St. Petersburg as first secretary from 1884 to 1888, was an object of his malediction. In Bülow's litany of complaints to his friends in the Foreign Office, Schweinitz was denounced not only as mistaken in his analysis of Russian affairs but as lazy, touchy, devious, disagreeably priggish, false, egotistical, and tiresome. There was much truth in what Bülow wrote, although he was oblivious to the fact that many of his pejoratives could as easily have been applied to himself. But William I and Bismarck liked Schweinitz and showed no signs of placing a more sympathetic envoy in the Russian capital. Bülow was therefore glad to be appointed minister to Rumania, a post of which, as he had earlier pointed out to Herbert Bismarck, he could make more than the former incumbent.[83] From Bucharest he kept up his campaign for advancement, one now directed against ambassadors whose more exalted posts he wanted.[84] Prince Reuss in Vienna and Count Münster in Paris both protested to Berlin that Bülow was trafficking in Austrian and French affairs. Bülow dis-

[82] PzE to Hohenlohe, Feb. 8, 1896, HohN, XXII.A.7; Monts to FvH, Jan. 9, 1896, HolN 3859/H194558–59; for another example see Pourtalès to Jagow, July 11, 1913, Dd 135, vol. 1, 345/00252–55.

[83] For Bülow's criticism of Schweinitz see BvB to Lindenau, Nov. 11, 1885, and Nov. 10, 1886, BüN 99; Count Friedrich von Vitzthum (second secretary at St. Petersburg) to BvB, n.d. [ca. Apr. 1887], ibid., 127; BvB to HvB, Sept. 1, 1886, BisN FC 2958/622–24. For Bülow's claim that he would be a good man for Bucharest see BvB to HvB, Apr. 27, 1886, BisN FC 2958/564.

[84] See Bülow's correspondence with Lindenau from 1888 to 1894 in BüN 99.

missed the charges by noting that all envoys suffered from paranoia that others were after their positions, but it is clear that he was in fact conspiring with his contacts in the Political Divsion to replace the aging Münster.[85]

The conditions of work imposed on German diplomats by the Wilhelmstrasse or by their own colleagues in the field thus were often onerous. As long as there was a firm hand exercised either by the chancellor or by the state secretary, the cabals and vendettas, the disorganization and drift in the Foreign Office were curbed. The Political Division performed the chancellor's will and diplomats worked hard to fulfill Bismarck's expectations and had little occasion for intrigues against one another. Business proceeded smoothly and advancement in the service was in the main determined by the chancellor's estimation of a diplomat's ability. In Bismarck's measurement, supinity had been a necessary, perhaps even a prominent, ingredient. For his diplomats, however, flattery and unctuousness had no place, since the chancellor was susceptible to neither. What he insisted on was obedience not servility. After 1890, obedience continued to be demanded, but now it was to be laid at the feet of William II, on whom sycophancy could be lavished in the expectation, one seldom frustrated, that imperial grace and favor would result. The habit of obedience in the German diplomatic service, long cultivated under Bismarck, was thus transferred to the kaiser, whose good will was far more decisive for a diplomat's career than any chancellor, state secretary, or other superior. But there was an important difference in the relationship between he who

[85] Nowak and Thimme, *Erinnerungen; Monts*, pp. 152–53; BvB to Lindenau, July 20, 1887, and Oct. 13, 1892, BüN 99. See also Bülow's letters to Lindenau of Apr. 9, and June 1, 1890, and Oct. 17, 1892, in ibid. Baron Edmund von Heyking, general consul in Calcutta, was also after Münster's post. See Elisabeth von Heyking, *Tagebücher aus vier Weltteilen, 1886/1904*, 2d ed. (Leipzig, 1926), p. 133. For other examples see Bülow, *Denkwürdigkeiten*, III, 36–38; Herbert von Hindenburg, *Am Rande zweier Jahrhunderte: Momentbilder aus einem Diplomatenleben* (Berlin, 1938), p. 220; Lindenau to FvH, Mar. 15, 1887, HolN 3820/E340991–92.

led and they who followed, for if Bismarck was served questioningly William II was played up to.

Under Bismarck, if diplomats were allowed only a limited initiative they could at least be confident that they were serving Europe's preeminent statesman and that the policies they would be expected to implement would be reasonable and coherent. But the last kaiser was neither the man nor the diplomat that Bismarck had been, and one might expect that under his rule some incidence of resistance could be discovered. Although pessimism and misgiving were privately expressed by German diplomats, there were almost no signs of open opposition in the Wilhelmstrasse. Indeed, the leading spokesman for the royal sway was a diplomat, Philipp Eulenburg, and in his abject sycophancy to William II he was rivaled only by another commanding personality in the Foreign Office, Bernhard Bülow. In an autocracy, one should not expect public reproach of the crown, but it is striking that even the quieter signs of disaffection are missing. From 1890 to 1914, there is not a single resignation from the service—if one excepts the departure of Rudolf Lindau as a Political Division counselor as well as Holstein's chronic and peevish letters declaring that he intended to surrender his office—that was prompted by disgust or apprehension at the quality and character of the kaiser's leadership.[86] Those who left the service for reasons other than physical or mental frailty did so because they were disappointed office seekers; those who remained were dependent on their august patron. William II's diplomats, although privately alarmed by the sovereign's antics, were, in public, models of compliance to the royal will, and after 1890 they resigned themselves to foundering along under an immature ruler and under a procession of chancellors and state secretaries who lacked Bismarck's commanding presence. The Iron Chancellor's succession in the Wilhelmstrasse was a file of epigoni who proved unequal to the destiny thrust upon them.

[86] On Lindau's resignation see p. 269 below.

## CHAPTER VIII

Caprivi and Hohenlohe

Bismarck's heir as chancellor, General Leo von Caprivi, did not resemble the Iron Chancellor in background, experience, or personality. He came from a recently ennobled family of Italian or Slavic origin and had established a reputation as a talented military administrator. Caprivi was taciturn, discreet, and quite hardheaded. The total impression, to some observers, was a trifle flat.[1] Bismarck himself nominated Caprivi as his successor, and William II, who doubtless believed that he would prove more pliant than his first chancellor, agreed without hesitation even though he did not much like the dour general.[2] Caprivi, who was always realistic about his prospects, had no illusions about the difficulty of his new position under William II. Some years earlier he had on several occasions expressed concern at the arrogant young prince's inflated estimation of himself. As head of the navy from 1883 to 1888 Caprivi had found that William preferred the advice of his entourage to that offered by government officials.[3] Just before assuming the chancellorship, Caprivi observed to an acquaintance that there was much talk in Berlin of "the gravity of my heritage, of the difficulties of my situation, of those at home and abroad. But the problem of which one speaks the least

---

[1] Count Hugo Lerchenfeld-Koefering, *Erinnerungen und Denkwürdigkeiten* (Berlin, 1935), p. 369; Ladislaus von Szögyényi-Marich (Austro-Hungarian ambassador in Berlin) to Foreign Minister Count Gustav Kálnoky, Nov. 10, and 24, 1894 (44B, 46C), HHStA, 144–B.

[2] Radolinski to Holstein, Mar. 2, 1888, HolN 3859/H195037.

[3] Holstein diary, Aug. 22, 1885, June 28, 1897, ibid., 3861/ H196077–78, H196263.

and the one which is the most fearful—not to say one which is unsurmountable—is that which comes from On High."[4] Caprivi's misgivings were well founded. At first, to be sure, the kaiser declared to one and all that he was delighted with his new servant. "We are getting on very well with Caprivi," he wrote to his grandmother, Queen Victoria, on Christmas Day, 1890. "He is already adored by friends and revered by his opposition. I think he is one of the finest characters Germany ever produced."[5] But the chancellor, on the other hand, had become aware shortly after taking office that his relations with the kaiser had cooled, a development he attributed to the fact that he would not always submit to the ruler's will.[6]

One of Caprivi's major problems was the Foreign Office, for he was unfamiliar with its operations, untutored in Germany's relations with the other powers, and in fact not very interested in diplomacy or diplomats. William II trusted that the chancellor's well-known industry would result in his swiftly acquiring a mastery of his new responsibilities.[7] There was, however, some doubt among German diplomats that this in fact proved to be the case. The Prussian minister to the Vatican, Kurd von Schlözer, who was an ardent supporter of Bismarck, wrote in the summer of 1890 that "Caprivi has an absolutely stupid lack of knowledge in non-mili-

[4] Princess Marie Radziwill, *Lettres de la Princess Radziwill au Général de Robilant, 1889–1914: une grande dame d'avant guerre,* 4 vols. (Bologna, 1933–34), I, 31.

[5] George F. Buckle, ed., *The Letters of Queen Victoria,* 3d series, 3 vols. (London, 1930), I, 666.

[6] Szögyényi to Kálnoky, Nov. 11, 1894 (44C), HHStA, 144–B. See also ibid., letter of same to same of Nov. 24 (46C); Ludwig Raschdau, *Unter Bismarck und Caprivi: Erinnerungen eines deutschen Diplomaten aus den Jahren 1885–1894,* 2d ed. (Berlin, 1939), pp. 174–75; Lerchenfeld-Koefering, *Erinnerungen,* p. 371.

[7] E. Richter, ed., "Aus kritischen Tagen: Berichte der sächsischen Gesandten in Berlin, Grafen Hohenthal und Bergen, aus den Jahren 1889–92," *Deutsche Rundschau,* CXC (1922), 168.

tary matters. . . . One could just as well have made any battalion commander chancellor. What good is all his reputed loftiness of character?" Kiderlen, then a counselor in the Political Division, was only marginally more charitable. "A horse which has done well in the out-of-doors," he declared, "is not one to be stabled."[8] Other diplomats complained that the chancellor avoided the Wilhelmstrasse 76 and was particularly hostile to the Colonial Division, having on one occasion declared that "the less Africa [Germany has] so much the better for us."[9] Not having himself been trained in the civil bureaucracy, and sometimes giving indications that he did not consider this necessarily to be a disadvantage, Caprivi was regarded as an outsider, especially by Bismarck's allies, who, like Schlözer, feared that they might be purged from the service.[10] Foreign envoys were also critical of Caprivi, grumbling that he either avoided the diplomatic corps or was less communicative than Bismarck when he did agree to grant audiences.[11]

On Bismarck's retirement in 1890, William II had attempted to retain his son Herbert as state secretary. Herbert was an able diplomat with many years of service and thus would have consistuted a countervailing force to the inexperienced Caprivi. Herbert declined to remain in the Wilhelmstrasse, however, for he resented the kaiser's handling of his father and he had no confidence that the new chancellor would be able successfully to stand up either to the crown or to the Reichstag.[12] Caprivi wanted a Prussian as state secretary and his candidate was the lackluster min-

[8] Schlözer, *Letzte Römische Briefe* (Stuttgart, 1924), p. 158; Otto Hammann, *Der neue Kurs: Erinnerungen* (Berlin, 1918), p. 57.

[9] Raschdau, *Unter Bismarck und Caprivi*, pp. 191, 238; General August Keim, *Erlebtes und Erstrebtes: Lebenserinnerungen* (Hanover, 1925), p. 71.

[10] PzE to BvB, Nov. 1, 1894, BüN 75; Szögyényi to Kálnoky, Nov. 10, 1894 (44B), HHStA, 144–B; Schlözer, *Römische Briefe*, p. 177.

[11] Szögyényi to Kálnoky, May 28, 1892 (63C), HHStA, 142–B; also same to same, Mar. 22, 1893, ibid., 144–V.

[12] Raschdau, *Unter Bismarck und Caprivi*, pp. 134–35; Eulenburg

ister to Belgium, Friedrich von Alvensleben. William II agreed, but Alvensleben, who was aware that his experience exceeded his ability, prudently refused the offer. The kaiser, probably inspired by his uncle, the grand duke of Baden, then chose Baron Adolf Marschall von Bieberstein, who since 1883 had been the minister of Baden at Berlin.[13] Marschall seemed an unusual selection. He was, in the first place, not a Prussian but a South German. He had been a lawyer and bureaucrat for most of his life and his service in Berlin had not really provided him much introduction into the realm of great power diplomacy. He was, in Bismarck's bon mot, the *"ministre étranger aux affaires."*[14] Moreover, Marschall was a tart-tongued man of gruff manners. Like Caprivi, he knew only the bare rudiments of French and had little taste for the social functions that pertained to his office. Marschall was conspicuously happier raising fruit trees on his estates in Baden than entertaining dignitaries in the secretary's villa in the Wilhelmstrasse.[15]

---

diary, Mar. 19, 1890, EN, X, 280; Count August Eulenburg to PzE, Mar. 22, 1890, ibid., 295–97; Richter, "Aus kritischen Tagen," p. 167; Heinrich O. Meisner, ed., *Denkwürdigkeiten des General-Feldmarschalls Alfred Grafen von Waldersee* 3 vols. (Stuttgart, 1923–25).

[13] Norman Rich, *Friedrich von Holstein: Politics and Diplomacy in the Era of Bismarck and Wilhelm II*, 2 vols. (Cambridge, England, 1965), I, 289–92. Waldersee and Eulenburg may have contributed to Marschall's nomination. See Meisner, *Denkwürdigkeiten; Waldersee*, II, 118, 122.

[14] Bernhard von Bülow, *Denkwürdigkeiten*, 4 vols. (Berlin, 1930–31), IV, 639; also Baron Hermann von Eckardstein, *Lebenserinnerungen u. politische Denkwürdigkeiten*, 3 vols. (Leipzig, 1919–21), I, 131. For surprise at Marschall's appointment see Karl von Eisendecher (minister in Karlsruhe) to FvH, Apr. 4, 1890, HolN 3818/E339938; Friedrich Curtius, ed., *Denkwürdigkeiten des Fürsten Chlodwig zu Hohenlohe-Schillingsfürst*, 2 vols. (Stuttgart, 1907), II, 497–98; Meisner, *Denkwürdigkeiten; Waldersee*, II, 139; also Holstein diary, Jan. 24, 1908, HolN 3842/H196999.

[15] Raschdau, *Unter Bismarck und Caprivi*, p. 142; Karl F. Nowak and Friedrich Thimme, eds., *Erinnerungen und Gedanken des Botschafters Anton Graf Monts* (Berlin, 1932), p. 372.

Since Caprivi had only a limited interest in foreign affairs, he tended to leave the operations of the Foreign Office to Marschall, much in the way that Otto Bismarck had let Herbert have his way there.[16] But Marschall often shirked his diplomatic responsibilities. His talents were frequently expended on parliamentary battles involving questions remote from foreign affairs, for he had considerable rhetorical gifts and more expertise in political affairs than in diplomatic maneuvers. Some diplomats did not think it made much difference whether Marschall spent his time in the Wilhelmstrasse or in the Reichstag since they interpreted his appointment as a sign that in the future it would be William II, not Marschall or Caprivi, who would direct foreign affairs.[17]

Since both the chancellor and the state secretary were novices in diplomacy and unable to communicate easily in French with envoys accredited to Berlin, both were forced to rely heavily on the Wilhelmstrasse staff. The new chancellor depended on Karl Göring, an old school friend and a counselor in the legal section, for advice in economic matters.[18] Caprivi's inexperience in diplomacy meant that Holstein, the senior counselor in the Political Division, now assumed an even more vital role in all aspects of German diplomacy. He was, as Bismarck's son-in-law Count Kuno von Rantzau, minister in The Hague, noted, the only person in the Foreign Office who knew what was going on.[19] In 1890, Holstein thus had a promising future. But he also had a compromised past, for he was suspected of having been responsible as a young legation secretary in Paris for the dismissal and subsequent indictment for treason of Ambassador von Arnim.[20] During the 1880s he enjoyed great favor

[16] Raschdau, *Unter Bismarck und Caprivi*, pp. 227, 314–15.

[17] BvB to Karl von Lindenau, June 1, 1890, BüN 99.

[18] KvR, "Autobiographische und andere Aufzeichnungen, 1903–1909," BisN FC 3030/597.

[19] Ibid., 700.

[20] The Arnim affair is treated in George O. Kent, *Arnim and Bis-*

with the Bismarcks, father and son, and became their most influential ally in the Foreign Office. By the middle of the decade his relations with Rantzau had soured, and by 1886 disenchantment with the entire tribe had set in. Holstein did not approve of the Reinsurance Treaty concluded with Russia in 1887, a mistake he attributed to Otto's senility and Herbert's vainglorious Russophilia. Nor had he countenanced any of Bismarck's reactionary plans for dealing with internal problems. By the time William II came to the throne, Holstein had concluded that the time had come for the chancellor to go. Holstein's expert biographer has settled very succinctly the question of whether he played an important part in the Iron Chancellor's fall: "He did."[21]

To his few intimates, Holstein was a loyal and even personable friend, but his public face was usually forbidding, his manner cold and distant, his mode of life furtive and peculiar. Declining promotion, he chose to remain behind the scenes, asking envoys to avoid mentioning his name in their reports.[22] He preferred to stay behind the closed door of his office, which adjoined Caprivi's, and only reluctantly did he see German or foreign diplomats.[23] Holstein was a man of prodigious energy and often displayed acute diplomatic judgment, but unfortunately he also had an irrepressible disposition to make trouble. He was a master of the

---

marck (Oxford, 1968); Gerhard Kratzsch, *Harry von Arnim: Bismarck-Rivale und Frondeur. Die Arnim Prozesse, 1874–1875* (Göttingen, 1973). Holstein's role in it is treated more fully in Rich, *Holstein*, I, 74–86.

[21] Holstein diary, Jan. 13, 1886, HolN 3861/H196151; Rich, *Holstein*, I, 280–83; see also Bülow, *Denkwürdigkeiten*, II, 216. On Holstein's relations with Rantzau see Rantzau's "Autobiographische Aufzeichnungen," BisN FC 3030/689–90, 693–94; for his analysis of the errors of the Bismarck's Russian policy see his undated memo in HolN 3842/H196879–99.

[22] Count Imre Széchényi (Austro-Hungarian ambassador in Berlin) to Kálnoky, Feb. 25, 1892 (21), HHStA, 144–B.

[23] Friedrich Rosen, *Aus einem diplomatischen Wanderleben*, 4 vols. in 3 (Berlin, 1931–59), I, 19, 23, 76.

poisonous innuendo; he gleefully passed along the most malicious gossip; he knew how to destroy friendships which once had been cordial. His most pronounced characteristic was his deep-seated paranoia; he was easily offended and relentlessly vindictive. To both Caprivi and Marschall, Holstein quickly became indispensable. The Austrian ambassador, Count Imre Széchenyi, early in 1892 described Holstein as the most important man in the Foreign Office; without consulting him neither the chancellor nor the state secretary would act. Moreover, according to Széchenyi, Holstein enjoyed the admiration of William II, who had never met him and whose bestowal on Holstein of the Hohenzollern order in 1892 was therefore all the more remarkable.[24] "I hear," the kaiser declared to an envoy the next year, "that I have an excellent official in the Foreign Office, Herr von Holstein. I haven't yet succeeded in getting to make his acquaintance."[25]

As the leading figure in the Political Division, Holstein was often consulted in policy formulation, and soon after 1890, finding that neither the chancellor nor the state secretary were inclined to challenge him, he began to meddle more actively in personnel as well. Such matters were officially the province of the *Personalreferent* of section *B* of the Political Division, Georg Humbert, who, however, lacked the will to stand up to Holstein. After 1890, Holstein began to make appointments himself or to entrust them to his confidants in section *A*.[26] Holstein's authority in person-

[24] Széchenyi to Kálnoky, Feb. 25, 1892 (21), HHStA, 144–B; PzE to FvH, Feb. 4, 1892, HolN 3855/H192267–70; FvH to W2, Jan. 26 and 29, 1892, in ibid., 3853/H190376–78; Caprivi to FvH, Jan. 27, 1892, ibid., 3852/H189449; Eulenburg diary, July 17, 1892, EN, XXI, 517–19; Ludwig Raschdau, "Zum Kapitel Holstein," *Deutsche Rundschau*, LI (1924), 237.

[25] Szögyényi to Kálnoky, Mar. 22, 1893, HHStA, 144–V. Szögyényi did not record the name of the diplomat to whom the remark was made.

[26] Raschdau, *Unter Bismarck und Caprivi*, p. 195; Raschdau, *In Weimar als preussischer Gesandter: ein Buch der Erinnerungen an*

nel matters made him now more than ever a man to be treated with care, and most diplomats, young and old, were circumspect in their dealings with him. Many trooped to the salon run by his rather colorless friend, Helene von Lebbin. "The whole Wilhelmstrasse paid her court," a well-placed Berlin diarist noted. "Every ambitious diplomat ardently aspired to make her acquaintance." In her residence in the Wilhelmstrasse, rumor had it, both diplomatic assignments and policy were determined. The salon of another of Holstein's friends, Klothilde von Wedel-Malchow, was also a foyer of diplomatic manipulation.[27]

Staying on Holstein's good side, however, was a difficult matter, for he was often unreasonable in his demands and capricious in his relations with colleagues. Some diplomats fell from favor suddenly and could never determine the cause for this abrupt change in their fortunes.[28] Herbert Bismarck as well as his brother-in-law Rantzau noted how difficult Holstein was to work with on personnel problems because his opinion was rooted in prejudices concerning the various candidates for positions.[29] Ambassador von Schwei-

---

deutsche Fürstenhöfe, 1894–1897 (Berlin, 1939), pp. 12, 29; see also Count Karl von Pückler, Aus meinem Diplomatenleben (Schweidnitz, 1934), p. 59; Alfred von Bülow to BvB, Aug. 13, 1892, BüN 14.

[27] Rosen, Wanderleben, I, 19–20; Elisabeth von Heyking, Tagebücher aus vier Weltteilen, 1886/1904, 2d ed. (Leipzig, 1926), p. 89; Ottomar von Mohl, Fünfzig Jahre Reichsdients: Lebenserinnerungen (Leipzig, 1921), p. 120; Rudolf Vierhaus, ed., Das Tagebuch der Baronin Spitzemberg . . . : Aufzeichnungen aus der Hofgesellschaft des Hohenzollernreiches, 2d ed. (Göttingen, 1960), pp. 426–27, 432–33.

[28] TN, XI, 9; PzE to BvB, Sept. 11, 1901, EN, LVIII, 174; BvB to Lindenau, July 20, 1887, and May 6, 1891, BüN 99; PzE to BvB, Sept. 22, 1895, ibid., 75; Rantzau, "Autobiographische Aufzeichnungen," BisN FC 3030/693–94; Lerchenfeld-Koefering, Erinnerungen, pp. 387–88.

[29] HvB to BvB, Aug. 15, 1884, BüN 65; Rantzau, "Autobiographische Aufzeichnungen," BisN FC 3030/696–97; also Raschdau, Unter Bismarck und Caprivi, p. 369; Prince Alexander von Hohenlohe, Aus meinem Leben (Frankfurt/Main, 1925), p. 316; Hammann, Neue Kurs, pp. 68–69.

nitz, who knew Holstein well, declared that he was "not right in the head," a diagnosis shared by Under State Secretary Berchem insofar as Holstein's temperament in appointments was concerned.[30] Holstein was obsessed by the specter of a return of the Bismarcks to power, and almost every ally of either the father or the son found himself relegated to Holstein's blacklist. In the early 1890s, Holstein began to purge the service of his enemies. Those who had been on good terms with Bismarck or who earlier had had disagreements with Holstein feared for their futures. Kurd von Schlözer, who had served in Washington, described the situation as being similar to the American practice that all diplomats must submit their resignations to an incoming president. "We Bismarck partisans will slowly be eased out of our positions," he predicted with accuracy.[31] Schlözer was forced into retirement in 1892, while other diplomats were punished by being demoted to inferior posts or being replaced by Holstein's protégés. One such case was the banishment to Madrid of Johann Maria von Radowitz, ambassador in Constantinople, who was supplanted by Holstein's friend, Prince Hugo von Radolin. Spain had been made available for Radowitz by booting out Ferdinand von Stumm, a Bismarck ally who, although not yet fifty years old, was forced into retirement.[32]

[30] Marie von Bunsen, *Zeitgenossen die ich erlebte, 1900–1930* (Leipzig, 1932), p. 86; Hajo Holborn, ed., *Aufzeichnungen und Erinnerungen aus dem Leben des Botschafters Joseph Maria von Radowitz*, 2 vols. (Berlin, 1925), II, 326; also Bülow, *Denkwürdigkeiten*, II, 290–91.

[31] Schlözer, *Römische Briefe*, p. 177; also Raschdau, *Unter Bismarck und Caprivi*, pp. 207, 308; Helmuth Rogge, ed., *Friedrich von Holstein: Lebensbekenntnis in Briefen an eine Frau* (Berlin, 1932), p. 157 note 2; FvH to Harden, Aug. 5, 1906, HardenN 52; Vierhaus, *Tagebuch; Spitzemberg*, p. 471.

[32] Raschdau, *Unter Bismarck und Caprivi*, pp. 206, 222–23, 308–9; Meisner, *Denkwürdigkeiten: Waldersee*, II, 260; Bülow, *Denkwürdigkeiten*, I, 495; Heyking, *Tagebücher*, pp. 164–65; Rogge, *Holstein: Lebensbekenntnis*, p. 157 note 2. Another casualty was Bismarck's son-in-law, Count Kuno von Rantzau, minister at The Hague. See Rantzau's "Autobiographische Aufzeichnungen," BisN

As Holstein consolidated his control of personnel affairs, he built up a strong nucleus of younger diplomats who unquestioningly performed his will and who venerated him as the remaining vestige of the era of Bismarckian greatness.[33] A prominent disciple was Count Friedrich von Pourtalès, a wealthy aristocrat of Swiss extraction who from 1888 had served as first secretary in St. Petersburg. In the spring of 1890, Holstein had his protégé reassigned as a counselor in the Political Division. Shortly after Caprivi assumed the chancellorship, Holstein succeeded in having Pourtalès made *Personalreferent* and also saw to it that he was given ministerial rank, even though he lacked the seniority for such a distinction.[34] Another confederate was Kiderlen, who had become a counselor in the Political Division in 1888. Until he fell out of favor ten years later, he was the Foreign Office dignitary who often accompanied William II on his numerous trips abroad.[35] The Holstein-Pourtalès-Kiderlen clique could also count on the support of Paul Kayser, the head of the *Kolonial Abteilung*, who, as a bourgeois Jew, was a social outsider but a figure of influence with the kaiser.[36] In addition to these younger diplomats, Holstein had several friends among the senior envoys.

FC 3030/676–78. Prince Reuss, who was forced out of Vienna in 1894, was thoroughly disliked by Holstein. See ibid., FC 2965/930–31.

[33] Monts to FvH, Apr. 19, 1906, HolN 3859/H194643. For Holstein's encouragement of letters from junior officials in the field see Raschdau, *Unter Bismarck und Caprivi*, pp. 207, 222–23, 314–15.

[34] Raschdau, *In Weimar*, pp. 12, 28, 46.

[35] Count Erhard von Wedel, ed., *Zwischen Kaiser und Kanzler: Aufzeichnungen des General-adjutanten Grafen Carl von Wedel aus den Jahren 1890–1894* . . . (Leipzig, 1943), pp. 193–94; BvB to PzE, Aug. 22, 1897, EN, XLVIII, 460–66.

[36] Franz von Rottenburg to HvB, Sept. 1, 1889, BisN FC 2977/321–22; Meisner, *Denkwürdigkeiten; Waldersee*, II, 292; Raschdau, *Unter Bismarck und Caprivi*, p. 195; Kayser to unknown person, Sept. 26, 1895, KayserN 44. Hammann, *Neue Kurs*, p. 57, identifies Karl von Lindenau, a Political Division counselor, as a Holstein ally. William II eventually fell out with Kayser.

One was the Polish grand seigneur, Prince Radolin, an innocuous and pliant personality who managed the singular feat of being an intimate of all three German emperors. Radolin had left the diplomatic service in 1884 to become marshal of the court of the Prussian crown prince. In 1892, probably due to Holstein's influence, he returned to the Wilhelmstrasse and was made ambassador to the Porte.[37]

A much more influential ally was Count Philipp Eulenburg, whose stature was based, not on his position in 1890 as minister to Oldenburg, but on the fact that he, along with Prince Max Egon zu Fürstenberg, was Kaiser William II's most intimate friend. Holstein and Eulenburg first met in 1886 and shortly thereafter began to correspond with one another. Holstein, who had never met or had any dealings with the emperor, realized that he could use Eulenburg as an avenue for implanting the proper ideas in the imperial mind. "The Kaiser, if properly advised," he pointed out to Eulenburg in 1891, "is a *great* asset in our political inventory. We should not forget it."[38] Holstein's letters to Eulenburg therefore frequently addressed themselves to what Eulenburg should tell William. On occasion, Eulenburg let Holstein see his letters to the emperor before sending them on to the palace.[39] In Holstein's opinion, keeping a rein on the kaiser was important, for he feared, as did Eulenburg, that the sovereign was likely to prove headstrong. "In my corner, depending as I do on secondhand information," the reclusive Holstein wrote a week after William ascended the throne, "I have the feeling that our young ruler has his own ideas and will, I hope not too often, succeed in having his way."[40]

[37] FvH to PzE, May 23, 1891, EN, XV, 162–63.

[38] Johannes Haller, *Aus dem Leben des Fürsten Philipp zu Eulenburg-Hertefeld* (Berlin, 1924), p. 52.

[39] FvH to PzE, Mar. 20, and Nov. 7, 1892, EN, XVIII, 195–96 and XXI, 711–12. For examples of Holstein's use of Eulenburg to reach the kaiser see his letters to Eulenburg of Feb. 21, 1888, ibid., III, 18–19, and Mar. 27, 1890, ibid., X, 342.

[40] FvH to PzE, June 21, 1888, and PzE to FvH, Nov. 8, 1888,

What Holstein especially wanted to prevent was any reconciliation between William and the Bismarcks, for he himself, being the most prominent enemy of the family in the Foreign Office, would surely be among the first victims of such a development. In December, 1891, Holstein urged Eulenburg to strengthen the kaiser's resistance to a restoration of relations with Friedrichsruh, a request with which Eulenburg promptly complied. Thereafter, Holstein repeatedly enlisted Eulenburg's help in preventing any accommodation, threatening to retire if a reconciliation took place.[41] In January, 1894, however, William II decided to receive Bismarck in Berlin. Holstein's threats to resign were often rituals not designed to be taken seriously, and he did not act on his declaration to Eulenburg. Holstein continued the charade through the remaining months of Caprivi's administration. Shortly after Caprivi was replaced by Prince Chlodwig zu Hohenlohe-Schillingsfürst, he wrote to the new chancellor that he wished to resign so as not "to make more difficult the establishment of close relations with Prince Bismarck which His Majesty desires."[42] The chancellor, who had no desire to create confusion in the Wilhelmstrasse at the outset of his administration, declined to allow Holstein to relinquish his post and did nothing to diminish his influence.

With a neglectful chancellor and an inexperienced state secretary, the grand design of German diplomacy fell more and more into the hands of the strong-willed monarch, while the Foreign Office and its day-to-day operations became Holstein's domain. It was a system which immediately provoked the most invidious comparison with the Bis-

---

ibid., IV, 124–25, 172–73; PzE to FvH, Jan. 25, 1890, ibid., VIII, 59–60.

[41] FvH to PzE, Apr. 15, 1891, ibid., XV, 114–15; Dec. 12 and 13, 1891, ibid., XVI, 377–79, 382–85; May 3, 1892, ibid., XIX, 294–95; June 3 and 5, 1892, ibid., XX, 372–74, 382–83.

[42] FvH to Hohenlohe, Feb. 2, 1895, HohN, XXII.A.2.

marcks' firm leadership.[43] The diplomatic corps was alarmed by the purge after 1890 of Bismarck's allies, and Holstein's custom of maintaining a private correspondence with subaltern figures in foreign missions created further apprehension. The purpose of such exchanges, after all, could be to plot the "demolition" of an envoy's position.[44]

Some officials chose to resign rather than to await their dismissal or to see others receive posts or honors to which they themselves felt entitled. Rudolf Lindau, the Political Division counselor next in seniority to Holstein, swiftly became dismayed at the state of the Foreign Office after Bismarck's fall and in 1892 resigned to take a seat on the Ottoman Debt Commission. Three years later, Ernst von Bothmer, a longtime counselor in the *Handelspolitische* Division, left the service. He disliked Holstein's attempts to expand his influence into his division as well as into the legal section and particularly resented the fact that Pourtalès had been given ministerial rank although he was junior to Bothmer in both age and service.[45] Other diplomats were appalled at the curt manner in which the resignation of envoys who had fallen from grace was demanded.[46] Caprivi was held responsible for some of the collapse in morale, for there was widespread resentment at the chancellor's appointment in 1892–1893 of two generals as ambassadors or ministers. The minister to Sweden, Count Carl von Wedel, one of the military figures whose nomination to an envoyship had occasioned this criticism, wrote at the end of 1893 that the Foreign Office was "chaos and disarray, where

[43] MichahellesN, p. 55; also BvB to Lindenau, Apr. 9, 1890, BüN 99; Schlözer, *Römische Briefe,* pp. 149–50, 163.

[44] Raschdau, *Unter Bismarck und Caprivi*, pp. 164, 206–7.

[45] Ibid., pp. 205, 346, 356–57; Raschdau, *In Weimar*, pp. 29, 78; Hammann, *Neue Kurs*, p. 58. Another victim was Karl Göring, a counselor in the legal division, who resigned early in 1895. See Raschdau, *In Weimar*, pp. 15–16.

[46] Raschdau, *In Weimar*, pp. 40–41; Raschdau, *Unter Bismarck und Caprivi*, p. 308; Meisner, *Denkwürdigkeiten; Waldersee*, II, 348; III, 183.

everyone does what he wants to. . . . That pair, Holstein and Kiderlen, to whom Pourtalès attaches himself in a shameless way, and Eulenburg, the third party in the constellation, who takes care of relations with the throne, live and breathe nothing but intrigues and do not shrink from the dirtiest tricks. Oh, if only a deliverer would appear and sweep clean this Augean stable with a broom of iron. . . ."[47]

Although Caprivi managed to effect a number of reforms, notably in military and tariff questions, these victories alienated the conservatives and the army. By 1893, the chancellors' continuation in office was due only to William II, whose support was at best fickle.[48] In the next year, Caprivi declined to agree to a measure which would have severely repressed political radicals, especially anarchists. This legislation, the chief spokesman for which was Count Botho von Eulenburg, the minister-president of Prussia and an enemy of Caprivi, had the kaiser's approval. As on many prior occasions, the chancellor found himself with the liberals, while William II sided with the right. Caprivi's resignation, which occurred on October 26, 1894, resulted less from this specific difficulty than it did from the mixture of ennui and irritation which the chancellor's personality had eventually produced in the kaiser. The respect which he had initially felt for Caprivi turned to boredom. William was impatient and intemperate, Caprivi slow and judicious. The ruler, used to having his own way, finally found the chancellor's

[47] Wedel, *Zwischen Kaiser und Kanzler*, pp. 193–94. For other complaints at this time see Meisner, *Denkwürdigkeiten; Waldersee*, II, 292; Haller, *Leben Eulenburg*, pp. 108–9; Wilhelm von Schweinitz, ed., *Briefwechsel des Botschafters General v. Schweinitz* (Berlin, 1928), p. 301; Wilhelm von Schweinitz, ed., *Denkwürdigkeiten des Botschafters General v. Schweinitz*, 2 vols. (Berlin, 1927), II, 443. For resentment at military appointments, see pp. 138–46 above.

[48] Szögyényi to Kálnoky, May 27, 1893 (18B), HHStA, 143–B; same to same, Jan. 21, and Mar. 31, 1894 (4A–C, 17C), ibid., 144–B; letter of Dec. 25, 1893, with illegible signature and no addressee, ibid., 144–V; Wedel, *Zwischen Kaiser und Kanzler*, p. 193.

"eternal contrariness" vexatious.[49] William had declared to Philipp Eulenburg in the summer of 1892 that his relations with the chancellor were complicated by Caprivi's "indescribable obstinacy and by his insuperable feeling that he is dealing with a very young man. He entirely overlooks the fact that I have acquired political judgment through my long association with Prince Bismarck and through my own experience."[50] Even the chancellor's admirers admitted that his obdurateness was excessive. Caprivi was intransigent where honorable compromise was possible and he invested his position with aggravating self-righteousness. "His sense of honor was often exaggerated, even otherworldly," his friend the Bavarian envoy in Berlin, Count Hugo Lerchenfeld-Koefering wrote. "He regarded his position like a general to whom the leadership of a campaign is entrusted and who says to himself: I cannot change the plan but must conduct it according to the book."[51]

As Caprivi's successor the kaiser probably would have preferred Botho von Eulenburg, but he had to be ruled out because of the unpopularity of his archconservative position. On October 24, 1894, two days before he accepted Caprivi's resignation, William confessed to Philipp Eulenburg that he had no idea who should become chancellor. It was no easy task, Eulenburg replied, to find a candidate who was "neither conservative nor liberal, neither ultramontane nor progressive, neither clerical nor atheistic."[52] Eulenburg proposed Prince Hohenlohe, the Bavarian-born *Statthalter* of Alsace-Lorraine. Hohenlohe, one of whose

[49] Raschdau, *Unter Bismarck und Caprivi*, pp. 174–75; Szögyényi to Kálnoky, Jan. 21, and Nov. 24, 1894 (4A–C), HHStA, 144–B, 145–V; PzE to BvB, Nov. 1, 1894, BüN 75; Lerchenfeld-Koefering, *Erinnerungen*, p. 369.
[50] Eulenburg diary, July 17, 1892, EN, XXI, 517–19.
[51] Lerchenfeld-Koefering, *Erinnerungen*, p. 369.
[52] On Botho Eulenburg's candidacy see memo by PzE, Oct. 21, 1894, EN, XXXII, 808–10; on William's quandary see memo by PzE, Oct. 23–25, 1894, ibid., 828–29.

brothers was a cardinal, was a devout but independent-minded Catholic, a bureaucrat of proven ability, and a man identified politically with neither the left nor the right.[53] William immediately acted on Eulenburg's suggestion and on October 26, Hohenlohe was named chancellor.

The new head of government was seventy-five but his frail appearance belied his physical stamina and moral courage. The selection of Hohenlohe delighted the Foreign Office, for the new chancellor, unlike his predecessor, was an experienced and talented diplomat whose service from 1874 to 1885 as ambassador in Paris and temporary duty from 1880 to 1881 as acting state secretary had made him well acquainted with diplomatic operations in Berlin as well as in the field.[54] Like Caprivi before him, Hohehlohe had no illusions that dealing with William II would be easy. "From the day I took office," he wrote early in 1896, "I made it clear to myself that the emperor would not extend to me the same position which Kaiser William I granted to Bismarck. If I did not want it that way I should not for a minute have assumed the office. But after I accepted it I was obliged to take the Kaiser as he is. . . ."[55] But Hohenlohe, a mediatized grandee, felt no hesitation at presenting his opinion forthrightly to the ruler, who was his cousin by marriage. "As Your Majesty's senior counselor," he wrote to William II in 1896 in the course of a disagreement on a matter of policy, "I consider it the duty of my office to ex-

[53] Grand Duke of Baden to PzE, Sept. 25, 1894, ibid., XXXI, 704–11; Szögyényi to Kálnoky, Nov. 24, 1894, HHStA, 144–V; PzE to BvB, June 8, 1896, BüN 76.

[54] Szögyényi to Kálnoky, Nov. 10, 1895 (44B), HHStA, 144–B; PzE to BvB, Nov. 1, 1894, and to W2, Nov. 3, 1894, EN, XXXII, 850–56, 862–65.

[55] Karl A. von Müller, ed., *Fürst Chlodwig zu Hohenlohe-Schillingsfürst: Denkwürdigkeiten der Reichskanzlerzeit* (Stuttgart, 1931), pp. 192–93, 235; see also Müller, *Hohenlohe: Denkwürdigkeiten der Reichskanzlerzeit*, II, 529.

press my views freely. . . ."[56] Where his prerogative as chancellor was concerned, he was quite insistent. In 1897, for example, he categorically refused to follow William's order that journalists from the conservative *Kreuzzeitung*, which had irritated the kaiser, be barred from the Foreign Office.[57] For little more than a year, William tolerated Hohenlohe's independent attitude with equanimity, but by 1896 it had begun to remind him of the perpetual obstructionism of Caprivi.[58]

"Uncle Chlodwig," as William II usually addressed the chancellor, was equally fearless with envoys, reminding them that it was his right to criticize them and warned against complaining to the kaiser about such reproaches.[59] In the Wilhelmstrasse 76 itself, the new chancellor was more cautious, and he treated State Secretary Marschall and Holstein with care. This behavior did not proceed from any personal inclination for Marschall, for the two south Germans were too ill-matched in personality to have been able to develop a close relationship. According to the chancellor, Marschall's career in diplomacy unfortunately had never succeeded in effacing his past as a lawyer.[60] But Hohenlohe had a shrewd appreciation of the state secretary's abilities and of his own limitations, and he realized the difficulties to which the government would be exposed if Marschall left his post. The state secretary's parliamentary

[56] Müller, *Hohenlohe: Denkwürdigkeiten der Reichskanzlerzeit*, p. 310.

[57] FvH to BvB, Jan. 8, 1897, BüN 90. For another example of Hohenlohe's resistance to William II, see Szögyényi to Foreign Minister Count Agenor von Goluchowski, Dec. 21, 1895 (41A–D), HHStA, 146–B.

[58] For the decline in their relations, compare William's letter to PzE of Feb. 21, 1895, EN, XXXIV, 146–47, with Szögyényi to Goluchowski, Feb. 1, 1896 (4B), HHStA, 147–B, and same to same, Feb. 6 and 15, 1896, ibid., 148–V.

[59] Hohenlohe to Münster, Jan. 15, 1896, MünsterN 9; Münster to FvH, Jan. 13, 1896, HolN 3859/H194741–42.

[60] Count Bogdan von Hutten-Czapski, *Sechzig Jahre Politik und Gesellschaft*, 2 vols. (Berlin, 1936), I, 341.

talents would enable Hohenlohe to have an effective spokesman in the Reichstag, and Marschall's firm ties to the Catholic Center party would help keep it in the chancellor's fold. In the Prussian ministry, Marschall would serve as a counterweight to the reactionary element, for which Hohenlohe had little liking.[61]

Hohenlohe's determination to keep Marschall was related to his belief that Holstein was indispensable.[62] The day the new chancellor took office, Holstein had informed him that if Marschall was sacked he too would submit his resignation. For the next two years, Holstein was steadfast in insisting that Marschall be retained and, on at least one occasion, repeated his threat to resign if the state secretary were dismissed.[63] Holstein and Marschall had known one another for years and their common fate after 1890 as objects of vituperation by the Bismarcks created a new bond between them. But Holstein's trust in his colleagues was never complete, and from the beginning he was suspicious of Marschall.[64] Shortly after becoming chancellor and probably acting at Holstein's urging, Hohenlohe informed Marschall that he intended to keep personnel matters in his own hands. Thereafter the chancellor shifted several diplomats around without bothering to inform Marschall, who spluttered momentarily about resigning when he discov-

[61] FvH to BvB, Feb. 21, 1895, BüN 90; Müller, *Hohenlohe: Denkwürdigkeiten der Reichskanzlerzeit*, pp. 39, 45, 243.

[62] Rantzau maintained that part of the hold which Holstein had on Hohenlohe was due to the fact that Holstein knew certain particulars of Hohenlohe's life as ambassador in Paris. See Rantzau's "Autobiographische Aufzeichungen," BisN FC 3030/700.

[63] Müller, *Hohenlohe: Denkwürdigkeiten der Reichskanzlerzeit*, pp. 1–3; FvH to PzE, July 18, 1896, EN, XLII, 504–5; FvH to BvB, Feb. 21, 1895, BüN 90; HP, III, 506, 635; PzE to FvH, Feb. 19, 1895, HolN 3855/H192380–82.

[64] FvH to Eisendecher, Apr. 16, and July 20, 1890, HolN 3847/E359799–801; PzE to FvH, Aug. 1, 1890, ibid., 3855/H192177–78; Rich, *Holstein*, pp. 289–90.

ered what Hohenlohe had done.[65] Hohenlohe allowed many personnel matters to rest with Holstein, who strengthened his position in this respect in 1895 by having Humbert, the *Personalreferent*, removed from the diplomatic service and made under state secretary in the Prussian state ministry. He was replaced by Holstein's protégé, Pourtalès.[66] Still obsessed with fear that Bismarck might return to William's favor, Holstein's paranoia continued, as it had under Caprivi, to unsettle many Wilhelmstrasse officials. He succeeded in driving some diplomats out of the service, the most prominent being Bismarck's friend, General Bernhard von Werder, the ambassador in St. Petersburg from 1892 to 1895.[67]

After Caprivi's fall, the position of the Foreign Office, if in part improved because of Hohenlohe's interest and competence in diplomacy, at the same time suffered because of William II's increasing alienation from Marschall. During the four years of the state secretary's service under Caprivi, he and the kaiser had failed to develop any personal rapport, and by 1893 William had come to dislike Marschall. During 1895, the sovereign's attitude turned to hostility. The problem was in part a collision of personalities, for Marschall was quite as headstrong and imperious as the kaiser. "For years," Eulenburg wrote early in 1897, "we have found ourselves in the grinding mill between two incommensurable titans."[68] Marschall resented William's continuous intervention in foreign affairs. "Things are not going well with His Majesty," the state secretary wrote on Christmas Day, 1895. "He is forever intruding into diplomatic policy. A monarch must have the last word, but His Majesty

[65] Hohenlohe to Marschall, Feb. 26, 1895, HohN, XXII.A.2; memo by Hohenlohe, Nov. 22, 1894, and FvH to Hohenlohe, Jan. 17, 1895, ibid., XXII.A.1.

[66] Raschdau, *In Weimar*, p. 12.

[67] PzE to BvB, Oct. 6, 1894 and Jan. 7, 1895, EN, XXXII, 749–51, XXXIV, 8–10; Meisner, *Denkwürdigkeiten; Waldersee*, II, 340, 348.

[68] PzE to FvH, Jan. 13, 1897, BüN 92.

always wants the first one as well. That is a cardinal error."[69] William II, for his part, resented Marschall's disposing of diplomatic or political matters without prior consultation with the sovereign. He also tended to blame the state secretary for problems which arose between Caprivi and the crown.[70] But the essential difficulty between the two lay in Marschall's highly developed taste for parliamentary politics.

Already influential in the Reichstag under Caprivi, under Hohenlohe Marschall became—as Holstein put it—the government's *Sprechminister*.[71] Marschall, like the two chancellors under whom he served from 1890 to 1897 but unlike the sovereign, usually found himself on the side of the liberal parties in the parliament, joining them in supporting such measures as tariff revision and the reform of military courts martial. Suspect as a South German, Marschall quickly alienated the Prussian agrarian contingent in William II's entourage. Court circles were fervently evangelical, and although Marschall was a Protestant he was disliked by this group because of his parliamentary identification with the Catholic Center, which until 1897 was usually in opposition to the crown. The state secretary had particularly influential enemies in Friedrich von Lucanus, the chief of the Civil Cabinet, and Johannes von Miquel, the Prussian minister of finance, who resented Marschall's intrusion into financial affairs. Eulenburg, who was certainly in a position to know, observed that the state secretary had not a single friend at court.[72] The kaiser was frequently unsympathetic

[69] Marschall's diary for Dec. 25, 1895, in David B. King, "Marschall von Bieberstein and the New Course, 1890–1897" (Ph.D. diss., Cornell University, 1962), p. 180 note 1.

[70] Hohenlohe diary, July 1, 1896, HohN, XXII.A.8; PzE to BvB, Sept. 22, 1895, BüN 75.

[71] FvH to BvB, June 6, 1896, BüN 90; Müller, *Hohenlohe: Denkwürdigkeiten der Reichskanzlerzeit*, p. 352; PzE to W2, Feb. 14, 1895, EN, XXXIV, 98–101.

[72] PzE to FvH, Jan. 13, 1897 (2d letter of this date), BüN 92; see also PzE to FvH, Feb. 19, 1895, HolN 3855/H192380–82.

to his government's liberal proposals and he was quick to suspect that it was Marschall who was behind any opposition to the crown. He therefore resented the state secretary's mixing in internal affairs, criticizing his deficient appreciation of the proper "Prussian" perspective.[73] The kaiser instructed Marschall to restrict himself to diplomacy, an injunction the state secretary airily disregarded. Marschall later admitted that his involvement in parliamentary squabbles undermined his position with the crown, an opinion shared by Holstein, Hohenlohe, and Bernhard von Bülow, who regretted the strain Marschall's behavior put on William's relations with the Foreign Office itself. Early in 1897 Eulenburg wrote to Bülow that the kaiser's hostility to the Wilhelmstrasse was as great as it possibly could be.[74]

The tension between the state secretary and his sovereign was revealed in an episode which occurred early in 1895, shortly after Hohenlohe took office. "Our friend Marschall has recently behaved toward me at a court ball in a way which surpasses everything that has happened up to now," William wrote to Eulenburg. The cause, according to the kaiser, was Marschall's rude insistence in having him speak to Ernst Lieber, the Catholic Center leader, whose support Marschall hoped to enlist by managing this mark of royal favor. William loathed Lieber because of the deputy's earlier opposition to an army bill and he was furthermore outraged that he had not been informed that Lieber was on the guest list, believing that this had been done at the last moment at Marschall's behest. The state secretary's version of the incident was that it was not he who had initially in-

[73] PzE to BvB, Oct. 10, 1894, BüN 75; FvH to PzE, Oct. 11, 1894, ibid., 92; PzE to Hohenlohe, Oct. 1, 1895, HohN, XXII.A.5.

[74] PzE to BvB, May 31, 1897, BüN 76; Marschall to BvB, Sept. 4, 1897, ibid., 104; PzE to Hohenlohe, Oct. 1, 1895, HohN, XXII.-A.5, for Marschall. For Holstein, see his letter to BvB of June 9, 1897, BüN 90; for Hohenlohe, Szögyényi to Goluchowski, Jan. 15, 1898 (2A–E), HHStA, 150–B; for Bülow, see his letter to PzE, Dec. [?], 1894, BüN 75. See also PzE to BvB, Mar. 8, 1897, ibid.

vited Lieber and that his purpose in having William II greet him was to fulfill a wish earlier expressed by the kaiser to thank Lieber for his support of a naval bill.[75] Though Marschall may have acted innocently, the affair enraged the kaiser and it clouded his subsequent relations with the state secretary. Thereafter he cut Marschall socially and had almost nothing to do with him officially. By March, 1896, Eulenburg described William's hostility to the state secretary as "insuperable."[76]

Ordinarily, William's distaste would have been enough to fell Marschall, but in this case he was reluctant to move because Hohenlohe favored his retention and was even prepared to resign if the kaiser insisted on firing the state secretary. At the same time, the chancellor realistically acknowledged that, given William's hostility, Marschall could not last indefinitely.[77] But Hohenlohe faced the same dilemma both Bismarck and Caprivi had earlier encountered: what diplomat could, or would, assume Marschall's post? Both Hohenlohe and the kaiser considered Bülow, ambassador to Italy since 1894, to be a promising candidate, but Bülow had no desire to exchange Rome for Berlin, especially since he felt that becoming state secretary might undermine his chances of eventually succeeding to the chancellorship. Bülow's intimate friend, Eulenburg, argued the envoy's case very persuasively with William II, and the result was that the kaiser was for the moment deterred from sacking Marschall.[78]

[75] William's account is in his letter to PzE of Feb. 12, 1895, EN, XXXIV, 98–101; Marschall's is in his letter to PzE, Feb. 17, 1895, in ibid. See also PzE to BvB, Mar. 8, 1897, BüN 76.

[76] FvH to BvB, June 10, 1896, BüN 90; PzE to BvB, Mar. 31, 1896, EN, XL, 130–32.

[77] PzE to W2, Feb. 18, 1895, and Hohenlohe to PzE, Feb. 21, 1895, EN, XXXIV, 118–21, 139–41.

[78] On Bülow's resistance to the state secretaryship, see his letters to FvH of Jan. 15, and Mar. 10, 1895, Jan. 3, and July 7, 1896, in HolN 3854/H191304–7, H191314–15, H191367–69, H191432–33. For Eulenburg's intervention with the kaiser see PzE to W2, Feb.

The state secretary's position became intolerable in early 1897, when Holstein deserted him. Holstein had long been wary of Marschall but his suspicion turned to hatred when he discovered that Marschall had become involved with Count Guido Henckel von Donnersmarck, whom Holstein had challenged to a duel in 1894 because of an imagined affront by the count. On a more professional level Holstein resented what he described as Marschall's favoritism of the *Handelspolitische Abteilung* at the expense of the Political Division. The state secretary, he declared, was against everyone who was a Prussian, a noble, and a political official.[79] Hohenlohe, irritated by Marschall's failure to consult him on various matters, eventually became resigned to replacing the state secretary. The chancellor feared that his own continuance in office might be jeopardized if he insisted on retaining Marschall or otherwise became too closely identified with him. Indeed, in the winter of 1896 to 1897, William II on several occasions said that he intended to fire both the chancellor and the state secretary.[80] But William's reservations about Hohenlohe were uncomplicated by personal animosity and paled beside the acute dislike he felt for Marschall. There were, moreover, problems regarding the succession to the chancellorship, for Bülow, whom the kaiser and others regarded as Hohenlohe's even-

---

14, 20, 21 and 23, 1895, EN, XXXIV, 98–101, 131–34, 145–47, 152–54, and PzE to FvH, Dec. 30, 1895, HolN 3855/H192481–83.

[79] PzE to BvB, May 31, 1897, BüN 77; same to same, June 11, 1897, EN, XLVII, 336.

[80] Notes by Hohenlohe, ca. May 1896, HohN, XXII.A.8; PzE to W2, Feb. 14, 1895, Hohenlohe to PzE, Feb. 21, 1895, EN, XXXIV, 118–21, 139–41; Hohenlohe to PzE, July 16, 1896, ibid., XLII, 493, on the chancellor's reservations about keeping Marschall. For William's threats to remove the state secretary, see Eulenburg's notes of a conversation with the kaiser on Oct. 4, 1896, and his letter to BvB of Dec. 10, 1896, in EN, XLIV, 681–83, 813–17; W2 to PzE, Jan. 5, 1897, ibid., XLV, 40–41; Szögyényi to Goluchowski, Apr. 10, 1897, HHStA, 148–V.

tual successor, needed first to replace Marschall.[81] William II therefore decided against dropping the chancellor but persisted in his determination to get rid of Marschall. Kiderlen described the situation in a letter to Holstein on April 25, 1897. "H.M. is reluctant to let Marschall go without cause, but is *very* annoyed at him and would gladly use any pretext to let him go. However, H.M. will not get rid of Marschall in the forseeable future because he fears the poor impression it would make. . . . H.M. cannot bring himself to replace Marschall with someone else at the cost of Hohenlohe's departure."[82]

As matters turned out, it was the state secretary rather than William II who resolved the situation. In August, 1896, Marschall declared to Eulenberg that he wished to resign because of the kaiser's hostility. Eulenburg, deferring to Bülow's desire to remain in Rome, again managed to persuade William that Bülow was not yet ripe for the move to Berlin.[83] The kaiser, however, was adamant. "You must step to the front," he ordered the ambassador. "Marschall has betrayed me."[84] At the end of May, 1897, by which time Bülow had been won over to the idea of assuming the position, Marschall agreed to go on a three-month vacation, having been promised that he would be named to a European embassy. Marschall's heart was set on Constantinople, and it was rumored that in anticipation of receiving the sultry post he had put his winter clothes in storage before leaving Berlin for his estates in southern Germany.[85] On June 21, Bülow, who had insisted that he be given a written assurance that he would later be given an embassy, arrived

[81] Raschdau, *In Weimar*, p. 41; Radziwill, *Lettres*, II, 105; Müller, *Hohenlohe: Denkwürdigkeiten der Reichskanzlerzeit*, p. 250; Haller, *Leben Eulenburg*, p. 225.

[82] HolN 3858/H194273.

[83] PzE to W2, Aug. 16, 1896, EN, XLIII, 582–84.

[84] BvB to Friedrich Wilhelm von Loebell, May 9, 1912, LoebellN 27.

[85] Alexander Hohenlohe to Chlodwig Hohenlohe, Oct. 14, 1897, HohN, XXII.A.12; PzE to BvB, May 31, 1897, BüN 77.

in Berlin to become deputy state secretary. In October, Marschall resigned to assume his ambassadorship and Bülow succeeded him at number 76.

Bülow took up his new position protesting its burden and complaining of the pleasures he had been forced to leave behind in Rome. He received some consolation from his French chef, who declared his intention to follow the envoy to Berlin. "Quand on a partagé les beaux jours de ses maîtres," the servant assured his master, "on ne doit pas les quitter dans la misère."[86] Bülow's dedication to self-interest was total, and he had so carefully planned his career that it seems very likely that the move to Berlin was one which he not only privately wanted but which he had sedulously arranged.[87]

No diplomat could have had a more impressive background for the state secretaryship than Bülow. He had grown up in a diplomatic family and entered the service in 1873, the year in which his father had become state secretary. He had served in several important capitals and all the while maintained close contacts with a number of counselors in the Foreign Office, as well as with other diplomats (including a brother and several cousins). The new state secretary possessed many diplomatic gifts: he spoke several languages effortlessly, he delighted in society, he wrote well, and his manners were deft and courtly. But even his friends admitted that his gestures were contrived and overblown. Bülow's responses such as "as you have just so cogently observed" were unconvincing when they followed commonplaces; his conversation too often verged on oratory and his deportment could sometimes be more oleaginous than polished. Bülow, however, considered his exaggerated suavity an assert rather than a liability. "Über

[86] Otto Hammann, *Zur Vorgeschichte des Weltkrieges: Erinnerungen aus den Jahren 1897–1906* (Berlin, 1919), p. 1.

[87] Eulenburg, in a letter to Bülow on the occasion of his assuming the chancellorship, reminded him of how they had planned his ascent to this office. Letter of Oct. 20, 1900, HA, Rep. 53a, no. 63.

Frankreich sprach ich pomadig," he once boasted of a parliamentary effusion.[88] His confidences, like his observations, were sometimes ridiculously inflated. Even the high-spirited Donna Laura Minghetti deplored this attribute of a son-in-law she otherwise found to be ideal. "Bernhard makes a secret of everything," she said. "He takes you by the arm, leads you to the window and says: Don't say anything, but there's a little dog down there who's pissing."[89] What passed for charm was essentially falseness, and while Bülow often captivated or at least titillated he seldom inspired respect. His own brother said of him once that "he would be quite a fellow if his character could only attain the height of his personality."[90] Bülow's resplendent manner masked a shallow character, and from the beginning William II recognized the new state secretary as one of his own.

"I adore him," the kaiser wrote to Eulenburg on August 20, 1897, contrasting Bülow with his predecessor. "Mein Gott, what a difference from the South German high traitor." The emperor called on the state secretary every morning but visited Hohenlohe conspicuously less frequently.[91] Bülow's initial estimate of William, expressed in a letter to Eulenburg of August 22, was more measured than the kaiser's adulation of the new state secretary. "As a man, His Majesty [is] charming, touching, enchanting to the point of adoration; as a ruler [he is] threatened by temperament, lack of nuance, and sometimes by judgments made by eye, by a preponderance of will . . . over calm, clear reflection

[88] Rogge, *Holstein: Lebensbekenntnis*, p. 284; cf. Bülow, *Denkwürdigkeiten*, II, 415.

[89] Hartmut Pogge von Strandmann, ed., *Walther Rathenau, Tagebuch 1907–1922* (Düsseldorf, 1967), p. 143.

[90] Princess Herbert Bismarck, "Meine Erinnerungen an Bernhard von Bülow," BisN FC 2958/968–69.

[91] W2 to PzE, Aug. 20, 1897, EN, XLVIII, 453–57; Szögyényi to Goluchowski, Feb. 2, 1898, HHStA, 151–V.

. . . unless he is surrounded by wise and especially by *completely loyal and trustworthy* servants."[92]

There was every reason for the two men to be compatible, for they had in common a love for the theatrical, a casual attitude toward rigorous work, and a taste for the arts as well as for salacious gossip. But both also had an overweening determination to be the center of attention, and since this last characteristic could lead to collision, Bülow was careful to truckle to the kaiser. "Bernhard the Obliging," one of his critics named him, seldom contested the sovereign's will directly, arguing that what he might prevent by pliancy was more significant than what he might lose by being obdurate.[93] Field Marshal Count Waldersee, not an uncritical observer, found Bülow's handling of the kaiser very talented. "He treats the ruler to a great deal of flattery," Waldersee wrote in 1899, "and never says 'no' to him, but often afterward he would do otherwise, for he knew that the kaiser frequently changes his opinion and also often forgets what he has said in haste."[94]

Six months after taking over as state secretary, Bülow again wrote to Eulenburg about William II. There is a lusher vein in this letter than in the one written on August 22, perhaps because he believed or hoped that Eulenburg would show it to the kaiser. "He is so *bedeutend*!! Of all the great kings and *Kurfürsten* he is by far the most significant Hohenzollern who has ever lived. He combines, in a manner such as I have never before known, geniality, the truest and most profound geniality, with the clearest good sense. He possesses a fantasy which raises me on eagle's

[92] BvB to PzE, Aug. 22, 1897, EN, XLVIII, 460–66.
[93] Baron Colmar von der Goltz, *Denkwürdigkeiten* (Berlin, 1929), p. 260; Count Robert Zedlitz-Trützschler, *Zwölf Jahre am deutschen Kaiserhof: Aufzeichnungen* (Berlin, 1924), pp. 88, 236–37; Bernhard Schwertfeger, ed., *Kaiser und Kabinettschef: nach eigenen Aufzeichnungen und dem Briefwechsel des Wirklichen Geheimen Rats Rudolf von Valentini* (Oldenburg, 1931), p. 73 note 1.
[94] Meisner, *Denkwürdigkeiten; Waldersee*, II, 433.

wings above all pettiness and thereby gives me the clearest appreciation of the possible and the realizable. And, added to that, what energy! What memory! What swiftness and certainty of viewpoint! Today at the privy council I was simply overwhelmed!"[95]

Getting along with William II was one thing, managing the Foreign Office another, but Bülow approached his new post with aplomb and he eventually emerged with success. The diplomatic corps approved his appointment, for Bülow was a professional who had made his way up in the ranks and ingratiated himself with his junior colleagues as well as with his peers. He enjoyed excellent relations with Hohenlohe, under whom he had served in the Paris embassy and whose wife's financial interests he later represented in St. Petersburg.[96] Bülow had an able and amenable under state secretary in Baron Oswald von Richthofen, who obediently followed the state secretary's orders. The problems which faced Bülow, insofar as they did not proceed from William II, lay with what the state secretary identified as the *Hauptgruppe* of Holstein and his two satellites, Kiderlen and Pourtalès.[97]

Herbert Bismarck had first introduced Bülow to Holstein in 1870, and over the years Bülow had developed a high regard for Holstein's ability as a diplomat. In the 1870s, Holstein kept a watchful eye on the young secretary and Bülow felt a lasting appreciation for the arts Holstein had taught him. The advantage was mutual, for Holstein realized the uses to which the son of a state secretary could be put.[98] At the same time, Bülow never trusted Holstein, just as Holstein never trusted him. The state secretary was too false to

[95] BvB to PzE, Feb. 15, 1898, EN, L, 40–41.

[96] Wedel to BvB, June 26, 1899, BüN 129; Monts to Marie von Bülow, Jan. 10, 1898, ibid., 106. Cf. Hohenlohe to Münster, July 4, 1897, MünsterN 9. Bülow's correspondence with Hohenlohe is filed in BüN 89.

[97] BvB to PzE, Aug. 22, 1897, EN, XLVIII, 460–66.

[98] BvB to Lindenau, Feb. 3, 1893, BüN 99; Bülow, *Denkwürdigkeiten*, IV, 454–55.

instill confidence and Holstein was too suspicious to extend it. State Secretary Bülow *père* had not liked Holstein, probably because of his complicity in the Arnim affair, and Bernhard's brother Alfred, also a diplomat, warned Bernhard that Holstein was not what either of them would call a gentleman.[99] By 1887, Bernhard began to fear that Holstein was conspiring against him, a discovery that mystified him because he claimed that he had always been one of the counselor's greatest admirers. The first real difference between the two occurred in 1890, for Bülow persisted in maintaining his cordial relations with the Bismarcks after their fall from office. Even so, Bülow believed that Holstein should be retained in the Foreign Office, for there was no one in the service who was so professionally expert. Yet he declared in 1894 that he himself would not accept the state secretaryship as long as Holstein served in the Wilhelmstrasse.[100]

Like many things Bülow said, this was something he did not mean. When Bülow assumed the position three years later, he did nothing to remove Holstein, who declared that he felt like a father to the new state secretary.[101] Bülow told Otto Hammann, the Political Division counselor in charge of press affairs, that he intended to take three things into his own hands: personnel questions, the press, and the political police.[102] Eulenburg reported to Bülow on August 23, 1897, that William II was disposed to give him a free hand in diplomatic appointments. *"Don't forget* that!" Eulenburg enjoined him. "Build your nest as you need and want it, without *hesitation and without quibble.* Even the monster of the

[99] Bülow, *Denkwürdigkeiten,* II, 112; IV, 454–55; Alfred von Bülow to BvB, n.d. [ca. 1882], BüN 14, pp. 21–23.

[100] For Bülow's deteriorating relations with Holstein, see BvB to Lindenau, July 20, 1887, Apr. 9, and Sept. 17, 1890, May 6, 1891, and Feb. 3, 1893, BüN 99; also BvB to PzE, Dec. 13, 1894, EN, XXXIII, 955–59.

[101] BvB to PzE, Aug. 22, 1897, EN, XLVIII, 460–66.

[102] Hammann, *Vorgeschichte,* p. 6.

labyrinth begins to moan, groveling before your feet."[103] Eulenburg clearly was referring to Holstein, with whom he had had a number of disagreements and whom Eulenburg suspected of trying to demolish his position as ambassador in Vienna.[104]

The principal difference between Holstein, on the one hand, and both Bülow and Eulenburg, on the other, was the fact that Holstein was alarmed at the increasing interference of William II in diplomatic matters, for he believed that the ruler was totally unfit for such a role.[105] He wanted Eulenburg and the state secretary to use their influence to restrain the kaiser's intervention so that the Foreign Office —and thus, at least in part, Holstein—could chart Germany's diplomatic path. Holstein believed that Bülow, unfortunately, was too weak to do this.[106] Both Eulenburg and the state secretary, being intimates of the emperor, had more reason to be tolerant of William II's Caesarean instincts. The two men, who were very closely allied, seem to have believed that they could employ their influence to see that the kaiser's authority, salutary if properly applied, was used to further their own devices.[107] Under such a conception, Holstein's role would be merely to carry out the policies and personnel decisions arrived at by William II and his two confederates in the Wilhelmstrasse.

In his aspiration to take over personnel, Bülow had to be careful of Holstein, who stood well with Hohenlohe, and his sidekick Pourtalès. The state secretary could not at first al-

[103] BüN 77.

[104] PzE to BvB, Mar. 8, 1897; PzE's notes for Apr. 20, 1897; PzE to BvB, Apr. 24, 1897, in BüN 76; FvH to BvB, Mar. 24, 1897, ibid., 90; Theodor von Holleben (ambassador in Washington) to PzE, Feb. 4, 1900, EN, LV, 46.

[105] Hutten-Czapski, Sechzig Jahre, I, 466.

[106] Rogge, Holstein: Lebensbekenntnis, p. 244; HP, IV, 245.

[107] BvB to PzE, Dec. [?], 1894; PzE to BvB, Sept. 22, 1895, BüN 75; notes by PzE for BvB, Oct. 27, 1896, ibid., 76; Hohenlohe to BvB, Mar. 3, 1897, ibid., 77; FvH to PzE, Jan. 1, 1895, Jan. 7, and June 15, 1897, ibid., 92.

ways get his way. Holstein's bitter enemy, Ludwig Raschdau, minister to Saxony, who in the winter of 1896 to 1897 had argued intensely that Holstein be retired, had to be sacrificed in 1897 when he refused assignment to Lisbon because that capital lay in Holstein's jurisdiction within the Political Division.[108] Bülow had one very great advantage, however, for by the time he took over as state secretary William II's admiration for Holstein had cooled. The cause of Holstein's declining favor is obscure, but it probably was related to the increasing differences of opinion which had emerged between the sovereign's confidant, Eulenburg, and himself. In April, 1897, the kaiser declared to Eulenburg that Holstein was "an old man full of specters and hallucinations for whom I broke many, many lances; a man who now and then has made the Wilhelmstrasse crazier than it already was."[109] By 1898, Bülow had consolidated his position in the Foreign Office to the extent that the emperor announced jubilantly to Eulenburg that "the sway of the counselors [in the Wilhelmstrasse] has almost stopped. Who talks nowadays of Herr von Holstein? What is Herr von Holstein? . . . Since Bülow now has the reins in his hands, one no longer knows the names of his advisors."[110] In the following year, Bülow further strengthened his position by removing Pourtalès as head of personnel, replacing him with Hohenlohe's cousin, Prince Karl Max Lichnowsky. This Silesian magnate had become a close friend of Bülow's while serving under him in Bucharest in the early 1890s. Lichnowsky, whose independence of mind and arrogance were pronounced, refused to be intimidated by Holstein, who therefore resented his influence with the state secre-

[108] Raschdau, *In Weimar*, pp. 164–66; Hohenlohe diary, Oct. 28, 1897, HohN XXII.A.12.

[109] PzE to BvB, Apr. 24, 1897, EN, XLVII, 258–63; Meisner, *Denkwürdigkeiten; Waldersee*, II, 399; Otto Hammann, *Bilder aus der letzten Kaiserzeit* (Berlin, 1922), p. 33.

[110] PzE to BvB, July 13, 1898, EN, LI, 150–51; same to same, July 12, 1899, ibid., LIV, 160, on Kiderlen's waning influence.

tary.[111] After Bülow succeeded Marschall as state secretary in 1897, Hohenlohe took less and less interest in personnel matters, and the state secretary filled important posts without even bothering to consult the chancellor.[112] In July, 1899, the Austro-Hungarian envoy advised Vienna that Hohenlohe was now leading a "contemplative existence," and four months later he reported that in diplomatic affairs Bülow had pushed aside the eighty-year-old chancellor, who did not appear troubled since his flagging energy was now entirely devoted to internal problems.[113]

Hohenlohe was determined that he would not be a straw man to William II, and early in 1900, worn out by age and office and irritated by the fact that the kaiser ignored him, he at last began to think seriously of retiring. "A chancellor whom the kaiser avoids has a ridiculous position," he lamented to his son Alexander.[114] Finally on October 16, 1900, the chancellor asked to be relieved of his office, for Bülow, clearly William II's favorite, was becoming anxious to have his place.[115] The kaiser accepted Hohenlohe's resignation with ill-concealed delight and at once appointed Bülow chancellor. "Bernhard," he declared to Eulenburg, "will one day be my Bismarck."[116]

[111] ThimmeN 24, 3–4; Rosen, *Wanderleben*, I, 25–26.

[112] Meisner, *Denkwürdigkeiten; Waldersee*, II, 439.

[113] Szögyényi to Goluchowski, Nov. 22, 1899 (47C), HHStA, 152–B; same to same, July 5, 1899, ibid., 152–V.

[114] Hohenlohe diary, May 22, 1897, HohN, XXII.A.11.

[115] Müller, *Hohenlohe: Denkwürdigkeiten der Reichskanzlerzeit*, pp. 554, 582.

[116] PzE to W2, Oct. 22, 1900, HA, Rep. 53a, no. 63.

## CHAPTER IX

Bülow and Bethmann Hollweg

The career which Bülow had long and sedulously planned had now come to its ultimate stage. A settled tenure in office stretched before him, for the kaiser had declared in 1896 that Bülow was the man he wanted as chancellor because he would have the ability to hold the office for twenty years or perhaps even longer.[1] Bülow's appointment, which was widely acclaimed, was especially well received in the Wilhelmstrasse 76, for in his term as state secretary from 1897 to 1900 Bülow had proven a popular leader. He was singularly devoid of enemies among diplomats, the only exception being Count Karl von Dönhoff, the minister in Dresden, with whose wife Bülow had made off in the 1880s. Some of the new chancellor's colleagues felt that he was wanting in character, but even they found that it was hard not to like the man. He was forever amiable and indulgent, an acknowledged *Feinschmecker*, a genial host and a fabled raconteur. His charming and energetic wife was equally well liked. As state secretary, he had succeeded in making a number of changes in personnel, in particular the appointment of Lichnowsky to succeed Pourtalès as *Personreferent*, which had strengthened his hand. During Bülow's three-year incumbency as state secretary, no less than thirty-two appointments were made to the forty-one existing envoyships. These included the accreditation of his brother Alfred to Berne and his stepson, Count Nicolas von Wallwitz, to Brussels. The changing of the guard had begun.

Immediately on taking office as chancellor, Bülow laid down the rules under which the Foreign Office would be

[1] PzE to BvB, May 24, 1896, BüN 76.

run. First of all, there was to be no question that it was he who would be in charge and that the state secretary and the counselors would do his bidding. The chancellor had no lack of self-confidence, and he approached his task feeling sure that he could overcome any obstacle, internal or external, and convert his critics into allies.

One of his first tasks was to organize the chain of command. Bülow offered the position of state secretary to Holstein, who declined it. With some difficulty, he persuaded William II to agree to elevate Baron von Richthofen, the under state secretary.[2] Richthofen was a pedestrian personality but an efficient bureaucrat, and one who was insistent that his authority, if subservient to the chancellor's will, was not to be contested by any subordinate officials in the Wilhelmstrasse. Richthofen was especially concerned about Holstein, whom he had long disliked and whom he suspected of conducting his own diplomacy behind the back of other Foreign Office officials. Richthofen, who only reluctantly would have anything to do with Holstein, insisted as a condition of taking office that all documents leaving the Foreign Office were to have his authorization. To the chancellor, this was a picayune squabble which could not be tolerated. As far as Bülow was concerned, neither Richthofen nor Holstein were to have the upper hand in the Wilhelmstrasse, but the state secretary-elect was less useful than Holstein and would have to be put on notice. Bülow therefore instructed Lichnowsky to tell Richthofen to overcome his sensitivity about Holstein. "As long as I am in power," the chancellor wrote to Lichnowsky, "nothing will be done in the Foreign Office against my wishes. . . . Please inspire in Richthofen a little courage as well as *des idées plus larges*. This is not the moment that I can let myself be de-

---

[2] On Holstein's decline see HP, IV, 376; Arthur von Brauer, *Im Dienste Bismarcks: persönliche Erinnerungen* (Berlin, 1936), pp. 410–11; on William II and Richthofen see BvB to Lichnowsky, Oct. 19, 1900, BüN 98; Bernhard von Bülow, *Denkwürdigkeiten*, 4 vols. (Berlin, 1930–31), I, 393.

tained by petty personal considerations."[3] Richthofen acceded to the chancellor's directions and accepted the post unconditionally. Holstein, however, continued to transmit documents without bothering to show them to the state secretary.[4]

There was never any effective challenge to Bülow's leadership in the Foreign Office and his command of diplomats in the field was equally firm. He would not countenance complaints by ambassadors to the emperor about their assignments and he had no hesitation in reprimanding envoys whose performance left something to be desired.[5] The chancellor retained the ultimate voice in personnel questions for himself, but he had perfect confidence that Lichnowsky would not propose unsuitable candidates. In 1904, the death of his father necessitated Lichnowsky's resignation from the diplomatic service in order to manage his landed estates, and thereafter personnel was handled by another confidant of Bülow's, Arthur Zimmermann, appointed a counselor in the Political Division in 1905. Two other counselors on whom the chancellor leaned heavily were Otto Hammann, a resourceful and ambitious bureaucrat who since 1894 had been in charge of press affairs, and Karl von Lindenau, with whom Bülow had kept up an intimate correspondence during the years that he served in the field.[6]

[3] Lichnowsky to BvB, Oct. 18, 1900, and BvB to Lichnowsky, Oct. 19, 1900, BüN 98.

[4] For an example of Holstein's independence, see Otto Hammann, *Bilder aus der letzten Kaiserzeit* (Berlin, 1922), pp. 29–30.

[5] BvB to FvH, Sept. 15, 1905, HolN 3855/H191676; BvB to European embassies and Washington, Feb. 2, 1904, Dd 149, vol. 8, 280/00340–42.

[6] Friedrich Thimme, ed., *Front wider Bülow: Staatsmänner, Diplomaten und Forscher zu seinen Denkwürdigkeiten* (Munich, 1931), p. 235; Bülow, *Denkwürdigkeiten*, III, 159; Count Bogdan von Hutten-Czapski, *Sechzig Jahre Politik und Gesellschaft*, 2 vols. (Berlin, 1936), II, 5; Ladislaus von Szögyényi-Marich (Austro-Hungarian ambassador) to Foreign Minister Count Agenor von Goluchowski, Nov. 14, 1900 (54E), HHStA, 154–B. The Lindenau correspondence, in BüN 99, is very rich and covers the years 1883 to 1905.

The only problem which Bülow faced in the Foreign Office was Holstein, and until the counselor's resignation in 1906 Bülow treated him with great care. If the new chancellor entered office with considerable advantages which could be, and were, applied to establishing his unquestioned leadership, Holstein's star was beginning perceptibly to wane. His grip on personnel matters had been loosened by Pourtalès' removal from the Political Division in 1899, the same year in which Kiderlen, another of Holstein's protégés, had been exiled to Rumania. Many of Bülow's allies in the Wilhelmstrasse were precisely those officials who, like Lichnowsky and the dutiful Richthofen, were Holstein's enemies. The chancellor's attachment to Holstein was nevertheless still strong, for he was attracted to the ageing counselor by sentiment, self-interest, and perhaps by fear. Bülow retained his appreciation for the training Holstein had given him two decades earlier; he acknowledged Holstein's diplomatic gifts; and he was aware that, as an enemy outside the Foreign Office, Holstein could cause far more trouble than he could by remaining at his desk in the Political Division.

The chancellor found ways in which to placate Holstein. The offer of the state secretaryship was a handsome gesture, but given the new chancellor's intention of directing foreign affairs personally it is likely that Holstein was expected to refuse the post, just as he had in 1890 when Caprivi had made a similar overture.[7] Radolin, Holstein's *Duzbruder* and most devoted admirer in the ranks of German diplomats, was at Holstein's insistence given the embassy in Paris in 1900 and allowed to stay there for ten years even though he proved to be only a mediocre envoy.[8]

[7] Helmuth Rogge, ed., *Friedrich von Holstein: Lebensbekenntnis in Briefen an eine Frau* (Berlin, 1932), p. 168; Prince Alexander von Hohenlohe, *Aus meinem Leben* (Frankfurt/Main, 1925), p. 312.

[8] Bülow, *Denkwürdigkeiten*, I, 495–97; Friedrich Rosen, *Aus einem diplomatischen Wanderleben*, 4 vols. in 3 (Berlin, 1931–59), I, 166–67.

Bülow ordered Richthofen to be cordial to Holstein and to consult him on the appointment of a new under state secretary. The result was that Otto von Mühlberg, whose entire career had been in the Wilhelmstrasse and who was close to Holstein, was given the position.[9] Two other associates of Holstein, Friedrich Rosen and Alexander von Kries, were transferred from the consular service and became counselors in the Political Division.[10]

Although Bülow was prepared to make these personnel arrangements to ingratiate himself with Holstein, the two men found that they could not always agree on matters of policy. Holstein deplored the chancellor's distaste for England, which he attributed to Bülow's Danish ancestry and the unfortunate influence of the Bismarcks. Bülow, like the kaiser, was inclined to believe that France, which Holstein considered to be irremediably revanchist, or Russia, which to Holstein was irremediably Germanophobe, might be won over.[11] Holstein was also irritated that in formulating these errant policies the chancellor seemed to be linking himself ever more closely with Richthofen, whom Holstein disliked intensely. In the summer of 1905, Holstein mounted a campaign against the state secretary which resulted in Bülow's very reluctantly granting Holstein the right to countersign all documents leaving the Political Division except those concerning personnel or the press. This gave Holstein the same authority which the directors of the other sections of the Foreign Office enjoyed.[12] Bülow also granted Holstein's request that whenever he needed to see the chancellor they would meet alone, for Holstein had no tolerance for "*Völk-*

[9] Szögyényi to Goluchowski, Nov. 14, 1900 (54E), HHStA, 154–B.
[10] On Rosen's relations with Holstein, see Rosen, *Wanderleben* I, 8–13, 40, 79–80; on Kries, ibid., p. 21.
[11] FvH to BvB, Jan. [?], 1906, HolN 3855/H191703–13; Holstein's undated memo, ibid., 3842/H196977; Holstein's diary for Jan. 11 and Nov. 7, 1902, ibid., 3861/H196405–8, H196411–16; Rogge, *Holstein: Lebensbekenntnis*, p. 231.
[12] HP, IV, 289–311; Rosen, *Wanderleben*, I, 84–85. The Political Division first acquired a director in 1910.

erversammlungen" of other Wilhelmstrasse officials.[13] By these marks of accommodation, Bülow secured Holstein's support, which was of considerable value. The result was the gradual erosion of Richthofen's power in the Foreign Office. "Bülow," Holstein crowed in June, 1905, "gives me his full trust since we once again became reconciled last October. During these eight months, in the course of which one difficult problem followed another, I have dealt without conflict with him alone. Richthofen is completely excluded, although he is useful to Bülow in parliamentary matters and as a mediary with the other ministries. From time to time he inquires of me about the status of affairs."[14]

In identifying himself with Holstein, however, Bülow introduced a disturbing element into his relations with William II. The kaiser's displeasure with Holstein, first discernible in 1897, never changed, and nothing that William did after the mid-1890s indicated to Holstein that his analysis of the sovereign's ineptitude for diplomacy should be amended in the least. As far as William was concerned, with a diplomat as talented as Bülow at the helm Holstein was superfluous. The emperor's attitude toward Holstein is illustrated by his conduct on the single occasion on which they met. On November 12, 1904, Bülow arranged a dinner including both Holstein and the kaiser, the purpose being to provide an opportunity for the two men to become acquainted. Rosen believed that Holstein had asked the chancellor to arrange the meeting so that he could in person counteract misleading impressions which he feared his enemies had implanted in William's mind. Other observers held that the affair took place because William was merely curious to meet a man about whom he had heard so much for so many years.[15] The emperor's behavior, as well as Bü-

---

[13] Rosen, *Wanderleben*, I, 22–23.
[14] Rogge, *Holstein: Lebensbekenntnis*, p. 240.
[15] Rosen, *Wanderleben*, I, 85–86; Hohenlohe, *Meinem Leben*, p. 318; Count Hugo Lerchenfeld-Koefering, *Erinnerungen und Denkwürdigkeiten* (Berlin, 1935), pp. 391–92.

low's arrangements for the dinner, indicate that William had no great desire to establish a footing with Holstein, for both men were seated at a large table at which there was no chance for intimate conversation. The imperial remarks sent Holstein's way after dinner had to do with diplomacy, but also with duck hunting, a subject on which the kaiser had developed a formidable expertise. Holstein, in any case, went away satisfied that he had corrected any unfavorable impression that the kaiser might have had before their meeting.[16]

Holstein's relations with William II, if perhaps improved by this encounter, soon suffered a serious deterioration as a result of the Moroccan crisis of 1905.[17] The Anglo-French Entente Cordiale of April, 1904, convinced Holstein that unless Germany challenged this constellation it would in the future find itself powerless to extract concessions from either Entente partner. Following this policy, in June, 1904, the Foreign Office successfully confronted England with demands regarding Germany's economic interests in Egypt and as a result secured a slight improvement of its position there. In the same month, Holstein and Bülow came to the conclusion that a similar campaign must be waged in behalf of Germany's nominal interests in Morocco, where France had a commanding position. The kaiser opposed any unilateral action by Germany because he had earlier assured the sultan that Germany's interest in Morocco was purely economic. In January, 1905, the French and the sultan entered into negotiations which Holstein believed would eventually lead to France's absorption of the country. Hol-

---

[16] HP, IV, 312–13; Friedrich von Trotha, *Fritz von Holstein als Mensch und Politiker* (Berlin, 1931), p. 78; Rogge, *Holstein: Lebensbekenntnis*, pp. 236–37; Rosen, *Wanderleben*, I, 87.

[17] The best treatment from the perspective of the Foreign Office, on which the following account is largely based, is Norman Rich, *Friedrich von Holstein: Politics and Diplomacy in the Era of Bismarck and Wilhelm II*, 2 vols. (Cambridge, England, 1965), II, 682–713.

stein and Bülow now began to encourage the sultan to resist the French takeover, and to give an earnest of Germany's support of the potentate they proposed that William II call at Tangier in the course of a Mediterranean cruise which was planned for March. The kaiser initially agreed but became increasingly reluctant as he came to realize the political implications of his proposed visit. Bülow strengthened William's resolve by arguing that for the emperor to pull out would be interpreted in Paris and elsewhere as a capitulation. This appeal to the imperial vanity succeeded and the kaiser landed dramatically at Tangier on March 31, 1905, and assured the sultan of Germany's support of an independent Morocco.

The diplomatic conflagration was instantaneous, and Holstein was prepared to deal with it. He proposed an international conference in the course of which, according to his scenario, Germany would play a sympathetic role as the champion of Moroccan independence. France, clearly branded as the aggressor, would forfeit England's support and be required to abandon its plans for hegemony in the sultanate. France, Germany, and neighboring Spain could then divide Morocco into economic spheres of influence. Holstein's plan succeeded only insofar as the kaiser's call at Tangier did eventually lead to such a conference, which was convened in Algeciras in January, 1906. In the course of that meeting, however, the Germans found that because of the kaiser's coup de théâtre and the intimation by Berlin that war could result from the Moroccan complications, it was they and not the French who were regarded as the troublemakers. The other powers supported France and the result was that the settlement, while granting Germany some economic concessions, not only acknowledged France's paramount position in the sultanate but indicated, by the steadfast cooperation of England and France during the negotiations, that the German action had tightened rather than weakened the Entente. The diplomatic offensive designed by Holstein had been reduced to a shambles.

The Moroccan crisis had serious repercussions in the Foreign Office. It persuaded several officials, notably Otto Hammann, that Holstein's policy was in fact a threat of war with France, a prospect for which Hammann had no use.[18] Holstein became enraged at Hammann, with whom he had formerly had close relations, when he found that he would not support his Moroccan action. Holstein also became increasingly critical of William II who, throughout the long year of negotiations which resulted in the Algeciras treaty, exhibited what Holstein felt was a deplorable willingness to yield to France. The kaiser, who during this period genuinely wanted to bring about a measure of tranquility into Franco-German relations, became ever more exasperated at the Foreign Office, believing that it was responsible for frustrating this desire. Bülow was caught in the middle, a position not necessarily uncomfortable for one of his genius for maneuver. He approved of Holstein's firm resolve against France but he had also to be mindful of William II's preference for accommodation. The chancellor, calculating the relatively greater disadvantage which would result from resisting the sovereign, decided to follow the kaiser's lead.

The preliminary negotiations in Paris to work out an agenda for the Algeciras conference had meanwhile created additional difficulties in the Wilhelmstrasse since the chancellor entrusted Friedrich Rosen, the Political Division's Africa expert, with a special mission to France to arrange these details. Neither Bülow nor Richthofen felt that Holstein's admirer, Ambassador Radolin, was equal to so delicate and crucial a deliberation.[19] Radolin was furious at Rosen's appearance in Paris and he expressed resentment at being upstaged to both William II and the chancellor. Bülow replied very firmly that if Radolin could not manage to cooperate with Rosen, he would inform William II that

---

[18] Hammann, *Bilder*, pp. 35–39; Hammann, *Der neue Kurs: Erinnerungen* (Berlin, 1918), pp. 68–70.

[19] Rosen, *Wanderleben*, I, 151–58; HP, IV, 367 note 3.

either the ambassador or the chancellor would have to be replaced. Radolin's remonstrances ceased.[20]

Holstein's position was further damaged in January, 1906, when, at William's insistence, Heinrich von Tschirschky und Bögendorff, the minister to Hamburg, was appointed state secretary in succession to Richthofen, who had died after a short illness. Richthofen had despised Holstein, but this was an enmity which Holstein could easily tolerate, for the state secretary was only the creature of Bülow. Tschirschky was more difficult, for he, unlike Richthofen, was an intimate of the kaiser's and had accompanied him on several trips as the Foreign Office's representative. Tschirschky's appointment, apparently dictated by the kaiser without any consultation with Bülow or the Wilhelmstrasse, came as a surprise, for it had generally been assumed that Holstein's lieutenant, Under State Secretary Mühlberg, would be moved up as state secretary.[21] Holstein did not like Tschirschky, who was stiff and somewhat self-important and who at once indicated that he did not intend to seek Holstein out for advice.[22] To cover himself in the event that Mühlberg did not succeed to the state secretaryship, Holstein had decided, as Richthofen lay mortally ill, to try to fortify his position in the Foreign Office. On January 11, 1906, he demanded that Bülow create the post of *Direktor* of the Political Division for him, a move which would give Holstein control over all of the division, including Hammann's press section.[23] The chancellor agreed, but

[20] Bülow, *Denkwürdigkeiten*, II, 168–69; Rosen, *Wanderleben*, I, 166–67; BvB to FvH, Sept. 15, 1905, and Radolin to BvB, Sept. 10, 1905, HolN 3855/H191676, H191678–80; also BvB to Radolin, Sept. 14, 1905, ibid., 3860/H195398–400.

[21] Bülow, *Denkwürdigkeiten*, II, 214–15; Karl F. Nowak and Friedrich Thimme, eds., *Erinnerungen und Gedanken des Botschafters Anton Graf Monts* (Berlin, 1932), pp. 245–47; Brauer, *Im Dienste Bismarcks*, p. 416.

[22] Bülow, *Denkwürdigkeiten*, II, 214–15.

[23] FvH to BvB, Jan. 11, 1906, HolN 3855/H191730–32; FvH to Maximilian Harden, Aug. 5, 1906, HardenN 52; Rogge, *Holstein: Lebensbekenntnis*, pp. 244–45.

he delayed taking the next step, which was to ask the Reichstag to authorize the position.

Tschirschky, whom Bülow described as the mere echo of his imperial master, was acutely sensitive to William II's every mood, and, unlike Bülow, he had no ties to Holstein which needed to be cultivated.[24] The kaiser made no secret of his displeasure with the Foreign Office's handling of the Moroccan crisis, during the course of which the French press had argued with considerable accuracy that Holstein, and not the German sovereign or his government, was the party in Berlin who was responsible.[25] Tschirschky knew of William's distaste for Holstein, and it occurred to him, just as the thought simultaneously came to the chancellor, that Holstein might therefore conveniently be sacrificed in order to alleviate the crisis with France and also to restore the Foreign Office to the kaiser's favor. Holstein's removal would also eliminate the cause for much of the friction within the Wilhelmstrasse. In March, 1906, Tschirschky, backed covertly by the chancellor, therefore began to cut off Holstein from the planning of the German position at Algeciras, while both he and Bülow tried to discredit Holstein with the kaiser.

Holstein soon became aware that a fronde had been organized against him, but he believed that it was the kaiser and Philipp Eulenburg, and not Bülow, who stood behind the state secretary. Holstein, confident that Bülow would not abandon him, thereupon submitted his resignation, which was dated April 2, 1906. On the fourth, the chancellor advised Holstein that he intended to take no action on the matter until he had had a discussion with William II. But on April 5th, the chancellor, not yet having seen the kaiser, fainted on the floor of the Reichstag and was con-

[24] Bülow, *Denkwürdigkeiten*, II, 256–57; Otto Hammann, *Um den Kaiser: Erinnerungen aus den Jahren 1906–1909* (Berlin, 1919), p. 3.

[25] Rogge, *Holstein: Lebensbekenntnis*, p. 246; J. Lepsius et al., eds., *Die grosse Politik der europäischen Kabinette*, 40 vols. (Berlin, 1922–27), XXI, 566–67.

fined to his residence. From his sickbed, Bülow instructed Tschirschky to submit Holstein's resignation to William II. After some delay, resulting from the fact that both Bülow and Tschirschky wanted to make it appear that it had been the other who was responsible for forwarding the resignation, Holstein's letter was sent to the sovereign, who signed it without the least pretense of regret. The Holstein era was at an end. Holstein never suspected that Bülow, and not William II or Hammann or Eulenburg, had been responsible for his fall, and the chancellor was present at Holstein's bedside when he died on May 8, 1909, only two months before Bülow's fall from office.

From the elimination of Holstein in 1906 until Bülow's dismissal in July, 1909, the chancellor had few further difficulties in the Foreign Office. Tschirschky had no enthusiasm for his position as state secretary, and in 1907, after holding the office only little more than a year, he was made ambassador in Vienna. His successor was the amiable and elegant Baron von Schoen, who years before had ingratiated himself with William II. The choice apparently was dictated by the kaiser, who in giving up one favorite insisted on replacing him with another.[26] Schoen was courtly, wealthy, and refined, the first state secretary to have been born a bourgeois. Along with his title, the new state secretary had acquired all the suitably aristocratic notions of the diplomatic establishment, but neither his baronage nor his graceful manner spared him titters from diplomats of more ancient noble lineage.[27] No one thought of Schoen as a great mind or an energetic bureaucrat. Like other incumbents of the post, he seems to have had little desire to have it, complaining that his duties would be too arduous and repre-

[26] On the kaiser's role in Schoen's appointment, see Bülow, *Denkwürdigkeiten*, II, 301–2; Hammann, *Um den Kaiser*, p. 36; Hartmut Pogge von Strandmann, *Walther Rathenau: Tagebuch, 1907–1922* (Düsseldorf, 1967), p. 141. Cf. Thimme, *Front wider Bülow*, pp. 268–69.

[27] Bülow, *Denkwürdigkeiten*, II, 301–2.

senting the government before the Reichstag too unpleasant. In addition, Schoen anticipated that the management of the Political Division, which had no director and therefore stood directly under the state secretary, would be difficult now that the omniscient Holstein was no longer there.[28] Schoen's somewhat lackadaisical attitude toward his office did not trouble Bülow, who intended to direct foreign affairs himself. But it did concern some German diplomats, who felt that the state secretary's frivolity gradually led the Wilhelmstrasse into a state of anarchy in which every envoy simply did as he pleased.[29]

Schoen, in keeping with his agreeable manner, had few strong views on foreign policy. His essential responsibility was to return the Foreign Office to William II's good graces and to represent the kaiser's foreign policy before the Reichstag. At both he proved to be entirely adequate. He got on famously with the sovereign, who visited him almost every day and who was generally receptive to the state secretary's advice, and his performances in the parliament, if not equal to those of Marschall and Bülow in their day, were effective until late in 1908 in placating the Wilhelmstrasse's critics.[30] Bülow, according to Schoen's account, gave him a free hand in policy as well as in personnel decisions.[31] Schoen presided calmly over the Foreign Office, and in his three years in office he made only twenty-two envoy appointments to the forty-eight existing posts, as opposed to Bülow's thirty-

[28] Schoen, *Erlebtes: Beiträge zur politischen Geschichte der neusten Zeit* (Stuttgart, 1921), pp. 51–53. Cf. Ernst Jäckh, ed., *Kiderlen-Wächter der Staatsmann und Mensch: Briefwechsel und Nachlass*, 2 vols. (Berlin, 1924), II, 102.

[29] Jäckh, *Kiderlen-Wächter*, II, 16, 102.

[30] Schoen, *Erlebtes*, pp. 125–26; Bülow, *Denkwürdigkeiten*, II, 442; Hammann, *Um den Kaiser*, p. 36 on Schoen's relations with the kaiser; Jäckh, *Kiderlen*, II, 109, for a personnel question on which the state secretary had to yield to the royal will; also Szögyényi to Foreign Minister Count Lexa von Aehrenthal, July 7, 1910 (26B), HHStA, 168–B.

[31] Schoen, *Erlebtes*, p. 102.

two appointments to forty-one posts in the same number of years in office. Schoen introduced no alterations in foreign policy, and the only administrative change, not one of major significance, was his revival of the long dormant *Bundes-ausschuss* for foreign affairs.[32]

Bülow's administration might have endured for the twenty years the kaiser had hoped for had it not been for a quality of the chancellor's character which was as striking as it was potentially dangerous. Bülow was not lazy, but his working schedule was dictated by his personal convenience, not by the national interest. As long as he was merely an envoy or even state secretary such a disposition could be indulged, for there were others to do the work and a chancellor who could take the blame if things went wrong. But when Bülow himself became head of the government there was no longer an avenue for evading this responsibility. On assuming the chancellorship, however, Bülow's cavalier attitude toward his work did not change. He would not tolerate any interruption of his lunch hour, his evening pleasure, or his night's rest, save in the most pressing of circumstances, a condition which he defined very narrowly. He rarely, if ever, set foot in the Wilhelmstrasse 76, preferring to call counselors or the state secretary to his office at number 77, and he begrudged the claims made on his time by envoys.[33] His office, which he artistically referred to as the "studio" and where he consorted with diplomats, artists, and intellectuals, was as much a social as a business establishment. What industry the chancellor summoned was devoted for the most part to letter writing, to mollifying William II, and to perfecting his considerable gifts of

[32] Ibid., pp. 107–8.
[33] Bülow memo of Oct. 24, 1900, Dd 149, vol. 4, 280/00259; KvR, "Autobiographische und andere Aufzeichnungen, 1903–1909," BisN FC 3030/639; Herbert von Hindenburg, *Am Rande zweier Jahrhunderte: Momentbilder aus einem Diplomatenleben* (Berlin, 1938), p. 200; Thimme, *Front wider Bülow*, p. 221.

theater. His perorations before the Reichstag were elocutionary masterpieces and behind them lay the most elaborate preparation. Hammann's press department would make a draft which would be further refined by Robert Schöll, a counselor responsible for arts and letters. Bülow would then memorize the oration, synchronize the gestures appropriate to the text, and hold a dress rehearsal before selected members of the staff.[34] On vacations, he let the staff handle matters, while he lounged about reading French novels. When Rosen, recently selected to conduct the complicated negotiations with France in 1906 to settle the Moroccan crisis, spent several weeks with Bülow at Nordeney, the chancellor never bothered to discuss the problems which he was expected shortly to resolve.[35]

The casualness with which the chancellor operated finally came to light in the fall of 1908. On October 29, the London *Daily Telegraph* carried what purported to be a recent interview of William II by a person of "unimpeachable authority."[36] In this conversation, which the ruler had actually had earlier with Colonel Edward Stuart-Wortley, an English acquaintance, the kaiser protested that he was a friend of England but that this fact was unfortunately unappreciated in London. Among several examples of his loyalty, he pointed out that he had devised and forwarded to Queen Victoria a strategy to defeat the Boers which was in fact very similar to the one employed by Field Marshal Lord Roberts. The emperor's inference that it was he who had been the architect of victory in South Africa was very unfortunate and very inaccurate. The outburst against the kaiser in England was vituperative, while in Germany the interview provoked demands for abdication or for constitutional reform. What was particularly puzzling in both

[34] Thimme, *Front wider Bülow*, p. 223.
[35] Rosen, *Wanderleben*, I, 149–50.
[36] For the genesis of the interview, see the Edward [Montagu]–Stuart–Wortley papers, Bodleian Library, Oxford, MS Eng. hist. d.256.

capitals was the fact that no one in the German Foreign Office had questioned the publication of such an embarrassing document.

The furor caused by the *Daily Telegraph* interview ensured that everyone would try to evade being revealed as the responsible party. William II blamed Bülow, claiming that he had asked the chancellor to approve a draft of the conversation before authorizing its publication. Bülow, rather petulantly alleging that he was overworked and that the draft was written in a difficult hand on cheap paper, declared that the responsibility should be charged to the Foreign Office, to which he had referred the document. State Secretary Schoen promptly excused himself by noting that he had been ill at Berchtesgaden during the crisis. The details of what happened are murky, but William II clearly was not at fault. The kaiser, however impolitic his utterance, had in fact forwarded to the chancellor a draft of the interview, asking that he—and not the Foreign Office staff—approve it for publication. William II was of the naive, not to say fatuous, opinion that his observations would improve rather than harm Anglo-German relations. The draft was transmitted to Bülow by his nephew, Baron Martin von Jenisch, Prussian Minister to Hesse then temporarily assigned to William's entourage. Jenisch advised Bülow that the interview was diplomatically questionable and besides contained factual errors.[37] The chancellor, who may have been concerned with other matters but who was well aware of the danger of allowing any act of William II's to pass by uninspected, forwarded the draft to the Wilhelmstrasse, asking that it "carefully examine [the contents] and indicate

[37] Rudolf Vierhaus, ed., *Das Tagebuch der Baronin Spitzemberg* . . . : *Aufzeichnungen aus der Hofgesellschaft des Hohenzollernreiches*, 2d ed. (Göttingen, 1960), pp. 494–95; Hammann, *Um den Kaiser*, p. 66; Walter Görlitz, ed., *Der Kaiser* . . . : *Aufzeichnungen des Chefs des Marinekabinetts Admiral Georg Alexander v. Müller über die Ära Wilhelms II.* (Berlin, 1965), pp. 69–72.

any desirable corrections, additions, and deletions."[38] Since Schoen was ill, the document went to Under State Secretary Wilhelm Stemrich, who interpreted Bülow's directions— perhaps too narrowly but in the best tradition of bureaucratic obedience—to mean that he was only to clarify any errors of fact and not to express an opinion as to the appropriateness of publication.[39] Stemrich read the draft and sent it on to Reinhold Klehmet, who had been a counselor in the Political Division since 1896. Klehmet did not show the draft to any other counselors since, in his opinion, it was a "*geheime Kaisersache.*"[40] He merely assessed the accuracy of the facts contained in the interview and made a few corrections. Since Stemrich had meanwhile gone to Italy on vacation, Klehmet then sent the draft to the chancellor, calling to his attention the factual errors. Bülow in turn handed the document over to Jenisch, noting that he saw no reason to withhold publication. The kaiser thereupon informed Colonel Stuart-Wortley that it could be printed.[41]

In the eruption following the interview's publication, Bülow attacked Klehmet for misinterpreting his responsibility in looking merely for factual errors. The chancellor secured the kaiser's consent to the publication in the October 30 issue of the *Norddeutsche Allgemeine Zeitung* of a statement to the effect that the Foreign Office was responsible since Bülow had asked it to review the draft. Since the Wilhelmstrasse had made no objection, Bülow had assumed that the interview could be published. On November 10, the chancellor exonerated himself before the Reichstag, em-

[38] Thimme, *Front wider Bülow*, p. 77; Hammann, *Um den Kaiser*, p. 67.

[39] Vierhaus, *Tagebuch; Spitzemberg*, p. 494; Schoen, *Erlebtes*, pp. 97–98; Hammann, *Um den Kaiser*, p. 67.

[40] Hammann, *Um den Kaiser*, p. 67; Schoen, *Erlebtes*, pp. 97–98.

[41] General Friedrich von Bernhardi, *Denkwürdigkeiten aus meinem Leben nach gleichzeitigen Aufzeichnungen und im Lichte der Erinnerungen* (Berlin, 1927), pp. 290–91, 332, relating an account given by Theodor Schiemann, an intimate of William II.

ploying the same defense. William II was deeply wounded by the chancellor's failure to defend the purity of his motives in granting the interview and in not giving adequate stress to how punctilious the ruler had been in clearing the interview with the chancellor.[42] The Foreign Office was equally offended, for the chancellor's rather mechanical directions respecting the draft—he had after all spoken only of "desirable corrections, additions, and deletions"— indicated that he wanted only a determination of the factual accuracy of the contents. In the tradition established by Bismarck, the Wilhelmstrasse had considered its duty to follow orders, not to give advice. The Foreign Office felt that it had been Bülow's responsibility to pass on the advisability of publication after it had purged the draft of its errors of fact.

The vital point in the recriminations was whether or not the chancellor had in fact read the draft of the interview before sending it on to the Foreign Office or after receiving it back. If he had not, he was guilty of carelessness; if he had read it his castigation of the Wilhelmstrasse and his failure to absolve the kaiser were deceitful. In both the article published by the *Norddeutsche Allgemeine Zeitung* and in his Reichstag speech Bülow denied that he had read the draft. Schoen, Under State Secretary Stemrich, Zimmermann, and the kaiser were all convinced that he had.[43] One argument presented by those who believed the chan-

[42] Count Robert Zedlitz-Trützschler, *Zwölf Jahre am deutschen Kaiserhof: Aufzeichnungen* (Berlin, 1924), pp. 196–99; Schoen, *Erlebtes*, pp. 98–99; General Karl von Einem, *Erinnerungen eines Soldaten, 1853–1933* (Leipzig, 1933), pp. 119–23; Bernhard Schwertfeger, ed., *Kaiser und Kabinettschef: nach eigenen Aufzeichnungen und dem Briefwechsel des Wirklichen Geheimen Rats Rudolf von Valentini* (Oldenburg, 1931), p. 110 note 1; Klaus Meyer, *Theodor Schiemann als politischer Publizist* (Frankfurt/Main, 1956), pp. 159–61, 163–65.

[43] Thimme, *Front wider Bülow*, p. 78; Schwertfeger, *Kaiser und Kabinettschef*, p. 100 note 1; Meyer, *Schiemann*, pp. 159–61; Zimmermann, "Bülow und Holstein—Die Daily Telegraph-Affäre—Bü-

cellor knew the contents was that he realized what the reaction would be and hoped that, in having the interview published, the kaiser would be fearfully embarrassed, thus enabling Bülow to increase his own authority at the expense of the crown.[44] The chancellor, as though to advertise that the guilty party in the Foreign Office had been identified, deprived Klehmet of his counselorship and packed him off as general consul in Athens. None of Bülow's devices succeeded in dispelling William II's conviction that he had been betrayed. The Reichstag roundly condemned the sloppiness of the operation, and the Conservatives, already at odds with the chancellor over financial issues, were outraged because Bülow had let the crown be besmirched. In July, 1909, the chancellor's parliamentary foes joined hands to topple the government on a taxation bill. The kaiser accepted Bülow's resignation in a perfunctory manner and selected Theobald von Bethmann Hollweg, the Prussian minister of interior, as his successor.

Bethmann's tall, angular frame and his reticent, almost dour, mien alongside Bülow's Falstaffian rotundity and irrepressible self-dramatization do not exhaust the catalog of differences between the two men. Nowhere was the contrast greater than in diplomacy, for if Bülow was par excellence a man steeped from birth in the arts of negotiation and ingratiation, Bethmann was utterly untutored and untried. This was not necessarily a disadvantage. Although the new chancellor was ignorant, he was also unspoiled, and his plain speaking was therefore welcome after Bülow's sonorous but often empty rhetoric. Sir Frank Lascelles, the British ambassador in Berlin at the time, observed on Bethmann's takeover that there was now a man at the helm in

---

low und Bethmann Hollweg," *Süddeutsche Monatshefte*, XXVIII, no. 6 (Mar. 1931), 391–92; Vierhaus, *Tagebuch; Spitzemberg*, pp. 494–95; see also Bernhardi, *Denkwürdigkeiten*, pp. 290–91.

[44] Vierhaus, *Tagebuch; Spitzemberg*, pp. 494–95; Meyer, *Schiemann*, p. 161.

Berlin whom he and the English government could trust.[45] Bethmann made no secret of his lack of training, candidly admitting to the Austro-Hungarian envoy that he knew little of foreign policy.[46] But he wasted no time in trying to master the business of the Wilhelmstrasse 76. Zimmermann wrote to Kiderlen on August 25, 1909, that the new chancellor had a "colossal" interest in the Foreign Office and was having all ambassadors and ministers come to Berlin to pass in review.[47] The result of this inspection was that, in 1910, six envoys were retired and another eleven reassigned, while in the next year another five left the service and six were given new assignments.

The appointment of a diplomatic novice such as Bethmann occasioned little enthusiasm in the Foreign Office, but the firmness which he showed was welcome after the ruin brought about by Bülow's lax conduct of affairs.[48] One asset which Bethmann possessed, and one which the Wilhelmstrasse needed very much, was the kaiser's good will. The new chancellor never enjoyed the rapturous adulation which William II had felt for Bülow in the early years of their association, but he liked and respected Bethmann and realized that he had the confidence of foreign governments. The chancellor himself was not unappreciative of William's good qualities. The relations between the two were by no means frictionless, but in general, and especially in foreign affairs, they got on tolerably well.[49] One serious and con-

[45] Marie von Bunsen, *Zeitgenossen die ich erlebte, 1900–1930* (Leipzig, 1932), p. 80.

[46] Szögyényi to Aehrenthal, Aug. 3, 1909 (25A–C), HHStA, 167–B.

[47] The letter is in KWN, box 5, drawer 71, no. 73.

[48] Karl D. Erdmann, ed., *Kurt Riezler: Tagebücher, Aufsätze, Dokumente* (Göttingen, 1972), p. 167. Kiderlen believed that Bethmann's "weakness" would lead to William II's assuming the direction of foreign affairs. See Jäckh, *Kiderlen-Wächter*, II, 32.

[49] Vierhaus, *Tagebuch; Spitzemberg*, p. 523; Hans-Günter Zmarzlik, *Bethmann Hollweg als Reichskanzler, 1909–1914* (Düsseldorf, 1957), p. 38.

tinuing problem was the kaiser's selection in 1912 of Prince Lichnowsky, the former personnel counselor, to become ambassador to the court of St. James. In making this choice William II did not consult Bethmann, who did not get on well with Lichnowsky and who regretted the appointment.[50] Just as Caprivi, who like Bethmann was a person with no experience in diplomacy, had depended on Holstein, so the new chancellor relied very heavily on Hans von Flotow, a Political Division counselor responsible for personnel from 1909 to 1910 and thereafter envoy in Brussels and Rome.[51] Bethmann liked State Secretary Schoen and might have retained him in office had Schoen not expressed a desire to exchange his position for a European embassy. The means of accomplishing this change were found in Prince Radolin, ambassador in Paris, who was almost seventy and rather infirm, and who no longer had Holstein to argue for his continuation in office. Radolin was retired in 1910 and Schoen inserted in his post. The state secretaryship went to Alfred von Kiderlen-Wächter, minister to Rumania since 1899.

On leaving office in 1909, Bülow had advised the kaiser that with a new chancellor unversed in foreign affairs it would be necessary to appoint a diplomat of firmer mettle than Schoen as state secretary. William II, according to Bülow, had replied with his accustomed self-confidence: "Just leave foreign policy to *me*! I've learned something from you. It will work out fine."[52] Kiderlen was the candidate Bülow had in mind, and in the wake of the *Daily Telegraph* crisis he had called Kiderlen to Berlin to manage the Wilhelmstrasse during Schoen's illness, a summons which gave the kaiser no pleasure. Schoen resumed his duties on December 1, 1908, but Kiderlen stayed on in Berlin

---

[50] Bülow, *Denkwürdigkeiten*, III, 122–23; ThimmeN 24, 10.

[51] Zimmermann to Kiderlen, Dec. 24, 1909, KWN, box 5, drawer 71, no. 73; Hutten-Czapski, *Sechzig Jahre*, II, 5; Jäckh, *Kiderlen-Wächter*, II, 45.

[52] Bülow, *Denkwürdigkeiten*, II, 512; Philipp Hiltebrandt, *Erinnerungen an den Fürsten Bülow* (Bonn, 1930), p. 32.

until the following April.[53] The sovereign as well as the Wilhelmstrasse thus had a foretaste of what Kiderlen might be like as state secretary.

The only obstacle to Kiderlen's appointment as state secretary was William II. In the 1890s, the witty and earthy diplomat had become a great favorite of the kaiser, who took him on cruises and delighted in his Swabian anecdotes. But in 1898, Kiderlen, who found William and his entourage quite tiresome and who could never resist making fun of those who were stilted or ponderous, made a number of barbed comments at the expense of royalty and its satellites. Kiderlen's observations eventually found their way—he believed via Bülow—to the palace, and the kaiser's displeasure at being an object of derision resulted in 1899 in Kiderlen's exile to Bucharest.[54] Even as late as the spring of 1909 Kiderlen was still unforgiven, and William II would initially hear nothing of his appointment as state secretary, although he agreed that he might have an embassy.[55] The sovereign's objections to Kiderlen were supported by the puritanical kaiserin, who found Kiderlen's vulgarity loathesome and who was scandalized by the fact that he had lived for years with a widow whom he had no intention of marrying.[56]

If Kiderlen was objectionable for personal reasons, his

[53] Jäckh, *Kiderlen-Wächter*, II, 6–30; Hiltebrandt, *Erinnerungen an Bülow*, p. 32.

[54] Ludwig Raschdau, *Unter Bismarck und Caprivi: Erinnerungen eines deutschen Diplomaten aus den Jahren 1885–1894*, 2d ed. (Berlin, 1939), p. 175; PzE to BvB, July 4, 1898, EN, LI, 129–30; Nowak and Thimme, *Erinnerungen; Monts*, pp. 44–45; TN, XV, 8–9.

[55] Bülow, *Denkwürdigkeiten*, II, 512; Flotow to Kiderlen, Nov. 8, 1900, KWN, box 5, drawer 71, no. 62; Bethmann to Kiderlen, June 5, 1910, ibid., box 5, drawer 71, no. 71; Vierhaus, *Tagebuch; Spitzemberg*, p. 522; Hammann, *Um den Kaiser*, pp. 35–36.

[56] Rosen, *Wanderleben*, II, 10; Nowak and Thimme, *Erinnerungen; Monts*, pp. 44–45; Raschdau, *Unter Bismarck und Caprivi*, p. 175; Jäckh, *Kiderlen-Wächter*, I, 96.

expertise and experience in the Balkans, which were regarded as Germany's primary diplomatic challenge in 1910, made him a very desirable candidate for the state secretaryship.[57] In June, 1910, the kaiser therefore reluctantly agreed to Bethmann's entreaty that Kiderlen be called, warning the chancellor at the same time that he was thereby implanting a louse in his pelt.[58] It was a chance Bethmann was prepared to take, for Kiderlen's very abrasiveness was an attest that he would be a strong state secretary. Since he shared the chancellor's interest in improving Anglo-German relations, Kiderlen would be a valuable ally in Bethmann's struggle with Tirpitz and the naval party.[59]

The new state secretary was notorious for his gruff manner and for his capacity for drink, and he had lost none of his savor for a tale wittily told. Few of his colleagues denied that Kiderlen possessed great talent, but hardly anyone— the kaiser, the chancellor, the staff of the Foreign Office, or its envoys in the field—failed to be irritated by his cynical, somewhat misanthropic personality and his brusque manner.[60] William II's attempts to overcome his distaste for Kiderlen, never very earnest, were unsuccessful, and before long he was tartly referring to the state secretary as a "bull in the china shop."[61] He soon found that Kiderlen's policy toward France, which culminated in a second crisis over Morocco in 1911, was as detrimental to the imperial interest in cordial Franco-German relations as the initial conflict with Paris over Morocco engineered by Holstein in 1905

[57] Thimme, *Front wider Bülow*, pp. 89–90.

[58] KWN, box 5, drawer 71, no. 83 (1911).

[59] Hutten-Czapski, *Sechzig Jahre*, II, 28–29.

[60] On Kiderlen the man, see Otto von Glasenapp to Baron Hellmuth Lucius von Stoedten, Aug. 25, 1925, in StoedtenN, and Lerchenfeld-Koefering, *Erinnerungen*, pp. 395–98.

[61] Josef Redlich, *Schicksalsjahre Österreichs, 1908–1919: das politische Tagebuch Josef Redlichs*, 2 vols. (Graz, 1953–54), I, 117; Count Johann-Heinrich Bernstorff, *Memoirs*, trans. Eric Sutton (New York, 1936), p. 105.

had been.[62] For his part, Kiderlen despised the stuffy, self-righteous Prussian court and quickly found that the kaiser's daily calls at the Wilhelmstrasse were enough to make him sick.[63] Kiderlen was very insistent that he, and not the sovereign, be the channel for diplomatic dispatches, and in March, 1912, he threatened to resign when he discovered that the kaiser was communicating privately with Ambassador Metternich in London without informing the state secretary.[64]

Kiderlen's association with Bethmann was hardly more successful. No one expected that they would get on well, for their personalities and backgrounds were dissimilar. Although the chancellor's impression of the state secretary was initially favorable, the two soon began to go their separate ways and, before long, both began to charge the other with lack of trust. Kiderlen resented the fact that Bethmann did not always keep him informed of his conversations with foreign envoys in Berlin, and he deplored what he argued was the chancellor's tendency to assign envoys on the basis of where they would be least useful.[65] Given the state secretary's truculent personality, the chancellor's avoidance of contact is understandable, but in fact this evasion seems not to have been deliberate nor did it occur frequently. For the most part, Bethmann apparently stayed in close communication with Kiderlen, to whom he referred occasionally as "*Dickkopf.*" Kiderlen, on the other hand, constantly evaded the chancellor and there was nothing accidental about this development. The state secretary treated Bethmann—the "*Regenwurm,*" he called him—as a subordinate, according

[62] Princess Marie Radziwill, *Lettres de la Princess Radziwill au Général de Robilant, 1889–1914: une grande dame d'avant guerre,* 4 vols. (Bologna, 1933–34), IV, 155–57.

[63] Redlich, *Tagebuch,* I, 117; Kiderlen to Baron Carl von Weiszäcker, n.d. [1911], Kl. Erwb. 458F, 6.

[64] Kiderlen to W2, Mar. 6, 1912, KWN, box 5, drawer 71, no. 63.

[65] Vierhaus, *Tagebuch; Spitzemberg,* p. 523; Jäckh, *Kiderlen-Wächter,* II, 82–84; Kiderlen's notes for Aug. 26, 1912, KWN, box 5, drawer 71, no. 83.

to their friend Count Hutten-Czapski. When Czapski remonstrated this treatment, Kiderlen's reply was that he was too overworked to present matters to "the old man," which Bethmann, in any case, would not have understood. The chancellor's protests did no good, for Kiderlen simply told Bethmann that if he did not trust him he should appoint someone else state secretary.[66] Kiderlen's secretiveness sometimes placed Bethmann in an embarrassing position, for it made him appear to be either a mere cipher or a deceptive partner in negotiation. To a frustrated foreign envoy, who complained that he could pry no information out of the state secretary, Bethmann replied: "So. Do you think he tells me more?"[67] The chancellor got no help from William II, who reminded Bethmann that he had opposed Kiderlen's appointment.[68]

The Foreign Office approved of Kiderlen's nomination, for it expected that the Wilhelmstrasse would now play a more assertive role than it had during Schoen's casual administration.[69] This was certainly the new state secretary's intention. "An unbelievable rut," he wrote on becoming acquainted with the routine of business in the Wilhelmstrasse. "Officials work competently and dependably, but they are intimidated because they are drilled always to ask what will the press say, what will the Reichstag say? I must therefore step in and restore another way of doing things."[70]

[66] Hutten-Czapski, *Sechzig Jahre*, II, 28–29, 107; Erdmann, *Riezler: Tagebücher*, p. 179; Kiderlen to Hedwig Kypke, Jan. 16, 1912, KWN, box 5, drawer 71, no. 107. For Bethmann's protests at Kiderlen's invasion of his prerogative, see Konrad H. Jarausch, *The Enigmatic Chancellor: Bethmann Hollweg and the Hubris of Imperial Germany* (New Haven, 1973), p. 111.

[67] Vierhaus, *Tagebuch; Spitzemberg*, pp. 546, 550; also Jäckh, *Kiderlen-Wächter*, II, 82–84.

[68] William II, *Ereignisse und Gestalten aus den Jahren 1878–1918* (Berlin, 1922), pp. 111–12.

[69] Jäckh, *Kiderlen-Wächter*, II, 80–81, 102; Thimme, *Front wider Bülow*, p. 278; Vierhaus, *Tagebuch; Spitzemberg*, pp. 522–23.

[70] Jäckh, *Kiderlen-Wächter*, II, 81.

Kiderlen's way was a tyranny which brooked no opposition. Once he was installed in office, his firmness began to appear less attractive to those who were subordinate to him. Some diplomats, recalling Bismarck's equation of envoys with soldiers falling into line at his order, began to refer to Kiderlen as "Bismarck II."[71] Two months after the new state secretary assumed office, Baroness Hildegard Spitzemberg, the mother-in-law of Baron Hans von Wangenheim, minister in Athens, reported that Wangenheim had told her that "Kiderlen's hand already lies very heavy on those who worked hardest to get him where he is. There is even concern that he is not smart enough to distinguish between roughness and energy and thus will offend even the good element [in the Wilhelmstrasse]."[72]

A number of counselors in the Political Division were worried that Kiderlen, like Holstein, would persecute colleagues he disliked.[73] No one in the service was more apprehensive at Kiderlen's move from Bucharest to Berlin than Otto Hammann in the press department. Hammann appreciated Kiderlen's admirable prose style and his competence in diplomacy, but at the same time he complained that the state secretary was too old-fashioned. He had, Hammann noted, no understanding of the importance of economic affairs and therefore did nothing to integrate the work of the Political Division with that of the *Handelspolitische Abteilung*.[74] Hammann's essential reservation about the state secretary, however, was that he was unwilling to keep the press department sufficiently informed of the aims of German policy, although he was quite ready to confide details to outsiders who called at the Wilhelmstrasse. Kiderlen's

[71] Ibid.; Vierhaus, *Tagebuch; Spitzemberg*, p. 546.
[72] Vierhaus, *Tagebuch; Spitzemberg*, p. 524.
[73] Ibid., p. 533.
[74] Hammann, *Um den Kaiser*, p. 37; Hammann, *Bilder*, pp. 79–94, for Hammann's depiction of Kiderlen. Kiderlen did show some interest in training young diplomats in economic affairs. See Jäckh, *Kiderlen-Wächter*, II, 81.

exclusion of Hammann was intentional, for even before taking office he had been suspicious of the press director. On becoming state secretary, Kiderlen secured the chancellor's consent to curtail the distribution of diplomatic telegrams to Hammann and he later considered getting rid of him altogether by naming him to an overseas post or to a seat on the Egyptian Debt Commission.[75] Kiderlen also devised a plan whereby Hammann and his press staff, who handled all aspects of the government's press relations, would be transferred to the Reichskanzlei, where they would deal solely with internal matters. A new press organization would then be established in the Wilhelmstrasse which would deal solely with foreign affairs. The scheme foundered on the opposition of the chancellor, who liked Hammann and valued his services. As a result, Hammann continued to serve as the press chief until his retirement in 1917.[76]

German envoys also had their differences with Kiderlen. The state secretary did not always show the consideration to heads of mission that might have been expected from someone who had spent so much time in the field. As with the chancellor, Kiderlen was inclined to tell his envoys less than they felt they were entitled to know.[77] Like William II, he preferred to do things on his own. On July 7, 1911, Baroness Spitzemberg noted in her diary that German diplomats were complaining that Kiderlen negotiated directly with the representatives of foreign nations stationed in Berlin, rather than proceeding through his own diplomats. Baron Wangenheim's promotion in June, 1912, to the ambassadorship in Constantinople occasioned another unfavorable reference to Kiderlen in his mother-in-law's diary.

[75] Jäckh, *Kiderlen-Wächter*, II, 104; Hutten-Czapski, *Sechzig Jahre*, II, 84–86.

[76] Kiderlen's notes for 1910 and 1911–12, KWN, box 5, drawer 71, no. 83; Jäckh, *Kiderlen-Wächter*, I, 153–54, II, 81.

[77] For an example see Bernstorff, *Memoirs*, p. 106.

Hans will not have an easy time of it with this chief, about whom indeed the entire Office complains, even those who for some time expected and hoped for much from him. In the first place he is utterly lazy (which he always was), orients and instructs no one and in his directives to ministers and ambassadors writes either a few friendly lines to his protégés . . . or offensively, coarsely, and irrelevantly to those whom he does not like. A downright dismal and very disturbing anarchy prevails in the Office, because everything knuckles under to Kiderlen's insolence. For example, Marschall [ambassador in London] has the lowest thinkable opinion of his political and even statesmanlike talents, for he has persisted in the point of view acquired in Bucharest. He was [Marschall said] without any moral earnestness, ran his state secretaryship as though it were a subsidiary position, and undermined his colleagues in that neither orally nor in writing did he put them in a position to acquit themselves properly in their posts.[78]

Kiderlen's high-handedness proceeded from the low opinion he had of most of his envoys. In addition to Ratibor in Madrid and Pourtalès in St. Petersburg, only Gottlieb von Jagow, the ambassador to Italy, enjoyed his favor. Kiderlen regarded the other European ambassadors— Tschirschky (Vienna), Schoen (Paris), Marschall (Constantinople and then London), Lichnowsky (London)—as lightweights, and he did not care for Rosen in Bucharest or Baron Julius von Griesinger, minister to Serbia.[79] The state secretary's disregard for the opinions of his envoys did not prevent him from becoming aggravated when he was himself bypassed in diplomatic negotiations. This was especially true in the naval talks with England, in which the

[78] Entry of June 23, 1912, Vierhaus, *Tagebuch; Spitzemberg*, p. 546.
[79] Jäckh, *Kiderlen-Wächter*, II, 89.

kaiser, Tirpitz, and outsiders such as Albert Ballin of the Hamburg-American Line, played conspicuous roles.[80] The tension which Kiderlen had created with the kaiser, the chancellor, the Foreign Office staff, and with German diplomats abroad had not abated when on December 30, 1912, he was felled without warning by a stroke. Even those who liked him least, notably the kaiser, admitted that he would be very difficult to replace. Bethmann also confessed his sense of loss, noting that Kiderlen's impetuosity had been a good foil for his own more philosophical manner.[81] Finding a diplomat both capable and willing to take the post had always been difficult, but the suddenness of Kiderlen's death made it even more so. According to Under State Secretary Zimmermann's claim, the staff of the Wilhelmstrasse 76 hoped that he would succeed Kiderlen, but Zimmermann declined because of his health, his weakness in foreign languages, and his inability, as a bourgeois, to hold his own in Berlin society.[82]

The choice for the state secretaryship, one presumably made by the chancellor, fell on Ambassador Jagow. This diminutive and aristocratic Prussian was colorless in personality and limited in experience but well thought of by his diplomatic colleagues. His nomination probably owed much to the influence of Ambassador Lichnowsky, who promoted his candidacy with Bethmann.[83] Jagow had joined the service in 1895 as a protégé of Bülow's and thereafter spent

---

[80] Kiderlen's notes for Feb. 1912, KWN, box 5, drawer 71, no. 83; Jäckh, *Kiderlen-Wächter*, II, 153; Kiderlen to W2, Mar. 6, 1912 KWN, box 5, drawer 71, no. 63.

[81] Szögyényi to Foreign Minister Count Leopold von Berchtold, Jan. 15, 1913 (1A–B), HHStA, 170–B. Bernstorff, *Memoirs*, p. 105, suggests that Bethmann's realization of the complementary nature of their personalities led him to choose Kiderlen as his state secretary.

[82] Ernst Deuerlein, ed., *Briefwechsel Hertling-Lerchenfeld, 1912– 1917* . . . 2 vols. (Boppard, 1973), I, 194; Vierhaus, *Tagebuch; Spitzemberg*, p. 554.

[83] Lichnowsky to BvB, Jan. 3, 1913, BüN 98.

most of his meteoric career in Rome. William II was not enraptured at the thought of Jagow in charge at the Wilhelmstrasse, but he agreed when Bethmann presented his name. The candidate at least had the virtue of being the emperor's fraternity brother in the Bonn Borussen.[84] Jagow himself had no desire to have the position, for he felt himself neither physically nor professionally equal to the office. "Nothing has helped," he wrote plaintively to his patron Bülow on January 5, 1913. "I am appointed."[85]

Jagow, the last of the peacetime state secretaries, is the most difficult to reconstruct, not because he was in any way enigmatic, but because the contemporary record is virtually bare of any discussion of his personality, temperament, or his manner of administering the Foreign Office prior to 1914. His own memoirs, *Ursachen und Ausbruch des Weltkrieges* (1919), deal entirely with various diplomatic problems with which he had to wrestle, and his rejoinder to Bülow, with whom he fell out during the war, in *Front wider Bülow* (1931) is no more revealing. His *Nachlass* in Potsdam unfortunately contains papers only for the period between 1916 and 1919. The absence of significant comment on Jagow by diplomats is probably a reflection of the brevity of his tenure as state secretary before the war broke out and to the fact that his blandness enabled him to avoid friction in Berlin and in the field. His sterile snobbishness caused little distress in the aristocratic Wilhelmstrasse, and what appears to have been a somewhat self-effacing manner conveniently relegated him to the background, a position which he seems to have been happy to occupy. He had only a few friends among German diplomats—notably Count

[84] Pogge von Strandmann, *Rathenau Tagebuch*, p. 179; also Bülow, *Denkwürdigkeiten*, III, 33–34; Frederic William Wile, *Men around the Kaiser: Makers of Modern Germany* (London, 1913), p. 212. See Vierhaus, *Tagebuch; Spitzemberg*, p. 553, for the false rumor that William II had offered Tirpitz the post.

[85] BüN 46; also Otto Hammann, *Zur Vorgeschichte des Weltkrieges: Erinnerungen aus den Jahren 1897–1906* (Berlin, 1919), p. 2; Hindenburg, *Am Rande*, p. 261.

Bernstorff in Washington and Flotow, who succeeded him in Rome.[86] In his Prussian coldness and quiet orderliness, Jagow was utterly unlike his predecessor, and, after Kiderlen, he was doubtless a welcome relief.

Jagow and Bethmann quickly established excellent relations and William II found to his delight that the new state secretary was quite tolerable. Only a month after Jagow took over, the kaiser reported with obvious pleasure to the chief of the Naval Cabinet, Admiral Georg von Müller: "He's becoming admirably seasoned. The little man says he would be the first to recommend war to His Majesty if anyone tried to dispute Germany's rights in Asia Minor."[87] Jagow did not disappoint his sovereign when in 1914, as the specter of war hung not only over the Near East but over Europe in the aftermath of Sarajevo, he did not retreat. "We had the will to defend our position in the world," he wrote in 1919 in justification of Germany's going to war, "and the right to do so."[88]

[86] The Bernstorff correspondence is in Bernstorff, *Memoirs*, pp. 158–70; also Bülow, *Denkwürdigkeiten*, III, 33–36. See Hutten-Czapski, *Sechzig Jahre*, II, 107, for Jagow's connection with Flotow.

[87] Müller, *Der Kaiser*, p. 202.

[88] Jagow, *Ursachen und Ausbruch des Weltkrieges* (Berlin, 1919), p. 176.

## CHAPTER X

Diplomats and Deputies

Those who serve the state as bureaucrats possess an influence on policy only when the circumstances in which they hold their offices enable them to express their opinions freely and to have some measure of independence on acting on those ideas. Those who advise must be in a position to represent their points of view without fear of recrimination and those who lead must be prepared to hear, though not necessarily to follow, the advice presented by their counselors. From 1871 to 1914, the German diplomatic service did not function under such conditions, for throughout the period its members both in Berlin and in the field were, with few exceptions, not trusted lieutenants but rather orderlies of superior figures who allowed them little independence and who often dismissed their opinions as irrelevant or useless. German diplomats therefore were seldom decisive in the formulation of diplomatic policy.

For this reason, the interest in a study of the German diplomatic service lies less in what it might tell of the design of Berlin's policy than in illuminating not only how, as an institution, the service reflected the will and character of those who provided it with its orders but also how a bureaucratic office operated under such constraint. We should therefore expect an elaboration of our understanding of the crown and the chancellors as well as of the aristocratic body from which their servants in the Foreign Office were drawn.

Since the primary characteristic of the German diplomatic service was its dependence on superior dignitaries, its principal attribute was obedience. But between 1871 and

1914 there were different persons to whom German diplomats had to be compliant and consequently there were changes in the form which their obedience took.

Until his downfall in 1890, Bismarck was the power in imperial Germany to whom the Wilhelmstrasse was beholden, and the command which he exercised was absolute and unyielding. It was Bismarck's stamp which lies on the Foreign Office from 1871 to 1890, and it was one rooted in a thorough and professional knowledge of diplomacy. Bismarck presided over the daily business of the Wilhelmstrasse with a firm hand, and only when he became old and tired did he delegate some of his vast prerogative to the few diplomats—such as the elder Bülow and his own son Herbert—to whom he gave his complete trust. The Iron Chancellor's regime was one which exalted his person and cast all others, including Kaiser William I himself, into his shadow. This was exactly Bismarck's intention, for he had not a high opinion of mankind at large and he did not think that the sovereign or many of his diplomatic servants were notable for their ability. Diplomats in his judgment had to be closely watched and kept on a tight rein. He would provide them with orders and their role would be to carry out his directives to the letter. The result was a system in which both the design of policy and the discipline of the diplomatic service depended on a single indispensable figure. Bismarck encountered no opposition from his subalterns in the Foreign Office, for German diplomats understood that their role was implemental, not consultative. If the chancellor was remote and tyrannical, he was also admired and honored as the most illustrious statesman of his time. Under Bismarck, diplomacy was an arduous career but one which would provide great satisfaction.

With the accession of William II, the role of the Foreign Office changed only in that it was now the creature of the crown rather than of the chancellor. The habits of obedience ingrained under Bismarck were now simply transferred to the young kaiser. However, obedience to William

321

II was grounded not in admiration but in servility, and if Bismarck expected quiet, unquestioning dutifulness from his subordinates, William was very susceptible to more exaggerated forms of deference. And the kaiser's control over the Wilhelmstrasse, although as Caesarean as Bismarck's, was only sporadic in application. Between the outbursts of imperial activity in the field of diplomacy, the Foreign Office enjoyed a degree of independence in its internal affairs that was undreamed of under Bismarck. Since the chancellors and state secretaries after 1890—with the exceptions of Bülow, who was lazy, and Kiderlen, who served too briefly to have a lasting effect—were either weak or occupied with other matters, the rivalries and enmities between diplomats and between branches of the Wilhelmstrasse, which had been suppressed under Bismarck, were now able to surface. Officials in Berlin began to disregard those in the field, who in turn snubbed the Wilhelmstrasse and complained to the kaiser. Diplomats abroad, aided by their confederates in the capital, labored to "demolish" their rivals, while the military figures involved in diplomacy took advantage of the situation to assert their independence from the Foreign Office and aligned themselves more closely with the crown. In such a chaotic situation, intrigue, cabals, and vendettas were able to proliferate, and out of this morass a figure such as Holstein was able to exercise such malignant influence. Under Bismarck the Wilhelmstrasse had been strenuous and demanding, but under William II it became the undisciplined and noxious *Giftbude*.

If obedience, in changing forms and with different results, was the primary characteristic of the diplomatic service, its other distinctive feature was its persistent allegiance to the aristocratic ascendancy in Prussia. The preponderance of nobles in the Wilhelmstrasse did not have any demonstrable effect on policy since this was controlled by Bismarck and after 1890 by William II. It seems entirely possible, given the impress of two such autocratic leaders, that had the diplomatic service been composed entirely of bourgeois it would have discharged its responsibilities in much the same manner as the aristocratic Wilhelmstrasse did. Bourgeois diplomats, in any case, did not think or behave differently than their noble brethren.

The hold of the nobility on the Foreign Office is of considerable interest, however, for what it reveals of that class. A dissection of the Wilhelmstrasse indicates the depth of hostility which underlay social relationships in imperial Germany. The rigorous segregation of middle-class diplomats into mediocre positions, the specification of diplomatic talent in terms calculated to favor recruits of noble birth, the intimacy of its association with the Prussian army, the emphasis on style rather than *Sachlichkeit,* and the premium put on connections all testify to the self-satisfaction of the nobility with its own traditions and to its distaste for the bourgeoisie. The disdain expressed for non-European posts, the lack of interest or training in economic affairs save those pertaining to agriculture, and the failure of the Political Division to pay much attention to trade or colonial policy all illustrate the static outlook of most German diplomats and their inability or disinclination to comprehend the forces which were altering imperial Germany. Finally, the supinity of diplomats, including those of noble birth, before their royal or bureaucratic masters was striking, even though the alleged independence of mind of the aristocracy was held by some diplomats to be the very justification for populating the ranks of the service with men drawn from that class. If the German nobility viewed the lower orders with ineffable condescension, its willingness to accommodate itself with those in power was almost total.

Germany thus moved toward 1914 with a diplomatic service remarkably like that which it had had in 1871. It was still noble, though the Junker element was now rather more attenuated; it was still quite martial in character, although fewer generals were now appointed as envoys; it continued to apply the same aristocratic and financial standards in the recruitment and promotion of diplomats; and it persisted in limiting its interest to traditional matters. German diplomats remained essentially courtiers engaged in European *Hofpolitik.*

Few Germans in the diplomatic service thought that it was perfect, an admission which was rare before 1890 but quite common thereafter. Even Bismarck realized that the Foreign Office had faults, but his reaction was to draw diplomatic affairs still more tightly into his own hands. Most of the complaints by diplomats who served under the Iron Chancellor's successors concerned the decline in professionalism of the Wilhelmstrasse, while the criticism of those who stood outside the Foreign Office tended to concentrate on the composition of the diplomatic service, which in turn was mistakenly held responsible for Germany's increasingly unenviable position in Europe. The kaiser's leadership could not be openly attacked, but no law or convention protected the Foreign Office from abuse. The target for the Wilhelmstrasse's critics was that feature of the service which was so visible and so archaic: its aristocratic preponderance. Those who deplored the condition into which the Foreign Office had fallen included businessmen, officials in other branches of the government, foreign statesmen, and rulers, but the chief foe of the Wilhelmstrasse were the deputies in the Reichstag. Its criticism of the Foreign Office was not constant and never really trenchant, however, and its determination to introduce reforms was somewhat deficient in zeal. This is perhaps a byproduct of the unfortunate tendency of most deputies to regard diplomacy as a *Staatsgeheimnis* beyond the pale of parliamentary scrutiny.[1]

The first intensive parliamentary attack on the Foreign Office did not occur until late in 1906. It was led by the National Liberal leader, Ernst Bassermann, and it concentrated on the aristocratic monopoly in the Wilhelmstrasse. Bassermann and his associates among the Progressives and

[1] See, for example, the remarks by the prominent Socialist deputy, Georg Ladebour, in the Reichstag, Mar. 5, 1901, pp. 1697–98.

Social Democrats believed that any reform of the diplomatic establishment had to attack the way in which diplomats were recruited and trained. They argued that diplomats were being drawn from too narrow a social background, a proposition with which at least one Conservative deputy agreed and to which Chancellor Bülow made an evasive and vacuous response.[2] The debate led to no alteration of the Foreign Office's practices, though it may have contributed to the abolition in May, 1908, of the requirement that candidates for the diplomatic service provide evidence of private wealth. Although this proof was thereafter not a formal part of the Wilhelmstrasse's initiation rites, it continued to be covertly applied.

The *Daily Telegraph* crisis of November, 1908, with its revelations of royal indiscretion and bureaucratic incompetence, intensified the Reichstag's attack. The fiasco illustrated the dangers both of an indolent chancellor and of a Foreign Office staff which never challenged but only fulfilled orders. Bülow skillfully shoved the blame for his own carelessness on the Wilhelmstrasse and, in the Reichstag, the diplomatic service rather than the chancellor had to assume the brunt of the charge. The Foreign Office was castigated as the preserve of aristocratic incompetents, men who were overly schooled in the intricacies of the law but profoundly ignorant of Germany's life-blood of trade and industry, men who were denizens only of the most rarefied society and who therefore had no understanding of the real world. The Foreign Office, its parliamentary critics argued, was indistinguishable from an aristocratic regiment in the Prussian army.[3] Deputy after deputy from the ranks of the

[2] Reichstag, Nov. 14, 1906 (Wiemer), p. 3646; Apr. 30, 1907 (Bassermann), p. 1247. The Conservative was the duke of Hatzfeldt-Trachenberg, Apr. 30, 1907, p. 1247.

[3] On the necessity of drawing diplomats from a broader base see Reichstag, Nov. 10, 1908 (Bassermann), pp. 5378–79; Nov. 11, 1908 (von Dirksen), p. 5436; Dec. 11, 1908 (Heckscher), p. 6161; Mar. 31, 1909 (Stresemann), pp. 7907–9; Dec. 7, 1909 (Lehmann),

National Liberals. Progressives, and Social Democrats rose to argue that only by a more democratic recruitment policy, by the effective abolition of economic qualifications for entry into the service, and by a reformed examination system could the Wilhelmstrasse become a competent agent of the Fatherland's interest. Diplomats might then understand something of trade and industry, of the concerns of ordinary people both in Germany and abroad. Such reforms, it was argued somewhat inaccurately, would parallel the social and economic democratization which had been brought about in the diplomatic services of other nations.[4] Several deputies suggested that one way this might be accomplished would be to combine the consular service, overwhelmingly bourgeois in composition and largely concerned with economic matters, with the diplomatic service.[5]

The defense of the system offered by State Secretary Schoen in replying to these attacks was wan, his arguments that the old emphasis on birth and wealth was vanishing were unconvincing.[6] The Reichstag's dissatisfaction resulted in the introduction of a resolution by Bassermann in Feb-

---

p. 154; Nov. 11, 1911 (Frank), p. 268. On diplomats' legal training see Bassermann's two speeches on Dec. 5, 1908, and Mar. 29, 1909, pp. 6017, 7812. For an earlier complaint on this point see a speech on Apr. 19, 1904, by Münch-Ferber, pp. 2204–5. On the social exclusivity of the diplomatic corps see Dec. 9, 1908 (Schrader), p. 6094; Mar. 29, 1909 (Bassermann), p. 7812; Mar. 31, 1909 (Stresemann), pp. 7907–9; May 18, 1912 (David), p. 2087; on the similarity with the army see Bassermann's two speeches of Mar. 29, 1909, and Mar. 31, 1909, pp. 7812, 7907, and Apr. 15, 1913 (Müller-Meiningen), p. 4779.

[4] Reichstag, Mar. 29, 1909 (Bassermann), p. 7812; Nov. 11, 1911 (Frank), p. 7778; May 18, 1912 (David), pp. 2085–87.

[5] Reichstag, Mar. 29, 1909 (Liebermann von Sonnenberg), p. 7830; May 18, 1912 (David), pp. 2085–87; Apr. 14, 1913 (Baron von Richthofen), pp. 4747–48.

[6] Reichstag, Mar. 31, 1909 (Schoen), pp. 7914–16; Mar. 16, 1910 (Schoen), pp. 2168–69.

ruary, 1912, demanding that the conditions of entry into the diplomatic service be regulated by law.[7] Three months later a group of National Liberals and Progressives brought forward a rider to the 1912 budget calling for the renunciation of any financial requirements for entry. The motion was passed without difficulty but over the strong objections of State Secretary Kiderlen, who pointed out that all professional men must be professionally educated and that such training cost a great deal of money.[8] Since the Reichstag lacked the authority to implement its resolution, nothing was done. In 1913, the same parliamentary coalition successfully attached a rider to the budget demanding that "entry into the diplomatic service be made possible for the most capable candidates without regard to their financial means." State Secretary Jagow argued in response that private wealth was necessary in a diplomatic career, although he evaded the question of whether the Wilhelmstrasse actually required candidates to give evidence of private incomes. Jagow's forensic talents were meager and he argued, no more persuasively than had Kiderlen, that reforms were in fact underway in the Foreign Office.[9] In the spring of 1914, the Reichstag passed a third resolution, this time one which called for a revision in the examination system so that in the future the panel responsible for interrogations of diplomatic aspirants would consist of economic experts and businessmen as well as Wilhelmstrasse officials.[10]

The Foreign Office treated these resolutions with olympian indifference, and the system of recruitment, examination, and promotion continued in the old manner. Private wealth and aristocratic background remained the essential

---

[7] Germany, Reichstag, *Verhandlungen des Reichstages: Anlagen zu den stenographischen Berichten*, vol. 299, no. 474, pp. 499–500.

[8] Reichstag, May 18, 1912 (Kiderlen-Wächter), p. 2103.

[9] The resolution is printed in *Verhandlungen des Reichstages: Anlagen*, vol. 301, no. 890, p. 1222; Jagow's remarks are in Reichstag, Apr. 15, 1913, pp. 4759–60.

[10] *Verhandlungen des Reichstages: Anlagen*, vol. 305, no. 1549, p. 3118.

ingredients in a successful application for entry and the examinations continued to stress the law. The correlation between noble birth and professional advancement persisted. Consequently, in August, 1914, when imperial Germany went to war, the Foreign Office, enveloped in its sacrosanct traditions, was undefiled by association with a world both at home and abroad which it could not comprehend. The recumbent sphinxes in the vestibule at number 76, as more than one diplomat had observed, were an appropriate symbol of the Foreign Office's inscrutability. The world went by, but the Wilhelmstrasse, watching with a weary and disapproving eye, sprawled in immutable repose.

Bibliography of Manuscript Sources

Bismarck *Nachlass* (BisN) Bundesarchiv, Koblenz. An enormous collection of 116 reels of microfilm of the originals at Friedrichsruh, bearing the archive classification numbers FC 2936 through 3052. Cited by reel/frame numbers. Of particular interest are *Bestand* B (FC 2952–2987), consisting of correspondence to and from Otto and Herbert Bismarck and others; *Bestand* D (FC 3003–3023), correspondence to and from Herbert Bismarck; *Bestand* E (FC 3027), correspondence to and from Wilhelm Bismarck; *Bestand* F (FC 3028–3030), correspondence to and from Count Kuno von Rantzau, Otto von Bismarck's son-in-law, as well as Rantzau's important autobiographical memoir. This *Nachlass*, the nonpolitical part of which was not filmed, can be used only with the permission of H.S.H. Prince Ferdinand von Bismarck. This collection is more fully described in Lamar Cecil, "The Bismarck Papers," *Journal of Modern History*, XLVII, no. 3 (Sept. 1975), pp. 505–11.

Bülow *Nachlass* (BüN) Bundesarchiv, Koblenz. A large and vital collection of papers of Bernhard von Bülow. Cited by folder number. Of particular interest are the following folders, all of which consist of correspondence to and from Bülow unless otherwise noted.

13–14 Adolf von Bülow (page numbers are provided for those folders in which the letters are undated.)

15 Karl von Bülow

22 Amtliche Schreiben und Beamte

23	Count Paul von Hatzfeldt-Wildenburg
46	Schreiben verschiedener Persönlichkeiten
61	Beamte des Auswärtigen Amtes
65–66	Count Herbert von Bismarck
75–77	Count (Prince) Philipp zu Eulenburg-Hertefeld
89	Prince Chlodwig zu Hohenlohe-Schillingsfürst
90–92	Friedrich von Holstein
95	Robert von Keudell
96	Alfred von Kiderlen-Wächter
98	Prince Karl Max von Lichnowsky
104	Baron Adolf Marschall von Bieberstein
112	Kaiser William II
114	Joseph Maria von Radowitz
127	Count Friedrich von Vitzthum
129	Count Carl von Wedel
151	Merkbücher (miscellaneous notes)
153	Numerierte Zettel betr. 1859–1910

Busch *Nachlass* (BuschN) National Archives, Washington, filed in T–291, reel 2, frames 00001–00828. The voluminous but largely insignificant papers of Clemens Busch. Cited by frame number.

Castell *Nachlass* (CN) Fürstliches Castell'schen Archiv, Castell, Bavaria. A rich collection of materials relating to Count Siegfried zu Castell-Rüdenhausen, who died in 1903 while minister to Chile. Of interest are Castell's diary for 1889–94 in folder IeVI/29 and his letters to his mother in folder IeIII/76. Cited by folder number.

Deutschland 122 (Dd 122) National Archives, Washington, filed in T–149, reel 280, frames 00762–00802. Microfilm copy of Foreign Office file Deutschland 122 No. 2, "Das Auswärtige Amt," vol. 3. Cited by volume, reel/frame numbers. In spite of its promising title, the papers are of only routine interest.

Deutschland 135 No. 1, no. 1 (Dd 135) National Archives, Washington, divided into two sections. The first is a microfilm copy of Foreign Office file Deutschland 135, "Akten betr. die deutschen Missionen im Ausland

(Generalia)," vol. 1, filed in T–149, reel 281, frames 00044–00086. Cited by volume and reel/frame numbers. The second is a microfilm copy of Foreign Office file Deutschland 135, "Akten betr. die deutschen Missionen im Ausland (Botschaft Konstantinopel)," vols. 1 and 3, filed in T–139, reel 345, cited by volume and reel numbers and by frame numbers where decipherable. Both sections are of limited importance.

Deutschland 149 (Dd 149) National Archives, Washington, filed in T–149, reel 280, frames 00055–00493. Microfilm copy of Foreign Office file Deutschland 149, "Der Geschäftsgang bei der Politischen Abteilung," vols. 1–13. Cited by volume, reel/frame numbers. This collection is of considerable significance for the internal affairs of the Wilhelmstrasse.

Eulenburg *Nachlass* This collection consists of three parts, all of them of great value.

(Asseverat 45) (1) Politisches Archiv des Auswärtigen Amtes, Bonn. Forty-three letters or memoranda by Count Philipp zu Eulenburg-Hertefeld to Baron Adolf Marschall von Bieberstein, 1890–1896.

(EN) (2) Bundesarchiv, Koblenz. "Eine preussische Familiengeschichte," vols. I through LXIX, filed as folders 1 through 59 of the Eulenburg *Nachlass*. This is a typescript of a collection of papers assembled by Eulenburg before his death in 1921. It contains extracts from his diaries and correspondence as well as Eulenburg's subsequent observations on events in which he participated. Cited by volume and page numbers.

(EN) (3) Bundesarchiv, Koblenz. Folders 61, 63 and 64, containing additional important correspondence with Holstein, Herbert von Bismarck, and others.

Gebhardt *Nachlass* (GN) National Archives, Washington (Military Records Division), filed in T–120, R5289. A microfilm copy of a file assembled by Professor Peter von Gebhardt, a *wissenschaftlicher Hilfsarbeiter* in the Foreign Office from 1940 to 1945, consisting of information drawn from personal dossiers of numerous diplomats. Cited by manuscript page number.

Generalia 1 AA.a.40 (Gen 1 AA.a.40) National Archives, Washington, filed in T–149, reel 279, frames 00442–00483. Microfilm copy of Foreign Office file Generalia 1 AA.a.40, "Acta betr. die den deutschen Missionen usw. ertheilten Instruktionen," vols. 2–4. Cited by volume, reel/frame numbers. Of limited value.

Generalia 1 AA.a.61 (Gen 1 AA.a.61) National Archives, Washington, filed in T–149, reels 279–280, frames 00513–00816, 00001–00042. Microfilm copy of Foreign Office file Generalia 1 AA.a.61, "Acta betr. den Geschäftsgang bei der Politischen Abteilung," vols. 1–7. Cited by volume, reel/frame numbers. Similar in content and interest to Deutschland 149 above.

Generalia 1 AA.a.68 (Gen 1 AA.a.68) National Archives, Washington, filed in T–149, reel 280, frames 00597–00662. Microfilm copy of Foreign Office file Generalia 1 AA.a.68, "Die Instruktionen für die Militär-attachés sowie die Behandlung der Militärberichte." Cited by reel and frame numbers only since there are no volume numbers. Important.

Harden *Nachlass* (HardenN) Bundesarchiv, Koblenz. Folder 52, to which all citations refer, contains letters by Friedrich von Holstein to Maximilian Harden.

Haus Archiv (HA) Geheimes Staatsarchiv, Berlin-Dahlem. This collection from the archive of the royal household contains important correspondence by William II and others in Repertorium 53a, especially in folders 54 (Tsar Alexander III), 31 (Bismarck), 44 (Prince Max von Ratibor und Corvey) and 65 (Philipp zu Eulenburg). Cited by Repertorium and folder number.

Haus-, Hof- und Staatsarchiv (HHStA) Vienna. File entitled "Preussen III," containing the correspondence of the Austro-Hungarian ambassadors in Berlin with the Foreign Ministry in Vienna. For each year there is a volume of numbered reports (*Berichte*) and unnumbered correspondence (*Varia*). Cited by document number in parentheses (where applicable), followed by a hyphen and the designation B (*Bericht*) or V (*Varia*). The observations in both series are penetrating and of the greatest importance.

Hepke *Nachlass* (HepkeN) Bundesarchiv, Koblenz, filed in Kleine Erwerbung 319. Folder 2 contains the useful diary which Hepke, a counselor in the Foreign Office, kept in the 1870s. Cited by folder number.

Hohenlohe *Nachlass* (HohN) A large collection containing Chancellor Chlodwig zu Hohenlohe-Schillingsfürst's correspondence and diaries. This very illuminating material also contains the small but interesting *Nachlass* of Chlodwig's son Alexander. Cited by folder numbers.

Holstein *Nachlass* (HolN) National Archives, Washington, filed in T–120, reels 3815–47, 3851–61. This is a microfilm of the original in the Politisches Archiv of the Foreign Office in Bonn. Reels 3815–47 consist of the originals of Holstein's correspondence and diaries, while reels 3851–61 are a typescript copy. Cited by reel/frame numbers. This collection is of vital importance for the Foreign Office.

Kayser *Nachlass* (KayserN) Staats- and Universitätsbibliothek, Hamburg. The papers of Paul Kayser, the director of the Colonial Division of the Foreign Office, are of great importance for colonial affairs but only of occasional interest for the Wilhelmstrasse itself. Of particular significance are the following folders of correspondence: 5 (Alfred von Bülow), 8 (General Consul Hermann Gabriel), and 44 (miscellaneous). Cited by folder numbers.

Kiderlen-Wächter *Nachlass* (KWN) Sterling Library, Yale University, New Haven, Connecticut. This collection, filed in the Robert M. House papers, is very ill organized and is in the process of being reordered.

333

The material is extensive but yields little on the operation of the Foreign Office. Kiderlen's political correspondence and memoranda are for the most part in box 5, drawer 71, numbers 63 through 108. His letters to his mistress, Hedwig Kypke, are filed in MS 312, numbers 1 through 108. Cited by box, drawer, and number of letter or other document.

Kleine Erwerbung (Kl. Erwb.) Bundesarchiv, Koblenz. File 458F, folder 6 contains correspondence of interest by Kiderlen-Wächter, while folder 10 has some important letters to Paul Kayser. Cited by file and folder numbers.

Loebell *Nachlass* (LoebellN) Bundesarchiv, Koblenz. The correspondence of Friedrich Wilhelm von Loebell, the under state secretary of the Reichskanzlei, with Bernhard von Bülow in folders 6 through 9 is of interest, as is Loebell's two-volume manuscript entitled "Ein Leben um Deutschlands Aufstieg und Werde: Erinnerungen" in folder 27. Cited by folder numbers, and in the case of folder 27, by volume and page numbers.

Michahelles *Nachlass* (MichahellesN) National Archives, Washington, filed in T–291, reel 4, frames 00014–00198. Microfilm copy of the original in Bonn, consisting of a typescript of interest entitled "Im kaiserlichen Dienst: Erlebnis." Cited by manuscript pagination rather than microfilm numbers, which are illegible.

Miquel *Nachlass* (MiquelN) National Archives, Washington, filed in T–291, reel 5, frames 00185–00255. Microfilm copy of the original in Bonn. Folder 1/1 contains 22 interesting memoranda which Miquel wrote on his career. Cited by frame numbers.

Münster *Nachlass* (MünsterN) Gräfliches Münstersches Familien- und Gutsarchiv, Derneburg, Hanover. Folders 4, 9, and 10, containing Münster's correspondence with other diplomats, are of some value. Cited by folder numbers.

Pourtalès *Nachlass* (PourtalèsN) National Archives, Washington, filed in T–291, reel 3, frames 00611–00727. Of limited significance. Cited by frame numbers.

Richthofen *Nachlass* (RichthofenN) This collection is in two parts, both of marginal interest. Cited by folder numbers.

(1) Politisches Archiv of the Foreign Office, Bonn, folder 1/2, containing a small amount of correspondence, most of which is to and from other diplomats.

(2) Bundesarchiv, Koblenz. Of interest are Richthofen's letters in the following folders: 1 (Hartmann von Richthofen), 6 (Prince and Princess Max von Ratibor und Corvey), 7 (Otto von Mühlberg), 13 (miscellaneous).

Rottenburg *Nachlass* (RottenburgN) Bundesarchiv, Koblenz. The papers of Franz von Rottenburg, originally a diplomat and later under state secretary of the imperial Interior Office. Folder II/2 has correspondence of note by Herbert von Bismarck. Cited by folder number.

Schlözer *Nachlass* (SchlözerN) National Archives, Washington, filed in T–291, reel 3, frames 00728–00818. Microfilm copy of the original in Bonn. Schlözer was longtime Prussian envoy at the Vatican. Of limited interest. Cited by frame numbers.

Stoedten *Nachlass* (StoedtenN) Politisches Archiv of the Foreign Office, Bonn. Of interest only for an important letter of Otto von Glasenapp to Baron Hellmuth Lucius von Stoedten of Aug. 25, 1925, in folder 5/1 G–2. Cited by folder number.

Thimme *Nachlass* (ThimmeN) Bundesarchiv, Koblenz. Papers of the historian Friedrich Thimme. Folder 17 contains memoirs of Gerhard von Mutius. Folder 24 contains a valuable undated memo by Wilhelm von Stumm, head of the Political Division after 1910. Cited by folder and page numbers.

Treutler *Nachlass* (TN) In the possession of Baroness Anne-Katrin von Ledebur, Schwenningdorf/Westphal. A very valuable autobiographical manuscript written between 1922 and 1930 by Karl Georg von Treutler, whose last post was minister to Bavaria from 1912 to 1917. Cited by chapter and page numbers.

Index

Library of Congress Cataloging in Publication Data

Cecil, Lamar.
  The German diplomatic service, 1871–1914.

  Bibliography: p.
  Includes index.
  1. Germany. Auswärtiges Amt. I. Title.
JX1796.Z7C42   354'.43'00892   76–3250
ISBN 0–691–05235–2